THE POETICS OF PSYCHOANALYSIS

The Poetics of Psychoanalysis

In the Wake of Klein

MARY JACOBUS

OXFORD

UNIVERSITY PRESS

OXFORD
UNIVERSITY PRESS

Great Clarendon Street, Oxford OX2 6DP

Oxford University Press is a department of the University of Oxford.
It furthers the University's objective of excellence in research, scholarship,
and education by publishing worldwide in

Oxford New York

Auckland Cape Town Dar es Salaam Hong Kong Karachi
Kuala Lumpur Madrid Melbourne Mexico City Nairobi
New Delhi Shanghai Taipei Toronto

With offices in

Argentina Austria Brazil Chile Czech Republic France Greece
Guatemala Hungary Italy Japan Poland Portugal Singapore
South Korea Switzerland Thailand Turkey Ukraine Vietnam

Oxford is a registered trade mark of Oxford University Press
in the UK and in certain other countries

Published in the United States
by Oxford University Press Inc., New York

British Library Cataloguing in Publication Data

Data available

Library of Congress Cataloging in Publication Data

Data available

Typeset by Newgen Imaging Systems (P) Ltd., Chennai, India
Printed in Great Britain
on acid-free paper by
Biddles Ltd., King's Lynn, Norfolk

ISBN 0–19–924636–X   978–0–19–924636–6

1 3 5 7 9 10 8 6 4 2

Preface and Acknowledgements

The Poetics of Psychoanalysis grew out of a wish to explore the literary aspects of the twentieth-century psychoanalytic tradition in England that has come to be known as British Object Relations. Its specific focus is Melanie Klein's legacy to psychoanalytic writing between the late 1920s and the late 1970s. My emphasis is not only on Klein but on the work to which hers gave rise both before and after the Second World War. This is not a psychoanalyst's book, however, nor does it set out to be a history of Kleinian or post-Kleinian thought. Although I inevitably deal with some of the main ideas developed by Klein and those who came after her, I try to do so in ways that are accessible to non-psychoanalytic readers. My approach to writing about psychoanalysis is primarily that of a literary critic, and my focus is on its making and shaping, its literary elements and aesthetic concerns, as well as its informing ideas.

Beyond this, I have tried to do two things: to pay close attention to a body of writing that is often sidelined by literary critics with an interest in psychoanalysis (by comparison with Freud or post-structuralist Continental psychoanalysis); and to make fruitful connections with particular works of literature and art. I have sometimes found myself turning to British Object Relations psychoanalysis in the light of pressing contemporary issues, or making connections with other kinds of literary criticism and theory that interest me. All the psychoanalysts I have included wrote richly about literary, aesthetic, and cultural subjects as well as about psychoanalysis. But they also drew on literature, art, and culture as they struggled to formulate their own psychoanalytic ideas. Like Melanie Klein, or her contemporary Ella Freeman Sharpe, the writers who came after them—Joan Riviere and Wilfred Bion, Marion Milner and D. W. Winnicott—saw psychoanalytic writing as a contribution to the culture of their time. I have structured the book to reflect a roughly chronological trajectory, but individual chapters can be read both as free-standing critical essays and as linked to each other by a common thread of ideas.

Psychoanalytic theory never stands still. Part I ('Transitions') emphasizes the shifts that spanned the period of Klein's own life and work. Starting with Ella Sharpe's emphasis on 'body poetics' (the concrete and corporeal aspects of language), Chapter 1 explores Sharpe's literary and linguistic analysis of dreams and Shakespeare's plays—forms of analysis that attracted Lacan's attention when it came to his own emphasis on the importance of language and desire for the formation of the subject. Chapter 2 quarries the epistolary record of Joan Riviere's analysis with Ernest Jones, seeing it as the autobiographical basis for her ideas about femininity and her emphasis on the negative therapeutic reaction; her deep interest in literature later led her to develop the concept of a composite 'personality' that is defined by literary memory. Chapter 3 concentrates on the last phase of Klein's writing, during the 1950s until her death, when she turned to the topics of identification, envy, and forgiveness. Her reading shows her modifying and revising her earlier ideas through allegorical readings of poetry, fiction, and the *Oresteia*. Klein finds a mirror for her theories in books, but books reflect on her theories as well as mirroring them back.

Part II ('Mediations') focuses on specific links between psychoanalysis, literature, and art, and especially on the mediating role of Milner and Winnicott as they evolved their ideas in tandem or in tension with Klein's. Chapter 4 traces the evolution of Klein's early play technique through the writings of Susan Isaacs, Marion Milner, and D. W. Winnicott, suggesting that the tendency of magic to surface in close proximity to theories of play signals an unacknowledged stowaway within psychoanalysis: aesthetics. In Chapter 5, Milner's case-history of a schizophrenic woman artist prompts questions about the role of violence in both therapy and art, as well as the relation between aesthetic production and the concept of psychic space which preoccupies contemporary artists. Chapter 6 develops a comparison that is often made between Winnicott and Wordsworth, given their interest in the growth of the mind; here they are read alongside one another, not for the congruence of their views but for the shared implication of an ultimately incommunicable self. The work of the negative in Wordsworth and Winnicott problematizes both autobiography and writing while posing a question: to what extent do psychoanalysis and literature speak to each other at all?

Klein's legacy is most radically transformed by the work of Wilfred Bion from the 1960s onwards. Despite its literary and theoretical originality, his writing is less read by critics than by practising psychoanalysts, not necessarily only Kleinian. Part III ('Transformations') spans the effect of Bion's war experiences on the formation of his ideas and his ambitious attempt to define the role of aesthetics within psychoanalysis. Chapter 7 draws on Bion's war writings about his years as a tank officer in the First World War to throw light on his construction of a personal myth of traumatic experience, as well its aftermath in his work with leaderless groups during the Second World War. In Chapter 8, the language of psychosis derived from Bion's clinical work offers an approach to the language of terror, along with the psychology of the Burkean Sublime; as in Shelley's Romantic drama, the psychotic patient writhes on a Promethean couch of suffering created by the concreteness of his language and thoughts. Chapter 9 confronts Bion's ambitious attempt to consider the role of aesthetics in psychoanalytic work, its representation, and its characteristic action: interpretation; despite his attempt to mathematize psychoanalysis, his thinking foregrounds the problematics of vision as well as hallucination. Working at the borders of aesthetics and psychoanalysis, Bion suggests that psychoanalysis (like reading) involves being willing both to see and not see. Finally, the 'Envoi' brings the wheel back full circle to the question of women, in the future-past autobiography that Bion wrote at the end of his life, when the question of psychoanalysis was again being posed by 1970s feminists fifty years after the debate between Freud and the feminist psychoanalysts of the 1920s and 1930s.

This book grew out of the excitement (and sometimes the bafflement) of learning about, struggling to understand, teaching, and writing about a particular psychoanalytic tradition. During the middle decades of the twentieth century, psychoanalysis was part of mainstream cultural activity, and it can be read as a form of proto-modernist discourse in its own right. Yet, with the notable exception of Winnicott, few of the writers I deal with have been taken up by contemporary literary criticism, although Klein's work has deservedly attracted its share of attention from philosophers, cultural theorists, and feminist critics, and Joan Riviere has made her mark on both gender theory and film theory. Not obviously hospitable to post-structuralism, British Object Relations psychoanalysis often challenges contemporary literary criticism and theory to find a foothold. Part of my intention has been to counter the misplaced separation of Continental and British psychoanalytic theory. Another aim has been to maintain a literary-critical approach. Rather than 'applying' British Object Relations psychoanalysis to literature and art, or using literature as a pedagogical vehicle to explain psycho-analytic ideas, I have tried to read psychoanalytic writing in literary ways. Historians and philosophers of science (and philosophy too) are alert to the metaphors, myths, and constructions employed by scientific writing. It is hard to imagine being interested in psychoanalysis without taking at least some of its truth claims seriously and without an awareness of its continuing life as a clinical practice. But the literary reader may find that it also repays reading for what I have called its 'poetics'.

Psychoanalysis is capable of providing profound and unexpected insights into literary texts and art objects—and minds, or what Bion calls the 'personality'. But it is certainly not my contention that psychoanalysis invariably does so (it may often go the other way), although I have found it both pleasurable and illuminat-ing to read literature and psychoanalysis together. Given its importance, the British Object Relations tradition deserves the attention of literary and cultural historians. But it also forms the basis for a living, changing, and contestatory body of clinical ideas—ideas that are constantly evolving in relation to contemporary clinical practice, theory, and intellectual exchange. While arguing that the writings of British Object Relations psychoanalysts repay literary attention (and trying to show how they do), I also hope that this book holds something for practitioners. What I have learned from them has helped me to be a better reader.

I am grateful to the many friends and colleagues over the years who have shared, enabled, or sustained my passion for British Object Relations, especially, among others, David Armstrong, Isobel Armstrong, David Bell, Peggy Dieter, John Forrester, André Green, Betty Joseph, Max Hernandez, David Hillman, Laura Marcus, Michael Parsons, Lyndsey Stonebridge, and Margot Waddell. Among those who have generously provided comments, criticism, or information, I should like to thank Mieke Bal, Etienne Balibar, Francesca Bion, Rachel Bowlby, John Forrester, Geoffrey Hartman, Athol Hughes, Pearl King, Meira Likierman, Scott McMillin, Irma Brenman Pick, Polly Rossdale, Gordon Teskey, and Andrew Webber. For their intellectual companionship, I thank my graduate students at Cornell University and the University of Cambridge, as well as participants in seminars at Cornell given under the auspices of the National Endowment for the Humanities and the School of Criticism and Theory, and members of the Cambridge psychoanalytic reading group. I am particularly indebted to Sara Wasson for her expert research assistance and enthusiasm for the topic at an early stage, and to Mary Flannery for her careful editorial work in preparing the MS. I have also received generous assistance in the form of research leave from the National Endowment for the Humanities in the USA and from the Arts and Humanities Research Council in the UK, for which I am grateful.

I should like to acknowledge the Melanie Klein Trust and the British Psycho-Analytical Society Archives for permission to quote from the letters of Joan Riviere, and to reproduce photographs of Melanie Klein's toys; John Milner and the Milner Estate for permission to reproduce Susan's drawings from *The Hands of the Living God*; and the Van Gogh Museum, the Tate Gallery, Anish Kapoor, the National Monuments Record Office, and the Archbishopric of Olomouc, Kromeriz, for permission to reproduce paintings and photographs.

Chapter 1, Part 1, was previously published in Helen Small and Trudi Tate (eds.), *Literature, Science, Psychoanalysis, 1830–1970: Essays in Honour of Gillian Beer* (Oxford: Oxford University Press, 2003). Chapter 4 appeared in *Psychoanalysis and History*, 7 (2005), and a shortened version as a catalogue essay for the Compton Verney exhibition, *Only Make-Believe*, curated by Marina Warner. A section of Chapter 9 originally appeared in Peter Brooks and Alex Woloch (eds.), *Whose Freud? The Place of Psychoanalysis in Contemporary Culture* (New Haven: Yale University Press, 2000), and in *Diacritics: Trauma and Psychoanalysis*, 28 (1998). The 'Envoi' first appeared in the Millennium issue of *Women: A Cultural Review*, 11 (2000).

Note

The term 'phantasy' is used throughout (so spelled) in its Kleinian sense to imply unconscious phantasy, as distinct from 'fantasy' in its more ordinary usage.

Contents

List of Illustrations

List of Abbreviations

E&G   Melanie Klein, *Envy and Gratitude and Other Works 1946–63* (London: Hogarth Press, 1975).

LGR   Melanie Klein, *Love, Guilt, and Reparation and Other Works 1921–1945* (London: Hogarth Press, 1975).

SE   Sigmund Freud, *The Standard Edition of the Complete Psychological Works of Sigmund Freud*, ed. James Strachey, 24 vols. (London: Hogarth Press, 1953–73).

PART I

TRANSITIONS

1

Body Poetics: *Ella Sharpe*

'BROWNIE' SHARPE AND THE STUFF OF DREAMS

The dream is the matrix from which art is developed. 'We are such stuff as dreams are made of.'

Analytic technique is an applied art and as in all art its principles are conditioned by the limitations of its medium.

Ella Freeman Sharpe, *Dream Analysis*, 1937[1]

What is the medium of dream-analysis? And what is the 'stuff' of dreams? One answer, at least since Freud's *Interpretation of Dreams*, would be metaphor. But there are others. For D. W. Winnicott, it might be a holding medium, like oil, which helps the wheels of the dream to go round; for Wilfred Bion, alpha-function, making raw sensations and perceptions available for dreaming; or for André Green, negative states trying to accede to symbolization.[2] Formulations such as these—whether visceral or highly abstract—offer ways to imagine the always

---

[1] Ella Freeman Sharpe, *Dream Analysis: A Practical Handbook for Psycho-Analysts* (1937; rpr. London: Karnac Books, 1988), 59, 124; subsequent references in the text (*DA*) are to this edition. Sharpe's book was presented as a series of lectures to students in training at the London Institute of Psycho-Analysis during the 1930s. The Shakespearian reference is to *The Tempest*, IV. i. 156–7.

[2] See, for instance, D. W. Winnicott, 'Withdrawal and Regression' (1954), in *Through Paediatrics to Psycho-Analysis* (1958; rpr. New York: Bruner/Mazel, 1992), 256–7. Winnicott tells his patient, 'you imply *the existence of a medium*' (his emphasis) to which his patient replies: 'Like the oil in which wheels move'. For the friendly spaces of intrauterine existence, see Michael Balint, 'Flying Dreams and the Dream Screen', in *Thrills and Regressions* (New York: International Universities Press, 1959), 75–6. For Bion's views on dreaming, alpha-function, and the contact barrier, see W. R. Bion, *Learning from Experience* (1962; rpr. London: Karnac Books, 1988), 6–7: 'As alpha-function makes the sense impressions of the emotional experience available for conscious and dream-thought, the patient who cannot dream cannot go to sleep and cannot wake up' (ibid., 7; for the 'contact barrier', see ibid., 24–7), and Gérard Bléandonu, *Wilfred Bion: His Life and Works 1897–1979*, trans. Claire Pajaczkowska (London: Free Association Books, 1994), esp. 151–5. See also André Green, 'Negation and Contradiction', in *On Private Madness* (Madison, Conn.: International Universities Press, 1986), 254–76, and 'The Intuition of the Negative in *Playing and Reality*', in Gregorio Kohon (ed.), *The Dead Mother: The Work of André Green* (London and New York: Routledge, 1999), 205–21. The central preoccupations of André Green's work and their bearing on questions of representation are well summed up by Adam Phillips: 'Dreams and affect, and states of emptiness or absence have been the essential perplexities of Green's work because they are the areas of experience (or anti-experience) in which the nature of representation itself is put at risk'; see 'Taking Aims: André Green and the Pragmatics of Passion', in *The Dead Mother*, 165.

incomplete transformation of bodily experience and affect into unconscious phantasy and dreaming. I want to begin by exploring the part played by the body and its metaphors in Ella Freeman Sharpe's psychoanalytic writing, starting with her 1937 sequel to Freud's dream-book, *Dream Analysis: A Practical Handbook for Psycho-Analysts*. Donald Meltzer credits Sharpe's *Dream Analysis* with taking such 'a quietly divergent view from Freud's . . . that hardly any notice has been taken of it'.[3] Perhaps this is because of its practicality. But an intriguing cluster of associations suggests that 'Brownie' Sharpe (as she was known to her friends and colleagues) was more than the first practical critic of psychoanalysis. A former teacher of English literature, she practises an art that is 'applied' in the sense of bringing the techniques of literary-critical analysis to bear on the poetics of dreaming.[4] However, she thinks of her medium in ways that go well beyond the formal analysis of poetic diction or tropes for which she is often cited (simile, metaphor, metonymy, and so on).[5] For her, the language of poetry and dreams is always concrete and corporeal. Metaphor may be what we get in exchange for ceasing to express emotions through the body, but the origin of metaphor in forgotten bodily experience leaves its imprint on dream-language.

In his introduction to the 1977 reprint of *Dream Analysis*, Masud Khan (who claims to have been her last patient) praises Sharpe both for taking on the grammatical legacy of Freud's dream-book—'the grammar of how man dreams'—and for anticipating Lacan's *dictum*, '*l'inconscient est structuré comme un langage*' (*DA* 10, 9). But Green (among others) has since taken issue with Lacan, objecting that the Freudian unconscious is structured not by (or 'like') a language, but by

[3] See Donald Meltzer, *Dream-Life* (Perthshire: Clunie Press, 1983), 27. Meltzer fruitfully suggests that Ella Sharpe's work 'builds a bridge to the field of aesthetics in general' (ibid., 113), as well as investigating the dream as an aesthetic object.

[4] Sharpe was co-head teacher at the Hucknall Pupil Teachers Training Centre (for boys and girls aged 15 to 18 years old), where she taught from 1904 until 1916. In 1917, aged 43, she moved to London as a patient and then student at the Medico-Psychological Clinic in Brunswick Square (which treated mainly women until the war produced a need for the treatment of shell-shocked soldiers), and entered analysis with James Glover. After the war, she went to Berlin in 1920 for a period of analysis with Hanns Sachs, continuing with him during summers for several years, and became a full member of the British Psycho-Analytical Society in 1923. She is said by Sylvia Payne to have undertaken more training analyses than any other analyst in England. At the time of her death, she was writing a novel. For an overview of Sharpe's work, see Carol Netzer, 'Annals of Psychoanalysis: Ella Freeman Sharpe', *Psychoanalytic Review*, 69 (1982), 207–19; and see also Payne's obituary of Sharpe, *International Journal of Psycho-Analysis*, 28 (1947), 54–6. Sharpe's papers on technique have been usefully republished with an account of her life and work, with essays by contemporary analysts; see Maurice Whelan (ed.), *Mistress of Her Own Thoughts: Ella Freeman Sharpe and the Practice of Psychoanalysis* (London: Rebus Press, 2000).

[5] See, for instance, Meltzer, *Dream-Life*, 27: 'Her central creative contribution to the theory of dreams was to point out the mountains of evidence that dreams utilize what she chose to call the "poetic diction" of lyric poetry. By this she meant that dreams employ the many devices of simile, metaphor, alliteration, onomatopoeia etc. by which the language of poetry achieves its evocative capacity.' For Sharpe's association of dreams and literature, see also Susan Budd, 'The Shark Behind the Sofa: Recent Developments in the Theory of Dreams', in Daniel Pick and Lyndal Roper (eds.), *Dreams and History: The Interpretation of Dreams from Ancient Greece to Modern Psychoanalysis* (London and New York: Routledge, 2004), 268.

thing-presentations; affect ('the signifier of the flesh') both seeks and resists linguistic representation.[6] Khan writes revealingly of Sharpe's recognition that metaphor 'is a *collage* of mind and body' and insists on her 'uncanny' knowledge that 'all language is born of the body' (*DA* 9,10). His own metaphors suggest that Sharpe troubles a strictly Lacanian account of the language of the unconscious. While *collage* implies the layering of material surfaces, her knowledge is 'uncanny' in revealing what ought to remain hidden (in this case, a female birth-body, as often in her patients' dreams). Sharpe's writing, in fact, frequently represents dream-thoughts and phantasies concretely in terms of their manufacture, and even as a woven texture—literally, as textile—rather than metaphorically, as a linguistic 'text'. Nor is the dream-text, for her, necessarily cut from the same fabric as the literary text. Analytic technique, she writes, has to take into account the individual's relation to the environment if it is to be 'a subtler instrument than the yardstick which measures every type of cloth' (*DA* 124). Her technique in *Dream Analysis* is attuned to the idiolect of the dreamer and its manifestation 'in individual settings'.[7] This is the expressive medium in which she works, a medium as material as 'Oils and water colours, clay and stone, violin and piano, lyric and novel' (*DA* 124).

After Sharpe's death, a colleague recalled that Sharpe treated her patients 'as if she were handling some fragile piece of pottery'—inadvertently letting slip the concreteness of Sharpe's psychoanalytic world as well as her careful handling of her patients.[8] Even the analytic setting, as Sharpe evokes it in her writing, has a unique texture to which her analysands bring their own tastes, styles, and emotions. Every analysand is aware that the room in which the analyst works is charged with as much phantasy and feeling as the analytic relationship itself. Sharpe's view of analysis as an applied art emphasizes its situatedness, along with its materiality. But at the same time—cannily—she asks questions about the corporeality of metaphor. If metaphor is indeed born of bodily experience, as she

[6] Green comments: 'Lacan is saying the unconscious is structured like a language . . . [But] when you read Freud, it is obvious that this proposition doesn't work for a minute. Freud very clearly opposes the unconscious (which he says is constituted by thing-presentations and nothing else) to the pre-conscious. What is related to language can only belong to the pre-conscious; Lacan tried to defend himself by emphasizing that he said "like a language", but that's not true. In other instances he says the unconscious *is* language'; see 'The Greening of Psychoanalysis: André Green in dialogue with Gregorio Kohon', in *The Dead Mother*, 24. On Green and affect, see also Adam Phillips, 'Taking Aims', ibid., 163–72.

[7] The same attunement to the nuances of her analysands' communicative styles distinguished Sharpe as a practitioner; see, for instance, the former analysand cited by Netzer: 'The most striking impression to me was Ella Sharpe's great sensitivity to the nuances of verbal and non-verbal expression, and particularly to the implications hidden in the use of words and phrases which characterize most clichés' ('Annals of Psychoanalysis', 207). For a less sympathetic view, see Margaret Little's account of her disastrous analysis with Sharpe, 'Psychotherapy with Ella Freeman Sharpe, 1940–1947', in *Psychotic Anxieties and Containment: A Personal Record of an Analysis with Winnicott* (London: Jason Aronson, 1990), 31–8.

[8] Quoted by Wahl, in Franz Alexander (ed.), *Psychoanalytic Pioneers* (New York: Basic Books, 1966), 267.

proposes, is this because all language bears the traces of affect and the drives? Or is it merely by virtue of the pervasiveness of corporeal analogy itself? Sharpe's model makes bodily continence the price paid for language and language itself a form of materiality. Her 1940 essay 'Psycho-Physical Problems Revealed in Language' argues that metaphor arises when the infant achieves control over its messy products and bodily orifices. Instead of faecal matter, the child produces language ('the immaterial expresses itself in terms of the material'). Motions become emotions when they take the form of verbal representation. Sharpe posits a mysterious 'subterranean passage between mind and body [that] underlies all analogy', and defines speech as an 'avenue of "outer-ance" present from birth'. Her coinage, 'outer-ance', equates the achievement of sphincter control with linguistic discharge: 'The activity of speaking is substituted for physical activity now restricted at other openings of the body, while words themselves become the very substitutes for the bodily substances.'[9] Words assume the qualities of substitute substances. They function as projectiles, weapons, gifts, or magical performances. Speech (utterance) becomes metaphorical 'outer-ance'.[10]

Sharpe's account of utterance as the unmediated substitution of words for bodily substances short-circuits what Lacan, in his seminar 'The Object and the Thing' in *The Ethics of Psychoanalysis*, calls 'the problem of sublimation'. Lacan is briskly dismissive of a Kleinian aesthetics of reparation involving the maternal body.[11] Otherwise respectful of Sharpe's acumen, he is equally contemptuous of what he calls the 'puerile results' yielded by her papers on sublimation.[12] Although Sharpe calls sublimation 'the very woof and weft of civilization', she tends to see it as magical, primitive, and delusory.[13] Still, Lacan is intrigued that her paper 'Certain Aspects of Sublimation and Delusion' (1930) sites the first form of artistic production in an underground cave. For Lacan, cave-painting defines the elusive

[9] Ella Freeman Sharpe, *Collected Papers on Psycho-Analysis*, ed. Marjorie Brierley (London: Hogarth Press, 1950), 156–7 (*CP*). For a perceptive discussion of Sharpe's writing on aesthetics, figuration, and incorporation, see Lyndsey Stonebridge, *The Destructive Element: British Psychoanalysis and Modernism* (London: Macmillan, 1998), 85–93.

[10] 'So we may say speech in itself is a metaphor, that metaphor is as ultimate as speech' (*CP* 157). Sharpe is paraphrasing John Middleton Murray here: 'Metaphor is as ultimate as speech itself, and speech as ultimate as thought' (*CP* 155 and n.).

[11] Lacan objects: 'I can tell you right away that the reduction of the notion of sublimation to a restitutive effort of the subject relative to the injured body of the mother is certainly not the best solution to the problem of sublimation'; see Jacques Lacan, 'The Object and the Thing', in Jacques-Alain Miller (ed.), *The Ethics of Psychoanalysis 1959–1960: The Seminar of Jacques Lacan*, Book VII, trans. Dennis Porter (London and New York: Routledge, 1992), 106. Lacan returns to the problem of Kleinian sublimation, reparation, and aesthetics in his next seminar, referring to Klein's account of the artist Ruth Kjär; see Lacan, '*On Creation* ex nihilo', ibid., 116–17.

[12] Lacan, 'The Object and the Thing', ibid., 107.

[13] See 'Certain Aspects of Sublimation and Delusion' (1930): 'If for us the idea of the dead is freed from the cruder superstitions and fears of past ages, it is because we are phalanxed right and left, behind and before, by a magical nullification of fear in *sublimation* that is the very woof and weft of civilization' (*CP* 136). Sharpe claims, among other things, that art '*springs from the same root as the delusion of persecution*' (*CP* 131); the 'magical performance' of dancing involves an omnipotent phantasy of incorporation of, and primal identification with, parental power.

'place of the Thing' as a 'construction around emptiness'—a way of mastering what lies beyond signification via 'the figuration of emptiness' and painting's mastery of the illusion of space.[14] Sharpe herself vividly compares cave-painting to the darkened theatre of the 1930s 'moving picture', and (like other modernists such as the writers H.D. and Bryher) celebrates the cinema, calling it 'the most satisfying illusion the world has ever known' (*CP* 136).[15] Here, after all, Lacan may point the way to a reading of Sharpe's body-based theory of signification. Sharpe connects the illusion of the movies—'The great figures will move and live . . . as they did even in life'—with the cave-artist painting his bison. Both film and painting, she writes, aim to 'reconstruct . . . life that has passed away' (*CP* 136, 125). The moving image stands between ourselves and the absent object. For all its focus on poetic language and metaphor, *Dream Analysis* is underpinned by Sharpe's recurrent appeal to recent (and not-so-recent) technologies of material production and visual projection. In this respect, her writing anticipates the idea of the dream-screen—since the late 1940s, one of the organizing metaphors of contemporary dream-theory. But Sharpe's emphasis on the concreteness of psychic representation, or what she calls 'concrete image thinking' (*DA* 58), gives her aesthetics a distinctively modernist inflection. Her writing modifies any simple assumption that concreteness (as opposed to concrete thinking) is antipathetic to symbolization. Indeed, her work implies that some degree of concreteness is foundational to all symbol-formation, even if in the last resort symbolization also involves the mourning and linguistic letting go of the object that contemporary Kleinian aesthetics (and recent Kristevan theories of writing) tend to associate with the depressive position.[16] This bodily understanding of metaphor informs Sharpe's reading of the dream-text.

[14] *The Ethics of Psychoanalysis*, 139–40. For a succinct account of 'the Thing' in Lacan's seminar of 1959–60, see Dylan Evans, *Dictionary of Lacanian Psychoanalysis* (London and New York: Routledge, 1996), 204–5; 'the Thing' is both the beyond of the signified and the forbidden object of sexual desire. Evans's entry takes issue with those who, like André Green, question the linguistic aspect of the unconscious, emphasizing Lacan's distinction between *das Ding* and *die Sache* in Freud's account of thing-presentation.

[15] H.D. and Bryher, like Sharpe before them, became analysands of Hanns Sachs (and H.D. also of Freud) later in the 1920s. For their involvement in the cinema, and their contributions to the journal *Close Up*, see James Donald, Anne Friedberg, and Laura Marcus (eds.), *Close Up 1927–1933: Cinema and Modernism* (Princeton, NJ: Princeton University Press, 1998); for the links between cinema and psychoanalysis, as well as Sachs's collaboration with Pabst, see especially Laura Marcus, ibid., 240–6 (and, for Sachs's contributions to *Close Up*, see ibid., 254–6, 262–7). Virginia Woolf also makes the link between cinema and primitive experience in her 1926 essay 'The Cinema'; see Rachel Bowlby (ed.), *The Crowded Dance of Modern Life* (Harmondsworth: Penguin, 1993), 54–8. Barbara Low, another British analyst who went into analysis with Hanns Sachs, regards cinema as similarly connected with primitive thinking and magical wish-fulfilment; see 'Mind-Growth or Mind-Mechanization? The Cinema in Education' (1927), rpr. in *Close Up 1927–1933*, 247–50.

[16] For a brief statement of Kleinian aesthetics in relation to symbolization and the depressive position, and the relation between 'concrete thinking' and 'symbolic equation', see Hanna Segal, 'The Function of Dreams', in Sara Flanders (ed.), *The Dream Discourse Today* (London and New York: Routledge, 1993), 101: 'Only when separation and separateness are accepted and worked through does the symbol become a representation of the object, rather than being equated with the object'.

'*REALLY*, MISS SHARPE'

Sharpe's 1940 paper 'Psycho-Physical Problems Revealed in Language: An Examination of Metaphor' ends by demonstrating how an apparently meaningless word like 'really' can point to the core of a serious illness. Her patient, a poet and translator, 'was the last person *really* to use meaningless words, since they were the stuff [*sic*] of imagination for him.' Studying his use of 'really', Sharpe observes: 'Whenever he was surprised into saying something critical about me, my belongings, or the analysis, he put up his hands in a beseeching way and said in an apologetic deprecating voice: "*Really*, Miss Sharpe...."' Sharpe comes to understand that this beseeching gesture with its deprecating 'really' represents an underlying infantile situation, repeated in the transference, that involves criticism, anger, and fear. These emotions reproduce others originally aroused, for instance, by 'the appearance of a new baby, the awareness of parental inter-course... the sight of the female genital, the sight of menstrual blood', and even his own emotions. For instance, ' "Another baby, really?—Really!" ' or ' "Made by father and mother, really?—Really!" ' or ' "A person without a penis, really?—Really!" '; or even ' "I feel like killing, really?—Really!" ' In this patient's idiolect, 'Really!' signifies disavowal of his perceptions, thoughts, and feelings: ' "I see these things, know these things, but they are not real; I feel like this, but I mustn't feel like this, not really" ' (*CP* 167–8). Both external and psychical reality are negated by an unconsciously freighted expression of disbelief.

I want to notice another apparently innocuous word—so neutral as to seem equally meaningless—that recurs in Sharpe's own idiolect. This word is 'material': for instance, what the analysand gives to the analyst; the raw material of art, drama, psychoanalysis; everything that is kept in the storehouse of memory and experience; even language itself. How material is the 'material' for Sharpe, really? What does the 'stuff' of reality (and imagination) consist of for her? Among the early meanings of 'stuff', in the sense of 'equipment, stores, stock', is both an aux-iliary force or reinforcement and a defensive padding used under, or in place of, armour (other meanings include an army's stores, its material, baggage, provisions, moveable property, and furniture (*OED*)). Sharpe's 'stuff' could be equated with 'supplement' or even 'defence', as well as the everyday baggage and furnishings of our lives. In another and more familiar sense, the word 'stuff' includes the idea of a substance to be wrought or matter of composition (building materials; what persons—or dreams—are made of; and even 'material for literary elaboration'). Finally, 'stuff' in a more specific sense has the meaning of woven material, a textile fabric or woollen cloth. A pervasive feature of Sharpe's own usage is the way in which the 'stuff' of dreams is tugged towards a specific association with woven

---

Cf. also Cecily de Monchaux: 'De-differentiation between the thing symbolized and the symbol is the basis for the concrete thinking of the schizophrenic; for the cathexis of words...as if they were objects' ('Dreaming and the Organizing Function of the Ego', in *The Dream Discourse Today*, 207).

material. Paradoxically, this form of materiality also lends itself to literary elaboration, including the pleasing fiction that we could really finger or even munch on the texture of metaphor. If dreams, to use a submerged pun, are the 'matter' as well as *mater* (the matrix) of art, Sharpe imagines the 'stuff' of which they are made as a homespun forerunner of what we know today (in the wake of Lewin's dream screen) as the dream-envelope. This is the name Didier Anzieu gives to the visual dream-film, the fine, ephemeral membrane which he thinks of as replacing the tactile envelope of the ego's vulnerable skin under the stress of daytime and instinctual excitation.[17]

Anzieu's metaphor for the repair-work of dreams is weaving. Whereas Penelope unravels at night the 'shroud' she weaves by day, 'The nocturnal dream . . . re-weaves by night those parts of the skin ego that have become unravelled by day'.[18] Early on in *Dream Analysis*, in a chapter called 'The Mechanisms of Dream Formation', Sharpe establishes weaving as a symbolic representation of the primal scene. A woman has an infantile memory of visiting the country when she and her parents slept in an old-fashioned four-poster bed: 'The big four-square loom was equated with a bed, the flying shuttle with the penis, the thread with semen, the making of the material from the thread with a child' (*DA* 55–6).[19] Subsequently, the silk-weaving looms of this rural district gave Sharpe's patient a chance to see 'the swift flinging of the shuttle'. The weaver at his work took over in phantasy from the scenes witnessed by the small child in the four-poster bed. Local silk-weaving became a screen memory for the scene of parental intercourse, whether witnessed or phantasized. For this patient, thread, silk, cotton, and string—milk, water, and semen—were at once the material (the matrix) of dreams and unconscious phantasy, and what goes into making a baby, symbolically represented as 'woven material'.[20] Indeed, Sharpe notes: 'There was not an operation relevant to the work of weaving that did not appear as symbolic of unconscious phantasies'—and also, for that matter, of the production of unconscious phantasy itself. For Sharpe, the work of weaving stages the primal scene of the dream's manufacture. Her metaphor for the dream-space is the bed-loom of a home-based technology (in keeping also with a modernist emphasis on the home-made crafting of objects).[21] Pontalis, who uses the phrase 'dream machine' for this

[17] See Didier Anzieu, 'The Film of the Dream', in *The Dream Discourse Today*, 137–50.

[18] Ibid., 141.

[19] The word 'loom', as Sharpe would have known, once meant a tool or implement, and only later took on the meaning of an instrument for weaving; see George Willis, *The Philosophy of Speech* (New York: Macmillan, 1920), 56. Sharpe cites Willis—'those bridges of thought which are crossed and recrossed by names in their manifold mutations' (ibid., 55)—on the importance of naming (see *DA* 29, 39).

[20] For a series of dreams linked by this 'all-dominating theme of thread', see *DA* 182, and n. 31 below.

[21] Cf. the account of modernism offered by Douglas Mao in *Solid Objects: Modernism and the Test of Production* (Princeton, NJ: Princeton University Press, 1998); Mao argues for 'a variety of ways in which modernists were affected by certain images of production—above all, the image of the individual maker crafting the individual object' (12). See also Hugh Kenner, *A Homemade World: The American Modernist Writers* (New York: Knopf, 1975).

homely mode of production, suggests that the dream also fosters the illusion 'of being able to reach that mythical place where nothing is disjointed: where the real is imaginary and the imaginary real, where the word is a thing, the body a soul, simultaneously body-matrix and body phallus.'[22] For Sharpe's patient, and perhaps for Sharpe herself, the place of this mythical rejoining of body-matrix and body-phallus is an old-fashioned four-poster bed.

The loom's association with the arts and crafts movement, as well as with modernist modes of production, makes it an apt figure for Sharpe's applied art.[23] Sharpe herself is most vividly communicative when it comes to the good-enough-to-eat, mouth-watering woven material that appears in her patients' dream associations. Here is her description of a woman analysand (presumably the same one) for whom different types of material produce intense bodily sensations. 'For this patient', she writes, 'an oatmeal coloured material had a "crunchy" feeling', making her teeth tingle, while

A cherry coloured silk will make her mouth water and she longs to put her cheeks gently on its surface. The range of colours for this patient are in terms of cream, butter, lemon, orange, cherry, peach, damson, wine, plum, nut brown, chestnut brown. Materials can be crunchy like biscuits, soft like beaten white of eggs, thick like cake. Threads can be coarse like the grain of wholemeal bread, shine like the skin of satin.   (*DA* 92–3)

Sharpe concludes: 'I do not let any reference to colour or material or to dress escape me in the dreams this patient brings' (*DA* 93). One thinks of Lewin's derivation of the 'dream screen' from the sight and feel of the mother's breast as the well-fed baby falls asleep.[24] In this rich cornucopia of taste sensations, Sharpe conveys her own pleasure in colour, surface, and texture. But notice how she signs her writing. When she questions her patient's remark that she has a feeling about a name 'lying about somewhere'—'"How do you *feel* a *name* lying about?"' (*DA* 100)—we begin to see how the feel of a name literally colours the dream-associations of this exceptionally clothes- and colour-conscious patient (Payne's obituary, incidentally, recalls Sharpe herself giving her paper on sublimation in 'a soft brick-red dress' that threw her dark colouring into relief).[25]

---

[22] See J.-B. Pontalis, 'Dream as an Object', in *The Dream Discourse Today*, 120–1, where the dream-screen is also compared to Freud's 'protective shield' (ibid., 119).

[23] Visitors to the Freud Museum can see the loom on which Anna Freud wove, sometimes incorporating the hair of the Freuds' chow into her weaving.

[24] See Bertram Lewin, 'Sleep, the Mouth, and the Dream Screen', *Psychoanalytic Quarterly*, 15 (1946), 419–34, and 'Reconsideration of the Dream Screen', *Psychoanalytic Quarterly*, 22 (1953), 174–99.

[25] This was the red dress in which Sharpe gave her paper on 'Sublimation and Delusion' in 1928: 'She was capable of being a great actress . . . On this particular occasion she wore a soft brick-red dress; her dark hair and dark eyes, and rather dark complexion were thrown into relief by the warm colour.' Payne goes on to note that 'the paper was not an intellectual communication, but a living thing to which she was giving birth'; see *International Journal of Psycho-Analysis* 28, 55. Elsewhere, Sharpe reads her own name in her patients' submerged word-play on 'sharp' and 'flats' (for 'Sharpe' she reads 'flat' or 'block of flats'; see *DA* 38).

In an engaging approximation to her patient's mindless stream of consciousness—'Free association means for her a recounting of all that has happened in reality' (*DA* 98)—Sharpe highlights the colour 'brown' until we grasp its transferential associations with the dark-complexioned analyst, 'Brownie' Sharpe herself:

The flowers in that vase of yours are lovely. The flowers in the other are not as good, the colour of the vase isn't right; it's the wrong brown, but the others are lovely. . . . I'm longing to get on with my jumper. I'd like it finished at once. I've a new stitch to do. I want to see how the jumper looks when it's made. The trouble is about wool. Strange how shops don't stock the right brown, the brown I want. You see the wool in made-up things—in jumpers already knitted—but one can't get the actual colour in wool and make it oneself. *I want wool like the dark brown of your cushion.* (*DA* 100; my italics)

And so on. In case we missed the reference, Sharpe interprets: 'the mother transference within the analysis is shown by reference to the brown colour of the cushion which she wants for herself and to the flowers in the vases' (*DA* 105). For her, this patient's feminine aesthetics—her attentiveness to colours, clothes, knitting, and furnishings—are the sign of a phantasy life strongly under repression. Bion might see it as an approximation to the beta-element screen, a dream-like state that is not a dream, but a confused jumble of sensations and perceptions.[26] Her preoccupation with the world of flower vases, knitting wool, cushions, and, of course, shopping (the locus of modernist aesthetic consumption and consumer desire) presents a particular difficulty for the analyst: 'she is immensely occupied by reality' (*DA* 98).[27] Preoccupation with reality functions here—like 'Really!'—as a defence against unconsciously disturbing thoughts and feelings (for instance, the idea of a sexual link between her parents). As Sharpe writes elsewhere, clearly alluding to the same analysand's denial of psychic reality, 'just because she is intensely occupied with reality I must be aware of her denial of reality' (*DA* 152).[28] Sharpe's patient is like Mrs Dalloway, but without a mind of her own—a sense of her internal world—let alone a room.[29]

[26] See Bion, *Learning from Experience*, 22, where the screen of beta-elements is defined 'as indistinguishable from a confused state and in particular from any one of those confused states which resemble dreaming'; for Bion, the beta-element screen may be designed, among other things, to destroy the analyst's potency, to withhold information, or even to prevent common-sense interpretations occurring to the patient, and is apt to elicit a desired counter-transferential response from the analyst (ibid., 23).

[27] See Douglas Mao, *Solid Objects*, 40: 'Many readers of *Mrs Dalloway*...have noted that Clarissa's gift extends to that still purer form of consumption known as shopping'.

[28] This patient 'will not believe there was any connection between her parents so long as she blots out real situations of her own life' (*DA* 154).

[29] See Robert Caper, *A Mind of One's Own* (London and New York: Routledge, 1999), esp. 111–26. Ella Sharpe had been Adrian Stephen's analyst from 1926 to 1927; she also refers to, and quotes from, *A Room of One's Own* (with particular reference to the manx cat) in her lectures on 'The Technique of Psycho-Analysis' (1930); see *CP* 95; see also Elizabeth Abel, *Virginia Woolf and the Fictions of Psychoanalysis* (Chicago: University of Chicago Press, 1989), 16, 19.

The medium of Sharpe's applied art, she tells us, is the displaced and variable manifestation of human emotions and idiolects 'in individual settings'. The brown cushions and flower-filled vases of her consulting room—the analytic 'setting' in a different sense—are filled with with her patients' unconscious phantasy. This metaphorical filling provides the material for Sharpe's object-lesson mode of interpretation:

> I said, 'You see the wool you want for your work in jumpers that are already made. It is to be had, people do have it and yet it is inaccessible to you. You want to make something, you want to have what others can have. I have cushions of the colour you want.'
> I now referred to the new baby she had mentioned. Then I gathered together the references that indicated an unconscious phantasy concerning the making of babies, the brown wool for jumpers, the putting of things together neatly . . .   (*DA* 103).

One plain, one purl. Sharpe herself neatly knits together feminine desire, envy of the analytic breast, untidiness, the small child's sudden evacuation of her bowels on a long-forgotten holiday, and her patient's unconscious phantasy about the making of babies: '*I want wool like the dark brown of your cushion*' (my italics). Her patient's 'want' allows Sharpe to furnish her mind. What does a woman *really* want when she knits a new woollen jumper, or shops for wool of a colour she associates with her analyst? 'It is to be had, people do have it, and yet it is inaccessible to you.' Should this be coded as the everyday form of Kleinian envy, or as Lacanian desire? As Lacan puts it mischievously, 'the phallus as a signifier plays a central role beneath a transparent veil'.[30] He makes this well-known remark in the context of a back-handed tribute to none other than Sharpe herself, whom he praises for having given pride of place to a literary background in analytic training, while deploring her failure to recognize the veiled role of the phallic signifier (he has well-dressed salmon in mind, not shopping for knitting wool). But it is Lacan, in his reading of Freud's dream of the witty butcher's wife—with her unsatisfied desire for smoked salmon (when what she really wants is a caviar sandwich)—who insists that 'Desire must be taken literally.' The butcher's wife expresses a gratuitous desire—a longing for something she doesn't really want or need. Was there ever a wittier argument for a new sweater?[31]

---

[30] Jacques Lacan, 'The Direction of the Treatment and the Principles of its Power', in *Écrits: A Selection*, trans. Bruce Fink (New York: Norton, 2002), 240.

[31] Sharpe later records a series of dreams and nightmares linked by 'this all-dominating theme of thread', each representing a stage towards the unravelling of her patient's ongoing psychic struggle: ' "*I found a piece of cotton in my mouth and began to pull it out. After pulling a long time I dared pull no longer for I felt it was attached to some inner organ which might come out with it. I awoke in terror*" '; ' "*I said to you I only understand the process of introjection by thinking of the muscles which run into and form the eyeball itself*" '; 'a dream in which the patient was again taking a hair out of her mouth. It came out quite easily, it was not attached to anything, and no anxiety was felt in the dream' (*DA* 182). Sharpe comments that 'The element of "cotton," "thread," "hair" . . . bridged the unconscious phantasy with real experiences from early infancy to late childhood' (*DA* 182). The term 'bridged' recalls her quotation from George Willis, *The Philosophy of Speech*, 55: 'those bridges of thought which are crossed and recrossed by names in their manifold mutations'; cf. Sharpe: 'The bridges of thought are crossed and

'OUR PRIVATE INNER CINEMA'

Sharpe's aesthetics are not reparative in the strictly Kleinian sense, although they turn out to involve the maternal body. What interests Sharpe is the Kleinian dream-theatre of childhood phantasy. Invoking *The Psycho-Analysis of Children*, she writes: 'as Mrs. Klein has shown, the child plays its dream, develops apprehension, enacts roles' (*DA* 59).[32] Sharpe defines drama much as she defines dreaming: as the overcoming of painful external reality and the playing out of instinctual fears and internal dangers in a manageable form; drama and dreams both have their origin in trauma and unconscious phantasy. Sharpe's reference to the child's theatricality and use of personification as a means to master anxiety coincides with her professional interest in, and extensive writings on, Shakespeare—and perhaps even her well-attested gift for dramatic expression.[33] But in *Dream Analysis*, drama slides imperceptibly towards a specifically modern medium: film. Alongside the phantasy of the bed-loom, Sharpe's chapter 'The Mechanism of Dreaming' includes a section on 'dramatization' (alongside sections on condensation, displacement, and symbolism). Sharpe defines 'dramatization' in cinematic terms as the dreamer's projection of visual images onto an interior screen: 'A film of moving pictures is projected on the screen of our private inner cinema. This dramatization is done predominantly by visual images...' (*DA* 58).[34] 'Our private inner cinema' involves what Sharpe calls 'the reversion to concrete image thinking' (*DA* 58). For her, drama and poetic diction—along with psychosis,

re-crossed by names and names have manifold mutations' (*DA* 29, 39). Willis also writes that 'language develops along the framework of the real'—a framework evoked by the concrete structure of Sharpe's dream-loom.

[32] Sharpe is referring to Klein's 'The Significance of Early Anxiety Situations in the Development of the Ego' in *The Psycho-Analysis of Children* (1932; rpr. London: Hogarth Press, 1975), 176, as well as to 'The Psychological Foundations of Child Analysis', ibid., 8. In 'A Note on "The Magic of Names"' (1946), Sharpe is critical of the tyranny of the terms 'good object' and 'bad object' on the grounds of their unconscious appeal to the super-ego and to a regressive belief in white and black magic—evidently a reaction against Kleinian terminology.

[33] See, for instance, Sharpe's essays on *Hamlet* (1929, and unfinished) and 'From *King Lear* to *The Tempest*' (1946) in *CP*. Payne writes in her obituary that Sharpe 'knew Shakespeare's plays in the same way as a devoted priest knows his Bible', comparing her to their common analyst, Hanns Sachs. Payne also pays tribute to Sharpe's dramatic skills in delivering papers ('She was capable of being a great actress if other things had not interfered') and in her seminars, where 'she used unconsciously her acting gifts and could reproduce a session with a patient in an unique way' (*International Journal of Psycho-Analysis* 28, 55).

[34] By 'dramatization', Sharpe seems to mean more than Freud's 'dramatizing' of an idea, or 'the transformation of thoughts into situations' (*SE* iv. 50, v. 653); rather, she follows one strand in Freud's thought when she accords cinema the status of hallucination ('dreams *hallucinate*... they replace thoughts by hallucinations' (*SE* iv. 50), emphasizing the pictorial and literal aspects of both dreaming and cinematic visualization. See also L. Saalschutz, 'The Film in its Relation to the Unconscious' (1929), in *Close Up 1927–1933*, 256–60, emphasizing the regressive aspect of the cinema: 'The dreamer is usually looking on at the dream enactments as a spectator surveys the stage... and this is called Regression by Freud; we call it cinema' (ibid., 258).

hallucination, and dreaming—share their reversion to the concrete image. Already a vehicle for modernist fascination with the image, film technology provides a handy projective analogy for twentieth-century dreaming.[35] But Sharpe's cinematic analogy also draws on the material properties of film itself, considered as a medium that combines surface with transparency. The image is the product of a light-diffusing, light-sensitive membrane—Anzieu's *'pellicule'*.[36] The cinematic dreams of Sharpe's patients adhere to this permeable, flexible, clinging film surface.

Sharpe's theory of drama envisages the distribution of different parts of the dramatist throughout the dream scenario: 'Could we analyse a play in terms of the inner life of the dramatist, we should find the plot and all the characters taking part in it to be aspects of himself, projections of himself into imaginary characters' (*DA* 59).[37] Prospero—a magician with the power to create and dissolve airy spectacles and to dispense sleep—becomes the type of the film director: 'We are such stuff | As dreams are made of'. Sharpe views dramatic aesthetics in Romantic terms, as the magical resolution of discord, or 'a unity of creation within which discordances resolve into harmony' (*DA* 60). Dreams, she writes, can be 'a kind of abortive drama'; dream mechanisms are an attempt to make unity out of 'the raw material of conflicting forces'. But when it comes to her use of the cinematic analogy, Sharpe focuses instead on mechanisms of image production and on the materiality and iterability of film. In a telling illustration, 'The Mechanisms of Dreaming' enlists cartoon technology to illustrate how a stereotyped dream symbol becomes 'real and fresh again'. The dream of a train from which the patient and other passengers get out—but *'I never saw them inside, I never saw them get out or get in'*—is initially associated by the dreamer herself with a feeling of boredom. But later in the same session, she gives an enthusiastic description of Mickey Mouse jumping into a giraffe's mouth: 'The long neck had a series of windows down it, and one could see Mickey all the time, you didn't lose sight of him, you saw him go in, and come out' (*DA* 57). We know how Mickey gets in

---

[35] See, for instance, Marcus's account of the relation between dream theory and film theory in her introduction to Laura Marcus (ed.), *Sigmund Freud's The Interpretation of Dreams: New Interdisciplinary Essays* (Manchester: Manchester University Press, 1999), esp. 33–43. Marcus examines the history of psychoanalytic interest in the cinematic apparatus as well as cinema's interest in the mental apparatus by which the mind represents its unconscious workings to itself. Touching on Lewin and Anzieu, as well as Sharpe, Marcus notes the shift to an emphasis on 'the play of sign on surface' in recent theoretical writing. For the sustained engagement of psychoanalysis with cinema, see also Marcus, in *Close Up 1927–33*, 240–6.

[36] See Anzieu's definition in 'The Film of the Dream', in *The Dream Discourse Today*, 137: 'the French term *"pellicule"* designates a fine membrane which protects and envelops certain parts of plant or animal organisms . . . In its second sense, *"pellicule"* means the film used in photography; that is the thin layer serving as a base for the sensitive coating that is to receive the impression. A dream is a "pellicule" in both these senses.'

[37] In this respect, Sharpe's view of dramatization in dreams is similar to the account of fantasy given by Jean Laplanche and J.-B. Pontalis in 'Fantasy and the Origins of Sexuality' (1964), rpr. in Riccardo Steiner (ed.), *Unconscious Phantasy* (London: Karnac Books, 2003), 107–43. See also Sharpe's reading of *The Tempest*, 'From *King Lear* to *The Tempest*', in *CP* 237–40.

(through the giraffe's mouth), although how he gets out is left to the imagination. This 'new and exciting world without and within' includes both the discovery of the inside of the human body (the train) and the mysterious process by which babies (and symbols) are made. But the windows in the giraffe's neck also allude, cinematically, to the serial frames of a film-strip. The stereotypical symbol of the body as a train becomes new and exciting when it animates cartoon culture. The moving film revitalizes tired Freudian symbolism.

Dream Analysis posits the primal scene as the privileged site not only for the production of phantasy but for the infant director's first film. Talkies in the age of mechanical reproduction introduce a new dimension to dreaming. The following chapter narrates an anxiety dream: 'A man is acting for the screen. He is to recite certain lines of the play. The photographers and voice recorders are there. At the critical moment the actor forgets his lines. Time and again he makes the attempt with no result. Rolls of film must have been spoilt' (*DA* 75–6). Sharpe explains: 'The photographers and voice recorders cannot get the actor to perform although they are all assembled for that purpose. He forgets his lines' (*DA* 76). The infantile situation, reconstructed on the basis of the dreamer's associations, involves a reversal: 'the dreamer was once the onlooker when his parents were "operating" together. The baby was the original photographer and recorder and he stopped his parents in the "act" by noise. The baby did not forget his lines!' (*DA* 76). Sharpe tells us that the one thing the infant onlooker could do by way of interruption was to 'make a mess and a noise that brought the operations to a standstill' (*DA* 77). Readers of 'The History of an Infantile Neurosis' (1918)—Freud's *tour de force* of dream analysis—will recall that in his reconstruction of the primal phantasy behind the Wolf Man's enigmatic dream, the baby similarly interrupts his parents.[38] Here too ' "rolls of film [i.e. 'a huge amount of faecal matter'] must have been wasted" ' (*DA* 76). Sharpe's own account of the dream's mechanisms underscores the importance of the cinematic dream-screen: 'The modern invention of the screen of the cinema is pressed into service as the appropriate symbol, the screen being the modern external device corresponding to the internal dream picture mechanism' (*DA* 77). But her interpretation of the dream itself recycles Freud's text, reminding us of the iterable aspect of film. In Sharpe's cinema, nothing is spoiled, nothing wasted. The analyst does not forget her lines, even if the dreamer prefers visualization to sound.

Film in *Dream Analysis* also clings to and denotes the body, especially the female body. Another of Sharpe's patients, a man whose main problem is his terror of the maternal body, has the following dream of a semi-naked woman: ' "*I saw a lady who had black stuff round the top of her body covering the breasts and black stuff round her hips hiding her genitals, only the middle part of her body was naked*" '

[38] See also Marcus (ed.), *Sigmund Freud's The Interpretation of Dreams*, 36–7, for the resemblance between Sharpe's interpretation and the primal scene of looking which underlies the Wolf Man's childhood dream.

(*DA* 107). Sharpe notes that the dream was an anal gift after the week-end. But the patient quickly turns to what really interests him—a long story whose scientific technicalities take half an hour to relate, involving an account of the production of physiological illustrations 'drawn by a medical colleague for the purpose of making slides for a lantern' (*DA* 108). The illustrations are reproduced first on large sheets of paper, coloured red, then reduced in scale. But 'when the slides were eventually shown the colour was wrong. Then the patient laughed and said "only if it had been possible to use a black light would those diagrams have shown red on the sheet" '. Interpreting this close-up as a cover-up, Sharpe accentuates the change of colour in her response: ' "From black we can infer red" '—to which her patient replies impatiently: ' "It can be what bloody colour you like" ' (*DA* 108). His angrily repeated 'bloody' functions for Sharpe as the return of the repressed, the red, raw, and inflamed appearance of the mother's genitals, hugely magnified to a child's eye: 'The expletive is symbolical of the thing ejected at the being of whom he was and is afraid' (*DA* 109)—including, presumably, his woman analyst. Language is hurled like a missile against a bit of embodied female reality. When the matrix of dreams is no longer a metaphor, but a much-feared and needed mother ('genitals and breasts as nursing homes'), language takes on fiercely primitive energy. As Bion reminds us, 'bloody' ('By Our Lady') belongs both to the archaic turmoil of the angry infant and to the realm of the sacred.[39] Uncovering a piece of concrete thinking, Sharpe shows how the maternal body gets under the skin-ego of the baby and becomes Lacan's 'Thing'—the prehistoric, unattainable object of infantile incestuous desire.[40]

Sharpe brings *Dream Analysis* to a close with an eloquent and moving 'last dream' (so named by her) that contains an emblem of her recomposed poetics. The penultimate chapter had illustrated the way in which analysed persons are able to 'knit together' (Sharpe's telling phrase) body ego and psychical ego (*DA* 195). The psyche finally receives its due; analysis is the technician's art, but 'the new synthesis is brought about by the forces within the psyche itself' (*DA* 199). The psyche is at work as well as the analyst. Sharpe goes on to link Psyche to both Eros and Thanatos. This 'last dream', dreamed by an 83-year-old woman three days before her own death, movingly condenses the vicissitudes and illnesses of a long life into a single image: ' "*I saw all my sicknesses gathered together and as I looked they were no longer sicknesses but roses and I knew the roses would be planted and they would grow*" ' (*DA* 200). Here Sharpe lets us see how symbolization and mourning go together. In her dreamer's bouquet, a sickness is a rose is a rose-bed—imagery that is at once pastoral, commemorative, and horticultural. Sharpe's 'A Note on the "Magic of Names" ' disagrees with the saying that 'a rose by any other name would smell as sweet' on the grounds that 'Poetic words have always an individual significance' (*CP* 107). The dream pays tribute not just

[39] See 'On a Quotation from Freud' (1976), in *Clinical Seminars and Other Works* (London: Karnac Books, 1994), 307.   [40] See '*Das Ding*', in *The Ethics of Psychoanalysis*, 53, 67.

to the psyche, not just to psychoanalysis, but to the significance of these particular roses—and the dreamer's individuality, too: 'She shared in her old age the interests of youth and any movement that promised fairer and better conditions for mankind in the future appealed alike to her mind and heart, and among these was psycho-analysis.' The dream reveals the knowledge that sustains and consoles her in the face of death. In the words that conclude *Dream Analysis*, 'It is Eros alone who *knows* that the roses will be planted and grow' (*DA* 201). With this elegantly understated gesture, Sharpe lays her own psychoanalytic knowledge at the feet of Eros: 'Eros . . . *knows*'. Eros, of course, is an anagram for 'rose'.[41] Eros is also the nightly visitor who woos Psyche under cover of sleep and darkness and prohibits looking. Recomposing the letters of the rose as an allegorical figure—a verbal representation of thought—requires a momentary fading of the concrete image and a letting-go of the object, so that its multi-layered associations can bloom (beauty, poetry, life, mortality, and love). For Ella Sharpe, '*imagiste*', the rose takes on a spectral afterlife when it flourishes as a linguistic symbol.

In Sharpe's culturally gendered aesthetics, psychoanalysis is a legacy to be passed on via the maternal line. This 'last dream' represents Sharpe's own dream of psyche as matrix—memorialized as a progressive and psychoanalytically minded old woman, still finding comfort in dream-life. *Dream Analysis* ends by redefining the matrix of art, not just as a womb or a place of origin but also a 'medium in which something is "bred", produced or developed' (*OED*). For Sharpe, the matrix *is* the medium. We might recall Pontalis's account of dreaming as 'above all an effort to maintain the impossible union with the mother'.[42] With this impossible union in mind, I want to revisit Sharpe's statement that dream-analysis is an art 'conditioned by the limitations of its medium' (*DA* 124). Here are the words with which Sharpe begins *Dream Analysis*: 'Dreaming is . . . a psychical activity inseparable from life itself, for the only dreamless state is death' (*DA* 13). Sharpe's 'last dream' marks the limit-point, before the dreamlessness of death intervenes. Pontalis defines the unplumbed navel of the dream as the vanishing-point of the seeable, and the unseeable as the face of death: 'The dream is the navel of the "seeing-visible" (*voyant-visible*; Merleau-Ponty). I can see my dreams and see by means of it. Death, as we all know, is not something to be looked at in the face.'[43] Sharpe's dreamer allows us to see life, for a moment, as if through the eyes of the still-dreaming dead—as a posthumous after-image on the dreaming eye. The dream makes roses bloom in the unimaginable emptiness beyond. The visual economy of *Dream Analysis* quietly revises Freud's view that the function of dreams is to prevent the dreamer from waking. Instead, Sharpe implies that one function of dreams may be to plant images between ourselves and the faceless, dreamless state of death. But the allegory enacted by her 'last dream' also reminds

---

[41] See Lyndsey Stonebridge, 'Bombs and Roses: The Writing of Anxiety in Henry Green's *Caught*', *Diacritics* (special issue on trauma and psychoanalysis), 28 (1998), 25–43.
[42] 'Dream as an Object', in *The Dream Discourse Today*, 113.   [43] Ibid., 119.

us (as Eros knows) that the object can only be recovered as a symbol when it has been let go of as a Thing.

AIR WARS: *HAMLET* AND THE MAGICAL PHALLUS

> Air, noise and words, when they are implied metaphors for flatus and excreta, become violent, aggressive attackers of the ear.
>
> Ella Freeman Sharpe, 'An Unfinished Paper on *Hamlet*', *CP* 248

> She was like a bird, was a bird. She was it and it was herself. That is, she was the magical phallus. The dancing was in her.
>
> Ella Freeman Sharpe, 'Certain Aspects of
> Sublimation and Delusion' (1930), *CP* 128

In her wartime contribution to the 'Controversial Discussions' that raged between Kleinians and Anna Freudians during the 1940s, Sharpe returned to the theme of concreteness. Susan Isaacs's paper 'The Nature and Function of Phantasy' (1943) cites Sharpe in support of the derivation of metaphor from bodily experience. In the unconscious mind, Isaacs continues, 'where everything remains concrete, sensorial, or imaginal, introjection is always experienced as incorporation'.[44] Sharpe's diplomatic response (a quest for common ground) acknowledges her debt to Klein's views on unconscious phantasy, singling out the infant's breast hallucination—'the initial wish psychosis'—as the point of agreement between Kleinians and Freudians.[45] The belief in 'the good concrete object within', she writes, 'preserves the illusions of non-bodily separation'. The aim of primitive introjection and projection is to deny the reality of bodily separation; even the mystic shares this belief (like God, the mother is 'in me and I in her'). Sharpe defines the work of mourning and separation—the depressive position—as at once the last birth throes and the *sine qua non* of symbolization. But she ends by acknowledging that the wish for concreteness is never entirely relinquished:

The ineradicable infantile wishes for concrete realization never cease. The acceptance of a symbol, the capacity for mental imagery, means not that infantile wish and hope are relinquished, but that belief in reality separation has occurred and substitutes must be found. The introjected corporeal object no longer commands entire belief. Reality is reached via mental image.

It may well be that in all of us something of this wish-psychosis returns, it is the degree that matters.[46]

[44] See Pearl King and Riccardo Steiner (eds.), *The Freud–Klein Controversies 1941–45* (London and New York: Routledge, 1991), 275. Isaacs later notes that Sharpe's 1930 paper on sublimation and delusion had developed ideas about the relation between early anxiety situations and creativity in Klein's 'Infantile Anxiety Situations Reflected in a Work of Art and in the Creative Impulse' (1929); see *The Freud–Klein Controversies*, 457.   [45] Ibid., 338.
[46] Ibid., 339–40.

Sharpe's difference with Klein is not so much over the return of the recalcitrant wish-psychosis, or disbelief in 'the existence of illusions of bodily incorporation', as over the problems of technique that are involved for the analyst in bringing the patient to face reality. How, she asks, is the illusion of bodily incorporation and 'actual objects inside' ever to be dispelled or weakened?

Sharpe's short but telling contribution emphasizes the difficulty of eradicating what she calls the 'wish-psychosis'. Acceptance of a substitute symbol means that the belief—not the wish—has waned. Reality is reached via the capacity for thought ('mental imagery'). The issue of symbol formation proved almost as central to the 'Controversial Discussions' as that of unconscious infantile phantasy, the ostensible point of disagreement. Klein's 1944 paper on the infantile depressive position invokes the crucial role played by symbol formation in relation to both external objects and sublimation.[47] A few years later, in her unfinished paper on *Hamlet*, Sharpe returns to central strands in her own thinking—concreteness, metaphor, and sublimation. Her intention is to demonstrate 'the organic, emotional and mental unity of the play', as well as the manic-depressive cycle of creative functioning which she set out to trace in her unfinished book, *The Cyclic Movement of Shakespeare's Plays*. Her other surviving chapter, 'From *King Lear* to *The Tempest*' (1946), plots the movement from the depressive storm within Lear to the storm in *The Tempest* that marks the psyche's re-emergence after depression. Sharpe reads both plays as the poet's way of resolving his inner conflicts. Her departure from Victorian readings of Shakespeare (focused on the plays' characters) situates the meaning of the text firmly in the operations of the poet's mind. But Sharpe's interpretation differs from the 'applied psychoanalysis' of her own time in its orientation towards the image-focused Shakespearean criticism of the 1930s (represented by Caroline Spurgeon and Dover Wilson).[48] While her reference-point remains psycho-biographical reconstruction—specifically, reconstruction of the infant poet's psychic drama—she finds her evidence in the language of the play.

Sharpe's interpretative stance corresponds to the analogy-making poetics that Francis Thompson, the subject of her earliest published piece of psychoanalytic literary criticism, had attributed to Shelley. In the passage quoted by Sharpe, Shelley is credited with 'An instinctive perception ... of the underlying analogies, the secret subterranean passages, between matter and soul ... He stood thus as

---

[47] See Melanie Klein, 'The Emotional Life and Ego-Development of the Infant with Special Reference to the Depressive Position', *The Freud–Klein Controversies*, 782: 'I consider symbol formation which is bound up with unconscious phantasy life as one of the fundamental methods by which the growing relation to external objects is achieved and as a basic factor for all sublimations, since it is by way of symbolic equation that various activities and interests become the subject of libidinal phantasies.' Klein's paper was later included in Melanie Klein, Paula Heimann, Susan Isaacs, and Joan Riviere (eds.), *Developments in Psychoanalysis* (1952; rpr. London: Karnac Books, 1989), 198–236.

[48] See Caroline Spurgeon, *Shakespearean Imagery* (Cambridge: Cambridge University Press, 1935); J. Dover Wilson, *The Essential Shakespeare* (Cambridge: Cambridge University Press, 1932). Sharpe includes both in her references to 'From *King Lear* to *The Tempest*', along with two other books of the 1940s, S. L. Bethell, *Shakespeare and the Popular Tradition* (London: P. S. King and Staples, 1944), and John Palmer, *Political Characters of Shakespeare* (London: Macmillan, 1945).

[at?] the very junction-lines of the visible and invisible . . . He could express as he listed the material and the immaterial in terms of each other (*CP* 183–4).[49] Thompson's metaphor, the 'secret subterranean passages, between matter and soul', surfaces in Sharpe's 1940 paper on metaphor, where she refers similarly to 'the subterranean passage between mind and body [that] underlies all analogy' (*CP* 156). Sharpe resists the temptation to think of Shakespeare's characters 'as persons speaking their own speeches' (*CP* 220). Instead, she uses the discipline of psychoanalytic listening in which she was trained to trace the unconscious phantasies—the inarticulate, unspoken, and unconscious '*meaning before words*' (her italics)—that underlie Shakespeare's imagery.[50] The body constitutes a crucial aspect of this meaning. Her unfinished essay on *Hamlet* defines 'organic' not as the aesthetic relation of part to part or part to whole but rather as the subterranean passage that leads from metaphor to 'the body as a functioning organism'. Sharpe reads *Hamlet* in terms of its fidelity to long-forgotten bodily events and body functions, and the infantile emotions associated with them. The prototype for her theory of sublimation in *Hamlet* is the creative process by which language, via symbol, metaphor, and psychic ordering, conveys this reconstructed, historical totality of body, emotions, and mental functioning.

In Sharpe's reading, Hamlet's procrastination becomes the symbolic equivalent of the child's withholding and release—a version of discharge which 'clears the system, physically and emotionally' (*CP* 245). The basis for this pattern of bodily purgation (Aristotelian catharsis) 'must be understood in its setting of personal relationships' (*CP* 245). For Sharpe, the play's organic unity is an effect of the playwright's early object relations. Shakespeare's poetic genius lies partly in his ability to access these 'long forgotten psycho-physical experiences' via 'symbolic and metaphorical word-bridges' (*CP* 245).[51] But besides reconstructing the furious bowel-evacuations of the poet-to-be, and his restoration to infant bliss by means of his mother's angelic ministrations, Sharpe turns her attention to the metaphor of language as such—specifically, to the concrete meanings attached to air, noise, and words in *Hamlet*. Dramatic performance is freighted with the same incorporatory and omnipotent delusion. Properly speaking, there are no actors in Sharpe's Shakespearean criticism: there is only the psyche. Her theory of drama consists of Shakespeare's ejection of his various 'incorporations' in the form of dramatic characters.[52] The papers on sublimation consistently view mimesis as a

---

[49] 'Francis Thompson: A Psycho-Analytical Study' (1925); Sharpe's responds to this passage as encapsulating 'what one feels from the standpoint of psycho-analysis to be the *sine qua non* of poetic genius' (*CP* 183).

[50] For instance, Sharpe traces the hidden relation in *King Lear* between the motifs of 'sport, hunting, sound, and silence' (*CP* 221–2).

[51] Cf. 'the bridges of thought . . . crossed and recrossed by names' (*DA* 29 and n. 31).

[52] Cf. Sharpe's view on the role of dramatization in dreaming (*DA* 59). For a brief discussion of Sharpe's contribution (especially her emphasis on melancholia, incorporation, and bodily metaphor) in the context of psychoanalytic criticism of *Hamlet*, see Norman N. Holland, *Psychoanalysis and Shakespeare* (New York: McGraw-Hill, 1964), 91–3.

form of delusion in which the performer magically appropriates the power of an incorporated object. Sublimation and delusion spring from the same persecutory root. But Sharpe's deluded performers believe that they have the phallus in them, rather than the mother or God (like the mystic). This desire *in* rather than desire *of* is the hook that will draw Lacan into the argument by way of his interpretation of the role of desire and the phallic signifier in *Hamlet*.[53] Lacan's reading of *Hamlet* takes Sharpe's main emphasis as its point of departure for an account of the subject's problematic relation to desire, signification, and mourning. Although admiring the literary and metaphorical aspects of Sharpe's analysis, Lacan is corrective of the Object Relations psychoanalysis represented by Sharpe herself, who always has in mind the object-related aspects of language and desire. For her, after all, Shakespeare's plays represent the renunciation of fulfilment in the interests of poetry. But she never forgets the murderousness that lines the wish for concrete realization. The ear is the target of the word's attack in *Hamlet*, while the Elizabethan stage becomes 'the actual battlefields of Europe' (*CP* 240). Wars of words and weapons are the modern manifestations of omnipotent phantasy, played out in contemporary history and among analysts themselves.

WINDS AND WORDS

Sharpe melds the poetry of *Hamlet* to a precise 'fit' with the bodily and emotional experiences of the infant bowel. The images she explores cluster around the idea of 'air', 'noise', and 'smell'. The ghost is 'as the air, invulnerable' (*Hamlet*, I. i. 145), accompanied by 'airs from heaven or blasts from hell' (I. iv. 41), and 'scent(s) the morning air' (I. v. 58). Hamlet's words are 'wild and whirling' (I. v. 133). He rails against his mother 'in noise so rude' (III. iv. 40), or, in his grief, exhales 'windy suspiration of forc'd breath' (I. ii. 79). But, Sharpe remarks, air is also 'the element in which birds fly'. Air, birds, and angels are linked 'because of their winged flight' (*CP* 248). Hamlet is sung to Heaven by 'flights of angels' (V. ii. 371). Claudius's prayers 'fly up' while his thoughts 'remain below' (III. iii. 97). Words are 'pregnant'. When the 'fit' is not upon him, Hamlet is 'as patient as the female dove | When that her golden couplets are disclos'd' (V. i. 309–10), silently brooding on poetry. Sharpe invokes Ernest Jones's compendious essay 'The Madonna's Conception through the Ear' (1914) in support of the idea of the fertilizing breath of the Dove and the sexual equivalency between speech and impregnation, and discovers an

[53] See 'Desire and the Interpretation of Desire in *Hamlet*' (1959), trans. James Hulbert, in Shoshana Felman (ed.), *Literature and Psychoanalysis: The Question of Reading, Otherwise* (Baltimore, Md.,: Johns Hopkins University Press, 1982), 11–52. Lacan's discussion of *Hamlet*, of which this translation is an abridged version, originally formed part of Seminar VI, *Desire and its Interpretations* (1958–9); selections were published as '*Hamlet*, par Lacan', *Ornicar?*, 24 (1981), 1–31; 25 (1982), 13–36; 26–7 (1983), 7–44. The concerns in Seminar VI are developed in 'The Subversion of the Subject and the Dialectic of Desire in the Freudian Unconscious' (1960); see Jacques Lacan, *Écrits: A Selection*, trans. Bruce Fink (New York: Norton, 2002), 281–312.

implicit contrast in *Hamlet* between divine procreation and carnal sexuality.[54] She also detects a Christological motif of rising and setting—'Hamlet dies and goes to heaven' (*CP* 250)—which she relates to the manic-depressive cycle of creative renewal. In this respect, Sharpe's reading of *Hamlet* reveals the latent pull towards a redemptive, even Christianized, version of the Kleinian depressive position.

Sharpe argues that Hamlet's procrastination about avenging his idealized Ghost-father and killing Claudius (his real or 'carnal' father) gives rise to linguistic excess. As for Shakespeare himself, Sharpe asserts simply that 'The poet transferred his allegiance to the Muses' (*CP* 258). Sublimation is the outcome of his 'substitution of immaterial, symbolic fulfilment' for the literal fulfilment of incestuous and murderous Oedipal wishes. But *Hamlet* also dramatizes the word's capacity to injure and poison in phantasy. Words themselves 'become violent, aggressive attackers of the ear' (*CP* 248), cleaving and splitting. After talking with the players, Hamlet imagines the actor who would 'cleave the general ear with horrid speech' (II. ii. 589); he criticizes the noisy actor who out-Herods Herod and 'split[s] the ear of the groundlings' (III. ii. 9). Air bites and nips, as in a snatch of dialogue early in the play (not cited by Sharpe), when Hamlet says that 'The air bites shrewdly' and Horatio replies: 'It is a nipping and an eager air' (I. iv. 1–2). This is the biting air that brings the Ghost on stage to goad Hamlet's conscience. Later, Hamlet's windy sighs are so strong that they threaten, famously, 'to shatter all his bulk | And end his being' (II. i. 95–6), and Polonius asks if Ophelia has given him 'any hard words of late' (II. i. 107) as if sighs and words had physical force. Unpregnant of his cause, Hamlet tries to rouse himself to anger as if given the lie 'i' th' throat | As deep as to the lungs' (II. ii. 601–2). Throughout *Hamlet*, 'air' tends to migrate towards the (aurally) adjacent aperture, 'ear'. The Ghost's account of his death, rendered to 'ears of flesh and blood' (I. v. 22), exposes the abuse of 'the whole ear of Denmark' (I. v. 36). The abuse of the ear of Denmark is concretized in the Ghost's lurid narrative of his murder by Claudius—'and in the portals of my ears did pour | The leperous distilment' (I. v. 63–4)—and later re-enacted for us in the play-within-the-play. Reproached by Hamlet, Gertrude exclaims 'These words like daggers enter in mine ears' (III. iv. 95). Claudius diagnoses in Ophelia's madness 'the poison of deep grief' (IV. v. 76). A usurper via the ear, Claudius worries that Laertes 'wants not buzzers to infect his ear | With pestilent speeches of his father's death' (IV. v. 90–1) and fears that he will stick at nothing in his campaign 'Our person to arraign | In ear and ear' (IV. v. 93–4). Bad-mouthing is infectious and can lead to the downfall of kings.[55]

The play's literalization of dying from a poisonous word in the ear brings to light the phantasy that language can kill. Sharpe's 1929 essay 'The Impatience of Hamlet' argues that Shakespeare both is all the characters and murders them too.

[54] See *Essays in Applied Psycho-Analysis*, 2 vols. (London: Hogarth Press, 1951), ii. 266–351.
[55] For the ear as textual organ signifying delay and deferral (a 'figure of momentous suspense') in *Hamlet* and in Shakespeare generally, see Joel Fineman, 'Shakespeare's Ear', *The Subjectivity Effect in Western Literary Tradition* (Cambridge, Mass.: MIT Press, 1991), 222–31.

This is how he survives: 'He has killed them and himself by writing the play. He has ejected all of them symbolically' (*CP* 205). The Ghost in *Hamlet* threatens to disrupt this symbolic system. Something is rendered corporeal that should remain incorporeal. When the Ghost appears to Hamlet, Gertrude asks why he holds discourse 'with th'incorporal air' (III. iv. 118). The Ghost embodies the return of the repressed phantasy of incorporation that underlies primitive introjection and projection. Sharpe goes out of her way to remind us that the Ghost is not just Hamlet's Oedipal phantasy, but 'projected in visible form from the mind of Shakespeare through Hamlet' (*CP* 252). Her insistence on the Ghost's projective status makes him more than 'the disembodied voice' (*CP* 254) of Hamlet's Oedipal grievances. The fate of this all-too-solid Ghost is the occasion for Sharpe's most obtrusively concrete stab at meta-narrative: 'The child poet was poisoned in the ear by what he heard, i.e., the parents in a marital embrace. This turned everything sour within him and then he let out his own poison.' (*CP* 255) We have witnessed this primal scene in the parental bedroom before, in *Dream Analysis*; appropriately, Sharpe's super-egoic Ghost inhabits 'the bowels of the earth' (*CP* 256) as a sign of his archaic origins. The civilized aspect of Shakespeare triumphs when Fortinbras exercises control over the rage and grief once evacuated by the furious infant. 'Spilling' (Sharpe's term) is contained by the play itself. The murderous Oedipal wish-psychosis has been successfully subsumed and hidden. As in a satisfying dream, the hiding of the wish is what makes possible its 'magical fulfillment' (*CP* 261).

Importantly, creativity for Sharpe is driven not by sin and repentance (the Christian equivalent of Kleinian reparation and forgiveness) but by the symbolic pursuit of displaced libidinal wishes. Her emphasis on the laid ghost of Oedipal desire is the point of contact between her reading of *Hamlet* and Lacan's. In 'Desire and the Interpretation of Desire in *Hamlet*' (1959), Lacan transforms an economy of substitution into an economy of loss: 'swarms of images, from which the phenomena of mourning arise, assume the place of the phallus'.[56] Lacan's *Hamlet* is dominated by the figure of mourning. His reading of the play as an account of melancholic subjectivity under the precarious sway of the phallic signifier follows a series of seminars that tease out at length a case-history drawn from Sharpe's *Dream Analysis*, the case of the patient who barks like a dog to put people off the scent (the metaphor is hers).[57] Sharpe's patient is a Hamlet figure

[56] *Literature and Psychoanalysis*, 38. For a Lacanian reading of Lacan's discussion of *Hamlet*, see also Julia Reinhard Lupton and Kenneth Reinhard, *After Oedipus: Shakespeare in Psychoanalysis* (Ithaca, NY: Cornell University Press, 1993), 67–88.

[57] See *The Seminar of Jacques Lacan: Desire and its Interpretation 1958–1959*, Book VI, trans. Cormac Gallagher from unedited French MS (n.d.), for the discussion of Sharpe's case-history and her patient's dream in Seminars 8–12 (from 14 January 1959 until 11 February 1959), running on into the *Hamlet* discussion in Seminars 13–19 (4 March 1959 until 29 April 1959). Seminar numbers are accompanied by parenthetical references to the dates and internal page numbers of Gallagher's translation. French transcripts of Seminar VI are to be found online at http://www.ecole-lacanienne.net/seminaireVI.php3

whose father died when he was a small boy, and who unconsciously believes that he has killed his father out of rivalry for his mother. Unable to work, he has problems with female sexuality (including his mother's), represses all bodily feelings, and eschews aggressive physicality; both his movements and his speech are tightly controlled. But one day Sharpe becomes aware ('with great joy', she notes) of 'the smallest and discreetest of coughs' (*DA* 130) before he enters her consulting room. The cough is the bodily manifestation of her patient's unconscious phantasy that he is about to disturb a sexual scenario. As a 15-year-old, he would cough discreetly before entering the drawing-room to warn his brother, in case he and his girlfriend would be caught embracing. The little cough produces a comically canine association which Lacan, struck by the acuteness and subtlety of Sharpe's analysis, reads as an allegory of the disappearing phallus, the sign of desire in the other.

The patient relates a phantasy 'of being in a room where I ought not to be, and thinking someone might think I was there, and then I thought to prevent anyone from coming in and finding me there I would bark like a dog. That would disguise my presence. The "someone" would then say, "Oh, it's only a dog in there"' (*DA* 132). Being where one ought not to be (doing what one ought not to be doing) and barking like a dog repeat a still earlier, infantile, interruption. The cough (a noisy exhalation of air) has the meaning of the 'explosive flatus' (*CP* 146) by which he had formerly tried to separate his parents—cleaving the parental ear with his horrid sounds. For Lacan, however, 'this little cough', the patient's discreet 'bow-wow', signals the effect of the signifier. His cough is his message—or rather, his question ('What is this signifier of the Other in me?'), although instead of a question, he constructs a phantasy. He is not a dog, 'but thanks to this signifier . . . he is other than he is'.[58] Not only does he absent himself from the place where he is but he also signals his otherness by calling attention to his life as a dog. In Lacan's understanding of the phantasy scenario, the canine impersonator enacts not only his own disappearance but the fading (Jones's *aphanisis*—the disappearance or making to disappear) of the phallus, including one that might be found in the wrong place or misbehaving. The disappearing phallus, however, signifies not so much the phallic woman he simultaneously fears and finds reassuring (Lacan spends a long time on Sharpe's exploration of the meaning of the maternal Thing) as desire—that is, the desire of, and in, the other. Desire itself has been made to disappear, although it reappears in signification: castration anxiety symbolizes its loss. Lacan credits Sharpe with a profound understanding of 'the signifying character of things' that anticipates his own emphasis on the element of linguistic substitution, and on the fact that the phallus, although never where it is expected to be, 'is there all the same'.[59] In so far as the dog-man is a speaking

---

[58] *Desire and its Interpretation*, Seminar 9 (21.1.59: 7, 11). For a discussion of Lacan's Seminar VI, one of the few to mention the extended commentary on Sharpe's case-history that precedes Lacan's discussion of *Hamlet*, see Herman Rapaport, *Between the Sign & the Gaze* (Ithaca, NY: Cornell University Press, 1994), 64–5.   [59] *Desire and its Interpretation*, Seminar 11 (4.2.59: 13, 14).

subject, 'He is and he is not the phallus. He is it because it is the signifier in language that designates him, and he is not it in so far as language . . . takes it away from him.'[60] Now you see him, now you don't. The phallus is a bit of a clown, like the barking boy who noisily announces his absence.

Lacan's playful, admiring, and corrective re-reading of Sharpe on the bodily symptom of the discreet cough prefaces his seminars on *Hamlet* as a tragedy of desire whose plot illustrates the hero's domination by the desire of the other—'the *Che vuoi?* of subjectivity constituted and articulated in the Other'.[61] Lacan's *Hamlet* becomes the tragedy of the subject's fading in the face of the signifier of desire (the phantasmal Ghost) whose meaning remains obscure to him. This unasked question ('Che vuoi?') is the true haunter of the text. In Lacan's scheme, deprivation defines the imaginary object of desire (Ophelia): 'The object takes the place . . . of what the subject is—symbolically—deprived of'.[62] Rather than being an object, a potential or actual source of satisfaction (Lacan's quarrel with Object Relations psychoanalysis), Ophelia is at once the locus of phantasy and the sign of Hamlet's alienation on account of his subjection to the desire of the (m)other (in this case, Gertrude's sexual desire for Claudius).[63] Lacan pretends to dismiss as preposterous the false etymology—introduced by himself in a previous seminar—'that Ophelia is *O phallos*' ('there's no need to resort to the etymology of "Ophelia"').[64] But he alludes in much the same vein to 'other things equally gross, flagrant, extravagant, if you just open the *Papers on Hamlet*, which Ella Sharp [*sic*] unfortunately left unfinished and which it was perhaps a mistake to publish after her death'.[65] It is, of course, Lacan himself who is being flagrant here. Perhaps he also has in mind the presence of things gross and flagrant in the play. Sharpe's 1929

---

[60] Ibid., Seminar 12 (11.2.59: 4).

[61] *Literature and Psychoanalysis*, 13. The reference is to the series of diagrams in Jacques Lacan, *Écrits: A Selection*, 300–2. For an ingenious mapping of the Lacanian graphs of desire (the 'Che vuoi?' schemata) onto psychoanalysis and Shakespeare, see also Lupton and Reinhard, *After Oedipus*, 232–47.   [62] *Literature and Psychoanalysis*, 15.

[63] Cf. Janet Adelman's Kleinian reading of *Hamlet* as a buried fantasy of the subjection of male to female, emphasizing the poisonous effects of sexual splitting; Janet Adelman, *Suffocating Mothers: Fantasies of Maternal Origin in Shakespeare's Plays* (London and New York: Routledge, 1992), 11–37. Like Sharpe, Adelman reads *Hamlet* as the vehicle for fantasy, albeit diffused and universalized rather than biographical.

[64] In the preceding seminar (Seminar 16), Lacan confesses that he 'had the curiosity to look up the derivation of "Ophelia", and . . . found a Greek reference' from Homer in which *Ophelio* means 'to make pregnant, to impregnate' and is linked to *Ophallos* (8.4.59: 12). Lacan is having fun here; see also Rapaport, *Between the Sign & the Gaze*, 66.

[65] *Literature and Psychoanalysis*, 20, 23. In Cormac Gallagher's translation, the reference to Sharpe is less ambiguous: 'I am only astonished that it has not been written that Ophelia is *ho phallus*, because we find things which are just as gross and just as striking (*'d'aussi gros et d'aussi énormes'*), by people who do not have bats in the belfry (*'de pas piqué des annetons'*), simply by opening the unfinished paper on *Hamlet*' (Seminar 17: 15.4.59: 13). In the phrase *'de pas piqué des annetons'*, *'annetons'* appears to be a mistranscription for *'hannetons'*; the colloquialism might be translated as 'excellent, first-rate; better than expected'. Sharpe, in other words, is not half bad. Apart from moments where he detects a 'wobble' or disagrees with her on theoretical grounds, Lacan gives frequent credit to Sharpe's interpretations.

essay on *Hamlet* had quoted the lines referring to the drowned Ophelia's garland with its phallic 'long purples' or 'dead men's fingers'—the *Orchis mascula* (botanically identified by Lacan himself), 'That liberal shepherds give a grosser name, | But our cold maids do dead men's fingers call them' (IV. vii. 171–3). When Hamlet nullifies Ophelia as the signifier of his desire, 'gross' is just what she becomes—a phallic part-object, or, in Lacan's terms, 'rejected by the subject as a symbol signifying life'.[66]

Lacan's Hamlet can only win back reintegration of the *objet a* (here, the missing object of desire) 'at the price of mourning and death'.[67] An underlying concern of his seminar is to elucidate the enigmatic relation between mourning and desire. In this it takes its cue from Sharpe. Sharpe's essay on Hamlet's impatience had invoked the psychoanalytic legacy of Freud's 'Mourning and Melancholia' (1917) and Karl Abraham's account of the expulsion, destruction, and preservation of the object via the manic-depressive cycles of melancholia and mourning.[68] Hamlet's 'impatience'—as opposed to his delay—is his inability to wait out the temporal vicissitudes of mourning and melancholia short-circuited by action: the hasty killing of Polonius; Ophelia's suicide; the fatal duel with Laertes. Lacan picks up this temporal theme when he says that Hamlet never finds his own 'hour', his time, but instead is always at the hour of the other. His departure from Freud (and Sharpe) lies in putting new pressure on the concept of mourning. Freud had proposed failed mourning—melancholia—as a regression from object-love to identification (the shadow of the object falls on the ego). But for Lacan, there remains an unanswered question: 'What is the incorporation of the lost object? What does the work of mourning consist in? We're left up in the air . . . The question hasn't been posed properly.'[69] His seminar attempts to put things right.

But at this point Lacan's development of his argument takes an unexpected turn. Citing Hamlet's outcry when Laertes leaps into the grave to embrace the dead Ophelia (transformed by death into the impossible object of desire),

[66] *Literature and Psychoanalysis*, 23. For Ophelia as an object in the context of Lacan's larger scheme, see also Philip Armstrong, *Shakespeare in Psychoanalysis* (London and New York: Routledge, 2001), 71–6; and, for a helpful discussion of the *Hamlet* seminar in relation to larger shifts in Lacan's thought, see ibid., 61–90.

[67] *Literature and Psychoanalysis*, 24. For the *objet a* and for Ophelia as *objet a* (lost and found), see Lupton and Reinhard, *After Oedipus*, 68–71, 76–8. In Lacan's seminars of the late 1950s and early 1960s, the evolving concept of the *objet (petit) a* is viewed in the *matheme* of fantasy as the object of desire sought in the other; see Evans, *Dictionary of Lacanian Psychoanalysis*, 124–5, and, for a fuller discussion of the trajectory of Lacan's concept (a deliberate departure from British Object Relations psychoanalysis), see also Malcolm Bowie, *Lacan* (Cambridge, Mass.: Harvard University Press, 1991), 165–78.

[68] See Karl Abraham, 'A Short Study of the Development of the Libido' (1924), *Selected Papers of Karl Abraham*, trans. Douglas Bryan and Alix Strachey (1927; rpr. London: Karnac Books, 1988), 418–501.

[69] *Literature and Psychoanalysis*, 37. Some air has got in here—literally, '*on reste dans un vague*' (vagueness, uncertainty, vacancy). Cf. *Desire and its Interpretation*, Seminar 18 (22.4.59: 12); Gallagher translates the phrase as 'in a state of vagueness'.

Lacan asserts the unbearableness of the death of someone essential to us, and the impossibility of experiencing one's own death: 'The one unbearable dimension of possible human experience is not the experience of one's own death, which no one has, but the experience of the death of another.'[70] Here Lacan overlooks Sharpe's injunction that 'To learn what the Ghost is we must listen to what the poet makes him say' (*CP* 252). His assertion tacitly ignores the fact that the Ghost returns to testify—in lurid and excruciating detail—to the manner of his own dying ('Cut off even in the blossoms of [his] sin, | Unhous'led disappointed, unanneal'd' (I. v. 76–7)).[71] The Ghost exposes what should remain hidden, a body hideously 'bark'd about, | Most lazar-like, with vile and loathsome crust' (I. v. 71–2). Not content with revealing his murder through the ear, he usurps the 'fair and warlike form . . . of buried Denmark' (I. i. 47–8). The Ghost embodies the fantasy of melancholy phallic incorporation and the disappearance of the phallus from the symbolic order (the phallus should play its part veiled by the mark of linguistic substitution which acknowledges symbolic castration). Lacan argues—by inverse analogy with psychosis, where what is foreclosed from the symbolic register is projected onto the real—that in mourning what is lost in reality migrates to the symbolic: 'the hole in the real that results from loss, sets the signifier in motion'.[72] Hence the swarming of images that Lacan notices in *Hamlet*. Sharpe sees Shakespearean metaphor as the compensatory yield of culture. But, for Lacan, symbolization is the phantasmic yield of loss. Psychosis and mourning move into alarming proximity. The subject is forever lacking by virtue of his relation to the signifier—and so is the symbolic, by virtue of its relation to the real. 'Up in the air' is just where we should be left when it comes to incorporation, since (for Lacan, at any rate) the lost object can only enter through the ear, via verbal introjection. Melancholia, by contrast, encrypts the retroactive phantasy of concrete incorporation, a poisonous form of intake and ingestion.

Lacan's most startling and revisionary reading of *Hamlet* is not that desire is founded on impossibility, but that mourning, too, turns out to be all but impossible. His chiasmus, or inverted analogy between psychosis and mourning (loss of the real as opposed to the reality of loss), intertwines madness with mourning in ways that illuminate a crucial aspect of *Hamlet*. The death of Hamlet's father, both because his death has lacked the proper rites, and because the Ghost is in improper possession of the experience of his own death, throws the signifying system into disarray. By virtue of his return in the real, the Ghost is a sign of the potential foreclosure of mourning at the level of the symbolic. Lacan claims (erroneously) to

---

[70] *Literature and Psychoanalysis*, 37.

[71] Scott McMillin, 'Lacan's Ghost: The Player in *Hamlet*' (unpublished paper), notes the oddity of Lacan's assertion that no one can experience their own death, citing the Ghost's lurid account as 'an all-around engrossment which threatens the boundary between inside and outside . . . This is what you get with a father just come from the tomb' (quoted by kind permission of the author).

[72] *Literature and Psychoanalysis*, 38. See the discussion of the relation between psychosis and mourning by Marjorie Garber, *Shakespeare's Ghost Writers* (New York: Methuen, 1987), 132–7.

be the only commentator to have remarked that 'from one end of *Hamlet* to the other, all anyone talks about is mourning'.[73] Hamlet's private madness represents the collective, communal madness of any attempt to memorialize the dead. Lacan implies that this collective falling-short results from the inherent limitations of signifying systems themselves. While acknowledging that 'The work of mourning is accomplished at the level of the *logos*', he argues that it is 'first of all performed to satisfy the disorder that is produced by the inadequacy of signifying elements to cope with the hole that has been created in existence.'[74] The signifying system is inadequate to the task. No rituals of mourning can patch the gaping hole (*béance*) opened up by mourning. Hence, Lacan suggests, the association in folklore of 'refusal of something in the satisfaction of the dead, with the appearance of ghosts and spectres in the gap left by the omission of the significant rite'.[75] There are never enough words—or rites—to do justice to the dead.

Sharpe's biographical reading of *Hamlet* uncovers the drowning in Stratford-upon-Avon of a young woman named Katherine Hamlett, whose burial rites were curtailed, and behind that, the death of the poet's sister, Anne (who received a costly funeral). The recovery of buried memories in the graveyard scene is Sharpe's alternative figure for the return of the dead father: 'As the bones are thrown up, they bring the living memories, and the man lives again' (*CP* 260). Lacan insists on Hamlet's privation ('that self-sacrifice, that pound of flesh which is mortgaged [*engagé*] in his relationship to the signifier').[76] By contrast, Sharpe had privileged the fullness of memory: 'Here, rather than in the Ghost, is the tribute of memory to the real father of childhood' (*CP* 260). Shakespeare lives.

THE MAGICAL PHALLUS

Sharpe's paper on sublimation, 'Certain Aspects of Sublimation and Delusion' (1930), traces dramatic performance back to an ancient form of ritual mourning—dancing—derived from Egyptian funerary rites: 'The impersonation of ghosts, the enacting of the resurrection of the dead person by the dancer, points to the same motivation in the origin of dancing... The dead are made alive by magical acts' (*CP* 127). Drama ('the impersonation of ghosts') has its origins in funeral ceremonies, she asserts; the masked actors are 'for the time being the incarnations of the spirits of the dead' (*CP* 127). Resituating *Hamlet*'s thematization of actors and acting in the graveyard, the Ghost comes to personify the ancient origins of drama. As Ivor Brown puts it (the quotation is Sharpe's), 'The swaddling clothes of drama are the winding sheets of the hero king' (*CP* 127). Shakespeare's *Hamlet* emerges, for Sharpe, from the winding sheets of an unlaid Ghost. Sharpe's two essays on sublimation during the 1930s are under-girded by her fascination with phallic performance. She endorses Freud's statement that 'the first and most

---

[73] *Literature and Psychoanalysis*, 39.   [74] Ibid., 38.   [75] Ibid., 39.   [76] Ibid., 28.

important identification of all, [is] the identification with the father' (*CP* 134).[77] Her 1935 paper comparing 'The Sublimations of Pure Art and Pure Science' argues that 'harmonious rhythmic representation in a symbolical way' (*CP* 144) serves to recover the union of primal identification and infantile object-love.[78] But she also explores the problematic aspects of the performer's identification with, and phantasied incorporation of, the phallic signifier. Art becomes a form of self-preservation and reassurance in the face of overwhelming anxiety: 'It is *life* that is danced' (*CP* 128). But the communication made by picture or statue, drama or novel, masks an underlying hostility.

In a passage that both performs and appropriates the rhythmic power she attributes to the dancer, Sharpe's 1930 paper evokes a patient who

knew herself *how* to dance. She knew how to have control over her muscles. To see new steps, a new dance, was to receive a picture through her eyes. She could then practise 'in her head.' Like a negative she had taken the image. Then it could be reproduced as a picture taken from a negative. She was the negative and she reproduced the picture. Sounds of music suggested dance. Sound and movement went together naturally. The body bent this way and that, swayed and moved as though it were one thing—all one thing—as a bird in flying is all one thing. She was like a bird, was a bird. She was it and it was herself. That is, she was the magical phallus. The dancing was in her. She had become the thing she once saw through eyes of desire, love and hate. She had incorporated it and after the manner of cannibalistic beliefs she had become endued with the power of the thing incorporated.   (*CP* 128)

How can we tell the dancer from the dance, let alone primal identification from object-love? 'She had become the thing she once saw . . . She had incorporated it . . . she had become endued with the power of the thing incorporated.' Sharpe implies that the problem has been resolved via symbolization; omnipotence is subjected to the demands of reality at the level of the body. But her deliberate switching between metaphor and identification, figure of speech and unconscious phantasy ('like a bird', 'was a bird'), signals the inevitably fused, confused, and retroactive relation between symbol and symbolized. We can only posit this rhythmic representation as a trace of the infant's union of self-preservation and pleasure. The phantasy of embodiment is itself an after-effect, and belongs inevitably to the realm of representation. The infant has long ago had recourse to substitutes in the face of what Sharpe calls 'the unmanageable frustrating object outside' (*CP* 146).[79]

---

[77] Sharpe cites Susan Isaacs, 'Privation and Guilt' (1929), to support her view that 'Freud's primary identification may perhaps play in the total drama a greater part than was originally thought' (*CP* 134); see Susan Isaacs, *Childhood and After: Some Essays and Clinical Studies* (London: Routledge & Kegan Paul, 1948), 10–22.

[78] 'The unconscious omnipotent good control of the parental imagos results in the projection of a harmonious rhythmic representation in a symbolical way in reality. This in terms of actual experience means a recapture of periods in infancy when primal identification and object-love were united' (*CP* 144).

[79] See Stonebridge, *The Destructive Element*, 85–93, for a perceptive discussion of this aspect of Sharpe's writing in connection with the role of rhythm generally; Stonebridge's discussion is acute on the way in which rhythm 'ceases to signify a continuity between the primary processes and art, and

The dancer's delusion depends on (and appears to celebrate) a primitive, cannibalistic form of object relation. Mimesis repeats this originally rivalrous identification with the phallus: 'Eyes have seen and ears heard and body felt, and the ego ... says "I can do that"' (*CP* 128). Rivalry, as well as love, drives the flying rhythms of the dancer's phallic appropriation, and even the mimetic dance of Sharpe's own writing as her words take flight.

The wish-psychosis invoked by Sharpe's distinctive contribution to the 'Controversial Discussions' is fuelled by persecution. Perfect dancing (like perfect writing?) assuages anxiety—ultimately, Sharpe suggests, anxiety about the mother. Significantly, her performers are all women: 'On to the mother had been projected those wishes that were inimical to life itself' (*CP* 129). Hamlet's murderous Oedipality becomes the girl's destructive death-wish against the retaliatory mother who has deprived her of what she wants (milk, babies, and phallus). This is the Kleinian subtext of Sharpe's thinking during the late 1920s and early 1930s: 'As she would have taken those things from her mother she desired and envied, from milk to children and the father's penis, so there had been projected on to the mother intents as destructive to herself' (*CP* 129). But Sharpe's writings on sublimation recoil from the next step in Kleinian aesthetics. Delusion takes the place of reparation: 'she is saved by perfect dancing. She becomes the magical phallus. She restores in herself what her hostility wished to take away, to destroy ... The father is restored to the mother; the penis, the child, are back again magically in the womb' (*CP* 129). This is magical restoration without the experience of guilt; bodily reunion without the pain of separation. Rather than being the dance of death that it really is, it banishes death, dancing death away. The very compulsion of Sharpe's singing and dancing women patients to impersonate the phallus is the cause of their artistic inhibitions. Sharpe's over-trained singer only recovers her voice when she finds it metaphorically and poetically—'You are a bird flying up in your voice' (*CP* 130)—and becomes at once the Orpheus and the Siren of literary song: 'Orpheus drew sticks and stones. The Sirens drew men to destruction' (*CP* 130). By vocalizing her phantasy of parental potency (the semen and milk that she pours out 'like water, like cream'), the singer moves others with her voice as she has been moved herself.

Evoking the artist's double movement of introjection and projection, Sharpe alludes fleetingly to the melancholic painter Ruth Kjär in Klein's 'Infantile Anxiety Situations Reflected in a Work of Art and in the Creative Impulse' (1929). Quoting Klein, Sharpe writes that 'painting is a restitution too. The blank space is filled' (*CP* 131).[80] But the persistence of persecutory anxiety and the

instead becomes caught up in a chain of metaphoric substitutions ... [T]he rhythmic dance itself comes precisely to *stand in* for something which is lacking—the phallus' (ibid., 88–9). Stonebridge suggests that the key to understanding this shift lies in Sharpe's concept of incorporation and acceptance of figurative language as a substitute for the lost object.

[80] Cf. Ruth Kjär's lament (' "There is an empty space in me, which I can never fill!" ') and the triumphant conclusion to Karin Michaelis's narrative: ' "The blank space has been filled" ' (*LGR* 215, 217).

recalcitrance of the delusion produce a slight but significant shift away from Kleinian aesthetics that has its parallel in the later writings of Marion Milner and D. W. Winnicott. Sharpe implies that reality is only reached through a compensatory detour, via the illusion of omnipotence. The child-artist keeps mother and baby together in a bower of roses, just as Sharpe's singing, dancing, and painting women exercise control over their first loved and feared objects: 'Every stroke of the brush is a power over the parents' (*CP* 131). A reduction in the intensity of the persecutory anxiety allows the blocked artist to perform. But, Sharpe insists (the emphases are hers), '*The sublimation springs from the same root as the delusion of persecution*' (*CP* 131). This provenance of sublimation in delusions of persecution has disturbing political implications. One of Sharpe's psychotic patients, for instance, has a fixed delusion, guarded over by a lady doll holding a baby. Surrendering the delusion allows her to shrink the doll from magical talisman to signifier of an unconscious Oedipal trauma (she becomes a student of history). But along the way, she takes on a dangerous masculine identification, 'played out by being a warrior. She massacred her dolls' (*CP* 133). The risks of a delusory, body-based psychic economy include not only doll-massacre, but nationalisms, ideologies, fascism, and suicide.

With hindsight, the Sharpe of the wartime 'Controversial Discussions' can write that belief in an actual good or bad object 'results in . . . a Hitler-ridden Germany'. Hence, the deadly combination (psychotic persecution of others, on one hand, and complacent denial of all destructiveness, on the other) found among those in the grip of self-righteous delusion: 'God's in his heaven'—and on one's side.[81] At stake for Sharpe in the Klein wars was the phantasy of embodiment which, she strongly implies, is the pathology of Kleinianism. 'Good' and 'Bad', she wrote later (apropos of 'The Magic of Names'), are 'the flags under which nationalisms and ideologies march, gaining recruits through a contagious belief in a good object. "Good" and "Bad" are the magical words of propaganda by which mass psychology is manipulated' (*CP* 107). Surely, she also has in mind the tendency of Klein's followers at the time to turn her ideas into a closed system with its own terminology.[82] In her 1935 paper, Sharpe pays tribute to Klein's researches, which 'have enabled us to realize to the full the hostile sucking and biting phantasies of grinding into pieces and swallowing' (*CP* 143). But she also warns that hostile phantasies can be acted on, whether with biting words or with knives. For Van Gogh, she reminds us, the failure of sublimation resulted not only in the psychotic rhythms of the melancholia-laden pictures painted at the end of his life, but in his murderous attack on Gauguin, in cutting off his own ear, and

[81] See *The Freud–Klein Controversies*, 340; and cf. Stonebridge, *The Destructive Element*, 90–1; as well as linking the war and the 'Controversial Discussions', Stonebridge argues that Lacan is mistaken in assuming that Sharpe's account of sublimation ignores its social implications.

[82] Similarly, Sharpe implies that Klein sees the baby as a closed system, rather than taking into account 'a complete situation' (what Winnicott will call 'the maternal environment'); see *The Freud–Klein Controversies*, 808.

finally in his suicide. 'Hate and aggression, chaos, loss of rhythm' are the tragic yield of the artist's loss of contact with reality—not to mention the uncontained hostilities unleashed in war and theoretical controversy within the psychoanalytic institution. Sharpe quotes Van Gogh's comment that his entire work 'was a race for life' (*CP* 147). Sublimation may preserve what is only destroyed in phantasy. But 'the race for life' can also be a defence against ever-present and unacknowledged destructive elements within the psyche. Death, as well as self-preservation, drives the artist's hectic rhythms.

Sharpe's 1930 paper on sublimation and delusion ends by quoting 'the English magician', Prospero abjuring his powers at the close of *The Tempest*. His broken staff and drowned book—'I'll break my staff...And, deeper than did ever plummet sound, | I'll drown my book' (*The Tempest*, V. i. 54–7)—become the symbols of Magian omnipotence finally submitted to reality. Seemingly without irony, Sharpe closes with Prospero's boast of waking the dead:

> Graves, at my command,
> Have wak'd their sleepers, op'd and let them forth
> By some so potent art.
>
> (*The Tempest*, V. i. 48–50)[83]

These sleepers waked from the grave recall the 'last dream' of *Dream Analysis*, where life is momentarily glimpsed through the eyes of the dead, or even the Ghost of Hamlet's father, returning to testify to his own excoriating death. Prospero's resurrected sleepers embody the illusions that we never fully relinquish. Clinging to the ineradicable wish-psychosis, Prospero enacts Sharpe's recognition that 'wishes for concrete realization never cease', and that literature bears the traces of these unceasing wishes. But her wartime contribution to the 'Controversial Discussions' ends on a warning note.

Sharpe writes pointedly of the need to relinquish belief in 'the incorporated psychoanalyst'—that modern version of the magician, whether individual, representative, or symbolic:

I do not believe in the omnipotence of the analyst or of psychoanalysis. That is still illusion that ignores many facts. The *psychical* delivery of the patient (no matter what magical results are achieved) is only brought about by the patient: relinquishing the belief in the incorporated analyst. For if not, the fundamental wish psychosis remains.[84]

---

[83] Prospero's boast forms the culmination of a speech which might well fuel thoughts about omnipotence: 'I have bedimmed | The noontide sun, called forth the mutinous winds, | And 'twixt the green sea and the azured vault | Set roaring war . . .' (IV. i. 41–4). Sharpe comments acutely (apropos of his torrential poetic energy) that 'Prospero is as unrepentant at heart as Caliban', even though 'he returned to normality by *actual* "waves" ' (*CP* 239).
[84] *The Freud–Klein Controversies*, 340.

Sharpe's closing gesture re-performs Prospero's surrender of his potent art, but to very different effect. Belief in the omnipotence of the incorporated analyst is the final wish-psychosis. But delivery from illusion is not the same as being disillusioned. Without the concrete effects of language, metaphor, and rhythm—without body-knowledge and its richly figurative yield—neither analysis, nor writing, nor dancing would be able to attain their magical results. Sharpe's body poetics pay tribute to aesthetic transformation.

2

Stolen Goods: *Joan Riviere*

I think in analysis it is as necessary to keep in mind how strong the *not* seeing and *not* knowing is to us as to learn all we can about what is unconscious in the mind.

What I am speaking of now springs from another of Freud's sayings to me. In my analysis he one day made some interpretation and I responded to it by an objection. He then said: 'It is *un-conscious*.' I was overwhelmed then by the realization that I knew nothing about it—I knew nothing about it.

Joan Riviere, 'A Character Trait of Freud's' (1958)[1]

Joan Riviere is best known for her account of 'womanliness' as a defensive masquerade. Her bleak view of femininity as pathology—only ever at best a performance—has been appropriated for a variety of de-essentializing and deconstructive versions of gender as performance (most influentially, in late twentieth-century feminist and film theory).[2] Riviere's critique of femininity emerged from her own struggle for personal and professional recognition during a period that coincided with the suffragette movement and the official founding of psychoanalysis in England. She entered analysis with Ernest Jones during the First World War, looking for a solution to personal problems that included depression, chronic ill-health, a breakdown, and lack of sexual fulfilment.[3] Gifted, snobbish,

---

[1] Athol Hughes (ed.), *The Inner World and Joan Riviere: Collected Papers 1920–1958* (London: Karnac Books, 1991), 353–4 (*IW*). 'A Character Trait of Freud's' appeared in John D. Sutherland (ed.), *Psycho-Analysis and Contemporary Thought* (London: Hogarth Press, 1958), 145–9, as the postscript to a series of lectures commemorating the centenary of Freud's birth in 1956; other contributors included Winnicott, Bowlby, and Milner.

[2] See, for instance, the classic discussion by Stephen Heath, 'Joan Riviere and the Masquerade', in Victor Burgin, James Donald, and Cora Kaplan (eds.), *Formations of Fantasy* (London: Methuen, 1986), 45–61; Mary Ann Doane, 'Film and the Masquerade: Theorizing the Female Spectator' (1982), in Katie Conboy, Nadia Medina, and Sarah Standbury (eds.), *Writing on the Body: Female Embodiment and Feminist Theory* (New York: Columbia University Press, 1997), 176–94; and Elizabeth Wright (ed.), *Feminism and Psychoanalysis: A Critical Dictionary* (Oxford: Blackwell, 1992), 242–3.

[3] For a short biographical account, see Hughes's account of Riviere's life and work (*IW* 1–43), and Athol Hughes, 'Joan Riviere and the Masquerade', *Psychoanalysis and History*, 6 (2004), 161–75. For overviews of Riviere's work, see Janet Sayers, *Kleinians: Psychoanalysis Inside Out* (Cambridge: Polity, 2000), 49–67, and Lisa Appignanesi and John Forrester, *Freud's Women* (London: Weidenfeld & Nicolson, 1992), 352–65, esp. for Riviere's role as translator and her triangular relations with Freud

and intellectual, with a strong interest in the arts, she emerged from the debilitating despair and neurosis of the war years, from her angry failed analysis with Jones, and from the remedial analysis with Freud that followed, to become a formidable psychoanalytic presence from the 1920s onwards. She was a founder-member of the British Psycho-Analytical Society when it was established by Ernest Jones in 1919, and played a respected (and, by all accounts, feared) part in its later activities, as well as being a distinguished training analyst and close colleague of Melanie Klein.[4] Although she herself did not work with children, her analysands during the 1930s included not only Susan Isaacs but Donald Winnicott and John Bowlby—two of the most influential child analysts to emerge from the post-war period.[5]

As a devoted, skilful, and literary translator of Freud's writings (she had been sent to Germany for a year after leaving school), Riviere deserves a special place in the history of the dissemination of psychoanalytic ideas. Freud was quick to see her potential value for psychoanalysis even before she came to him for analysis in the early 1920s, and supported her claims over those of Jones when it came to the project of translating his work into English. But Riviere's own writing—from the

and Anna Freud (her analytic sibling). Born Joan Verrall in 1882, a niece of the Cambridge classicist Arthur Verrall, she married a barrister, Evelyn Riviere, in 1906, and had a daughter, Diana. Her circle overlapped socially and intellectually with the Bloomsbury Group, and in 1913 she also attended meetings of the Medico-Psychological Society, a glimpse of whose ethos from 1913 until its closure in 1923 (when many of its analysts had died or moved to the British Psycho-Analytical Society) can be found in Suzanne Raitt, *May Sinclair: A Modern Victorian* (Oxford: Clarendon Press, 2000), 135–9. It was against this background of suffragism and eclectic psychoanalytic treatment, focused on women until the war intervened, that Riviere entered analysis with Ernest Jones in 1916. Although Riviere seems not to have been a student herself, a number of other women associated with the Medico-Psychological Clinic later came to play a major part in the British Psycho-Analytical Society: Marjorie Brierley, Susan Isaacs, Sylvia Payne, Nina Searle, and Ella Freeman Sharpe all passed through the Medico-Psychological Clinic before becoming analysts (see ibid., 139).

  [4] After her death, James Strachey (acknowledging that he came from a similar middle-class, professional, late-Victorian background) included not only himself but also Jones among those who had been afraid of her: 'And indeed, she was a very formidable person'; see his obituary of Riviere, *International Journal of Psycho-Analysis*, 44 (1962), 230.

  [5] Susan Isaacs dedicated her second book, *Social Development in Young Children: A Study of Beginnings* (1933), to Riviere. The theoretical part of Winnicott's membership paper, 'The Manic Defence' (1935), read to the British Psycho-Analytical Society the same year as Riviere's paper on the negative therapeutic reaction, emphasizes the internal world and the denial of depression, possibly reflecting Riviere's influence; see D. W. Winnicott, *Through Paediatrics to Psycho-Analysis: Collected Papers* (1958; rpr. New York: Brunner/Mazel, 1992), 129–36. For the period of Winnicott's analysis with Riviere, see F. Robert Rodman, *Winnicott: Life and Work* (Cambridge, Mass.: Perseus Publishing, 2003). This was Winnicott's second analysis (his first was with James Strachey), lasting from 1933 to 1938; Bowlby's analysis lasted ten years, from 1929 to 1939. Winnicott and Bowlby complained that their analyses with Riviere had been too narrowly focused on the inner world as opposed to the environment, and Bowlby felt that his had been over-long (see *IW* 34; Rodman, *Winnicott*, 81). Riviere's wartime supervisees later included Herbert Rosenfeld, Hanna Segal, and Henri Rey (*IW* 33), who all pay tribute to her originality, intellect, sensitivity, kindness, and culture, as well as to her sharp tongue and forcefulness. Marion Milner, however, saw her as a 'bully'; see Phyllis Grosskurth, *Melanie Klein: Her World and her Work* (Cambridge, Mass.: Harvard University Press, 1987), 396.

late 1920s to the 1950s—has striking originality, passion, and eloquence. It also stages the gendered drama that continued to preoccupy her. Paradoxically, it was the fall-out from Riviere's disastrous analysis with Jones between February 1916 and April 1918 that provided the basis for her insight into the pernicious form of masking she came to associate with so-called 'womanliness'. The analysis had foundered on the confrontation between what Jones (with some justification) announced to Freud as Riviere's 'colossal narcissism' and what Riviere herself originally saw, uncritically, as her 'womanliness'. Arguably, it also failed because of Jones's difficulty in recognizing Riviere as a woman and as a colleague. He proved spectacularly unable to deal with the transferential and counter-transferential aspects of their stormy analytic relationship—aspects that included not only her mingled love and rage but his own relations to women, and especially his feelings about dominant women. From its beginnings in the mid-1920s, Riviere's friendship with Melanie Klein provided a less agonized and agonistic context for her personal and professional development in the years that followed. Klein's ideas gave Riviere a lens through which to view her analytic experience, and from the late 1920s onwards her writing reflects both her support for Klein's work and their close and productive intellectual collaboration.

Riviere often presents Kleinian ideas in ways that are more accessible and elegant than Klein's densely packed papers, and she may also have helped Klein to express herself more effectively in English. But she was much more than simply an editor, an advocate, or a spokeswoman for Klein's views.[6] She articulated and even anticipated crucial theoretical developments (for instance, the Kleinian emphasis on reparation), while her most telling contributions mined the complexities of her own psychic and emotional life with imagination and acerbity. Despite adopting the impersonal tone of her time and class, Riviere's best-known papers explore aspects of her own psychoanalytic experience in highly charged and individual ways. Their drama—their distinctive combination of insight, melancholy, and harshness—derives partly from seeming to occupy the psychic terrain they open up. Their literary quality and range of reference inevitably link her to the Bloomsbury Group, with whose class-marked cultural background and aesthetic interests (though not its bohemianism) she has much in common, even beyond their immediate social overlaps in London and Cambridge. Riviere's statuesque beauty and personal elegance—she had started her professional life as a court

---

[6] Riviere was well placed to deliver one of the exchange lectures with the Viennese Society during 1935–6, 'On the Genesis of Psychical Conflict in Early Infancy' (1936), which provides a lucid introduction to Klein's thought. Hughes calls it 'the clearest and most beautifully expressed outline of Kleinian theory as it was at that time' (*IW* 271). During this period Riviere also published her joint volume with Melanie Klein, *Love, Hate and Reparation* (1937). She later wrote the general introduction to the flagship volume of papers paying tribute to Klein's influential ideas; see Melanie Klein, Paula Heimann, Susan Isaacs, and Joan Riviere, *Developments in Psychoanalysis* (1952; rpr. London: Karnac Books, 1989), 1–36. However, by the 1950s Riviere was dissociating herself from the circle of disciples who surrounded Klein; see Pearl King and Riccardo Steiner (eds.), *The Freud–Klein Controversies 1941–45* (London and New York: Routledge, 1991), p. xix.

dressmaker—often become a synecdoche for her work. The elevated, hyperbolical quality of Riviere's writing is one of its distinctive features, perhaps even a stylistic equivalent of the 'colossal narcissism' of which Jones complained. Riviere can be conversational and direct, but she also insists (and even bullies) with her eloquence. Elevation and depression, glimpses of bourgeois household management and tooth-and-nail nursery fury define the domesticated world of Riviere's inner theatre. Her writing explores the passionate vicissitudes of hate and love, negativity and reparation, in ways at once aesthetic and visceral. Imaginatively, she can pay tribute to the dizzying psychic allegory of Ibsen's *Master Builder* (1892) while also appreciating the solid foundations and systematic building up of the Freudian edifice. Riviere's single greatest debt to Freud may not only be for the insight he gave her into her feelings but for his encouragement to write about them, harnessing the narcissism latent in self-representation much as Ibsen himself had done in *The Master Builder.*

THE MASK OF INNOCENCE

Riviere's 1936 paper, 'A Contribution to the Analysis of the Negative Therapeutic Reaction', is widely regarded as her most important contribution to psychoanalytic theory. But it is also among her most uncompromisingly personal in its origins, drawing on the painful experiences bound up with her analyses with Jones and Freud. She writes not of the masquerade as performance but of something altogether more sinister—the mask of the narcissist. The omnipotent and narcissistic patients whom Riviere describes are mean, self-satisfied, and deceptive (Riviere's harsh terms). As Karl Abraham wrote in 1919, their envy makes them want to do everything themselves.[7] They employ a defence against analysis known as 'the manic defence'—a defiant denial of their need and dependence that includes contemptuousness of others, and an insistence that they themselves are doing the analyst's work, lest the analyst should gain any power over them:

Above all, however, the trait of *deceptiveness*, the mask, which conceals this subtle reservation of all control under intellectual rationalizations, or under feigned compliance and superficial politeness, is characteristic of the manic defence. This mask . . . is exploited in the manic position not as a defence in itself but as a cover for the defence of securing exclusive control.   (*IW* 141)

The manic defence—this mask of 'feigned compliance and superficial politeness'—conceals yet another defensive strategy: the need for control. Beneath the mask lies

---

[7] See Karl Abraham, 'A Particular Form of Neurotic Resistance against the Psycho-analytic Method' (1919), *Selected Papers of Karl Abraham*, trans. Douglas Bryan and Alix Strachey (1927; rpr. London: Karnac Books, 1988), 303–11. Abraham anticipates Klein's emphasis on envy (ibid., 307) in the form of the patient's destructive assault on the analyst's contribution, as well as emphasizing such narcissistic patients' stalling of the analysis: 'nothing is too dear for their narcissism' (ibid., 310).

a hidden core of emptiness and fear. The depressive kernel within contains the fear of suicide or madness, threatening chaos and ruin both to the self and to the analyst (whose destruction the patient at once seeks and fears). The question Riviere asks about this inner situation is why the need to secure exclusive control should express itself in the form of not getting well—in the so-called 'negative therapeutic reaction'. After all, the patient comes to analysis to be cured, not to deceive. Her answer is bound up with the graphic account she gives of the hidden depression against which the patient erects her manic defence.

Riviere's understanding of this depressive core qualifies and humanizes her devastating critique of the narcissist. Her paper can be read both as the record of her own psychic history, and as a penetrating work of retrospective self-analysis. Freud's account of the negative therapeutic reaction in *The Ego and the Id* (1923)—translated by Riviere herself in 1927—was written during a break in the period of her analysis with him. But whereas Freud emphasizes unconscious guilt as the motive for not getting well, Riviere's paper, written during the mid-1930s, puts the emphasis elsewhere.[8] Drawing partly on her analytic experience with Jones, partly on her experience with Freud, but above all on Klein's more recent formulation of the depressive position during the 1930s, Riviere focuses attention on the patient's despair about her inner world and her hopelessness about making reparation to the damaged objects it contains. Her paper evokes an internal disaster of epic proportions. Hers is the ground zero of the Kleinian depressive position, reactivated by 'this nightmare of desolation'—the unbearable pain of object-loss:

The content of the depressive position (as Melanie Klein has shown) is the situation in which all one's loved ones *within* are dead and destroyed, all goodness is dispersed, lost, in fragments, wasted and scattered to the winds; nothing is left *within* but utter desolation. Love brings sorrow, and sorrow brings guilt; the intolerable tension mounts, there is no escape, one is utterly alone, there is no one to share or help. Love must die because love is dead. Besides, there would be no one to feed one, and no one whom one could feed, and no food in the world. And more, there would still be magic power in the undying persecutors who can never be exterminated—the ghosts. Death would instantaneously ensue—and one would choose to die by one's own hand before such a position could be realized.   (*IW* 144)

Riviere writes from inside the ruins. Her account of an internal wasteland evokes a world haunted by ghostly persecutors and suicidal impulses, unalleviated by any comfort other than the grandiose gesture of suicide. This is what it means to feel like death—to feel death as a destructive force within the psyche (Riviere's definition of the death-drive), and to choose death as the only means of escape.

---

[8] Freud had written: 'The battle with the obstacle of an unconscious sense of guilt is not made easy for the analyst. Nothing can be done against it directly, and nothing indirectly but the slow procedure of unmasking its unconscious repressed roots, and of thus gradually changing it into a *conscious* sense of guilt' (*SE* xix. 50 n.).

As Riviere wrote in 'Hate, Greed, and Aggression' (1937), 'Death represents the farthest extreme of destructiveness that we can conceive of, and one's own death...represents the acme of inherent destructive forces operating *within* one-self (*IW* 175).[9] Empathy with the melancholy, tyrannical ego takes the form of stylistic ventriloquism. The relentless pressure towards identification generated by Riviere's use of free indirect discourse, her intensifying prose rhythms and sorrowing domestic vignette ('no one to feed one, and no one whom one could feed'), even the touch of fantastic imagination ('the ghosts'), make her a verbal performance-artist of the depressive position.

With this performative aspect of Riviere's writing in mind, I want to turn to the concept of the negative therapeutic reaction. This is the reaction that disables and prevents what Riviere (following Freud) calls the 'unmasking' process of psycho-analysis. Her paper identifies the internal wrecker as sadism. For all the patient's altruism and guilt, her real or ostensible caretaking of others, sadism lurks at the core along with the haunting fear of abandonment and breakdown. The loved ones within, by whom the patient fears to be abandoned, are at the same time revealed to be the objects of her undying hatred and cruelty. She yearns for uncon-ditional love and union with a perfect object, while being possessed by the murderous fury of disappointment and rejection. For all her appearance of loving compliance, the patient is a trickster and deceiver. To make reparation would be such an all-consuming task that an unending, fake analysis is preferable to 'cure'. In this scenario, guilt itself becomes suspect. Riviere cites Freud's footnote from *The Ego and the Id* about the patient who gets worse instead of better in the face of analytic encouragement: 'He says that this unconscious sense of guilt is sometimes a "borrowed" one, adopted from some other person who had been a love-object and is now one of the ego's identifications. And "if one can unmask this former object relation behind the unconscious sense of guilt, success is often brilliant."' (*IW* 161)[10] Even the patient's sense of guilt is 'borrowed' (like Riviere's quotations from Freud), and requires to be unmasked as belonging to someone else. Any apparent improvement may be a trick to evade the feeling of failure that haunts the analytic process. Nothing is proper to the patient—not guilt, not 'cure'; per-haps not even the identity on which the narcissist's sense of uniqueness depends.

---

[9] Cf. the visceral language in another paper of the same period, 'On the Genesis of Psychical Conflict in earliest Infancy' (1936): 'Not only do the hunger-pangs feel like foreign agents within one, like biting, gnawing, wasting forces inside one, against which one is helpless; but the intense wishes to seize and devour (the breast) which accompany such hunger at its inception will be identi-fied with these inner devouring agencies or pains' (*IW* 283); 'destructive forces operating *within*' feel like hunger-pangs.

[10] Making the link between 'the sole remaining trace of the abandoned love-relation' and 'what happens in melancholia', Freud writes: 'One has a special opportunity for influencing it when this Ucs. sense of guilt is a "borrowed" one—when it is the product of an identification with some other person who was once the object of an erotic cathexis...If one can unmask this former object-cathexis behind the Ucs. sense of guilt, the therapeutic success is often brilliant, but otherwise the outcome of one's efforts is by no means certain' (*SE* xix. 50 n.).

This unconscious deceit ('the *false* transference') is the hardest of all disguises to see through, according to Riviere, because it flatters the analyst's own narcissism and risks meeting with complicity and denial; the patient may be allowed to depart with her narcissism intact. In this exquisitely deceptive and deceived choreography, all that is truly proper to the patient is the concealed and disavowed kernel of her depressive illness.

In Riviere's essay on the masquerade, 'womanliness' is worn as a mask of innocence to hide an unconscious phantasy involving the theft of masculinity and to avert reprisals, 'much as a thief will turn out his pockets and ask to be searched in order to prove that he has not the stolen goods' (*IW* 94). Riviere's feminine trickster-thief—filled with hatred of other women as well as rivalry with men— wants to steal the father's masculine intellect and phallic attributes in order to wear the trousers. Just as there is nothing proper to an identity made up of borrowed identifications, there is nothing proper to femininity that rests on the wish to appropriate another's intellectual property ('stolen goods'). The mask of 'womanliness', with all the ideological freight the term conveys, covers over sadistic fury and destructive envy of the very masculinity it seeks to sooth and placate.[11] In the turbulent letters which record the aftermath of her failed analysis with Jones, Riviere clung desperately to the mask of 'womanliness' as a means to assuage her anguish and disguise the fury aroused in her by what she experienced as rejection. Riviere's letters to Jones can be read as the raw material—the untheorized pre-writing—which led her to the heart of the painful psychic dilemma later uncovered by her papers on femininity and the negative therapeutic reaction. In the one-sided correspondence that survives from this period, spanning the autumn of 1918 and the early months of 1919, Riviere made a desperate appeal to Jones to take her back into analysis, simultaneously mounting a destructive attack on his analytic authority. Her ultimate target was the analysis itself, which she linked to the question of her value to herself and to him.

Riviere's analysis with Jones had endured, with breaks due to illness, from February 1916 until he broke it off in April 1918.[12] Her letters show that she had found any break in the analysis difficult to bear, resenting even small disruptions to her analytic appointments. The period of her analysis had also seen Jones's impetuous marriage in early 1917 to a woman twelve years younger than himself, a gifted Welsh musician named Morfydd Owen—a marriage that Riviere was unable to forgive and insisted was a flight from Jones's feelings for her. After he had broken off the analysis with Riviere, Jones's young wife died suddenly in September 1918 from the complications of a ruptured appendix.[13] The tragedy

---

[11] See Athol Hughes, 'Personal Experiences—Professional Interests: Joan Riviere and Femininity', *International Journal of Psycho-Analysis*, 78 (1997), 899–911, for a speculative discussion of Riviere's troubled relation to her own femininity, including her experience as both daughter and mother.

[12] See Sayers, *Kleinians: Psychoanalysis Inside Out*, 52.

[13] For Jones's brief courtship and marriage, see Vincent Brome, *Ernest Jones: Freud's Alter Ego* (London: Caliban Books, 1982), 112–13.

and its emotional aftermath colours Riviere's letters to Jones, seeming to revive her fury even as she offers the 'womanly' sympathy appropriate to his bereavement and frantic state. Riviere's punitive and self-punishing letters enact the drama she later describes with such clear-sightedness. Her ostensible aim is to recover Jones for a shared project, the discontinued analysis. But she turns the analytic tables on him, appropriating the role of analyst for herself. She can do the job better than he could (as she has no hesitation in telling him). Her excoriating and self-castigating letters provide a glimpse of the workings of the deeply negative and destructive elements that Riviere later describes so vividly. But as well as testifying to an insoluble analytical *impasse*, the letters to Jones also show her confronting his view of her—and her view of herself. They reveal that most painful of all collisions, the challenge to narcissism posed by the impingement of another's view, and the collapse of a precarious self-idealization. Riviere's paper on the negative therapeutic reaction emphasizes the patient's suicidal despair after the inevitable wreck of this fragile defence. Her letters to Jones often express the wish simply to give up and die, or hint at suicide. These love-letters (more accurately described as hate-letters) are characterized by a deadly combination of grandiosity, denunciation, and bitter reproach, punctuated by moments of self-reproach and glimpses of what had been '*un*-conscious' in her feelings for Jones. Riviere's alternately condescending and dictatorial tone often gives way to pathetic expressions of dependence and need, and a plea for recognition as a woman—indeed, for recognition of any kind. This, she believed, was what Jones so cruelly withheld. It was what Freud would finally offer.

On the receiving end, Jones (only four years older than Riviere) later complained to Freud about Riviere's cleverness, cruelty, and sadism; she had 'devoted herself to torturing [him] without any intermission and with considerable success and ingenuity, being a fiendish sadist'.[14] With customary sang-froid, Freud expressed his relief that Jones had not actually slept with Riviere ('I am very glad you had no sexual relations with her as your hints made me suspect').[15] Whatever their relations, Riviere herself seems to have expected special treatment when she first entered analysis with Jones (she refers to having felt herself 'unique' at the outset), while Jones failed to contain the relationship within professional boundaries.[16] Her ensuing 'declaration of love' was followed, according to his self-serving account to Freud, by 'the broken-hearted cry that she had never been

[14] 22 January 1922; see R. Andrew Paskauskas (ed.), *The Complete Correspondence of Sigmund Freud and Ernest Jones 1908–1939* (Cambridge, Mass.: Harvard University Press, 1993), 454.

[15] 23 March 1922 (ibid., 464). Freud was well placed to know of Jones's history of problematic relations with women, including his women patients.

[16] Hughes has described Riviere's unsuccessful analysis with Jones, in the short-hand of psychoanalysis, as 'apparent unanalysed transference manifestations and acting out on the part of both patient and analyst'; see 'Letters from Sigmund Freud to Joan Riviere (1921–1939)', *International Review of Psycho-Analysis*, 19 (1992), 265. Or, as Hughes puts it tactfully, 'She experienced a deep transference love for Jones into which she appeared to have no insight, and apparently she was not helped to find it' (*IW* 11).

rejected before (she has been the mistress of a number of men)'.[17] Jones took responsibility for the débâcle, however, admitting that 'The treatment finally broke down over [his] inability to master this negative transference'.[18] Riviere's letters asking Jones to take her back into analysis after his wife's death in September 1918 (under pressure, he continued to see and work with her until she left for Vienna in June 1921) reveal her as deeply insensitive to Jones's grief, which she saw as an obstacle to the resumption of her analysis. Jones had mishandled the analysis from the outset, taking pity on Riviere to the extent of lending her his cottage for much-needed holidays (a cosily possessive letter from Riviere on the subject of interior decoration survives from one of her stays), and letting her look after his dog.[19] He subsequently asked her for advice on the occasion of his marriage—turning the knife in the wound—and then (in Freud's words) 'took her resistance too seriously and could not control her sadism after it came up as it had to do'.[20] Chagrined by her condescension, Jones complained to Freud of Riviere's 'strong complex about being a well-born lady' and the way she 'despises all the rest of us [i.e., analysts], and especially the women'.[21] This seems to have been true, judging from Riviere's letters, which compound snobbishness with anti-semitism.[22]

Jones's later remarks to Freud also express his resentment at being dominated by a woman (as he had been dominated by his common-law wife, Loe Kann). His self-confessed fear of maternal figures seems to have given Riviere a hostage in the struggle, as if mutual analysis was an aspect of their professional relations; Jones, after all, had been briefly in a 'didactic' analysis with Ferenczi in 1913.[23] But it was Jones's refusal to acknowledge or value Riviere's femininity (as well as her professional ambition) that became the most fiercely contested issue. During

[17] 22 January 1922; *The Complete Correspondence of Sigmund Freud and Ernest Jones*, 454.
[18] Ibid., 454.
[19] CRB/F07/35; see Hughes, *IW* 11. Not always dated, Riviere's letters are numbered in the sequence preserved in the Archives of the British Psycho-Analytical Society. They are quoted here by kind permission of the Melanie Klein Trust and the British Psycho-Analytical Society.
[20] 11 May [1922]; *The Complete Correspondence of Sigmund Freud and Ernest Jones*, 475. Freud makes further criticisms of Jones's handling of Riviere in another long letter of 4 June 1922: 'You seem to have soon lost the analytic superiority especially required in such a case...When Mrs. R. brought up her unpleasant reactions you seem to have treated her as a bad character in life but you never got behind her surface to master her wickedness' (ibid., 484).   [21] Ibid., 454.
[22] Writing to Riviere in 1923, Freud regretted that their analysis had not been longer: 'I might have succeeded in letting you see the connexion between neurosis and national or social prejudice, and we both may have derived some benefit from this study, perhaps after several stormy hours'; see Hughes, *International Review of Psycho-Analysis*, 19, 271. What he has in mind can be seen in Riviere's letter of 3 October 1922 describing her travel-companions *en route* for Berlin (*IW* 36), and even her first impressions of Freud's appearance—'not typically that of a medical man, nor was it particularly Jewish...The long pale face...might have suggested a learned professor' (*IW* 209). For the latent racism in Riviere's case-history of a southern woman in 'Womanliness as a Masquerade', see also Jean Walton, 'Re-placing Race in (White) Psychoanalytic Discourse: Founding Narratives of Feminism', *Critical Inquiry*, 21 (1995), 775–804; rpr. in Elizabeth Abel, Barbara Christian, and Helene Moglen (eds.), *Female Subjects in Black and White* (Berkeley, Calif.: University of California Press, 1997), 223–50.
[23] Jones undertook his brief Budapest analysis with Ferenczi, which he seems to have enjoyed, during June and July 1913; see *The Complete Correspondence of Sigmund Freud and Ernest Jones*, 200–14 and 214 n.

her struggle with Jones, Riviere wields 'womanliness' as a formidable weapon in her arsenal. Her disappointment gave rise to one of the most revealing records of amorous fury to have been preserved within the psychoanalytic archive—or indeed in the literature of spurned and abandoned women, from Dido to the present day. Written in a heroic and high-flown register, they reveal Riviere's gift for self-dramatization and swingeing critique, along with her thin-skinnedness and sensitivity to imagined slights (what Freud tactfully called her ' "agonistic" disposition').[24] The stakes were high. Riviere saw both the analysis and Jones as intertwined life-lines, and intensely feared their loss. However, this was no ordinary case of an angry woman pleading for the attention of a disinclined man. It was a struggle in which the patient sought to gain the upper hand. We see Riviere flexing her psychoanalytic muscles—not on her own psyche, however, but on Jones's. She is his patient, yet it is she who tells Jones that his grief is exaggerated and claims to know him better than he knows himself, especially when it comes to his unadmitted feelings for her. Another name for this might be 'reversible perspective'—a peculiar and deadly form of analytic *impasse* which defends against psychic pain.[25] The patient refuses to surrender the task of analysis to the analyst, but instead tries to cure herself. She will owe nothing to the analysis, which is thereby disabled. Riviere's letters to Jones reveal the negativity of this destructive misunderstanding.

'YOU HAVE NOT SEEN THE *WOMAN* IN ME'

Riviere's dealings with Jones none the less provided some basis for her complaint about his attitude to her as a woman. Jones may have taken Riviere on as a patient with a history of unhappiness and breakdown, but she also had an interest in psychoanalysis as well as her modern woman's quest for sexual and professional fulfilment.[26] Jones was a serial womanizer, and there are signs that Riviere tried her hand at free love. Initially, Riviere attempted to manage Jones as she tried to manage other men in her life, with so-called 'tenderness' and love. But every evidence of Jones's refusal to meet her emotional demands confirmed her sense

---

[24] See Freud's letter to Riviere of 13 March 1923; Hughes, *International Review of Psycho-Analysis*, 19, 273. Less flatteringly, writing to Jones on 25 June 1922, Freud—who was having a hard time himself—called Riviere 'that implacable woman'; see *The Complete Correspondence of Sigmund Freud and Ernest Jones*, 491.

[25] See Wilfred Bion, *Elements of Psycho-Analysis* (1963; rpr. London: Karnac Books, 1984), 48–63. Bion defines reversible perspective as 'evidence of pain; the patient reverses perspective to make a dynamic situation static' (ibid., 60). For a brief clinical account, see also R. Horacio Etchegoyen, *The Fundamentals of Psychoanalytic Technique*, trans. Patricia Pitchon (London: Karnac Books, 1991), 764–70.

[26] Jones's letter to Freud of 22 January 1922 diagnosed Riviere as 'a case of typical hysteria, almost the only symptoms being sexual anaesthesia and unorganized Angst . . . Most of her neurosis goes into marked character reactions, which is one reason why I was not able to cure her'; see *The Complete Correspondence of Sigmund Freud and Ernest Jones*, 453.

that he was incapable of doing so. If she was incurable, he had failed her. If he was unseducible, this was an insult to her femininity. Riviere also chose to believe that he had rejected what she offered in the way of support and friendship. The relationship became a deadlock, with Riviere meting out both self-punishment and punishment-by-letter. Tormented and unhappy herself, she tormented Jones, turning her intellect against him as she made use of the correspondence to gain self-understanding. A letter from Riviere, pre-dating the death of Jones's wife, indicates that she had drearily reconciled herself to ending the analysis ('there is probably no use in going on'). But even in her disappointment, she writes: 'I still cling unconsciously to the hope of finding everything I seek in you'. He has been patient—but she has been disappointed by his inability to help her. The analysis has stalled—but she still clings to him.

At the core, however, is a plea to him to communicate knowledge: 'what are the causes of this impasse? Can you analyse it? Please remember that I am completely in the dark & don't "know" or realize anything. I feel, as I always feel over these nightmares, that if only you would *tell me what it is* I would so willingly accept it. But I suppose this is self-deception.'[27] Self-deceived or not, what Riviere wants from Jones is not so much her own understanding as his: 'My peace of mind, such as it is, depends entirely on my *understanding* everything & your letter shows me that I still fail to do that . . . I therefore must beg of you to explain it all to me.'[28] Jones is to hand over his understanding so that she can acquire peace of mind. Riviere depicts him as unsympathetic to her sense of 'the despairingness of life' (a despair he shrugs off as wartime servant-problems).[29] Furious, she tries to shift the analytic burden onto Jones, accusing him of refusing to take responsibility and of 'wounded professional pride' as well as lack of sympathy. But above all, she complains, he persists in a 'hard & indifferent silence' in the face of her pleas. She follows this up with a thinly veiled threat of suicide: 'I certainly shan't care to live if I am not to be cured & if I didn't die I should have to kill myself.' The onus is on Jones to persuade her that the analysis is worth continuing, since she herself has no hope of cure.[30] But Riviere's next communication, a letter of condolence to the grief-stricken Jones, written on 26 September 1918 after receiving the news of his wife's sudden death, initiates a new phase. Riviere offers her solicitude in exalted terms: 'I believe so intensely in the value of love that I feel that it cannot be wasted or brought to nothing—however short it may be'. She has come to realize that 'psycho-analysis is now the only thing left [her] to care about'. But she also realizes that Jones's personal tragedy will mean 'another blow' for her analysis and that he 'will find a negative satisfaction in the fact'. She asks rhetorically: 'Will this be the

[27] CRB/F07/01 (emphases are Riviere's throughout). For a selection of linked excerpts from Riviere's letters to Jones, see Brome, *Ernest Jones*, 114–20.   [28] 4 November 1918; CRB/F07/07.
[29] Undated; CRB/F07/02: 'You passed the question of the difficulty of the analysis without a word—as usual—and all one gets is cheerful accounts of how other people live with no servants and so on . . . As if it is not the despairingness of life which is the problem but this you will never discuss.'
[30] Undated; CRB/F07/03.

last of the sacrifices I have been called upon to make for you, I wonder?'—hardly the way to address a man half-crazed by the loss of his wife.[31]

Riviere's letter of 25 October 1918 continues in the same vein: 'I have been through the hardest time of my life over all this—the final stage of the long tragedy of my relations with you.' In keeping with this tragedy, she has arrived at 'a realization so infinitely sad that you would call it cynicism...I have at last the satisfaction of completely understanding *you* and the strange story of it all.' She is 'left, to be haunted by the terrific irony of it all'—the irony of her inability to help him: 'I, who love and understand and ought to help you, am the one person who can I suppose, do nothing for you. Isn't that enough to make anyone cynical? *Even me.* Yes, even me, for I am not cynical.'[32] Riviere's rehearsal of her cynicism (simultaneously assumed and denied) is the mask for pain and rage. Claiming now to '*see the truth*', she writes that if she were truly cynical, she would either 'let it all come to an end' or respond to Jones's letter 'in a soothing & friendly strain'. No chance of that. In truth-seeing mode, Riviere tells Jones that his grief is 'too extravagant'. Perhaps, she suggests, he should try analysing the depth of his love and sorrow for his wife, turning the same light on his own tragedy that he has shed on the tragedies of others: 'What a lot you will learn from all this'. If she seems 'hard' to him, 'You must remember how often you have seemed hard to me'. As she now knows, ' "hardness" is a symptom of *feeling*, not of want of it!' The tables are turned:

Now I know why you were hard to me—and now I see that my inexpressibly bitter pain produced in me a hardness under which you failed to see that the suffering was conscious and extreme—When feeling has no outlet & is turned back upon itself, something must cover the torture. But that torture—that turning back of love—that's what I can't go through again. Even as I write to you as I must now is to hurt you—don't I have to be hard to myself first to do that?[33]

Therapeutic writing is both hurting and self-hurt; hardness, like cynicism, masks self-inflicted pain—the sado-masochistic excuse ('this hurts me more than it hurts you'). Dreading his response, she sees her letter as 'the last sacrifice' she will have to make. But she ends on a note of exaltation: 'For the hundredth time, I say to myself—"what a madman you are" and "how wonderful you can be." Which will you end as?'

Writing ('*un*-consciously') out of her humiliation and abandonment, Riviere focused on the 'case' of Jones. His problem is a 'mother-complex' (perhaps he had told her as much). In any case, she explains in her next letter: 'It is now clear that your feeling for me throughout has been very much greater than either of us has known or suspected—and it is *because* you never *have* realized its depths that you are now caught in this net'.[34] His assumed 'indifference' to her (she proposes) had

[31] Undated; CRB/F07/04.   [32] Undated; CRB/F07/05.   [33] Ibid.
[34] 31 October 1918; CRB/F07/06. See Brome, *Ernest Jones*, 115–17, for excerpts from a twelve-page document dated 30 October 1918, setting out the full history of their relations and including Riviere's analysis of Jones: 'I regard it as absolutely unquestionable that your wife was to you a substitute for me...It added very much to my pain that you should imagine there could be any substitute

been an attempt to prove it to himself, '*by means of showing to me* an indifference to me & to my feelings... In these letters there has hardly been a single word which was not *aimed* at showing me your indifference to me & my feelings.' In this hall of mirrors, Jones is seen as acting a part for his own benefit as much as hers; but he aims to hurt. Riviere interprets the 'purpose' of what she calls his 'grotesque & dreadful "blunderings"' at the time of his marriage as the story of the lover who tests and demeans his beloved by staging his marriage to another woman: 'It was simply the story of Patient Grizel acted out in real life in the 20th Century'. Patient Grizel she is not: 'whatever else you have wanted, you *have wanted* to hurt me'. Why has she been 'too afraid of hurting [him]'? But now she is 'almost too ill & exhausted to live'.[35] Yet in the midst of this contradictory mix of extravagant mourning and cynical suffering, Riviere arrives at the brink of realizing Jones's love for his wife. This precipitates a crisis. It meant that she had ceased to control reality and him.

Apparently in response to a letter from Jones, Riviere can humbly admit to being 'a good deal horrified' to find that an earlier letter contained 'such mistakes'.[36] Asking for help with her own neurosis, she describes herself as deeply distressed— unable to eat or sleep or do anything but 'wander about'. All her efforts to 'help' Jones in his own trouble have turned him against her, leaving her pathetically alone: 'I am so craving for help & comfort, and *I* can't rush about to anyone for it, you see. I have to get through it entirely alone.'[37] She is frightened of having another breakdown: 'I couldn't go through that again—so if that's it[,] it will have to end'. The next meeting is to be their last. In the face of her desperate appeal and implied threat, Jones surrenders. Five days later, Riviere thanks him in the wake of a helpful interview: 'I hadn't had the slightest expectation that you could do anything for me, in spite of the frantic appeal I had made—no appeals ever had before—I was surprised & touched too to find that you had read my letters with some attention—"for once" I might truly say too, but that would be ungracious!'[38] Jones's willingness to read her letters becomes a sign that he cares about her. Her estimation of him is raised; she hopes for his friendship and help ('friendliness & help which I need *much more* when I am "*hard and bitter*" than at any time'). Feeling life 'too depressing to be worth going on with', Riviere continues to insist on her need to be '*unique*' ('what in those first months you so often used to call me!') among women psychoanalytic rivals: 'the thought of *sharing* you & psychoanalysis with the multitude—a lot of grinning & enthusiastic frumps—though funny, is

---

for me, much less my exact opposite' (ibid., 116). This detailed final reckoning is not included among the letters preserved in the British Psycho-Analytical Society Archives.

[35] Undated; CRB/F07/06.   [36] 4 November 1918; CRB/F07/07.

[37] 6 November 1918; CRB/F07/08. In another distraught letter of 5 November 1918 (see Brome, *Ernest Jones*, 117), Riviere says she has been struggling between taking 60 grams of veronal (in the end she took only 16 grams) and the 'costly effort' of writing letters to Jones that 'haven't helped [him] and they've done [her] harm'. This letter is not included in the British Psycho-Analytical Society Archives.   [38] 11 November 1918; CRB/F07/09.

quite horrible to me'.[39] Theirs must be an exclusive relationship. Without irony, she wonders if Jones might find her a ' "poor girl" ' (a Patient Grizel?) to take into analysis.

Riviere represented herself as sufficiently punished: 'If you could realize my love you would realize what a punishment it is to me now to feel you fear me & cannot trust me for any generosity towards you in your sorrow & will not take any sympathy from me'.[40] As for her letter of condolence after his wife's death (26 September 1918), she feels 'not remorse perhaps—but you know that I can feel punishment'. The struggle shifts to Jones's rejection of her sympathy: 'You only showed me defiance & indifference—how should I suppose that less real than the indifference to my love & rejection of my appreciation & sympathy that you have always shown?' But, she begs, 'Don't punish me too much'. There are limits to her fury. Although Jones faced further tragedies in his own life that required her sympathy, Riviere persevered: 'My bitterness is mostly impersonal and is never shown to those who rouse it, my hate is totally suppressed to those I love. Only you (& my father) have ever heard an expression of it.'[41] Men especially receive and appreciate her wisdom, sympathy, and maternal feeling. Riviere's complaint against Jones finally emerges as his refusal to recognize her capacity for love ('Do you realize that in the early days you recognized my capacity for love & tenderness & often said so?'). The man has forgotten, but the analyst should have remembered. This is a lovers' quarrel. Retreating to the high ground of 'womanliness', Riviere presses her grievance, at once tenderly and sharply:

[Y]ou have not seen the *woman* in me—you will not see it. How striking it was the other day when you said 'you are a woman after all' & then turned suddenly & smiling said 'What a pity you are not more of a woman'...I am a great deal more of a woman than you know & that is why I said angrily that if I weren't I shouldn't be there now. You ought to know that it is my femininity that has saved my life more than once, too. My analysis has been conducted against your resistance as well as against mine. So it is not surprising that I have done most of it.[42]

'It is my femininity that has saved my life'. With this assertion, Riviere lays claim to 'womanliness'. But 'all men hate the maternal side of women, & you of course more than any, in me'. Her thumbnail sketch of her tactics with men (no fussing, no forcing, no inquisitiveness or interference, plenty of help and sympathy) is revealed as a costly masquerade: 'But they don't know how I think & ponder about them & the ceaseless longing I have to serve & guide them.' Riviere's unmasking had to wait until 'Womanliness as Masquerade' (1929), the paper that took Jones's observations on female sexuality as the starting-point for analysing 'a particular type of intellectual woman' (*IW* 91), herself.[43]

[39] Ibid.   [40] 18 December 1918; CRB/F07/10.
[41] 20 December 1918; CRB/F07/11.   [42] Ibid.
[43] Jones's paper 'The Early Development of Female Sexuality', *International Journal of Psycho-Analysis*, 8 (1927), 459–72 discusses 'aphanisis' (extinction of the capacity for sexual enjoyment) as the female equivalent of castration anxiety in men; he defines two types of female homosexuality, one oriented towards women, the other towards men.

'MY GREATNESS—MY PERSONALITY'

Jones's 'resistance' took the form of an understandable reluctance to read Riviere's letters. In the wake of one meeting, Riviere could hardly contain her anguish: 'in the first few minutes you told me that you hadn't been able to read it—hadn't been able to read it! You who spend hours every day analysing other people—hadn't even read my letter enough to know what I had said'.[44] Jones had responded to Riviere's protestations of her capacity for love and tenderness with a brutal catalogue of her failings: 'all that about narcissism & selfishness & hate & contempt— about *me*, my cynicism…I was stunned with horror—I simply cannot tell you what it was, what it is—It destroys me—.' In the midst of her 'stunned agony', Riviere refers to 'the crash—you said I was hurting you again. O it was beyond anything.' This 'crash' signals the collapse of the narcissistic structure to which 'womanliness' is the keystone. The rush of anguished explanation culminates in Riviere's realization that she 'was worthless, utterly selfish, utterly worthless'. She has been deluded in everything she believes about herself:

It is nothing to me *now* to say you will try & see good in me—You have just told me not that you can't see it, but that *there is none*. My life, my self-esteem, my right to live, my confidence is all built up upon my power to love, my power to see, to feel, to understand, & so to help—it is my greatness—my 'personality' which is everything to me—my other gifts are *nothing*. It is my belief in Life! Now you tell me that it is a delusion.[45]

If she neither understands nor loves, if her 'personality' (which is everything to her) is '*nothing*' in Jones's eyes, then she is annihilated. Her greatness is a delusion.

Riviere's letter replays the encounter, as if to mend matters ('I said "it is my cynicism directed against *myself*"—(I said "could you feel that & did you know how awful it was!")—It is my own defence against the truth, the disappointments I continually meet with in you.' Her expressions of bitterness are 'adaptation to reality—they are really not reproaches'. She has been very 'unconscious & guiltless about it', but Jones has taken them as directed at him rather than at herself: 'Evidently this has been a very big thing between us—& I am only just beginning to realize it'. If the crash is on a grand scale, so too is the misunderstanding, the 'very big thing' between them. Riviere pours out her despair as if her only resource were to write it: 'such horror & pain—& such numbness & emptiness. Now I feel almost utterly numb & despairing…I am stunned & bewildered—…I didn't know you saw my heart as quite empty & black.' And then: 'I have a sort of feeling that you have destroyed yourself to me'. If she is no good, neither is Jones; the two of them are in it together. All she can do is draw around her the remnants of her 'womanliness': her women friends tell her what '*patience*' she has with men. As the seven-page letter storms to its close, Riviere reframes her narcissistic collapse as

---

[44] 28 December 1918; CRB/F07/12.   [45] Ibid.

'a great & dreadful misunderstanding' between them. Perhaps Jones is unjust only because she has hurt him. She repeats their analytic credo ('I believe in narcissism, & sadism & masochism—as well as object love'), but then she adds an item of her own: 'we have a right to ourselves'. Wounded beyond her own powers of repair, Riviere adds a postscript reiterating her hurt, incomprehension, and remorse at wounds delivered to Jones: 'Indeed I don't understand it—I dread to understand it.' In *The Ego and the Id*, Freud calls this the clamour of life that proceeds from Eros—'And from the struggle against Eros!' (*SE* xix. 46).

Riviere's letters to Jones never again approach this emotional and psychic chaos, the depressive position at ground zero of a ruined narcissism. In January 1919 Riviere wrote to thank Jones for taking her back into analysis, acknowledging this proof of his 'greatness', dedicating herself to the resumption of analytic work in terms reminiscent of the contemporary First World War battlescape: 'I believe in the analysis—it will not fail us though we shall fail it. I am not blind to what it means. I know I've got to go through horror, mud & slime & deep waters—& drag you too . . . but I *shall* go and I shall not be drowned & I will not drown you—here *is* my omnipotence.'[46] Two days later, she is 'absolutely shattered' by a letter from Jones: 'I am so stunned now by your saying that I have no desire to live—or to recover' (perhaps the wish not to recover which she later associates with the burden of reparation).[47] But in the long letter that follows, Riviere rallies, insisting that she has a right to her feelings and to the resumption of the analysis. Her analysis is equivalent to his grief: 'I have my love, which is bound up with my neurosis, my grief, which is bound up with my analysis . . . Your grief is to you "the one engrossing & tremendous fact", my analysis is that to me—It is *my* work, upon which I am engaged . . . your grief is *your* work.'[48] In this economy, their respective suffering can be weighed in the same scales—her grief-work and his, her analysis and his mourning; her sacrifice if she were to give up the analysis, his in undertaking it: 'In this deadlock of irreconcilable feelings between us, who shall say which is to be sacrificed? We are both right.' The scenario of mutual sacrifice ('one of us *must* be sacrificed') redistributes the sacrificial portion so that Jones is drawn in to the masochistic economy. The result is stasis.

This is the last scene of a drama whose plot consists of Riviere's refusal to yield the high moral ground when it came to resigning her claim on Jones's time, emotions, and professional standing. Reverting to the language of the courtroom, Riviere re-poses the question of the analysis in terms of her 'potential value in the world': 'Is my life, my potential value in the world worth any sacrifice by you? That is the question I put to you. You can still say "no"—& in the sick shuddering horror & ghastliness of the present moment I should be thankful for the release it would be to me . . . Whatever you are suffering please believe that mine is . . . quite as great.'[49] Her suffering is equal to his. Not only their sufferings but their resentments are

---

[46] 5 January 1919; CRB/F07/13.   [47] 7 January 1919; CRB/F07/14.
[48] 11 January 1919; CRB/F07/15.   [49] Ibid.

alike: 'both our resentments are due to the same thing—"insults—felt though not real—against our loyalty & love." I can see now that your injuries to me were not real.' Magnanimity and equivalence resolve the problem of insult. A letter written the next day regrets her explanation ('I feel it was wrong of me to write yesterday & *explain* myself again'). It seems that her very existence makes things worse for Jones. But 'What am I to do? To think only of you I *ought* to die. If I am to live I can't help being hurt & suffering—though I know it's a crime. This feeling that my pain must recoil upon you, even without bitterness & resentment is too awful.' Riviere is caught in the system she has created. In the spirit of her commitment to the project of living, Riviere promises to make Jones's sacrifice worth while—the only way she can lighten Jones's burden 'except by dying'.[50]

'Except by dying': the struggle between Riviere and Jones engages with the death-driven language of the war which formed the backdrop to their correspondence—not only the mud, slime, and deep waters of a battle-scarred landscape, or the language of shared suffering, but its passive heroism, sacrificial despair, and disillusioned commitment to a cause no longer believed in. This, after all, was the aftermath of a war which had provoked its own protective 'cynicism' and hardness. The mood of doomed soldiers returning to the front colours Riviere's return to analysis, placing the interpersonal drama in a larger historical frame. Jones's grief for his wife was of a piece with the national grief-work. In a letter of 18 April 1919, Riviere looked back on the past and sums up her difficulties—'this peculiar & as it happens so painful process of identification, which unfortunately seems inherent in my neurotic attitude'. She lists her neurotic troubles in a striking parenthesis: '(impotence, anesthesia, not loving, coldness,—& sadism, wounding, & cutting off)'.[51] One might speculate that impotence, anaesthesia, and the inability to love, not to mention 'sadism, wounding, & cutting off', had as their context the more generalized helplessness, numbness, cruelty, and wounding of the First World War. By now, Riviere no longer expects Jones to see things her way: 'you must regard it all as a preposterous fiction of my brain'. But her identification with Jones (Klein will call it projective identification) as her sadism turns him into the persecutor has made it possible to see something previous unseen in herself: 'It seemed as if I cannot get at these things in myself except through you!' She can see that Jones neither has nor perhaps ever had a conscious wish to 'cut [her] off'. The worry that her letter will incur fresh 'resentments'

---

[50] Undated; CRB/F07/16.
[51] 18 April 1919; CRB/F07/17. Here, as elsewhere, the wording of Karl Abraham's account in 'A Particular Form of Neurotic Resistance against the Psycho-Analytic Method' (1919) is prescient: 'In place of making a transference the patients tend to identify themselves with the physician...they put themselves in his place. They adopt his interests...They tend to exchange parts, just as a child does...They instruct the physician by giving him their opinion of their own neurosis...In this way they abandon the position of patient, and lose sight of the purpose of their analysis. In particular, they desire to surpass their physician, and...claim to be able to "do it better" ' (Abraham, *Selected Papers on Psycho-Analysis*, 306).

makes her repeat that she writes out of her own 'misery & a desire if possible to make some amends for what pain I cause you'. Instead of 'sacrifice', she writes of making amends.[52]

The dénouement has a certain tragicomic inevitability: in the autumn of 1919, Jones announced his re-marriage.[53] In a letter written the day after his wedding, alternating between tenderness, dismay, and denunciation, Riviere wrote to him wanting to say ' "I am glad you are happy" '. Instead she questions the '*reality*' of anything he feels. Her verdict is 'Emotions enough & to spare—but so unrelated to reality.'[54] She is not surprised, since she had thought his grief of a year ago 'inordinate & in its way a madness', although this year he seemed 'so much sobered & ennobled & dignified by it, at last "grown up" '. But 'the old [Jones] is still there'— what she calls his 'Celtic' quality and his 'unreliability'. While she no longer condemns him, she no longer takes him seriously:

You are not a reasonable being, you are an irresponsible tempestuous, uncurbed child. That is why people are either indulgent to you or hard upon you—they don't take you seriously...In your place I should know the grotesqueness of the things you do, know it was a world of phantasmagoria that I was living in—not reality...One thing this shows me which I never saw before—the strength of the Reality principle in myself—[55]

But 'my truths never penetrate through the limelight of your emotions'. Still, she would be the last to deny the '*Lust prinzip*', for 'it is really what I so much love in you—you irresponsible Puck! Irresistible to women, meeting them on their own ground, the emotions! May you be always proof against reality.' Jones the fantasist is a bit of a woman, as well as a womanizer. By now seeing patients of her own, Riviere believes that her own hope of 'cure' is gone and that the analysis is at an end; in any case, she could never take 'truth' from him again ('it would be only prolonging the awful useless deadlock it has always been'). All she asks for is a face-saving gesture, so that she is not 'publicly thought to be in any way cut off from [him] by this'. She ends: 'God bless you & give you happiness—my dearly-loved one—my dear foolish one—my terrible one—weddings & funerals & weddings—how many more times will you kill me, Bluebeard & shall I always love you? I want you to be happy, yes, with *her*—das Ewig weibliche!' Bluebeard had done his work. But Riviere, like Scheherazade, lived to tell the tale.[56]

[52] Riviere later made the link between suicide ('that supreme instance of self-withdrawal [which] represents to the clouded mind a gift of one's life to ensure the happiness of another'), fantastic reparation, and a fresh start; see her 1937 paper, 'Hate, Greed, and Aggression' (*IW* 183), which was paired with Klein's 'Love, Guilt, and Reparation' (1937) in their joint book.

[53] On 11 October 1919, Ernest Jones married Katherine Jokl, an Austrian whom he had met in Switzerland and originally hoped to employ as his secretary and assistant in his analytic work with Freud.   [54] 12 October 1919; CRB/F07/18.

[55] Ibid.

[56] Riviere's allusions to folk-tales were infectious; when Winnicott, during his analysis with Riviere, announced his plan to write a book on the environment, 'She said to me: "You write a book on the environment and I'll turn you into a frog!" Of course she didn't use those words, you understand, but that's how what she did say came across to me'; see John Padel, 'The Psychoanalytic

'EINE ZWICKMÜHLE'

Apropos of the negative therapeutic reaction, André Green asks: 'By what deviation, by what process of turning away does the work of the negative turn here into a "negativistic" work?'[57] In January 1922, Jones heralded Riviere's arrival in Vienna with a poisonous letter of introduction in which he called her analysis 'the worst failure I have ever had'. He had hoped, he writes, 'to win her for the cause' (of psychoanalysis) but 'underestimated the uncontrollability of her emotional reactions... The treatment finally broke down over my inability to master the negative transference, though I tried all means in my power'. Despite her 'far-reaching insight', he complained, she had 'the most colossal narcissism imaginable'.[58] Freud salvaged the wreckage with kindness, diplomacy, and understanding. He supported Riviere professionally in the face of Jones's objections to having a woman placed over him in the hierarchy of the translation project, acknowledging Riviere as clever and forceful, but also understanding her need for recognition as a woman: 'In my experience you have not to scratch too deeply the skin of a so called masculine woman to bring her femininity to the light.'[59] Freud's relief at finding that Jones 'had no sexual relations' with her provoked a chagrined riposte: 'To satisfy her vanity she has always maintained the theory that I also was in love with her but was not honest enough to confess it... She is not the type that attracts me erotically.'[60] Jones's sexual insult is compounded by grudging admiration of Riviere's 'masculine' intelligence—admiration that did not extend to being able to tolerate her as anything but his assistant in the project of translating Freud's writings.

Ever the pragmatist, Freud saw that Riviere 'is a real power and can be put to work by a slight expenditure of kindness and ' "recognitions" '. In a pithy verdict, he conceded: 'To be sure she is a concentrated acid not to be used until duly diluted and she is not yet even with you'. But Jones was 'too hard in criticising her, took her resistance too seriously, and could not control her sadism after it came up

---

Theories of Melanie Klein and Donald Winnicott and their Interaction in the British Society of Psychoanalysis', *Psychoanalytic Review*, 78 (1991), 336; and see also Brett Kahr, *D. W. Winnicott: A Biographical Portrait* (London: Karnac Books, 1996), 65: 'By claiming, however jocularly, that Mrs Riviere had threatened to turn him into a frog, Winnicott thereby found himself betraying his view of her as a witch-like figure'.

[57] See André Green, *The Work of the Negative*, trans. Andrew Weller (London: Free Association Books, 1999), 95. Green sees the negative therapeutic reaction as 'an iatrogenic pathology... created by the analysis itself'. His account of a peculiar form of negativity in relation to a depressed mother may be relevant to Riviere, who was herself a 'replacement' baby born a year after the death of an older brother; see 'The Dead Mother' (1980) in André Green, *Life Narcissism, Death Narcissism*, trans. Andrew Weller (London: Free Association Books, 2001), 170–200, where transferential effects of early maternal loss include 'a *compulsion to think*' and a form of seduction 'in the area of the intellectual quest, the search for lost meaning, which reassures intellectual narcissism' (ibid., 151–2, 161).

[58] 22 January 1922; *The Complete Correspondence of Sigmund Freud and Ernest Jones*, 453–4.

[59] 23 March 1922; ibid., 464.   [60] 1 April 1922; ibid., 466.

as it had to do'.[61] Jones objected in return that Riviere had 'cleverly managed to introduce into her analysis with [Freud] the same difficulty as happened with [him], namely the intermixture of analytical considerations with external actual ones'. She was playing her past and present analysts off against each other, and her story of his unkindness 'is a pure myth':

She is known in the Society as my favourite, people wonder why I endure her behaviour, and I have never treated any other patient with such consideration, in both feeling and conduct. But every proof of kindness on my part was always ignored or taken as her natural right as a matter-of-course, or even regarded as an insult . . . she regressed to identification with her father and treated me . . . like her younger brother, whose sole function in life was to admit that he was nothing by the side of her greatness.[62]

Riviere had already scored palpable hits, and now she had managed to get Freud's ear as well. Worst of all, Jones 'could not endure cooperating with a domineering woman'.[63] According to Jones, Riviere was a hectoring woman, who treated other people 'like dirt beneath her feet'. In a further letter Jones complained that he would never 'be able to work under her orders because of the impossible tone in which she issues them'.[64]

Freud, who wanted to see the translation of his writings moving ahead, was forced reluctantly into playing the part of 'Pontifex maximus'. He represents Riviere's role cunningly as that of a secretary whose 'uncommon combination of male intelligence with female love for detailed work' (*sic*) would relieve Jones 'of most of the time-spending drudgery'.[65] The partnership he sketches is ineluctably gendered: 'She will act as a skilled secretary and be the strongest power at work, while you continue to be the directing mind of the whole. I can imagine no better combination if you decide to collaborate with her . . .'. Freud's formula evidently made it possible for Jones to accept the situation. But at Freud's insistence, Riviere was not given the auxiliary role of 'revising translator' rather than 'translating editor'; Jones owed her something, as Freud had written in an earlier letter: 'I am of opinion besides that you owe her a compensation having aggravated her analysis by inconsequent behaviour as you confess yourself'.[66]

---

[61] 11 May 1922; ibid., 475.

[62] 22 May 1922; ibid., 478. The possibility that Winnicott experienced Riviere as an older-sister substitute may be relevant. Jones gives as an example of Riviere's response to any act of kindness the occasion when he left some books for her while she was ill in a nursing home: 'This she found to be insulting, for it shewed that that was *all* I was willing to give her' (ibid., 478). When it came to arranging celebrations for Riviere's seventy-fifth birthday in 1958, while Winnicott was President of the British Psycho-Analytical Society, he incurred her wrath for sending out notices too early ('I warn you that if you attempt to get up any present for me, I shall refuse it'). Winnicott replied, 'For some reason or other you are, I think, unduly sensitive about this matter'; see F. Robert Rodman (ed.), *The Spontaneous Gesture: Selected Letters of D. W. Winnicott* (1987; rpr. London: Karnac Books, 1999), 118; and for Riviere's letter, see Kahr, *D. W. Winnicott: A Biographical Portrait*, 63–4.

[63] *The Complete Correspondence of Sigmund Freud and Ernest Jones*, 479; possibly a reference to Jones's earlier relationship with his common-law wife, Loe Kann, about which Freud would have known.   [64] 26 May 1922; ibid., 482.

[65] 4 June 1922; ibid., 486–7.   [66] 6 April 1922; ibid., 468.

It has been suggested that Freud became enmeshed in an enactment with Riviere. But he addresses the triangulated situation head-on:

Somehow I imagine I guess your opinion of me in this matter. You think Mrs R. has put on her sweetest face and moods, has taken me in completely and seduced me to defend her against you in a chivalrous manner, so that now I am a puppet in her hands, show her the letters I get from you and give you away to her. I am sure you are wrong and I feel rather sorry there should be a need to point it out to you.[67]

In taking Riviere's part he is simply doing his duty as an analyst: 'It would not have worked, had I announced from the very beginning your dissension with Dr. J. must not be mentioned in our analysis or: Be sure, whenever you were at variance with him you must have been wrong and he right . . . Better not to have started her analysis at all!' As Freud puts it, he had to give Jones away before he could get him back. There was no chance of Riviere seeing 'the abnormality of her reactions' unless she received some acknowledgement of Jones's errors. Here Freud levels with Jones: 'And in fact I cannot praise the way you handled her'. Not only did Jones lose 'the analytic superiority especially required in such a case', but when Riviere 'brought up her unpleasant reactions', he simply 'treated her as a bad character in life'.[68] In other words, Jones too had been guilty of mixing analytical considerations with real life.

Freud's well-known account of Riviere as an analysand provided the basis for her later understanding of the negative therapeutic reaction. Far from playing the '*intriguante*' with him and insisting on her 'sweetness', Riviere had rapidly shown her true colours: 'She soon became harsh, unpleasant, critical even with me, tried to provoke me as she had done with you.' Freud's profound insight identified the double-bind of negativity:

She cannot tolerate praise, triumph or success, not any better than failure, blame and repudiation. She gets unhappy in both cases . . . So she has arranged for herself what we call '*eine Zwickmühle*' [a dilemma] . . . Whenever she has got a recognition, a favour or a present, she is sure to become unpleasant and aggressive and to lose respect for the analyst. You know what that means, it is an infallible sign of a deep sense of guilt . . . To be sure this conflict, which is the cause of her continuous dissatisfaction, is not known to her consciousness; whenever it is revived she projects her self criticism to other people, turns her pangs of conscience into sadistic behaviour, tries to render other people unhappy because she feels so herself.[69]

[67] 22 June 1922; ibid., 483. For Freud's use of what he calls 'active therapeutics' in Riviere's case, see Anton O. Kris, 'Freud's Treatment of a Narcissistic Patient', *International Journal of Psycho-Analysis*, 75 (1994), 649–64. Kris argues that Freud made greater therapeutic use of his personality to support and affirm the patient than his advocacy of analytic 'abstinence' would indicate, and suggests not just that Freud exceeded the bounds of proper analytic technique but that 'addressing the patient's self-criticism was the first step in the treatment of narcissistic patients'; Freud's linking of unconscious guilt and narcissism represents an unacknowledged technical and theoretical departure (ibid., 75.656).   [68] *The Complete Correspondence of Sigmund Freud and Ernest Jones*, 484.

[69] Ibid., 484. In a later letter, of 25 June 1922, Freud criticizes Jones for deviousness: 'what made the case so hard for me was the fact that accuracy and plainness is not in the character of your dealings with people . . . Whenever I had to examine a case between you and her in detail I had to find that you were to be doubted while that implacable woman . . . could not be refuted' (ibid., 491).

As Freud admits, 'Our theory has not yet mastered the mechanism of these cases.'[70] But Freud did explore the mechanism of unconscious guilt in 'The Dependent Relations of the Ego', the final section of *The Ego and the Id*, which he began writing in July 1922 during the summer break in Riviere's analysis. Here he describes patients who 'behave in a quite peculiar fashion during the work of analysis. When one speaks hopefully to them or expresses satisfaction with the progress of the treatment, they show signs of discontent and their condition invariably becomes worse'. Any praise, appreciation, or partial solution offered by the analyst merely exacerbates their illness: 'they get worse during the treatment instead of getting better. They exhibit what is known as a "negative therapeutic reaction"' (*SE* xix. 49).

Riviere's paper on the negative therapeutic reaction cites Freud's footnote on 'the slow procedure of unmasking' the unconscious roots of guilt and 'gradually changing it into a *conscious* sense of guilt.'[71] Freud had written in *The Ego and the Id* of 'this new discovery...an "unconscious sense of guilt"' as especially bewildering in the obstacles it placed in the way of recovery (*SE* xix. 27). The activities of unconscious self-criticism and conscience were peculiarly intractable; the clinical facts illustrated that the super-ego was 'farther from consciousness than the ego is'. The hard-to-reach super-ego is the seat of sadism, as well as the reason why patients like Riviere 'cannot endure any praise or appreciation'. It is the ' "moral factor", a sense of guilt, which . . . refuses to give up the punishment of suffering' (*SE* xix. 49). The super-ego 'develops such extraordinary harshness and severity towards the ego' and 'rages against [it] with merciless violence, as if it had taken possession of the whole of the sadism available in the person concerned . . . What is now holding sway in the super-ego is, as it were, a pure culture of the death instinct' (*SE* xix. 53). For Freud, the fear of death is the negative apogee of the unconscious, 'a difficult problem to psychoanalysis', since (unlike the dread of an object) 'death is an abstract concept with a negative content for which no unconscious correlative can be found' (*SE* xix. 58). Fear of death is the most inaccessible of all fears because it evades representation even in the unconscious. No wonder *The Ego and the Id* had begun with Freud's musings on the difference between 'Consciousness and What is Unconscious', a discussion preceded by his unpublished paper of September 1922, 'Some Remarks on the Unconscious' (the topic he discussed with Riviere during her analysis).[72] Returning to the

[70] Freud speculates that Riviere's sexual freedom was 'an appearance, the keeping up of which requires conspicuous compensatory attitudes as haughtiness, majestic behaviour, etc.' (22 June 1922; ibid., 484).

[71] Kris takes issue with Riviere's citation (*IW* 151), arguing that she is less precise than usual in her conflation of two different aspects of Freud's footnote, 'which may reflect persistence of the characteristic transference she is describing'; see Kris, 'Freud's Treatment of a Narcissistic Patient', *International Journal of Psycho-Analysis*, 75, 660 n.

[72] See the abstract reprinted in Strachey's introduction to *The Ego and the Id* (*SE* xix. 3–4): the facts of resistance from the ego in analysis and of an unconscious sense of guilt show that 'in the ego too there is an unconscious'.

unconscious sense of guilt in 'The Economic Problem of Masochism' (1924), Freud reiterated that it was hard for patients to believe in it, since 'They know only too well by what torments—the pangs of conscience—a conscious sense of guilt, a consciousness of guilt, expresses itself, and they therefore cannot admit that they could harbour exactly analogous impulses in themselves without being in the least aware of them' (*SE* xix. 166).[73] As Freud unforgettably told Riviere, ' "It is *un-conscious*" ' (*IW* 354).

Freud believed that the analyst could not play the part of a prophet, saviour, or redeemer; he could only 'give the patient's ego *freedom* to decide' (*SE* xix. 50 n.). His verdict on Riviere was not hopeful—'I cannot say that I have much altered the other party . . . I don't think I could impress her in a noticeable degree . . . I fear she will require special care and regards indefinitely.'[74] Translating *The Ego and the Id* in 1927, Riviere's return to the period of her own analysis must have provided a retrospective view of the 'dilemma' on whose horns she had impaled herself.[75] Her own paper on the negative therapeutic reaction warns, pessimistically, that while the analyst may not use a 'trick method', the patient will inevitably try to trick the analyst; apparent improvement may be based on a manic defence: 'The patient exploits us in his own way instead of being fully analysed' (*IW* 152).[76] Riviere's injunction 'that we should not be deceived by the positive aspects of [the patient's] narcissism but should look deeper, for the depression that will be found to under-lie it' recognizes melancholia as the negative vicissitude of narcissism (*IW* 138). But it is precisely here (building on Abraham and Klein) that Riviere makes her distinctive contribution to the understanding of the 'nightmare of desolation' which she had experienced (*IW* 145). The offer of analysis is unconsciously felt as seduction and a betrayal, since it means 'an offer to help [her] to abandon [her]

---

[73] At the end of his life, in 'Analysis Terminable and Interminable' (1937)—translated by Riviere herself for the *International Journal of Psycho-Analysis*—Freud again referred to the intractability of the negative therapeutic reaction and the sense of guilt as 'unmistakable indications of the presence of a power in mental life which we call the instinct of aggression or of destruction . . . and which we trace back to the original death instinct.' He continued: 'we must bow to the superiority of the forces against which we see our efforts come to nothing' (*SE* xxiii. 243).

[74] 25 June 1922; *The Complete Correspondence of Sigmund Freud and Ernest Jones*, 491. For Freud's continuing correspondence with Riviere, see Hughes, *International Review of Psycho-Analysis*, 19, 265–84. On 10 September 1922, he responds with understanding to her '*slight uneasiness about the critical remarks*' (in English in the original), adding 'I hope that you will now be better able to bear a word of appreciation in private' (ibid., 270–1). His next letter, dated 30 January 1923, regrets that he had not been able to keep her for a further six months: 'I might have succeeded in letting you see the connexion between neurosis and national or social prejudice' (ibid., 271).

[75] For a re-reading of Freud's account of 'The Economic Problem of Masochism' in terms of both narcissism and negativity, see André Green, *Life Narcissism, Death Narcissism*, 131–57.

[76] See ibid., 152, where Green takes up the technical implications of the treatment of 'moral narcissists' and the analyst's temptation to modify the analytic situation in order to break the deadlock: 'Since the least guilt-inducing variant is kindness, the analyst offers his love . . . here the analyst is making a technical error because he is responding to a desire of the patient . . . Since it is a matter of moral narcissism, the analyst then becomes a substitute analyst, indeed a priest.' Elsewhere, Green restates Freud's emphasis on the 'unconscious sense of guilt' as 'a "narcissistic" sense of guilt' or 'an *unconscious sense of guilty narcissism*' (Green, *The Work of the Negative*, 103).

task of curing the others first' (*IW* 147). The only good thing the patient has is her 'buried core of love', the altruistic wish to make herself better by making things better for others. The problem, for Riviere (echoing Freud), is that these 'unconscious aims are really *unconscious* and that we cannot use them directly as a lever to help on the analysis' (*IW* 148). The unconscious motive of being cured in order to help others, 'the one slender positive thread on which the analysis hangs', is constantly weakened, obstructed, and undermined, not only by the patient's despair and unmanageable sadism but by the fear of deceiving and betraying the analyst (*IW* 149). Apropos of the resistances that mask the depressive position, Riviere slips in a revealing sentence that can be read at once professionally and confessionally: '*This has been my own experience*' (*IW* 146; my italics).

'WRITE IT, WRITE IT'

In 1928, the year before the publication of 'Womanliness as a Masquerade', Freud welcomed Riviere's promise to write something for publication: 'Anything you write about yourself personally is sure of my interest'.[77] In her tribute to Freud, at the very end of her life, Riviere went out of her way to redefine 'that quality we call greatness' not as a grandiose or heroic self, but as creativity—the quality she saw in Freud's capacity to build up a system of knowledge outside himself, thereby effecting 'a fusion of external reality and internal phantasy'. She recalls:

He once said something to me which had little meaning for me at the time but which later threw light on this problem for me. I suppose I had mentioned some analytic explanation that had occurred to me. He said: 'Write it, write it, put it down in black and white; that's the way to deal with it; you get it out of your system.'... In later years, as I acquired more understanding of him and his work... I came more and more to realize the underlying importance in him of the creative side of his work—his work must have meant to him a structure he was creating and building. He almost says so once or twice. This idea then linked up in my mind with his former remark to me: 'Get it out, produce it, make something of it—*outside you*, that is; give it an existence independently of you.' (*IW* 351)

Riviere celebrates Freud as the architect of a structure of ideas, 'a process of building up those ideas into a whole outside himself and inside the minds of others'. Rather than the need to influence others, what interested him (consciously or not) 'was to work out and construct the edifice of his thought into an intelligible whole by means of their co-operation' (*IW* 352). Perhaps this had been her own experience as Freud's analysand. But she did not forget his advice.

Two of Riviere's papers belonging to the 1950s—both included in the special issue of the *International Journal of Psycho-Analysis* marking Klein's seventieth birthday, and republished in *New Directions in Psycho-Analysis* (1955)—reveal the

---

[77] 9 September 1928; see Hughes, *International Review of Psycho-Analysis*, 19, 281.

extent to which her thinking about the inner world coincided with her literary interests.[78] 'The Unconscious Phantasy of an Inner World reflected in Examples from Literature' (1952) explores the meaning of 'an inner world' in everyday terms (including both conscious memories and unconscious phantasies of the figures first loved and hated in life). Riviere links the unconscious feeling that others are part of ourselves to Klein's account of narcissism as a relation to oneself 'unconsciously bound up with the inner world, the relation one has to the figures inside one and their relation to oneself' (*IW* 307). Her paper poignantly explores the poetic expression of the lover's wish to possess the absent beloved, 'the over mastering intensity of the love-longing and the terror of loss', and the way in which loss can trigger 'the destructive tendency that might be called the capacity for death in oneself' (*IW* 311, 314).[79] But in her analysis of a novel by Conrad, his fantastic and tumultuous *The Arrow of Gold* (1913), Riviere broaches a different aspect of love-relations. Here the beloved has been successfully incorporated by means of projection—or rather, 'projective identification' (Klein's term), which Riviere defines as 'phantasies of bodily incorporation, union, fusion, and inner possession' (*IW* 327). Meeting his beloved unexpectedly after a long absence, the lover explains:

'When I have you before my eyes there is such a projection of my whole being towards you that I fail to see you distinctly . . . I never saw you distinctly till after we had parted and I thought you had gone from my sight forever. It was then that you took body in my imagination and that my mind seized on a definite form of you for all its adorations—for its profanations too.' (*IW* 326)[80]

Riviere reads this passage as 'a direct statement of the phantasy of self-*projection* into the object which appears to be bound up and simultaneous with the process of *introjection* of the object' (*IW* 327). For her, Conrad's insight represents 'a most remarkable direct intuitive mergence into the author's conscious thought of the deepest unconscious processes' that have only now been uncovered by the work of Melanie Klein.[81]

---

[78] See Melanie Klein, Paula Heimann, and R. E. Money-Kyrle (eds.), *New Directions in Psychoanalysis* (1955; rpr. London: Karnac Books, 1985), 346–69, 370–83. Including Klein's paper, 'On Identification' (1955), the volume—which contained a number of contributions on literary and aesthetic topics (by Hanna Segal, Adrian Stokes, and others)—provides the representative statement of Kleinian thinking on aesthetics during the 1950s.

[79] For Riviere's discussion of absence in relation to a metaphysical love poem (*IW* 309–13), see also Mary Jacobus, *Psychoanalysis and the Scene of Reading* (Oxford: Oxford University Press, 1999), 55–8.

[80] *The Arrow of Gold: A Story Between Two Notes* (1919; rpr. Philadelphia, Penn.: University of Pennsylvania Press, 2004), 328–9. Riviere makes a short silent omission. In the previous chapter, the hero expresses his sense of his beloved's inner presence as 'more like the consciousness of you always being present in me . . . not only when we are apart but when we are together, alone' (ibid., 326). In her foreword to Riviere's work, Segal, who was supervised by Riviere, records their common admiration for Segal's Polish compatriot, Conrad (*IW*, p. xii); elsewhere she writes that 'working with Joan Riviere, a person of immense culture as well as a great analyst, was a particular inspiration. She did a lot to introduce me to English literature . . .'; see Hanna Segal, *The Work of Hanna Segal* (London: Free Association Books, 1986), p. xiii.

[81] Klein's paper, 'On Identification', in Klein *et al.* (eds.), *New Directions in Psychoanalysis*, explores the same phenomena at greater length; Klein also remarks on the apparent simultaneity of the processes of projection and introjection, although one actually follows the other.

Riviere underscores the idealization which defends against the ruthless egotism, greed, violence, and hatred of love, as well as the capacity of the absence of the love-object to transform love-longing into a 'nightmare'. The 'savage impulses' of love gain ground when they are frustrated and turn deadly. Bad objects are absent objects whose origins lie in our own disowned dangerous and evil tendencies. Even in the best of compromises between Eros and Thanatos, the impulse to possess and incorporate 'entails the imprisonment, subjection and torture of the loved, desired, and hated objects, and from that circumstance spring the torments and agonies suffered by them and by us in our inner worlds.' (*IW* 328) The same figure can be ideally perfect and protecting or vile, monstrous, and persecutory. Riviere's theory of identity undoes the narcissistic fiction of 'personality' which her analysis with Jones had painfully exposed as a delusion ('my "personality" which is everything to me— ... Now you tell me that it is a delusion').[82] For the Riviere of the 1950s, 'personality' is not a delusion but rather a richly diachronic and synchronous fabric of object relations—'a composite structure, which has been and is being formed and built up since the day of our birth out of countless never-ending influences and exchanges between ourselves and others' (*IW* 317). Identity depends on 'goods' that are begged, borrowed, and even stolen—debts denied by egotism and omnipotence: 'We cling to the fiction of our absolute individuality, our independence, as if we owed nothing to anyone and nothing in us had been begged, borrowed or stolen' (*IW* 318). Samuel Rogers's consolatory fiction of the ever-present dead—'Those whom he loved so long and sees no more, | Loved and still loves . . .'—tells us, not just that 'memories are always present with us', but that these loved figures lead a life unconsciously 'within us indivisible from ourselves' (*IW* 320).[83] Riviere evokes the meaning of death as the disappearance of a composite self, 'a living existence, an entity, a person, a personality, a most complex and composite structure of attributes, tendencies, experiences, memories, idiosyncrasies good and bad' (*IW* 316). Stolen goods become our most intimate possessions. They are ourselves.

Riviere's paper includes literature itself in the debt we owe to others. Her moving conclusion quotes Apollinaire's '*Cortège*' to illustrate 'that each of us is a company of many, and that our being is contained in all those others we have been and are occupied with as we live, just as they are contained in us' (*IW* 328–9). Apollinaire's poem describes the search for self in the passing of a funeral-train:

> The stream of life went past me and I looked for my body there
> All those who followed on and on and who were not myself
> Were bringing one by one the pieces of myself
> There I was built up piece by piece as one erects a tower...

(*IW* 329)[84]

[82] 28 December 1918; CRB/F07/12.
[83] Samuel Rogers, *Human Life, a Poem* (London: John Murray, 1819), 61.
[84] '*Le cortège passait et j'y cherchais mon corps | Tous ceux qui survenaient et n'étaient pas moi-même | Amenaient un à un les morceaux de moi-même | On me bâtit peu à peu comme on élève une tour . . .*'; see Guillaume Apollinaire, *Alcools: poèmes 1898–1913* (Paris: Editions de la Nouvelle Revue Française,

With Apollinaire's 'Nothing is dead but what is yet to come' ('*Rien n'est mort que ce qui n'existe pas encore*'), Riviere makes her peace with both past and future. The complex structure of a personality, built up piece by piece 'as one erects a tower' ('*comme on élève une tour*'), doubles for the process by which Riviere imagines the building up and creation of a structure that exists as 'a whole outside [herself] and inside the minds of others' (*IW* 352). The radical implication is that we are also what we quote, built up piece by piece from the 'complex and composite structure' of literary memory—the books and poems that we read, recall, and love. Literature expresses our thoughts and feelings better than we could do for ourselves.

Riviere's 'The Inner World in Ibsen's *Master Builder*' (1952) provides an apt companion piece, a work of 'applied' psychoanalytic criticism that treats Ibsen's play as a representation of the pathologies of the inner world.[85] Unlike Freud, Solness, the master builder, builds castles in the air (' "Castles in the air is all one *can* build" '), and it is this that leads to his vertiginous downfall.[86] At the foundations of Solness's apparent success lie his guilty conscience and the ashes of retribution (ruthless exploitation of others and the burned-down family mansion whose insurance had provided the financial basis for his success; his desolate home, depressed wife, and dead babies). Riviere sees Solness's *folie à deux* with Hilde as the enigma of the play, at once an ironic fulfilment of his fear of being destroyed by the younger generation and the embodiment of daemonic forces that seem to destroy him from within. Hilde, a fantasist in her own right, reawakens the fantasist in the middle-aged Solness, sending him to his death through her own excited masculine identification; she personifies the manic defence. For Riviere, 'the factor of illusion' expressed in both characters forms the play's central theme. Left alone on the stage at the end, after Solness's dizzy plunge to the ground, Hilde gazes upwards and 'suddenly cries out "*My—my* Master Builder!" She has lost the man himself, but in her inner world of illusion she seems to have gained him at last' (*IW* 347).

Solness's castle in the air is the antithesis of the Freudian edifice of ideas—lacking solid foundations, existing only in his own and Hilde's imagination. But, for Riviere, 'writing it' means more than simply externalizing one's dreams and daemons, or acknowledging their destructive power in the real world. Her own writing responds to Ibsen's implication that the literary dream-builder also

---

1920), 57. Riviere quotes only the last fourteen lines. Segal recalls that it was she who introduced Riviere to Apollinaire and drew her attention to '*Cortège*' and the translation is Segal's (information by courtesy of Athol Hughes; personal communication).

[85] *The Master Builder* (1892) had been performed in London in 1948, and broadcast on radio by the BBC in 1950 and 1951, as well as on television in 1950. For the biographical background to the writing and reception of Ibsen's play, see James Walter McFarlane (ed.), *The Oxford Ibsen*, 7 vols. (Oxford: Oxford University Press, 1966), vii. 519–42.

[86] André Green takes as his epigraph for his essay on the negative therapeutic reaction the passage from Milton's *Paradise Lost* that describes Satan enthroning himself omnipotently on high as a simulacrum of 'the highest'—'a resemblance...where faith and realty | Remain not' (vi. 114–16); see Green, *The Work of the Negative*, 89.

communicates and shares his phantasy.[87] In Apollinaire's '*Cortège*', the luminous past leaches the future of colour ('*Prés du passé luisant demain est incolore*'), but it is also what keeps the self alive. The harvest of the past yields the poetry of the present.[88] When it comes to the aesthetic—'what perfectly | Presents at once both effort and effect' ('*ce qui parfait | Présente tout ensemble et l'effort et l'effet*')—there is more to it for both Apollinaire and Riviere than getting one's feet on the ground. Deluded or not, imagination lives on the stolen goods of literature.

[87] Cf. Hanna Segal in 'A Psycho-Analytical Approach to Aesthetics' (the paper that immediately follows Riviere's in *New Directions in Psychoanalysis*): 'The neurotic's phantasy interferes with his relationships in which he acts it out. The artist withdraws into the world of phantasy, but he can communicate his phantasies and share them'; Klein *et al.* (eds.), *New Directions in Psychoanalysis*, 398. Segal's classic statement of the Kleinian position on aesthetics was originally presented to the British Psycho-Analytical Society in 1947. In a 1980 postscript to her 1955 paper, Segal revised her original emphasis on reparation, acknowledging the role of idealization ('an ideal object merged with the self, and an object perceived as separate and independent'); see *The Work of Hanna Segal*, 204. For a wide-ranging discussion of Segal's cultural and aesthetic context, see also Riccardo Steiner, *Tradition, Change, Creativity: Repercussions of the New Diaspora on Aspects of British Psychoanalysis* (London: Karnac Books, 2000), 229–72.

[88] Segal instances Proust in relation to the depressive position, reflecting a similar idea (and perhaps the influence of Riviere's supervision during this period): 'all creation is really a re-creation of a once loved and once whole, but now lost and ruined object, a ruined internal world and self. It is when the world within us is destroyed, when it is dead and loveless, when our loved ones are in fragments, and we ourselves in helpless despair—it is then that we must re-create our world anew, reassemble the pieces, infuse life into dead fragments, re-create life'; Klein *et al.* (eds.), *New Directions in Psychoanalysis*, 390.

3

The Mirror of Theory: *Klein's Books*

When art and literature effect a dynamic that is comparable to the ordeals of psychic survival that [Klein] has described, she enjoyed holding those texts up to the mirror of her theory, which she polished herself while sitting in her analyst's chair and listening to her analysands. Along the way, literature benefited from being in the spotlight, though it also jealously retained its enigmas.

Julia Kristeva, *Melanie Klein*[1]

Klein's relation to books is at once Magian and programmatic. Literature is held up to the mirror of her clinical theory, as Kristeva suggests, but it also serves as a powerful trope for symbolic action and creativity. Creativity is what the loved and envied breast means for the Kleinian infant. Psychoanalysis too both loves and envies what it sees in literature, while Kristeva personifies literature itself as jealously retaining its enigmas. Klein's focus on the dynamics of psychic processes in dramatic and fictional characters, and on the artist's symbolic resolution to emotional conflict, is especially evident in her posthumously published paper, 'Some Reflections on "The Oresteia"' (1963). She considers the characters of Aeschylus' trilogy in terms of their symbolic roles—the Furies, for instance, symbolize internal processes and injured internal objects. Her *Oresteia* allegorizes the divided and embattled psyche's struggle to free itself from the cycle of past suffering and vengeance, and to learn from experience. She also acknowledges external reality: Clytemnestra really is a bad mother to Orestes and Electra (even if her mourning for Iphigenia is sincere). But Klein's main emphasis is on the third and final part of the trilogy, *The Eumenides*, where Orestes is released from his persecution at the hands of the unforgiving Furies.

Klein invokes the Furies in the words of Gilbert Murray's translation. His 'Watcher in the breast' is the conscience or super-ego (unforgiving yet necessary) whose origins lie in infant destructiveness and primitive parental identifications: 'Times there be when Fear is good, | And the Watcher in the breast | Needs must

[1] Julia Kristeva, *Melanie Klein*, trans. Ross Guberman (New York: Columbia University Press, 2001), 191.

reign in masterhood' (*Eumenides*, ll. 517–20).[2] The miserable, misery-bearing Furies are the enraged and unforgiving, tortured and persecutory parts of the self. But the aspect of the Furies associated with fear of wrongdoing is re-inscribed in the order that reconciles justice and forgiveness at the end of the play. Klein implicitly links literature and psychic integration as well as symbolic action. Literature enacts the integration that is ultimately unachievable in the ordinary span of human life, serving as a counter-force to the Kleinian emphasis on destructiveness. Envy, aggression, and the death instinct do not have things entirely their own way in the furious *psychomachia* waged within infantile unconscious phantasy, and recapitulated in adult emotions. Negativity is mediated by Klein's belief in the infant's innate drive towards love, gratitude, and reparation.

Klein's reflections on the *Oresteia* embody her view that the ego, once it acknowledges its own destructiveness, becomes more tolerant, understanding, and forgiving. The forgiveness extended to Orestes himself at the end of the trilogy constitutes the point of comparison between Klein and another twentieth-century woman thinker whose achievement Kristeva has celebrated alongside Klein's: Hannah Arendt. Arendt's *The Human Condition* (1958) bases its redemptive system on the idea of human making or fabrication (*homo faber*). In 'Irreversibility and the Power to Forgive', Arendt refers to 'the interrelated faculties of action and speech, which produce meaningful stories as naturally as fabrication produces use objects'.[3] Meaning is the redemptive miracle. Her *animal laborans* is saved from the recurrent cycles of the life process by the human capacity for meaning-making. But, given the impossibility of being able to undo what one has done, the only way to redeem action is 'the faculty of forgiving'. The potentialities of action impose the predicament of irreversibility, for which the only remedy is forgiveness. Its partner is promising, the only remedy for unpredictability:

> The possible redemption from the predicament of irreversibility—of being unable to undo what one has done though one did not, and could not, have known what he was doing—is the faculty of forgiving. The remedy for unpredictability, for the chaotic uncertainty of the future, is contained in the faculty to make and keep promises. The two faculties belong together in so far as one of them, forgiving, serves to undo the deeds of the past, whose 'sins' hang like Damocles' sword over every new generation; and the other, binding oneself through promises, serves to set up in the ocean of uncertainty, which the future is by definition, islands of security without which not even continuity, let alone durability of any kind, would be possible in the relationships between men.[4]

---

[2] *E&G* 296. Quotations are drawn from Gilbert Murray, *The Oresteia Translated into English Rhyming Verse* (London: George Allen & Unwin, 1928), rpr. in *The Complete Plays of Aeschylus*, trans. Gilbert Murray (London: George Allen & Unwin, 1952). Klein's paper refers to Murray's introductory definition of *Hubris*, which he sees as a form of greed ('the habit of "having-more", or trying to have more'): ' "Hubris grasps at more, bursts bounds and breaks the order" ' (*E&G* 280; cf. Murray, *Oresteia*, 6–7).

[3] Hannah Arendt, *The Human Condition* (1958; rpr. Chicago: University of Chicago Press, 1998), 236.   [4] Ibid., 237.

Unless we can forgive and be forgiven, we remain the victim of consequences from which we can never escape, menaced by a trans-generational sword of Damocles. Just as forgiving unbinds the past, promising binds the incertitude of the future. Without promises we would lose our identities, 'condemned to wander helplessly and without direction in the darkness of each man's lonely heart.'

Redemption from this existential *impasse* is made possible by the existence of a political and legal community, 'for no one can forgive himself and no one can feel bound by a promise made only to himself'. The possibility of forgiving or promising depends on the extent to which one can be forgiven or promised by others. Arendt interprets forgiveness—a strictly secular concept—within a web of social relations. Unlike vengeance, which binds the actor to the original misdeed in a process like a chain reaction, forgiveness enables new beginnings. It becomes the only reaction that does not re-act, but instead 'acts anew and unexpectedly, unconditioned by the act which provoked it'.[5] But, for Arendt, forgiveness has to be accompanied by the possibility of punishment. Unlike vengeance, both forgiveness and punishment attempt to put an end to something that would otherwise continue endlessly. Arendt proposes that what is unpunishable cannot be forgiven, any more than what is unforgivable can be punished. As we shall see, Derrida takes issue with her on both counts; for him, forgiveness concerns what is essentially unforgivable and lies beyond 'prescription' by the Law.

Arendt points out that, whereas forgiving has been deemed inadmissible in the public realm, promises have always existed in the political realm (whether as Roman laws or as Biblical covenants). Promises perform the function of mastering the unpredictability of human affairs while refusing domination over oneself or others. They provide 'islands of certainty in an ocean of uncertainty', and guarantee 'limited independence from the incalculability of the future'.[6] Mutual promising is the only acceptable form of collective sovereignty that has a relatively reliable reality. Arendt identifies forgiving and promising as the foundation for morality— 'control mechanisms built into the very faculty to start new and unending processes'. Without the ability to undo or to control the consequences of what we have done, 'we would be the victims of an automatic necessity bearing all the marks of the inexorable laws which . . . were supposed to constitute the outstanding characteristics of natural processes'. Arendt's 'control mechanisms' are all that stand between us and something that resembles the death-drive—'The life span of man running toward death [which] would inevitably carry everything human to ruin and destruction if it were not for the faculty of interrupting it and beginning something new'.[7] Only new life brings the hope of new beginnings, new action, and new possibilities for living.

Arendt is bent on preserving the category of 'radical evil' (later to become Eichmann's 'banality of evil') as a category that can neither be punished nor

[5] Hannah Arendt, *The Human Condition* (1958; rpr. Chicago: University of Chicago Press, 1998), 241.   [6] Ibid., 244, 245.
[7] Ibid., 246.

forgiven, since it simultaneously transcends and destroys the realm of the human. In her final work, *The Life of the Mind* (1978), Eichmann embodies 'the banality of evil' not only because he is unable to speak for himself, but because he is unable to think. Specifically, he is unable to think in a way that involves the capacity to identify with anyone else:

The longer one listened to him, the more obvious it became that his inability to speak was closely connected with an inability to think, namely, to think from the standpoint of somebody else. No communication was possible with him, not because he lied but because he was surrounded by the most reliable of all safeguards against the words and the presence of others, and hence against reality as such.[8]

This is the passage that Kristeva quotes when she re-poses Arendt's famous question about Eichmann: 'whether the accused had a conscience'.[9] Eichmann's 'sheer thoughtlessness' is bound up with his incapacity either to inhabit meaningful discourse (his 'horrible gift' for ready-made words and consoling clichés) or to imagine the standpoint of others. He is unforgivable because he cannot identify with other people. Consequently, other people are unable to identity with him.

Unlike Arendt, Klein eschews any explicit political or social morality. Her ethics are predicated on a recognition of others as at once whole and other, and on what she believes is an innate drive (even in infancy) to undo the cycle of persecution and retaliation. We are only solitary or isolated to the extent that we defend ourselves against loving, hating, or the terror of abandonment. Like Arendt, Klein envisages built-in 'control mechanisms' consisting of the infant's capacity for love and gratitude, working to counteract the death-drive. Her 1955 paper 'On Identification' uses a novel by the Franco-American writer Julian Green to illustrate her theory of 'projective identification', a concept that radically revises previous psychoanalytic understanding of identificatory processes.[10] In Green's *If I Were You* (1949), the infernal pact made by his anti-hero involves splitting off his own thoughts and desires and projecting them into others. Separated from the world of attachment on which his emotional life depends, he becomes a party to desires and acts that he is unable to recognize as his own. I want to explore Klein's theory of identification, first in her account of the way adults are shaped by emotional lives of infants, and then in 'On Identification', before returning to the *Oresteia*. My argument will be that Klein not only holds books up to the mirror of her theory but that books shaped her theory of identification even though they retained their enigmas.

---

[8] *The Life of the Mind* (New York: Harcourt Brace Jovanovich, 1978), 192.

[9] Julia Kristeva, *Hannah Arendt*, trans. Ross Guberman (New York: Columbia University Press, 2001), 148.

[10] For an overview of the complex and evolving concept of projective identification, as understood by Klein, her followers, and by contemporary Kleinians, see R. D. Hinshelwood, *A Dictionary of Kleinian Thought* (London: Free Associations Books, 1991), 179–208. For a recent discussion of the difficulties and the potential involved in Klein's formulation of projective identification, see also Meira Likierman, *Melanie Klein: Her Work in Context* (London: Continuum, 2001), 156–71.

IMAGINATIVE THINKING

In their joint book, *Love, Hate and Reparation* (1937), Melanie Klein and Joan Riviere set out to show (as John Rickman wrote in his preface) 'that the unconscious of the adult is actually not so very different from the mind of the child'.[11] Riviere tackles the part played by hate, greed, and aggression in the emotional life of adults, while Klein broaches 'the equally powerful forces of love and the drive to reparation'. In each case, studying the complexities of love and hate means returning to their point of origin: the infant's relation to the mother's breast. This is not just a matter of desire or satisfaction, but the most primitive form of mental activity, 'that is, phantasy-building, or more colloquially, *imaginative thinking*' (*LGR* 308; my emphasis). For Klein, the baby's unconscious phantasying of the absent breast 'is the earliest form of the capacity which later develops into the more elaborate workings of the imagination' (*LGR* 308). 'Imaginative thinking' begins at the breast. Whether pleasurable or destructive, the baby's phantasies are characterized by their literalness; Klein emphasizes the baby's feeling that it '*has really destroyed*' the object of its destructive impulses (*LGR* 308). There is no 'as if' in the infant unconscious. Infantile phantasies of repair are equally omnipotent. The baby who phantasizes injuring his mother by biting and tearing her up 'may soon build up phantasies that he is putting the bits together again and repairing her' (*LGR* 308).

Enter literature. Illustrating the unconscious sense of guilt, Klein invokes Coleridge's *Christabel*: '... to be wroth with one we love | Doth work like madness in the brain' (*LGR* 309). The quotation comes from the passage in which Christabel's father, melancholic since the death of his wife, hears Geraldine's false tale of abduction and recalls the quarrel that had estranged him from her supposed father:

> Alas! They had been friends in youth;
> But whispering tongues can poison truth;
> And constancy lives in realms above;
> And life is thorny; and youth is vain,
> And to be wroth with one we love
> Doth work like madness in the brain.
>
> (Christabel, ll. 408–13)

Aroused by his memories as well as by indignation at Geraldine's tale of wrongs, Sir Leoline takes her in his arms (later he will angrily repudiate his own daughter).

Likierman points out that 'Klein offers a very unusual angle of the development of identity. She shows that it is not a question of simple and increasing self-awareness. The most intense and disturbing parts of the self are only accommodated after they have journeyed through the minds of others' (ibid., 160).

[11] Melanie Klein and Joan Riviere, *Love, Hate and Reparation* (1937; rpr. New York: Norton, 1964), p. vi.

The unconscious workings of love and hate disturb our relations with others, just as relations between parent and child are disturbed in Coleridge's gothic narrative of inter-familial alienation. For Klein, guilt and distress, along with anxiety and frustration, complicate the baby's growing feelings of love towards the mother.

The destructiveness of the Kleinian infant coexists with concern for the loved person on whom it depends—the drive not only to love her but to make sacrifices for her, and ultimately to identify with her:

> Side by side with the destructive impulses in the unconscious mind both of the child and of the adult, there exists a profound urge to make sacrifices, in order to help and put right loved people who in phantasy have been harmed or destroyed. In the depths of the mind, the urge to make people happy is linked up with a strong sense of responsibility and concern for them, which manifests itself in genuine sympathy with other people and in the ability to understand them, as they are and as they feel.   (*LGR* 311)

The Kleinian baby has the capacity that Eichmann lacks, 'genuine sympathy with other people' and 'the ability to understand them'.[12] The ability to identify with others makes love possible: 'To be genuinely considerate implies that we can put ourselves in the place of other people: we "identify" ourselves with them. Now this capacity for identification with another person is...a condition for real and strong feelings of love' (*LGR* 311). Responsibility and concern for other people manifests itself in our understanding them. We can only 'put the other person's interests and emotions first, if we have the capacity to identify ourselves with the loved person' (*LGR* 311). Identification emerges as the foundation for reparation and, ultimately, for creativity as well.

Klein suggests that love is displaced from the earliest loved people to things, activities, and symbols. This displacement becomes the basis for aesthetic pleasure: 'By a gradual process, anything that is felt to give out goodness and beauty, and that calls forth pleasure and satisfaction' takes the place of the breast (*LGR* 333). Klein interprets the example of 'explorers who set out for new discoveries' in terms of the boy's unconscious aggressive and genital phantasies about the mother's body and his quest to repair it—an impulse that can also lead to violence against conquered peoples and the ruthless colonization of new lands. Leaving colonial conquest aside, Klein turns to science and the creative arts. Once more, her main example is literary. Keats's 1816 sonnet 'On First Looking into Chapman's Homer' uses the discovery of new worlds as a metaphor for discovering a new book:

> Much have I travell'd in the realms of gold,
> And many goodly states and kingdoms seen;
> Round many western islands have I been
> Which bards in fealty to Apollo hold.

---

[12] This is close to the position that Riviere had taken in her 1936 paper on the negative therapeutic reaction, although she depicts the situation of the altruistic melancholic as less hopeful (see Ch. 2 above).

Oft of one wide expanse have I been told
That deep-brow'd Homer ruled as his demesne:
Yet did I never breathe its pure serene
Till I heard Chapman speak out loud and bold . . .

(ll. 1–8)

Klein comments that Keats responds to Chapman's Homer 'from the point of view of one who enjoys a work of art', comparing poetry to 'goodly states and kingdoms' and 'realms of gold'. Keats reading a book becomes the eagle-eyed explorer, Cortez, discovering 'a new land and sea' (*LGR* 335). The country of Keats's desire (presided over by the 'deep-brow'd' Homer) is not just that of 'art, beauty, the world', but the world as created by the father of all poetry (a blind man unable to see the ocean except in imagination). Klein's literalized reading of the exploration metaphor (beautiful lands equal longing for the mother) is less arresting than her aesthetic equation: 'In Keats's perfect poem the world stands for art, and it is clear that to him scientific and artistic enjoyment and exploration are derived from the same source—from the love for the beautiful lands—the "realms of gold" ' (*LGR* 335). Books, too, may be explored and conquered in unconscious phantasy, violently as well as lovingly. But for Klein, even guilt (unless it is overwhelming) provides an impulse towards creativity, since it awakens children to constructive expressions of the wish to repair, such as drawing, modelling, and speech.

Having surveyed the range of human relations (parenthood, marriage, childhood, and adult same-sex friendships), Klein ends with the most intriguing relation of all—'the rather odd phrase "the relation to ourselves" ' (*LGR* 340). Klein's eloquent and expansive definition of 'ourselves' suggests Riviere's influence:

But what are our selves? Everything, good or bad, that we have gone through from our earliest days onwards; all that we have received from the external world and all that we have felt in our inner world, happy and unhappy experiences, relationships to people, activities, interests, and thoughts of all kinds—that is to say, everything we have lived through—makes part of our selves and goes to build up our personalities. If some of our past relationships, with all the associated memories, with the wealth of feelings they called forth, could be suddenly wiped out of our lives, how impoverished and empty we should feel! How much love, trust, gratification, comfort and gratitude, which we experienced and returned, would be lost! Many of us would not even want to have missed some of our painful experiences, for they have also contributed to the richness of our personalities.   (*LGR* 338)[13]

Green's envious, shape-shifting character risks erasing all the experiences, relationships, memories, and feelings that make up a self (a 'personality', or the

---

[13] Compare Riviere on the death of the 'personality' in 'The Unconscious Phantasy of an Inner World Reflected in Examples from Literature' (1952): 'a living existence, an entity, a person, a personality, a most complex and composite structure of attributes, tendencies, experiences, memories, idiosyncrasies good and bad, as well as the body they belong to'; see Athol Hughes (ed.), *The Inner World and Joan Riviere: Collected Papers 1920–1958* (London: Karnac Books, 1991), 316.

personification of a 'person'). He becomes a man without identity, dissociated from his almost forgotten name. But for Klein, 'We keep enshrined in our minds our loved people.' The capacity to be at peace with ourselves depends on our capacity to forgive those we once loved and hated: 'If we have become able, deep in our unconscious minds, to clear our feelings to some extent towards our parents of grievances, and have forgiven them for the frustrations we had to bear, then we can be at peace with ourselves and are able to love others in the true sense of the word' (*LGR* 343). Klein's moving conclusion to 'Love, Guilt and Reparation' is the template for her reading of Green's novel *If I Were You*.

Twenty years later, Klein returned to the subject in 'Envy and Gratitude' (1957), her last major contribution to psychoanalytic theory.[14] The infant's underlying desire for an ever-present breast—the fount of inexhaustible goodness, patience, generosity, and creativity—makes it the foundation for all adult belief in goodness. Its unconscious significance far exceeds any actual capacity to give nourishment, while also being distinguished from an idealized breast whose function is to defend against persecutory anxiety. The infant's pre-verbal emotions and phantasies 'appear as "memories in feelings"' revived by the transference, 'reconstructed and put into words with the help of the analyst' (*E&G* 180 n.). And once more, with the help of the poet. Klein's reconstruction of the envy felt in the face of imaginary maternal plenitude is derived from a range of literary sources. Envy, for Klein, is projective (as opposed to greed, which is introjective), etymologically derived from the verb '*invideo*', to look askance at, look maliciously or spitefully into (*E&G* 181 n.), and distinct from jealousy. Envy in Klein's sense is envy of the first object, the breast on which it feeds. Milton's Satan and Augustine's account of envy illustrate the impulse to spoil creativity; Satan makes war because he envies God's creation. But Klein's most intriguing example is drawn from Spenser's *Faerie Queene*, bringing into view the habit of personification on which her own insistently allegorical system depends (love, guilt, and reparation; envy and gratitude).

Klein's schematic use of paired terms often provokes resistance because it produces the impression of a moralized binarism. Her system seems both to describe and to enact the psyche's own ambivalent splitting into good and bad. In *The Faerie Queene*, allegory similarly operates in the service of a constantly proliferating, splitting, and reconfigured narrative of affects, attributes, and characteristics—at once a fantasy-realm and a moral system, romance intertwined with didacticism. In Book I, Canto iv, the Redcrosse Knight (having abandoned Una) is guided by Duessa to the sinful house of Pride where he will do battle with

---

[14] See Likierman, *Melanie Klein*, 172–91, for a cogent account of the misgivings aroused by Klein's theory of envy, which took the place once occupied by sadism in infant unconscious phantasy. Likierman describes 'Envy and Gratitude' not as 'a single hypothesis that stirs a particular set of objects' but as 'a text that is having an argument with itself' (ibid., 180) since it tells two different stories: one about the infant's innate envy, and the other about reactive envy related to its own predisposition and the experiences it undergoes.

the knight Sansjoy. Pride is a figure of envy, surrounded by glistering gold and precious jewels; her very throne is outshone by her beauty, 'as envying her self, that too exceeding shone' (I. iv. 8), in the reflexive turn of phrase that often governs Spenserian allegory. Her 'exceeding' is compared to that of Phoebus' fairest child, who inflamed the skies when he attempted to drive his father's chariot: 'So proud she shyned in her Princely state' (I. iv. 10). Pride's alias is Lucifera (daughter of Pluto and Proserpina), a usurper who rules with the help of her six councillors, named for the other deadly sins: *Idlenesse, Gluttony, Lechery, Avarice, Envie*, and *Wrath*. The figure of envy—a ravenous wolf—is the deadly sin that hates not only good works and virtuous deeds but 'eke the verse of famous Poets witt | He does backebite, and spightfull poison spues | From leprous mouth on all, that ever writt . . .' (*E&G* 202; I. iv. 32).[15] Spenser's poetry, his 'witt', is attacked by a leprous mouth that spews poison instead of nourishment. Self-consuming envy manifests itself as perverse orality, a violent mutual devouring that has been described by one recent theorist of allegory as *allelophagy*, or 'the corporeal expression of the symmetrical otherness . . . in the word allegory'—that is, 'two bodies engaged in a mutual devouring'.[16] Envie devours himself, even as he devours the body of a poisonous toad:

> . . . still did chaw
> Between his cankred teeth a venomous tode,
> That all the poison ran about his chaw;
> But inwardly he chawed his own maw
> At neighbours wealth, that made him ever sad;
> For death it was, when any good he saw . . .
>
> (I. iv. 30)

Chawing one's own maw (because the envied breast must have no satisfaction in feeding, nor the envious psyche any satisfaction in being fed) is the aptest of all figures for Kleinian envy, with its underlay of melancholy ('that made him ever sad'). The good breast, or its analytic substitute, is poisoned at the source; its capacity for providing nourishment need never be acknowledged since it has been destroyed in the process of incorporation.

In a much earlier paper, 'Personification in the Play of Children' (1929), Klein had identified 'personification' (the symbolic or dramatic representation of qualities and ideas) as the chief mechanism driving children's wish-fulfilling phantasies.[17]

---

[15] Klein also footnotes Chaucer's references to backbiting and destructive criticism (*E&G* 202–3 n.).

[16] See Gordon Teskey, *Allegory and Violence* (Ithaca, NY: Cornell University Press, 1996), 8. Teskey's brilliant observation—that in allegory, 'The body of the other must . . . be annihilated in the only possible way possible: by devouring it'—points to an as-yet untreated dimension of allegory: its melancholic incorporation. Far from moving towards the realm of abstraction, Spenserian allegory enacts the concrete incorporation of its own objects as a way to capture them; Teskey calls this process 'violence'.

[17] Klein defines the operation of splitting that is the motor for personification (in adults as well as children) as 'a mechanism analogous to and closely connected with projection' (*LGR* 205). Published

Personification is allied to allegory's attempt to figure abstractions in the form of concrete actors who paradoxically resist their own abstraction. Where children's phantasies express themselves in the form of folk-tale narratives of quest, persecution, and rescue, 'Envy and Gratitude' displays the working of allegory and personification in a more adult mode: word-play and wit. A series of dreams from Klein's clinical practice illustrate her thesis that envy of the feeding breast drives attacks on the primal object, as 'the spoiling and destructive quality of envy... undermines the sense of gratitude' (*E&G* 230). Klein herself features in these symptomatic dreams as the object of mingled frustration, envy, and even satire. But once again, *allelophagy* is the order of the day. A woman patient, having missed sessions owing to a pain in her shoulder, feels uncared for and neglected. On her return, she reports a restaurant dream:

[S]he was in a restaurant, seated at a table; however nobody came to serve her. She decided to join a queue and fetch herself something to eat. In front of her was a woman who took two or three little cakes and went away with them. The patient also took two or three little cakes... There was a sudden doubt about the name of the cakes (actually *petits fours*) which she first thought were 'petit fru', which reminded her of 'petit frau' and thus of 'Frau Klein'. The gist of my interpretation was that her grievance about the missed analytic sessions related to the unsatisfactory feeds and unhappiness in babyhood. The two cakes out of the 'two or three' stood for the breast which she felt she had been twice deprived of by missing analytic sessions... The fact that the woman was 'determined' and that the patient followed her example in taking the cakes pointed both at her identification with the analyst and at projection of her own greed onto her... The analyst who went away with the two or three *petits fours* stood not only for the breast which was withheld, but also for the breast which was going to *feed itself*... To frustration had been added envy of the breast. (*E&G* 205)

Her patient's response to this allegorical interpretation, so Klein records, 'was a striking change in the emotional situation... She had tears in her eyes, which was unusual, and said that she felt as if she now had had an entirely satisfactory feed.' (*E&G* 205–6)[18]

In this formulation of the relation between a good feed and a good interpretation, the semantic slide from *petit fru* to *petit frau* (*kleine frau*) to *Frau Klein* replays the traditional alliance of allegory and wit; two or three things the patient knows about Klein add up to *petit fours*. Allegory, personification, and punning ('Poets witt') characterize the richly self-feeding psychoanalytic breast—not so much enviously chawing its own maw as savouring its own interpretations. No wonder Klein's patients are envious. One man dreams of her as a cow munching

the same year, 'Infantile Anxiety Situations Reflected in a Work of Art and in the Creative Impulse' (1929) is generally regarded as Klein's inaugurating paper on aesthetics; here, however, reparation verges on magical omnipotence since Klein has not yet fully worked out the depressive position (for Klein's foundational theory of play and her play technique, see Ch. 4).

[18] 'I have repeatedly heard the expression at the end of such sessions "I have been well nourished"' (*E&G* 206 n.).

an endless strip of blanket ('an endless stream of words'), making her eat her boring interpretations (*E&G* 207). Another patient dreams of a fish-baby in a laundry basket, dressed in green like the cover of a book in the *International Psycho-Analytical Library* series—catching her on the baited hook of one of her own books (*E&G* 211). Yet another (addicted to orality's prosthetic substitute) smokes a pipe 'filled with [her] papers which had been torn out of one of [her] books'; he, too, resents Kleinian interpretations which 'he had to "put into his pipe and smoke"' (*E&G* 214). For the pipe-smoker, 'one does not smoke printed papers' except to smoke out the self-consuming analyst as she holds books up to the mirror of her theory and turns them into allegory.

HOMO FABIAN

In 'Our Adult World and its Roots in Infancy' (1959), Klein distinguishes between identification with an object based on introjection ('acquiring some of the characteristics of this object and being influenced by them') and projective identification: 'in putting oneself into the other person (projecting), the identification is based on attributing to the other person some of one's own quali-ties' (*E&G* 252). Projective identification behaves like allegory, swallowing up the other. But putting one's own qualities, emotions, and thoughts into the other person can help us to understand other people: 'By attributing part of our feelings to the other person, we understand their feelings, needs, and satisfactions; in other words, we are putting ourselves into the other person's shoes' (*E&G* 22–3). By contrast, predominantly hostile projection impairs empathy with others. Like the interplay between introjection and projection, the character and extent of projection—benign or pathological?; moderate or excessive?—has the potential to enrich or impoverish the inner world, and to enhance or attack relations with others. Klein's formulation (too much introjection endangers the ego, while hos-tile projection impairs empathy) is the foundation on which Bion subsequently develops his theory of thinking.[19] Projective identification becomes the basic building-block for any form of emotional linking and communication, including thought itself, whether positive or negative.

Klein's fullest working-out of the concept of projective identification occurs in a literary context. Her 1955 paper 'On Identification' is based on her reading of Julian Green's post-war novel *If I Were You*, or *Si j'étais vous*... The paper is her contribution to the 'applied psychoanalysis' section of *New Directions in Psychoanalysis*, alongside other contributions on literature and aesthetics. Although Klein avoids dealing with the specifically fictional aspect of projective identification, Green's novel is an indirect expression of his own theory of fiction

---

[19] See Wilfred R. Bion, 'Attacks on Linking' (1959) and 'A Theory of Thinking' (1962), in *Second Thoughts* (1967; rpr. London: Karnac Books, 1987), 93–109, 110–19.

and of the self.[20] The hero of *If I Were You*, Fabian Especel, is a species of *homo faber*—a would-be writer who resembles the author as a young man. Trapped in the limits of his life and body, he attempts to escape his existential predicament with the help of a magic formula given him by the Devil's agent, the repellent M. Brittomart (an intriguingly Spenserian name). Like a sorcerer's apprentice, Fabian dreams of achieving his desires, only to find himself imprisoned yet more claustrophobically in the confines of his provincial *petit bourgeois* Catholic existence. Green's preface to the revised edition of his novel dates its inception to 1921, during his student years at the University of Virginia, when he conceived the 'bizarre idea' of a plot involving the ability to exchange one's personality with whomever one wished. Finding himself unhappy and surrounded by others who seemed satisfied with their lot, he longed to be like them. Envy gave him his plot.

In his account of the novel's origins, Green says that he thought he had created a new myth, ignoring his unconscious debt to Stevenson's *The Strange Case of Dr Jekyll and Mr Hyde* (1886), which he had read shortly before in his English class.[21] Green's other early story from this period, 'The Apprentice Psychiatrist', is a similarly disquieting tale of doubling in which an obsessed psychiatrist drives his morbidly sensitive pupil to nervous collapse and then shoots him, revealing himself as a raving maniac.[22] By contrast, the sensitive hero of *If I Were You*, caught between his longing for self-transcendence, his sensual appetites, and his religious scruples, dies from a brief but hectic career based on knowing too much about himself and others. Green put his plot aside for twenty years until he returned to it as a portrait of his youthful self-dissatisfaction—and as testimony to the secret and insatiable curiosity that drives the novelist to enter and possess his fictional characters: ' *"Qui est-ce? Que pense-t-il? Où va-t-il? Est-il heureux?" . . . Je voulais savoir tout cela, je voulais être tout le monde.*'[23] Green's preface rehabilitates the desire to know by invoking the spirituality of Meister Eckhard (to each his own especial cross), noting the tendency of advancing age to reconcile one to the limits of one's own personality. A later, revised edition shifts the emphasis from the hero's death to the writer's dream, adding a final section that frames the depressed, daemonic fable of 1949 with a writerly *mise en abyme*. We no longer know what world we have strayed into—supernatural or psychological, daemonic or dreamed? A newspaper item records the imminent arrest of a crook and extortionist called

---

[20] The fullest account of Green's views, life, and work is to be found in Robert de Saint Jean, *Julien Green par lui-même* (Paris: Editions de Seuil, 1967) and Robert de Saint Jean and Luc Estang, *Julien Green* (Paris: Editions de Seuil, 1990), as well as in the journals he published throughout his life; see also Glenn S. Burne, *Julian Green* (New York: Twayne Publishers, 1972) for a useful introductory survey. Homosexual love ('impossible love') is dealt with more explicitly in Green's later novels and plays from the mid-1950s onwards.

[21] See Julian Green, *Si j'étais vous . . .* (Paris: Librarie Plon, 1970), 10. Both Green's novel and Fabian's story-within-a-story are also reminiscent of Oscar Wilde's *The Picture of Dorian Gray* (1891) and his moralized fairy tales.

[22] See Julian Green, *The Apprentice Writer* (New York: Marion Boyars, 1993), 237–48; written May 1920 and published in *The University of Virginia Magazine.*   [23] Green, *Si j'étais vous . . .*, 12.

Brittomart, the name given to the Devil's agent who accosts Fabian in his 'dream',
which begins all over again . . .

Green's foreword to the original 1949 translation had addressed the riddle of
human identity—'why I was my particular self and not someone else'—in terms
of envy: 'Which of us, after all, has never said to himself: "If I were he," or: "If I
were you"? The novelist, who to a greater or lesser degree is part of every character
he creates, can on occasion, and with a great effort, transform himself into whatever shape he pleases.'[24] Otherness-envy (*allelophagy*) provides the motive for his
allegorical fiction. Driving the novel is 'that feeling of intense bitterness so forcibly
described by Milton in Samson Agonistes when he says: "Thou art become, O
direst of prisons, thine own dungeon"' (a quotation that struck Klein so forcibly
that she repeats it twice over in her paper).[25] Only poets and novelists, on one
hand, and mystics on the other, can escape the prison of the self—novelists by transforming the ego, mystics by transcending it. For Green, 'our innate discontent arises
from the perpetual sameness in which we are enveloped'. Existential *ennui* prompts
'the same ever-recurrent question, how we are going to keep ourselves going till
nightfall, or indeed till death'.[26] Green explores his theory of fiction in lectures
delivered during his wartime stay in America (where he acted as a cultural
spokesman for, and to, occupied France). In 'How a Novelist Begins' (1941), he
writes: 'A real novelist is neither a photographer nor a dreamer indulging in idle
fancies; he is a man with a strange power to substitute himself for life and to create
destinies.'[27] In 'Where Do Novels Come From?' (1941), he defines the novelist's distinguishing characteristic as his capacity to take on the identities of others ('A novelist
is a man who can transform himself into the character described in their [*sic*] book').[28]
Green compares the novel to an 'iceberg, floating blindly on what a psychoanalyst
might call the sea of the subconscious'. Fiction is an unconscious form of self-
betrayal: 'When an author writes "Chapter I" at the top of a blank page, he is starting
out on a strange and often dangerous adventure . . . What he wishes to do or say himself, but doesn't quite dare, he makes his characters say and do in his stead.'[29]
Wishing but not quite daring describes his pathetic creation, Fabian, in *If I Were You*.

Green's 1949 foreword reveals his subject as 'that double anguish which consists
in the knowledge that a man can escape neither his own destiny nor the approach
of death.'[30] Klein's account of the novel responds to this double anguish, as well as to
Fabian's envy, hatred, and claustrophobia; for her, fear of death is the source of 'the
feeling of chaos, of disintegration, of lacking emotions as a result of splitting'.[31] By

[24] Julian Green, *If I Were You* (New York: Harper, 1949), p. v; Klein uses the 1950 London edition, trans. J. H. F. McEwan.
[25] 'Thou art become (O worst imprisonment) | The dungeon of thyself' (*Samson Agonistes*, 155–6); see *E&G* 154, 166 n.   [26] Green, *If I Were You*, pp. v, vi.
[27] Green, *The Apprentice Writer*, 142.   [28] Ibid., 163–4.   [29] Ibid., 145–6.
[30] Green, *If I Were You*, p. vi.
[31] In 'Some Reflections on "The Oresteia"', Klein writes: 'I have dealt elsewhere with the excessive fear of death in people for whom death is a persecution by internal and external enemies as well as a threat of destruction to the good internalized object'; the reference is to 'On Identification' (*E&G* 287–8).

contrast, 'integration implies being alive, loving, and being loved by the internal and external good object' (*E&G* 144). She interprets Fabian as if he were a patient, seeing his mobile and driven identity as motivated by greed, envy, and an unconscious need to defend against depression. Intruded into by his own bad objects, just as the Devil's rapacious agent intrudes into him (and the author enters his characters?), Fabian projects disowned parts of himself into other people, then steals their lives. In one of his identities, he becomes a brutal murderer, in another, a religious paedophile, but he is touched most of all by his unfulfilled longing to be a young woman (an identification which the novel refuses to gratify). This violent and negative form of 'projective identification' gives a pathological spin to the processes of novelistic curiosity, which take the form of cruelty, murderousness, perversion, compliance, and voyeurism. Fabian's identity changes involve concrete flights from his own body and forcible invasions of another's, using Brittomart's magic formula as a form of seduction. His envious and opportunistic substitutions lead to confusion between his own emptied-out personality and his serially assumed personalities. In his increasingly desperate migrations, Fabian risks forgetting the magic formula (his own name) that safeguards the secret of his identity and allows him to recover his original form. Fabian Especel is special (or, as Kristeva quips, '*espèce-elle*', a woman-identified man) only when he recalls his birth name.

Klein reads Fabian's hectic progress as the story of a how an unhappy young man works through the paranoid-schizoid and depressive positions in the last three days of his life, before returning to his mother, recovering his infant love for her, and dying. *If I Were You* depicts the revival of infantile anxieties that takes place 'if death is felt as an attack by hostile internal and external objects' (*E&G* 174). On his deathbed, Fabian achieves integration and 'repairs what had gone wrong in his life' (*E&G* 175), dependent on his mother's ministrations as he had been in infancy. But this is an idealized version of the novel, putting right what has gone wrong, in literature as well as life. Klein's reading focuses on the greed, hatred, and repetitions of Fabian's shape-shifting career. In this context, his death represents not so much integration as a continuation of his flight from the psychic reality of depression into infant dependence. Ambiguous in his relations to religion (whether Catholic or Protestant), as well as to his own puritanical mother, Green holds out less hope for his character than Klein; indeed, our sympathy depends on the extent to which Fabian's life lacks any *telos* other than his serial flight from identity to identity and his final regression. This is not a saving fantasy, although it is partially redeemed by Fabian's frustrated rebelliousness and Green's discomfiting satire. The Devil may not get what is left of a beautiful soul, but Fabian keeps his assignation with a death foretold by earlier episodes of illness. The uncomprehending mother who watches over him as he lies dying (' "Say your prayers, my son" ') is the same one who had extracted his promise to make his annual confession during Holy Week, in spite of a sexual assignation. In the final scene, she hears only her own breathing and mistakes it for his, although 'Fabian himself had ceased to breathe'—the novel's last, ironic line.

Klein's method of 'applied psychoanalysis' focuses attention on symbolic moments when Fabian's internal objects manifest themselves as good or bad—the stars that attract him in the night sky are an aspect of his lost or distant good objects; the ticking watch inherited from his father stands for a good internalized father (as opposed to the bad father represented by Brittomart); a large-breasted baker-woman whom he longs to caress and possess stands in for the maternal breast; and so on. In the example of the baker-woman, 'the whole shop turns in his mind into the feeding mother' (*E&G* 156). Fabian's deprivation of love and satisfaction makes him choke on his fresh roll, such is the frustration and hatred she engenders. When he lights candles in a church, his indignation at the 'bone-dry' font corresponds to the child's sense of a mother neglected by the absent father. Fabian is the frustrated child of a frustrated mother. Hence his murderousness towards the sordid woman whom the handsome but brutal Paul desires and then strangles, or the propensity for obscene pictures which he discovers in the midst of the religious torment consuming the ascetic intellectual, Fruges. For Klein, Fabian's restless quest for other lives is an attempt to prolong the life of his dead (dead-beat) father. His envy and greed are figured by the damned gathered at the Devil's country house—those who envy or have misused the 'gift' now offered to Fabian himself. As Klein points out, the men whose identity he steals turn out to be either contemptible or weak. The unpleasantness of the novel lies partly in Fabian's disillusionment with the various identities he serially inhabits—the pompous employer, the brain-dead thug, the sordid intellectual, the weak and immature husband.

Klein implies that projective identification not only depletes and empties out the ego but (since it depends on an existing point of similarity) makes Fabian the dungeon of himself, no matter whose body he snatches. He invariably exchanges identities with people who magnify some pre-existing element in him—cruelty, murderousness, paedophilia, compliance. The concreteness of his projection into his object-victim is matched by what he re-incorporates as hostile, dangerous, and undesirable parts of himself, with ingredients added by the owner. This is the novel's true confession, the banality of identification: in other words, no identification at all in the sense in which Arendt understands it.[32] As Klein suggests, Fabian is unable to identify with his good objects; he does not want to be the baker-woman (or even her lover). Resistance to Fabian's magic formula or 'gift'— depicted throughout the novel as intimate seduction—occurs only at moments when others are imagined as genuinely other, or else spared because they contain some element precious to Fabian himself. This is the case in Fabian–Fruges's slavering attempt to seduce a little boy protected by his innocence, or in the

---

[32] Cf. Herbert Rosenfeld, 'A Clinical Approach to the Psycho-analytical Theory of the Life and Death Instincts', *International Journal of Psycho-Analysis*, 52 (1971), 169–78, for the perverse internal Mafia gang that inhabits Fabian. Like Bion's, Rosenfeld's work on projective identification and schizophrenia during the 1950s develops Klein's ideas; see Herbert Rosenfeld, *Psychotic States: A Psychoanalytic Approach* (1965; rpr. London: Karnac Books, 1982).

moment of truth delivered by Fabian–Camille to a young girl in love with her vacuous, handsome brother-in-law. He is safe from himself in the guise of a child, or an imaginary twin sister. Klein suggests that he preserves the parts of himself still capable of love or being loved (perhaps they are rendered impenetrable by their paradoxically envied narcissism). For Klein, Fabian's final return to his mother expresses his longing to rejoin these abandoned childhood parts of himself.

The child who briefly appears at the start of the novel is called 'Thief of the Wind'. He is created by the mind of a dreamer—Fabian himself. As well as being a frustrated sensualist, Fabian is an aesthete who haunts second-hand bookshops and collects fine books. He is a sordid incarnation of Benjamin's urban *flaneur*, a prowler in arcades where he loiters outside shop windows and waits for women who never arrive. Tormented by acquisitive appetites, he becomes a frustrated shopper in search of the sexual excitement that lurks around the corner or hides in display stands (Fruges collects obscene postcards). Instead, he meets the Devil. At the start of the novel, trying to resist the temptation to keep his assignation with a woman, he starts writing a story whose title comes to him unbidden: 'An Appointment with the Devil'. Green implies that this story-within-a-story is an allegory of Fabian's own story—and the novelist's. Fabian has no idea what comes next. Instead he stares at an ink stain on his blotting pad 'as if he expected to find the answer to his question there'. The oddly shaped stain resembles a hand with the thumb missing, and seems to move slightly from right to left: 'The long and slender fingers had about them something instinctively rapacious and at the same time spoke of an intelligent or it might even be spiritual rapacity; the hand was the hand of a robber but not necessarily one who steals gold.'[33] Like his eye, mirrored in the lid of his father's watch (reminding him of textbook diagrams of eyes 'with lines issuing from them to explain how the image reflected on the retina is reversed'), the scene is a reversed image of the writer reading his own writing. The inky hand—moving from right to left, rather than left to right—suggests both automatism and distortion, or writing beyond authorial control. Once set going, it makes allegory run by itself. The 'gift' offered to Fabian is that of imaginative possession. It, too, involves a reversal, since the omniscient author becomes the object/victim of his own auto-narrative.

Fabian's half-written story concerns a boy 'called "Thief of the Wind" because nothing, in spite of all he could do, ever succeeded with him'.[34] An idealized version of the young Fabian, 'Thief of the Wind' is a light-footed child who sings nonsense songs that come to him on the air and blow away 'to far countries that he himself would never see'. He plays happily and freely in the town until he is bound apprentice to a bookbinder in a dark little shop where his job is to mix the glue. One day he opens a customer's picture book 'and from that moment felt a longing to learn about everything'. Pictures and text disclose a world of mountains, lakes, and gardens: 'It gave him a feeling of such poignant joy that he clasped the book

33 Green, *If I Were You*, 17, 18.   34 Ibid., 18.

tightly to him as if he would incorporate it and all its lakes and mountains and gardens into his very being'. Rather than projecting parts of himself into others, he incorporates the imaginary vistas of books into himself; they become his inner world. When the book goes back to its owner, 'Thief of the Wind' quits the bookbinder's shop. His father sends him to college where he has to surrender his belief 'that the contents of a book are to be mastered by pressing it to one's heart'.[35] What he learns there deprives him of his childhood communication with the non-human world. In its place, he develops curiosity about the human world. He longs to know everything and possess everything, and, more than knowledge, he longs for love. Most of all he is irked by the thought of remaining trapped in the same personality and body for the rest of his life. An encounter with an old man who seems to know him (paralleling Fabian's encounter with Brittomart) introduces the idea of stealing souls rather than the wind. At this point the story breaks off, and Fabian's own seduction by Brittomart takes over. The 'gift' he is offered is that of omnipotent identification: ' "you are to have conferred upon you the gift of being able to exchange personalities with whomever you may choose... The whole vast experience of the human race is at your disposal... Fabian, to you I give the world" '.[36]

Fabian's grandiloquent 'gift' is the novelist's curse, binding him to the characters he invades and depleting him of his own identity. In its pathological form, projective identification allows for no recognition of otherness, but only identification with the ejected or disowned parts of the self located in others. Fabian's sole encounter with resistance occurs when confronted by the opacity of a child, or when he sees, in eyes that strangely resemble his own, the adolescent anguish of his imaginary female twin, Elise. Part Two of *If I Were You* opens by giving us the world from an entirely new fictional view-point. Immersed in a provincial family that is ruled by a sanctimonious and hypocritical uncle, we see through the eyes of an unhappy girl. The furniture and the view from the window are described from her perspective; we feel what it is like to brush her hair and languish in the summer heat, sweltering in the sexuality that defines her bourgeois *ennui*. She is the incarnation of Fabian's longing for love—longing, however, embodied in a girl's desire for a man. Fabian's true other, Elise represents the single character in the novel to whom the author lends himself freely. For once we get away from the claustrophobic adventures of his *alter ego*, as Fabian enters imaginatively into the confinement of family life, with its undercurrents of deception, manipulation, and domination. Into this world walks Fabian, now in the guise of Camille, the young married man whom Elise sees and desires every day. But at the point when Camille confesses that he should have married Elise instead, she recognizes that this is not Camille. Her dream-come-true turns out to be a deception, and she recoils from him. Not only is he not her: he is not himself either.

---

[35] Green, *If I Were You*, 19.   [36] Ibid., 55.

Fabian–Camille toys with the idea of becoming Elise and loving himself, Narcissus-like, in her familiar blue-grey eyes (a woman who loves and is loved by a man). Instead, he disabuses her, settles his scores with Camille's manipulative wife and tyrannical uncle, quits the house, retraces his steps, and person by person recovers his original half-forgotten identity. What are we to make of Fabian's volte-face? Ostensibly, he is motivated both by the boredom of being the hand-some, empty Camille, and by his altruistic wish to free Elise from her hopeless love. But the novel's shift of perspective from Fabian to Elise implies an alternative narrative. When Fabian–Fruges contemplates seducing a child but is unable to do so (an authorial taboo on paedophilia?), or when Fabian stops short of a sex-change that implies passive homosexuality (another authorial taboo?), we could read it as an attempt to go straight, or as self-imposed censorship. But this other story also represents a fictional prison-break. When Green enters the imagined world of another—Elise—the novel permits the possibility of a different kind of identification. Klein defines the friendly form of identification in 'Our Adult World and its Roots in Infancy' as the attribution of part of our feelings to some-one else in order to understand them: 'in other words, we are putting ourselves into the other person's shoes' (*E&G* 252–3). This is the redemptive aspect of the novelist's potential for inhabiting other people. Fabian's world is often described as 'banal'. He turns his back on banality (his own and others') when he makes his exit not only from the vacuous Camille, but from his poignant female other, Elise, whom he understands, pities, and tries to help. What Arendt calls Eichmann's inability 'to think from the standpoint of somebody else' is briefly overcome, by both character and author. It is this that allows Fabian to recover himself at the end of the novel.

Green's 'Lectures on Novel Writing' had admonished the writer to be in sympathy with his characters, since 'they are part of yourself'.[37] When he immerses himself in the imagined world of Elise's tormenting adolescent passion, the novel briefly achieves just such sympathy with split-off parts of the self. We glimpse a fictional form of the richer, more complex, diachronic sense of self that Klein eloquently describes as having been built up by 'all that we have received from the external world and all that we have felt in our inner world . . .—that is to say, everything we have lived through' (*LGR* 338). Experience changes the self. Green's fable of the writer's ambiguous gift in *If I Were You* touches indirectly on this more complex understanding of what it might mean to live through others' experience. What we receive from the external world and feel in our inner world enables us to 'think from the standpoint of somebody else' (Arendt's phrase). Bion's epistemological transformation of projective identification—Klein's defining theoretical concept during the 1950s—makes it the basis of both thinking and any emotional link between the self and its objects. Identification in the wrong place is better than none at all. In 'Attacks on Linking', Bion describes how infantile anxieties about

---

[37] Green, *The Apprentice Writer*, 161.

annihilation may be projected into a container that fails to contain, such as a dutiful mother (compare Fabian's uncomprehending mother) who responds to the baby's fear of death with an impatient ' "I don't know what's the matter with the child" '.[38] The result is an escalating attempt to achieve projective identification, such as we see played out in Fabian's story. But there are other ways to read Green's post-Second World War novel, for all its pre-war origins. *If I Were You* evokes the closed, collusive, and aversive atmosphere in which anti-semitism and fascism took root during the years of Green's American exile. But in this confined fictional world, Green's homosexual aesthetic as yet finds no overt expression, emerging only from the moment of incoherence when his allegory of an imprisoned identity comes up against what it cannot say about itself.

THE WATCHER IN THE BREAST

Gilbert Murray describes the *Oresteia* as Aeschylus' attempt 'to think out, in terms that are not quite our terms, one of the deep unsolved mysteries of life—the problem of Sin, Punishment, and Forgiveness'.[39] If the rule of revenge is that blood calls for blood (the order upheld by the Furies), he asks, 'would not forgiveness be a kind of monstrosity, a wanton breach in the law of Cause and Effect?'[40] Murray's terms are those of early twentieth-century Humanism. Derrida's 'On Forgiveness' (1999) points to a similar breach at the root of the Abrahamic concept of forgiveness, when he argues that its madness lies in forgiving the unforgivable. Forgiveness only has meaning (*pace* Arendt) if the crime is inexpiable, '*imprescriptible*', and lies beyond punishment according to the Law. For the post-Humanist Derrida, it 'must remain a madness of the impossible'; it is radical and unconditional, belonging to the philosophic realm of 'As if' from which new possibilities might emerge.[41] Forgiveness refuses meaning or intelligibility, resisting its contemporary reduction 'to amnesty or to amnesia, to acquittal or prescription, to the work of mourning or some political therapy of reconciliation'.[42] Forgiveness also poses problems for what philosophers of the emotions call 'empathy'. Martha Nussbaum, for instance, asking about the contribution made by emotions to ethical thought, invokes the cognitive structure of compassion as a special instance. Compassion, she writes, 'pushes the boundaries of the self further outward than love', as against other emotions that 'draw sharp boundaries around the self'.[43]

---

[38] See Bion, *Second Thoughts*, 104.   [39] Murray, *Oresteia*, 5.   [40] Ibid., 23.

[41] Jacques Derrida, 'On Forgiveness' (2001), in *On Cosmopolitanism and Forgiveness*, trans. Mark Doolley and Michael Hughes (London and New York: Routledge, 2001), 39. For Derrida's use of the phrase 'As if' to indicate the realm of possibility as well as impossibility from which new conditions might arrive, see, for instance, Jacques Derrida, 'The University Without Condition', in *Without Alibi*, trans. Peggy Kamuf (Stanford, Calif.: Stanford University Press, 2002), 202–37.

[42] 'On Forgiveness', 45.

[43] Martha Nussbaum, *Upheavals of Thought: The Intelligence of the Emotions* (Cambridge: Cambridge University Press, 2001), 300.

She points out that the term 'empathy' is often used (as she will use it) 'to designate an imaginative reconstruction of another person's experience without any particular evaluation of that experience' (whether pleasurable or painful, significant or insignificant).[44] She goes on to ask a series of disturbing questions about the mental operation of empathy: 'Does one actually think, for the time being, that one *is* oneself the sufferer, putting oneself in his or her own place? Does one imagine one's own responses as *fused* in some mysterious way with those of the sufferer?' To imagine that one is oneself the sufferer would, she argues, 'precisely have failed to comprehend the pain of another *as other.*'[45] These questions are relevant to Klein's theory of identification, as we have seen, and they complicate the displaced identifications of Green's *If I Were You.*

If empathy is not a requirement for compassion (as Nussbaum argues), even though it offers a psychological guide to understanding others, does that also mean that empathy is not a requirement for forgiveness? Distinguishing between the irreducible yet indissoluble poles of forgiveness, on one hand, and reconciliation, on the other, Derrida imagines an unconditional form of forgiveness that abjures power over the other—'*unconditional but without sovereignty*', whether the sovereignty is that of a strong soul or a state.[46] If, as Arendt claims, one can only forgive where one can also judge and punish, then putting in place an instance of judgement presupposes a form of sovereignty. This is the model envisaged at the end of the *Oresteia*, where Athene founds the Council of Areopagus (as well as the *polis*) in order to stage Orestes' judgement and forgiveness for murdering his mother, Clytemnestra. His tragedy—which is also a drama of political reform—is enacted at the heart of Athenian democracy. For Derrida, however, the act of forgiving comes from somewhere other than the state or the Law. Derridean forgiveness originates in an area that is inaccessible, both to consciousness and to others, whether as citizens or psyches. It resists any principle of identification that is based on 'putting ourselves into the other person's shoes', while directly confronting the problem posed by the unconscious for ethics. Derrida invokes 'a logic of the unconscious' that disturbs both knowledge and 'the work of mourning' associated with the processes of public and private forgiveness and reconciliation. Pure forgiveness cannot represent itself in consciousness without reaffirming some form of sovereignty and thereby assuming, or granting, the power to forgive. But in the register of the unconscious, it is impossible to know the nature of the crime— or even who is guilty of what and towards whom: 'alterity, non-identification, even incomprehension, remain irreducible. Forgiveness is thus mad. It must plunge, but lucidly, into the night of the unintelligible. Call this the unconscious or the non-conscious if you want.'[47] As soon as the victim 'understands' the criminal,

[44] Ibid., 301–2. Nussbaum's ambitious, personal, and often moving account of the cognitive structure and ethical value of emotions includes a substantial discussion of the emotions of infancy that draws on the psychoanalytic work of D. W. Winnicott (see ibid., 174–238, *passim*).
[45] Ibid., 327, 328.   [46] Derrida, 'On Forgiveness', 59.   [47] Ibid., 48, 49.

even if forgiveness is refused, the process of reconciliation has begun and a third party has entered the scene.

In forgiveness, Derrida argues, we have to accept something 'that exceeds all institution, all power, all juridico-political authority'. He imagines a hypothetical situation in which 'a victim of the worst, himself, a member of his family, in his generation or the preceding, demands that justice be done, that the criminals appear before a court, be judged and condemned by a court—and yet in his heart forgives'. This is the inaccessible zone of experience which Derrida tries to imagine (and asks us to imagine) in all its historical specificity, only to reassert the finite limits of his understanding: 'Imagine a victim of terrorism, a person whose children have been deported or had their throats cut, or another whose family was killed in a death oven. Whether she says "I forgive" or "I do not forgive", in either case I am not sure of understanding. I am even sure of not understanding, and in any case I have nothing to say.'[48] Forgiveness as Derrida envisages it here refuses the principle of identification. Rewriting Hegel's definition (everything is forgivable except the crime against the reconciling power of forgiveness), Derrida defines the unforgivable as the crime that deprives the victim of speech, and of the right to speech. But, in the last resort, unconditional forgiveness remains a form of madness, a possibility that may or may not arrive—as 'radical' in its own way as the evil which Derrida locates in the hatreds aroused by the terrible intimacy of familial, ethnic, or tribal violence. This is terrain of the *Oresteia*. Derrida retreads the same ground as Aeschylus, when (in Murray's words) he attempts 'to think out, in terms that are not quite our terms, one of the deep unsolved mysteries of life', the problem of forgiveness.

The plot of the *Oresteia* has traditionally been seen as the shift from the old blood law, with its trans-generational curse and vengeance exacted for parental wrongs, to the power of thought, linguistic persuasion, judgement, and understanding represented by Athene.[49] Conflict resolution wins out over retribution and blood-bathed destruction. This is in line with Klein's Murray-derived reading. But the Aeschylean plot is as much political as ethical, while the concept of *dike*—which undergoes a running redefinition throughout the trilogy—produces its own incoherence.[50] Ostensibly, Athene's founding of a special court, the Areopagus, involves an attempt to reconcile, limit, and combine the powers of the

---

[48] Derrida, 'On Forgiveness', 54, 55.

[49] For an innovative account of the role of the performative power of language at the end of the *Oresteia*, as well as its linguistic challenges and transgressions, see Simon Goldhill, *Reading Greek Tragedy* (Cambridge: Cambridge University Press, 1986), esp. 28–32; and for a critique of the tradition of reading the *Oresteia* as a myth of the origin of the institution of law, as well as for the rhetorical appropriation of *dike*, including its modern ideological appropriations, see ibid., 33–56. Goldhill's short guide, *Aeschylus: The Oresteia* (Cambridge: Cambridge University Press, 1992), offers a succinct discussion of differing critical approaches as well as a compressed account of his own.

[50] See Simon Goldhill, *Language, Sexuality, Narrative: The Oresteia* (Cambridge: Cambridge University Press, 1984), 208–83, for a detailed reading of the complex language of *dike* in the *Eumenides*.

old mythic order with the new order of the *polis* and its civic discourse.[51] The scene of judgement in any case requires special pleading on both sides about consanguinity and matricide (the mother is merely the vessel for the father's seed; marriage is equivalent to a blood-tie; and so on), as well as about the relation between *dike* (right) and *nike* (victory). But in the end the verdict turns on a casting vote for acquittal by Athene, the embodiment of Zeus' Thought. Klein points out that Athene has been engendered without a mother and therefore escapes deformation by Oedipal issues (she has no mother to love or hate).[52] In Klein's view, Athene votes for acquittal because she represents forgiveness based on understanding, given that her primary identification is with Zeus, the Father, who has himself been a suppliant for his crime of usurpation: 'He can forgive just because he understands' (Murray's formulation).[53]

In other words, Athene forgives neither because she is empathetic with the sufferings of Orestes nor because she identifies with Zeus, but because she identifies with his understanding. Derrida's swerve from the Abrahamic tradition towards the inaccessible zone of the unconscious and the inaccessibility of other people's experience renders empathic identification as problematic as it is in Green's novel and Klein's 'On Identification'. Murray notes that the appeal from the generality of the law to the person (ultimately the ethical appeal inherited from the Greeks by Pauline theology and by modern European Law) not only involves the idea of the wise or just intercessor but the idea of a law that can be loved: 'the offender who deserves pardon can be pardoned. But that is not all. The Law that is directed and put in force by one who can pardon and understand can itself be understood and loved.'[54] The Law that is understood and loved entails judgement not so much by one's fellow-citizens as by a sovereign power. This power abrogates understanding to itself, albeit at one remove. For Derrida, as we have seen, devolution from deity to his representative, or from city-state to citizenry, leaves the issue of sovereignty unresolved. This is the issue that Athene attempts to foreclose by her founding of the Areopagus as the ultimate court of appeal. In its benign aspect, identification—whether with the Father or with the

---

[51] For the political situation involving the Council of Areopagus—a court traditionally viewed as founded for the judging of homicide cases, but subject to successive interpretations and attempted reforms or curtailments of its powers—see the summary in D. J. Conacher, *Aeschylus' Oresteia: A Literary Commentary* (Toronto: University of Toronto Press, 1987), 197–206. For a critique of the tradition of reading the *Oresteia* as a myth of the origin of the institution of law, see Goldhill, *Reading Greek Tragedy*, 33–56. Goldhill points out that the approach to the *Oresteia* initiated by H. D. F. Kitto (the tensions of tragedy resolved by the mediation of social order) overlooks the fact that resolution comes about not through legal process but through linguistic persuasion.

[52] For a brief discussion of the 'male–female conflict' in the *Eumenides*, see Conacher, *Aeschylus' Oresteia: A Literary Commentary*, 206–12; see also Froma Zeitlin, 'The Dynamics of Misogyny: Myth and Myth-Making in the *Oresteia*', *Arethusa*, 11 (1978), 149–84. For a dissenting view of some feminist readings of the *Oresteia* (Athene's transgressive rejection of traditional gender roles versus Bachofen's interpretation of the trilogy as the overthrow of Mother-right), see Goldhill, *Reading Greek Tragedy*, 31, 51–5.   [53] Murray, *Oresteia*, 25.

[54] Ibid., 29.

'understanding' Law he represents—leads to stable social formations, as well as repeating the Freudian resolution of the Oedipus complex (one can be *like* one's father/mother, but not *be* or *have* him/her). Yet identification with a parental instance could still be said to involve a form of madness given the radical (im)possibility of putting oneself in the other person's shoes, whether or not one happens to share the same *polis*. The '*imprescriptible*' element of crimes against humanity—including matricide—involve thinking (as it were) beyond or outside the witness-box. This non-juridical, imaginative thinking is symptomized by Derrida's insistently doubled representation of the anonymous victim (whether forgiving or not) whose plight we are asked, twice over, to 'imagine'.

Klein's 'Reflections' on the *Oresteia* confronts the problem of identification from the perspective of the formation of the archaic and troublesome super-ego. The infant's earliest identifications involve both good and frightening aspects of the mother; but symbolization and the super-ego first arise in the context of a vicious cycle of persecutory anxiety that breeds destructiveness and yet more persecutory anxiety. Crime and punishment are the double-bind of the super-ego, and for Klein they begin at the breast. Greed and envy are first experienced by the infant in relation to the mother. They are accompanied by the expectation of punishment from someone 'who by projection turns in the child's mind into a greedy and resentful figure. She is therefore feared as a source of punishment, the prototype of God' (*E&G* 280). God's primitive prototype is an avenging mother, and the Erinyes are her hell-hounds. Athene's triumph (which can also be seen as the overthrow of female authority) is to curtail this punitive matriarchal power and subordinate it, not so much to male authority as to Zeus' forgiving Law. By her powers of verbal persuasion, Athene also converts the wrathful, persecutory, and distraught Erinyes into the domesticated Eumenides, who become the benign Guardians of family values although remaining apart from the city itself. For Klein, the ruthlessly persecutory Erinyes belong not only to the paranoid–schizoid position but also to the depressive position, where persecutory and depressive anxieties vacillate.[55] This is the cusp of the transition—the oscillation—which she sees in Orestes.

Klein remarks that Murray calls Orestes 'mad' and that he appears to have a manic-depressive illness: 'he shows the mental state which I take to be characteristic of the transition between the paranoid–schizoid and the depressive position, a stage when guilt is essentially experienced as persecution' (*E&G* 286). Remorse appears in Orestes as soon as he has murdered Clytemnestra. His guilt is the source of his wish to expiate the wrong he has done to his mother, but the relentless super-ego modelled on the vengeful, murdered matriarch will not let him off. The

---

[55] The working-through of the depressive position 'is impeded by a vacillation between persecutory and depressive anxiety' (*E&G* 279). Klein's formulation paves the way for Bion's concept of the oscillation between PS and D (PS← →D). Cf. also *E&G* 292–3, where Klein concedes that guilt feelings about injured internalized objects are operative during the paranoid–schizoid position as well as the depressive position.

unavenged dead, personified by the Erinyes, rage against forgiveness. Their talion principle is an instance of the negative potential involved in identification—that is, the relation between cruelty and retribution and its compounding of the infant's originary sadism:

> According to the talion principle, based on projection, the child is tortured by the fear that what he in phantasy did to the parents is being done to him; and this may be an incentive towards reinforcing the cruel impulses. Because he feels persecuted internally and externally, he is driven to project the punishment outwards and in doing so tests by external reality his internal anxieties and fears of actual punishment. The more guilty and persecuted a child feels... the more aggressive he often may become.   (*E&G* 290)

'Do as you would (not) be done by' has distinct disadvantages as an ethical code. No wonder the Erinyes foresee a chaotic reign of terror by guilty children over their parents if Athene has her way: 'by a knife | In a child's hand their bosom shall be torn' (*Eumenides*, ll. 496–7).

Paraphrasing Freud, Derrida writes that one may put an end to murder, but 'a psychic cruelty will always take its place'.[56] The Erinyes represent the most primitive and terrifying aspects of the super-ego, unmediated by love. Athene's casting vote for acquittal not only brings about Orestes' final 'cure' but leads to the pacification and assimilation of these furious, displaced, unloved women. Klein points out that they succumb quite cheerfully when Athene offers to share with them the love of men (i.e., the father) as therapy for their loveless and unfathered condition, and to provide them with an underground home of their own. For Klein, it seems, the father is a kinder, gentler basis for identification than the maternally tormented and tormenting super-ego. In the *Oresteia*, Zeus represents a tolerant form of con-science based on his own experience of having deposed his father, Chronos: 'To have recognized and understood one's destructive tendencies directed against loved parents makes for greater tolerance towards oneself and towards deficiencies in others' (*E&G* 295). So says Klein (personifying a combined parental super-ego). Something else is needed, beyond the guilty perpetrator's urge to make reparation, for the cycle to be broken. That necessary supplement is the capacity to learn from suffering, however unwillingly, as Zeus has done: 'Man by suffering shall learn...Aching with remembered pain...Wisdom comes against his will' (*E&G* 296; *Agamemnon*, ll. 177–81). In the new world order promoted by Athene, crime-induced suffering is not so much atoned for by penitence and penance (the Christian way) as reconciled with a mitigated super-ego that is able to take on board its own past wrong-doing and to learn from experience. The human drive towards integration makes possible the coming together of love and hate, reparative and destructive impulses. Aeschylus (read through the lens of Murray) provides the allegorical blueprint for Klein's ethics at the end of her life.

[56] See Jacques Derrida, 'Psychoanalysis Searches the States of its Soul: The Impossible Beyond of Sovereign Cruelty', in *Without Alibi*, 239. Derrida is discussing war and capital punishment—state cruelty—as well as the psychical cruelty specifically addressed by psychoanalysis.

Klein, however, does more than emphasize learning from experience. She models her position on Athene's when she argues that even 'the mild super-ego demands the control of destructive impulses'. We should not (and cannot) entirely rid ourselves of fear. Klein cites Athene's advice approvingly: 'And casting away Fear, yet cast not all; | For who that hath no fear is safe from sin?' (*E&G* 297–8; *Eumenides*, ll. 699–700). The mitigated super-ego still needs a portion of guilt.[57] Moreover, as Klein recognizes (perhaps from her own experience), 'Internal peace is not easily established' (*E&G* 298). The voters of the Areopagus are evenly divided. They come together in spite of their conflicting tendencies, but 'This does not mean that they can ever become identical with each other' (*E&G* 298)—any more than the peaceful coexistence that emerged from the warring factions of the British Psycho-Analytical Society during the 'controversial discussions' could resolve their theoretical differences. Like the ego, the Kleinian Areopagus is founded on the differences and contradictions of its multiple identifications. It becomes the psychic as well as institutional equivalent of the alterity that Derrida sees at the heart of the non-identical meaning(lessness)—the madness or unreason—of forgiveness. Klein's 'Reflections' on the *Oresteia* concludes by relating the symbolic roles in Aeschylus' trilogy to the coexistence of ambivalent unconscious processes and phantasies. The child puts all his love, hate, conflicts, satisfactions, and longings into the creation of the internal and external symbols that become part of his world. But at the heart of this drive to create symbols is the inevitability of maternal failure, since 'even the most loving mother cannot satisfy the infant's powerful emotional needs' (*E&G* 299). And, in fact, no reality situation could ever satisfy the insatiable and contradictory desires of phantasy life. With this admission of lifelong maternal deficit, Klein explains the artist's special capacities in terms of a childhood of (relatively) unimpeded symbol formation.

Kristeva's semi-satirical verdict on Klein's reading of the *Oresteia* is 'Get rid of your mother, for you no longer need her'.[58] But hold on to your symbols. Fear, frustration, envy, greed, destructiveness—these are the negative emotions that fuel Kleinian symbolization and Aeschylean tragedy. Yet, as we have seen (and as Nussbaum argues), these are also the negative emotions that impede compassion and make altruism suspect.[59] Klein claims that great literature like the *Oresteia* derives from Aeschylus' 'intuitive understanding of the inexhaustible depth of the unconscious' (*E&G* 299). Nussbaum—a liberal in literary criticism as in ethics—cites tragedy in support of her thesis that the resources of poetry and

---

[57] For a relevant reassessment of Klein's thinking on the depressive position in relation to tragedy and morality, see Meira Likierman, *Melanie Klein*, 112–35, esp. 119–21.

[58] We have symbols 'because the mother is insufficient—precisely because she is incapable of satisfying the child's emotional needs' (Kristeva, *Melanie Klein*, 133). Kristeva's reading of 'Some Reflections on "The Oresteia"' emphasizes the matricidal crime and its relation to deicide, reflecting her theory that symbolization depends on a symbolic killing of the mother: 'Klein's ode to matricide is a plea to preserve our symbolic capacity... although the mother is omnipotent, we can—and we must—make do without her' (ibid., 135).   [59] See Nussbaum, *Upheavals of Thought*, 335–50.

drama 'promote concern for someone different from oneself'. For her this is a good thing, because tragic dramas 'encourage pleasure of the most difficult type: the pleasure of contemplating our mortality and our vulnerability to the worst disasters in life'. For the eudemonistic philosopher, in other words, tragedy helps one to 'embrace the lives of others' as well as one's own.[60] But when Derrida asks us so insistently to 'imagine' the victim who calls for justice, 'and yet in his heart forgives', he does not endorse Nussbaum's position. Whether he invokes the inaccessible zone of the unconscious or the baffling incomprehensibility of someone else's experience ('Whether she says "I forgive" or "I do not forgive", in either case I am not sure of understanding. I am even sure of not understanding, and in any case I have nothing to say'), Derrida signals the limited extent of any understanding of the mind and emotions of another. Someone else's experience can only be imagined or spoken for at the risk of denying or appropriating its otherness (as Nussbaum readily acknowledges in relation to empathy).

Forgiveness—radical forgiveness in the Derridean sense—becomes the limit case for any ethical theory founded on the ability to put oneself into another person's shoes, whether in life or in literature. Held up to her well-polished clinical mirror, Klein's books help to define identification in both positive and negative terms, revealing its dark underside as well as its link to understanding. The enigmas of literature are those of the inexhaustible unconscious, where identification (like Derridean forgiveness) contains the potential for imagining the impossible as well as the impossibility of imagining. Like the impersonal workings of the figurative language with which they are coterminous, identificatory processes exist before or beyond what Derrida calls 'any personal figure', any personification, any allegorical self-identity.[61]

[60] Ibid., 352, 353.

[61] 'Cruelty there is. Cruelty there will have been, before any personal figure, before "cruel" will have become an attribute, still less anyone's fault' (Derrida, *Without Alibi*, 280). In his own use of the figure of 'cruelty' as a figure or personification, Derrida points to the impersonal and performative aspect of language.

PART II
MEDIATIONS

4

Magical Arts: *The Poetics of Play*

> People speak with justice of the 'magic of art' and compare artists to magicians. But the comparison is perhaps more significant than it claims to be. There can be no doubt that art did not begin as art for art's sake.
>
> Sigmund Freud, *Totem and Taboo* (1913); *SE* xiii. 90

Is there such a thing as 'art for art's sake'? Freud evidently thought not; for him, art always had a psychic function. Freud's comparison between magicians and artists has its parallel in the long-recognized link between magic and play. But here, too, from a psychoanalytic perspective, play seems never to be play for play's sake. To take an obvious example: Melanie Klein's 'The Psycho-analytic Play-Technique: Its History and Significance' (1955) looks back at her early work with children during the 1920s and relates how she first made use of a collection of small toys. Finding one 7-year-old girl unresponsive and withdrawn, she writes:

I left her, saying that I would return in a moment. I went into my own children's nursery, collected a few toys, cars, little figures, a few bricks, and a train, put them in a box and returned to the patient. The child, who had not taken to drawing or other activities, was interested in the small toys and at once began to play. (*E&G* 125)

From this improvised Pandora's toy-box came mighty consequences (Figures 1 and 2). Klein first conceived the play technique as a way for children to express their anxieties and unconscious phantasies. Interpreting children's play, she thought, was like interpreting adult dreams; symbolic language saturated every aspect of their toys and games: 'the brick, the little figure, the car, not only represent things which interest the child in themselves, but in his play with them they always have a variety of symbolical meanings as well' (*E&G* 137). Play for Klein was not necessarily fun, or creative, or even particularly playful. It was a serious form of meaning-making—often compulsive, repetitive, and anxious, with its own syntax, rules, and narrative conventions.[1]

Play told a story, but it also became a vehicle for Klein's theory of symbolization. Symbol-formation, as Klein wrote in 'The Importance of Symbol-Formation in

---

[1] See also Klein's account of the play technique in her first major book in English, *The Psycho-Analysis of Children* (1932; rpr. London: Hogarth Press, 1975), 16–34.

Figures 1 and 2 Toys used by Melanie Klein in her psychoanalytic work with children; Melanie Klein Trust.

the Development of the Ego' (1930), provided 'the basis of the subject's relation to the outside world and to reality in general' (*LGR* 221). A mechanism for the transfer of feelings from person to person, or from persons to things, symbol-formation performed a vital role in establishing children's relation to external reality. As well as communicating their unconscious phantasies, play was therapeutic because the formation of symbols allayed children's anxiety. But why, one wonders, should magic—along with myth, ritual, and folklore—surface so persistently in proximity to something much less obviously adapted to the claims of reality? Perhaps this is not so surprising as it might seem, given the long-standing connection between magic and theories of symbolism.[2] But in psychoanalytic theory, magic is often equated with omnipotence. As Freud writes in *Totem and Taboo*, 'the principle governing magic, the technique of the animistic mode of thinking, is the principle of the "omnipotence of thoughts"' (*SE* xiii. 85). Like neurotics and savages (and ordinary adults, too), children 'believe they can alter the external world by mere thinking' (*SE* xiii. 87). Not only this, but (Freud again) 'some of the primitive belief in omnipotence still survives in men's faith in the power of the human mind, which grapples with the laws of reality' (*SE* xiii. 88). No wonder magic is paired with play when it comes to the complex negotiation between phantasy and reality that is Klein's chief theoretical legacy to British Object Relations psychoanalysis. But my contention is rather different—that the ineluctable (yet uninspected) link between magic and play also provides a way to trace the persistence of aesthetic concerns within psychoanalysis.

Whether explicit or covert, the linkage between magic, play, and aesthetics can be traced from the early work of Klein and her followers onwards, surfacing with especial clarity in the writings of three analysts whose thinking was both deeply indebted to, and developed in tandem with—and eventually in reaction to—Klein's theories of unconscious phantasy: Susan Isaacs, Marion Milner, and D. W. Winnicott. Klein famously disagreed with Anna Freud over the extent to which it was either possible or useful to analyse young children.[3] But a much more far-reaching division eventually emerged within the sphere of Klein's immediate influence. This split was based on a difference of opinion over the nature and value of infantile omnipotence: was it controlling or creative?; pathological, or a crucial link between child and reality? As the playing child became the unconsciously phantasying baby, the issue of omnipotence displaced Freud's emphasis on primary narcissism and hallucination of the breast. For Klein, infantile omnipotence was not just the means by which the baby annihilated the frustration or persecution in the absence of the breast; rather, it came to represent a potentially despotic form of control of the object.[4] But for child analysts like Milner and Winnicott, protecting the infant's illusion of omnipotence against premature or traumatic impingement was a prerequisite for any subsequent creative partnership with external reality. Arguably, one function of Winnicott's concept of the transitional object was to preserve a buffer-zone of omnipotence, blurring Klein's over-sharp boundary between phantasy and reality, inner and outer. But while both omnipotence and the transitional object have received their share of attention from Kleinians

---

[2] See the extensive review of the literature by Daniel Lawrence O'Keefe, *Stolen Lightning: The Social Theory of Magic* (Oxford: Martin Robertson, 1982).

[3] For Klein's disagreement with Anna Freud, see 'Symposium on Child-Analysis' (1927), a response to criticism of the play technique, in Anna Freud, *The Psycho-analytical Treatment of Children*, trans. N. Proctor-Gregg (1927; London: Imago, 1946).

[4] See, for instance, 'Some Theoretical Conclusions Regarding the Emotional Life of the Infant' (1952): 'Denial in its most extreme form—as we find it in hallucinatory gratification—amounts to an annihilation of any frustrating object or situation, and is thus bound up with the strong feeling of omnipotence which obtains in the early stages of life' (*E&G* 65).

and Winnicottians respectively, magic remains (comparatively speaking) the joker in the pack. During the 1950s, one has to turn to anthropology for any sustained theorization of the role of magic in psychic, social, or cultural life. Why is this so?

One answer might be that magic exerts an inevitable pull in the direction of a disowned pre-scientific past. The psychoanalyst had to be sharply distinguished from the practitioner of magical arts—magical cures or shamanistic rituals—just as Freud had disowned the use of hypnosis and the laying on of hands in his early treatment of hysterics.[5] Whether magic involves attributing special power to persons, objects, words, or actions (in the form of magicians, talismans, spells, or rituals), it reveals—according to Marcel Mauss in *A General Theory of Magic* (1950)—the coexistence of scientific method alongside a fascination with the poetic and mystical thinking that secretly survives within it. Mauss sees the return of the magical as a reminder that shamans and sorcerers are the precursors of modern positivistic science. Hence, 'Magic can also function as a science and take the place of sciences not yet developed'.[6] Magic becomes the residue of an earlier mode of cognition, just as it had anticipated modern theories of causality. By contrast, Gésa Róheim, in *Magic and Schizophrenia* (1955), emphasizing the psychic rather than social function of magic, rationalizes it as a defence against both external and internal reality. Magic is the necessary illusion that protects us against frustration: 'We grow up through magic and in magic, and we can never outgrow the illusion of magic. Our first response to the frustrations of reality is magic; and without this belief in ourselves, in our own specific ability or magic, we cannot hold our own against the environment and against the superego.'[7] Substitute the term 'narcissism' for 'magic', and we find ourselves in Freud's company; emphasize the word 'illusion', and we encounter something like Winnicott's belief that if we outgrow illusion too soon, we shall be unable to bear too much reality.[8] For Róheim, both infant and adult need to preserve the illusion of magic-ally creating what they find, either to hold their own against the environment and the cruelty of the super-ego, or to retain their vital connection with creativity and culture.

Kleinian aesthetics are bound up with ideas about magical thinking. In 'The Role of the School in the Libidinal Development of the Child' (1923), she suggests that the child 'appears to find in drawing a "magic gesture" by which he can realize the omnipotence of his thought' (*LGR* 72). In 'Early Analysis' (1923), she speculates that 'the compulsion to make symbols . . . [is] the driving force in the cultural evolution of mankind' (*LGR* 104). Later, in 'Personification in the

    [5] For Freud's use of hypnotic techniques, see the case of 'Frau Emmy von N.' in *Studies on Hysteria* (1895; *SE* ii. 48–105).

    [6] Marcel Mauss, *A General Theory of Magic*, trans. Robert Brain (1950; London: Routledge & Kegan Paul, 1972), 63.

    [7] Gésa Róheim, *Magic and Schizophrenia* (Bloomington, Ind.: Indiana University Press, 1955), 46.

    [8] See John Turner, 'A Brief History of Illusion: Milner, Winnicott and Rycroft', *International Journal of Psycho-Analysis*, 83 (2002), 1063–82, for the importance of the concept of 'illusion' during the 1950s, before its occlusion by the categories of play and creativity.

Play of Children' (1929), she identifies 'personification' (the symbolic or dramatic representation of qualities or ideas) as the chief mechanism at work in children's phantasies.[9] Her small players are caught up in epic struggles between malignant persecutors, sublime overreachers, and benign helpers—the psychic prototype for Philip Pullman's anim(al)istic world in *His Dark Materials*.[10] The foundational paper for Kleinian aesthetics, 'Infantile Anxiety-Situations Reflected in a Work of Art and in the Creative Impulse' (1929), takes as its example Ravel's opera, *L'Enfant et les Sortilèges*, which Klein knew as 'The Magic Word' (*Das Zauberwort*). Drawing on an account of Colette's libretto in the *Berliner Tageblatt*, Klein allegorizes the opera's oversized nursery setting and toys—'made very large in order to emphasize the smallness of the child' (*LGR* 213)—in terms of the child's omnipotence and anxiety, along with his sadistic attacks on the maternal body.[11] The personifying power of unconscious phantasy animates and transforms the miniature world of the play technique: 'the child's anxiety makes things and people seem gigantic to him—far beyond any actual differences in size' (*LGR* 213). The 'magic word' of the title is 'Mama', the redemptive *sotto voce* call that restores the child to the helping human world at the chaotic climax of the action, when even the animal world falls to fighting.[12]

I shall argue that the poetics of play in British Object Relations preserves the most magical aspects of psychoanalytic thinking, if only in viewing the child as both origin and prototype of creativity. Susan Isaacs, an educationist-turned-psychoanalyst who advocated the enlightening effects of play on children's intellectual growth, was to be the designated spokesperson for Klein's theory of unconscious phantasy during the wartime 'Controversial Discussions'. For Isaacs,

[9] See Otto Fenischel's discussion of acting as a magical form of play in 'On Acting', *Psychoanalytic Quarterly*, 15 (1946), 141–60, which takes up Klein's suggestion that playing 'parts' assumes a dominant role in children's games.

[10] For a psychoanalytical account of the world of Pullman's trilogy, see Margaret Rustin and Michael Rustin, 'Where is Home? An Essay on Philip Pullman's *Northern Lights*', 'A New Kind of Friendship—An Essay on Philip Pullman's *The Subtle Knife*', and 'Learning to Say Goodbye: An Essay on Philip Pullman's *The Amber Spyglass*', *Journal of Child Psychotherapy*, 29 (2003), 93–105, 227–41, 415–28.

[11] Klein's paper sets out to refine Freud's account of the infantile-danger situation in *Inhibitions, Symptoms, and Anxiety* (1926)—i.e., castration for the boy, object-loss for the girl—in terms of her own theory of unconscious phantasy. For Colette's libretto, see *L'Enfant et les Sortilèges*, in Colette, *Oeuvres*, 5 vols. (Paris: Gallimard, 1991), iii. 151–69.

[12] Klein's second example is a story by the Danish writer Karin Michaelis, 'The Empty Space', which describes a wealthy socialite and art collector who is subject to unaccountable fits of melancholia but is inspired to paint by an empty space on her wall. This form of magical reparation only superficially anticipates the depressive position later associated with Kleinian aesthetics; for the classic statement, see Hanna Segal, 'A Psychoanalytic Approach to Aesthetics' (1955), *The Work of Hanna Segal* (London: Free Association Books, 1986), 195–205, and 'Art and the Depressive Position', *Dream, Phantasy and Art* (London and New York: Tavistock/Routledge, 1991), 85–100. For Klein's and Segal's aesthetics in relation to women, see Lyndsey Stonebridge, *The Destructive Element: British Psychoanalysis and Modernism* (London: Macmillan, 1998), 47–8 and 63–7; and for a re-reading of the depressive position in relation to both tragedy and morality, Meira Likierman, *Melanie Klein: Her Work in Context* (London: Continuum, 2001), 112–35.

metaphor itself constituted a form of magical action. Later, in 'The Role of Illusion in Symbol Formation' (1952), Marion Milner's artist-child—Klein's own grandson—re-enacts a mythic drama of destruction and renewal for which she finds parallels in Frazer's *The Golden Bough*; his ritualistic play kindles the psycho-analyst's sympathetic imagination, already charged with mythic significance from her own prior reading. For Milner, illusion is a privileged form of resistance to, as well as partnership with, the demands and frustrations of the real world. Finally, D. W. Winnicott's theory of transitional phenomena extends children's play from the nursery to the realm of cultural activity and aesthetic appreciation. The playing child is father of the cultural man. Winnicott's all-encompassing theory of play—diffused across the entire cultural field like Melanesian *mana*—comes to define 'the place where we live'.[13] His elision of creativity and culture installs magical thinking (what he calls 'private madness') as an aspect of the socio-cultural sphere, along with a bleak form of negativity. In Winnicott's late writings on transitional phenomena, the deepest attachment is to loss itself.

Mauss observes that 'A religion designates the remnants of former cults as "magical" even when the rites are still being performed in a religious manner.' A magical rite is defined as '*any rite which does not play a part in organized cults*'.[14] The survival of magic within a modern positivistic science invites an analogy with the secret life of art within psychoanalysis. This is not to say that the poetics of play include the covert rehearsal of art-rites, nor to suggest that play is always continuous with magic (play can be rigidly rule-based as well as make-believe). Rather, the magical pre-history of play reveals the pervasiveness of aesthetic concerns in British Object Relations writing. I want to trace the poetics of play in Isaacs, Milner, and Winnicott not only in terms of the negotiation between illusion and reality initi-ated by Klein but also in terms of evidence of the lasting entanglement between psychoanalysis and the 'magic of art'. Where magic was, there aesthetics will be.

ACTING OUT THE METAPHOR

Susan Isaacs's pioneering *Intellectual Growth in Young Children* (1930) makes the young child parent to the scientist. For Isaacs, play involves a perpetual form of experiment. Just as imaginative play has the effect of creating 'practical *situations*', play pursued for its own sake leads to actual or potential discoveries. Even in repetitive play, 'at any moment, a new line of inquiry or argument might flash out, a new step in understanding be taken'.[15] Isaacs's detailed observations of children's

[13] For an illuminating account of the poetics of play in Winnicott, see John Turner, 'Wordsworth and Winnicott in the Area of Play', in Peter Rudnytsky (ed.), *Transitional Objects and Potential Space: Literary Uses of D. W. Winnicott* (New York: Columbia University Press, 1993), 161–88.

[14] Mauss, *A General Theory of Magic*, 18, 24.

[15] Susan Isaacs, *Intellectual Growth in Young Children* (London: Routledge & Kegan Paul, 1930), 99 (*IG*).

play (based on records of the children she taught at the progressive Malting House School in Cambridge during the 1920s) burst with energy, insight, and humour.[16] Children's doings and sayings spring off the page with inventiveness, jokes, and games. The domestic setting of the school becomes a workshop for budding investigators and inventors. Children's daily encounters with the resistance, complexity, muddle, and basic mechanics of their environment provide a constant stimulus to intellectual and social development. Their make-believe games lead to technical and philosophical discussions about how things work (pulleys, for instance), and above all about causation: '*Because, look!*', they exclaim—their version of 'Eureka!' (*IG* 100). But what Isaacs calls children's '*circumstantial* relation' to the environment is always underpinned by infantile phantasy: 'the *first* value which the physical world has for the child is as a canvas upon which to project his personal wishes and anxieties, and his first form of interest in it is one of dramatic representation' (*IG* 101). The raw materials that come to hand are saturated with significance: 'engines and motors and fires and lights and water and mud and animals have a profoundly symbolic meaning' (*IG* 102). This rich mechanical–elemental–organic mix, fermented by unconscious wishes and anxieties, gives rise to symbol-formation.

For Isaacs, as for Klein, play enables the passage from symbol to reality: 'Imaginative play builds a bridge by which the child can pass from the symbolic values of things to active inquiry into their real construction and real way of working' (*IG* 102). Isaacs's child is a 'realist' in Piaget's sense—everything is equally real: 'he does not distinguish between a sign and the thing signified, between the internal and the external, the psychical and the physical'. Piaget's child is an animist who feels that he possesses magical powers, attributing consciousness to anything that is active and harbouring 'spontaneous ideas of a magical nature' (*IG* 76). But for Isaacs the argument only begins here. Magical performatives such as 'Save, save, *save!*', designed to establish a child's ownership ('bags I'), involve ideas about what she calls 'magical "pre-causality"'; they show how fluidly children move 'between the realms of pure phantasy and occasionally of magic, and those of practical insight and resource, and of verbal argument and reasoning' (*IG* 92). Yet in the face of Piaget's argument that children's egocentricity makes them resistant to knowledge, Isaacs insists, to the contrary, that their minds are 'egocentric, pre-causal, and magical' only *because* they lack knowledge and experience. Phantasy is involved at every level. Children are us: 'The child's mind moves in these ways of magic and "participation", of syncretism and precausality, in its

---

[16] Originally trained as a teacher, Isaacs became a full member of the British Psycho-Analytic Society in the early 1920s. In 1924, she accepted the post of principal at a Cambridge nursery school founded to put in practice a progressive educational philosophy in which children expressed themselves freely and found out what they could for themselves; the experiment lasted until 1927. She later became head of the new Department of Child Development at London University Institute for Education and underwent a second, Kleinian analysis. See Lydia A. H. Smith, *To Understand and to Help: The Life and Works of Susan Isaacs* (Rutherford, NJ: Fairleigh Dickinson University Press, 1995).

deepest layers—as do our own, in dream, in reverie and free association' (*IG* 94). Play becomes the prelude to thought: 'Make-believe may at any moment slip across into genuine inquiry', just as gaining a new bodily skill can turn into dramatic play (*IG* 99). Because imaginative play subsumes reality into its texture, phantasy is saturated with reality (and vice versa). The child's magical omnipotence leads to actual experiences of the external world, rather than being organized against reality, like primitive rituals or psychosis. Isaacs is already puzzling over the problem that will preoccupy Milner and Winnicott. Given the porous boundaries of internal and external worlds, how does the external world ever come to feel real?

Isaacs's later psychoanalytic writing explores the meaning of play that has become divorced from imaginative inquiry. Where Klein had focused on the mechanisms and meta-narratives of unconscious phantasy, Isaacs investigates its language. 'A Special Mechanism in a Schizoid Boy' (1939) concerns an adolescent's problematic use of metaphor—and a pulley.[17] The 'special mechanism' employed by her fifteen-year-old patient is '*the acting out of a metaphor*'. The child of divorced parents ('bohemian' and of 'advanced political views'), he has been brought up by his grandmother's strict nonconformist family, of whose provincial values his mother is fiercely critical. When his mother decides to bring him back to live with her, she precipitates a terrible conflict between his love for her and his love for his maternal grandmother, whom he now feels called on to reject. One day he tells Isaacs that he has been trying to make a parachute out of an umbrella, intending to attach it to a basket so that he can lower the cat ('of whom he was very fond') from the top floor of his house. In Isaacs's words, the demand that he should leave his beloved grandmother 'was felt by him as a demand that he should "throw her out"', along with the cat. Although the parachute project fails to materialize (and the cat survives with its nine lives intact), the game dramatizes the boy's wish not only to eject his grandmother, as his mother requires him to do, but to find a way to 'let her down gently'. In other words, 'in the parachute incident, he was *acting out a metaphor*'.[18] Footnoting other instances where she has decoded the boy's verbal acting-out of metaphors (such as 'giving him a smack in the face' or 'making him feel small'), Isaacs refers to Clifford Scott's telling distinction between 'charade' and 'play': 'It is always a charade, never a play' (*C&A* 123 n.). The analyst's role is to restore meaning to the charade's scattered component parts.

A charade entails the acting-out of words or phrases for an audience who has to decode and combine them in order to guess their meaning. For instance, in his sessions with Isaacs, the boy makes 'certain graceful pulling movements with

---

[17] Isaacs notes Freud's discussion of schizoid language in Section vii of *The Unconscious* (1915), where he reports changes in speech or what he calls 'organ speech' specific to schizophrenics (*SE* xiv. 197–9); she also refers to Ella Freeman Sharpe, 'Psycho-Physical Problems Revealed in Language: An Examination of Metaphor' (1940), rpr. in Marjorie Brierley (ed.), Ella Freeman Sharpe, *Collected Papers on Psycho-Analysis* (London: Hogarth Press, 1978), 155–69 and Melanie Klein, 'The Importance of Symbol-Formation in the Development of the Ego' (1930), *LGR* 219–32.

[18] Susan Isaacs, 'A Special Mechanism in a Schizoid Boy' (1939), rpr. in *Childhood and After: Some Essays and Clinical Studies* (London: Routledge & Kegan Paul, 1948), 123 (*C&A*).

his right hand and fingers' which turn out to represent the actions of a puppeteer, expressing how he unconsciously feels himself being manipulated and pulled about by his parents and family (both his external and internal family). His hand movements 'reversed the situation and represented him as being in control of other people and them as the puppets' (*C&A* 124). Leaving his grandmother amounts to killing her. Unable to sleep on the two nights before quitting his childhood home to rejoin his mother, he carries his bed downstairs and into the garden. As Isaacs translates, 'he "threw himself out" in a literal bodily way; but unconsciously he was throwing his grandmother out as his mother wished him to do', as well as expressing other fears—for instance, that his grandmother would throw him out for siding with his mother; or that he might even throw himself out of the window (*C&A* 124). In the end, his parachute project had failed to let either of them down gently. Something more drastic is required if he is to get rid of (throw out, or throw up—he literally vomits with anxiety) the much-loved grandmother, whom he feels to be part of himself. Caught in this no-win situation, the boy reacts with relief to Isaacs's verbalization: 'When I decode the boy's action... and put the reconstructed metaphor into words, it always receives his assent and usually the comment "of course"'. In contrast to his affect-free acting-out, 'Feeling is only recovered when the metaphor is stated in words' (*C&A* 125). Acting out the metaphor had defended him against the unbearable conflict created by his mother's demand.

Isaacs suggests that words are felt by the boy to get inside him in a persecutory way, precipitating actual psychic change. Thus 'His mother's criticism had literally and concretely poisoned the boy's mind against her' (that is, against the now-ruined and destroyed object, his grandmother, *C&A* 126). His sometimes blurred vision—a coded statement that ' "My parents cannot see straight" '—is an aspect of his problematic identification with his parents, who wear glasses and have given him precocious and disturbing knowledge through their own marital and sexual lives. Isaacs ventriloquizes his unconscious thoughts as a phantasy of the primal scene: ' "My parents inside me are in a terrible sexual intercourse... Their intercourse is destructive because it stirs up destructive feelings in me" ' (*C&A* 126). Invoking Freud's *The Unconscious* (1915), she argues that schizophrenic words take on special significance in their own right, 'as things in themselves' and 'far more real than actions'. Words in their most basic somatic form—breath, sound, sensation—are experienced not just as actions or events but literally, as concrete and invasive body parts:

The bodily experience of hearing or using words (the breath going in or out, the sound going in or out, the movements and sensations) remains for him an integral part of their reality and their meaning. Words are still felt by this boy, thus, to be the actual words of the people who were first heard to use them. Even in consciousness words are never signs, but always actions and events. In unconscious phantasy they are parts of people's bodies, 'bits' of those who used them; and they are now inside him. (*C&A* 127)

Words phantasized as 'bits' provide a last-ditch defence against pre-verbal phantasies involving oral and anal biting up or poisoning. Freighted with excessive feeling, metaphor has to be broken down into its discrete elements ('meaningless actions, hypochrondriacal symptoms, vomiting, defaecating', *C&A* 127). When he loses his purchase on language, the boy comes to inhabit an entirely somatic world in which words are no longer the bearers of affect, but instead 'are treated as having no meaning but their bodily existence'. Acting out the metaphor means divorcing feeling from meaning, much as his parents' marital breakdown led to their divorce. Isaacs lets slip her own metaphor: 'Words and actions alike are by their divorce degraded to mere bodily experiences. Only by bringing words and actions together can the life and meaning of each be restored' (*C&A* 127–8). The analyst can never reunite the parents, but she can bring words and actions together in all their affect-laden metaphoricity.

Isaacs is best known outside educational circles for her strategic statement of the Kleinian position on phantasy, a version of which was presented in 1943 during the British Psycho-Analytical Society's heated wartime 'Controversial Discussions'. The concept of unconscious phantasy has been seen as the central theoretical focus of the so-called 'Scientific Discussions', polarizing Anna Freudian and Kleinian views of the infant.[19] In 'The Nature and Function of Phantasy' (1948), Isaacs set out to provide a rigorously Freud-derived account of the centrality of the concept of unconscious phantasy for all aspects of psychic life, conscious as well as unconscious, from the moment of birth onwards (this was the truly 'controversial' claim for Anna Freud's group). While Kleinians saw unconscious phantasy as the source of new discoveries and meaning, Anna Freudians saw it as a source of dangerously unscientific (not to say magical) ideas. Edward Glover, disputing Isaacs's attempt to frame an account compatible with both Freud's and Klein's views, accused her of being 'addicted to a sort of psychic anthropomorphism' that confused concepts of the psychic apparatus with the psychical mechanisms at work in the child's mind.[20] This amounted in the end to an anthropomorphism of the baby, who was credited with ego-functions, object relations, and defences during the earliest months of life (in contrast to the Freudian baby, still locked in original primary narcissism).[21] In the version of her paper revised for the Kleinian flagship volume *Developments in Psychoanalysis* (1952), Isaacs invokes Freud's grandson in *Beyond the Pleasure Principle* (1920) as

[19] See Riccardo Steiner, 'Background to the Scientific Controversies', in Pearl King and Riccardo Steiner (eds.), *The Freud–Klein Controversies* (London and New York: Routledge, 1991), 242–5.

[20] See Riccardo Steiner, 'First Discussion of Scientific Controversies', ibid., 326.

[21] For the generic babies of psychoanalytic theory—Freudian (Viennese), Kleinian (London), as well as the indigenous British baby—see Riccardo Steiner, *Tradition, Change, Creativity* (London: Karnac Books, 2000), 106–21, 160–86; for Isaacs's contribution, see ibid., 187–95. For a comprehensive survey of the major figures in child analysis in Vienna and London, as well as the wartime arguments between them and developments in the post-war period, see also Claudine and Pierre Geissmann, *A History of Child Psychoanalysis* (1992; London and New York: Routledge, 1998), chs. 9, 10, and 11 *passim*.

the psychoanalytic prototype for the use of play to master anxiety—the *fort/da* game of the cotton-reel's disappearance and return.[22] Building on Freud's view that the baby hallucinates the breast in order to enjoy it, Isaacs sees the hallucinating baby (fearful of being poisoned by the breast it has lost) as retrospective evidence for Freud's belief in omnipresent infantile phantasy.

Isaacs, however, relies less on claims to psychoanalytic orthodoxy (combining the legacy of Freud and the authority of Klein) than on the observation of very young children. Her sweeping pan-instinctualism—'There is no impulse, no instinctual urge or response which is not experienced as unconscious phantasy'[23]— risks reducing the protean content and workings of phantasy to an instinctual aim; the drive (as Laplanche and Pontalis put it) 'intuits' or 'knows' the object with infallible intentionality.[24] But the defining moment in Isaacs's paper is not so much her insistence on phantasy as the primary content of unconscious mental processes as it is her retroactive linking of words and phantasy. It is phantasy that 'thinks' us, rather than language (making her an anti-pan-lingualist). Isaacs argues that meanings, along with feelings and phantasy, pre-date language: 'Meanings, like feelings, are far older than speech . . . In childhood and in adult life, we live and feel, we phantasy and act far beyond our verbal meanings.' Meaning infuses every aspect of painting and music, as well as the tones and gestures of everyday communication. Language has a referential dimension, but it is not synonymous with experience. Words are gestural rather than constitutive: 'Words are a means of *referring* to experience, actual or phantasied, but are not identical with it . . . Words . . . point to situations.'[25] Isaacs's example of how meaning pre-dates language is a 20-month-old child who screams with terror at the loose sole flapping on one of her mother's shoes. Fifteen months later, after the child has learned to talk, 'she suddenly said to her mother in a frightened voice, "Where are Mummy's broken shoes? . . . They might have eaten me right up" '.[26] For Isaacs's small child, language defends the endangered psyche against the terrifying phantasy of a devouring mouth—the form taken by her devouring feelings towards her mother. Words, Isaacs concludes, are a late development when it comes to expressing the inner world of phantasy. Freud's baby grandson's 'Baby o-o-o-oh' has a long history behind it.

Isaacs concludes, as one might expect, 'that spontaneous make-believe play creates and fosters the first forms of "as if" thinking'—the creative intentions that 'mark out the artist, the novelist, and the poet, but also . . . the sense of reality, the scientific attitude and the growth of hypothetical reasoning'.[27] Play evokes not

[22] See Melanie Klein, Paula Heimann, Susan Isaacs, and Joan Riviere, *Developments in Psycho-Analysis* (London: Hogarth Press, 1952), 72–3 (first published in the *International Journal of Psycho-Analysis* in 1948); rpr. in Riccardo Steiner (ed.), *Unconscious Phantasy* (London: Karnac, 2003), 145–98. The earlier version is repr. in Pearl and Steiner (eds.), *The Freud–Klein Controversies*, 265–321.   [23] *Developments in Psycho-Analysis*, 83.
[24] For a critique of Isaacs's intentionalist pan-instinctualism, see Jean Laplanche and J.-B. Pontalis, 'Phantasy and the Origins of Sexuality' (1968), rpr. in *Unconscious Phantasy*, 129–30.
[25] *Developments in Psycho-Analysis*, 89.   [26] Ibid., 91.   [27] Ibid., 111.

just the past but the future, 'the consequences of "as ifs" '. Yet words, even as they refer to an untold story or a theoretical 'as if', remain subtended by unconscious bodily phantasy. Without its support, what Isaacs calls 'reality-thinking' would be unable to operate: 'we continue to "take things in" with our ears, to "devour" with our eyes, to "read, mark, learn and inwardly digest" throughout life'.[28] We never let go of the magical omnipotence and pre-causality that precede language use (proper or improper). The proto-scientific children of Isaacs's Malting House experiment exclaim '*Because, look!*' But magic returns in the all-consuming metaphors of education, as we omnivorously 'read, mark, learn and inwardly digest'—a tamed and taming phantasy of the devouring mouth at work in the progressive schoolroom. Glover's 'psychic anthropomorphism' is the flapping sole attached to Isaacs's 'as if' theory of play.

PLAYING WITH FIRE

In 'The Role of Illusion in Symbol Formation' (1952), Marion Milner sets out to expand what had come to seem to her the restrictive and impoverished use of the term 'symbolization' within psychoanalysis (as opposed to epistemology, aesthetics, or the history of science) and to add to it a new concept: illusion.[29] Her best-known contribution to Kleinian theory and a gift to Klein on her seventieth birthday, it therefore marks a radical swerve from Klein's ideas.[30] Her clinical material is introduced via previous accounts of symbolism (Jones's classic 1916 paper and Klein's influential 1930 paper on symbol-formation) and aims to extend to art what Jones had written about scientific invention.[31] Milner links symbolization to what she calls 'ecstasy', suggesting that Jones's view of symbolism as regressive has left out the possibility of 'a regression in order to take a step forward'—that is, 'the possibility that some form of artistic ecstasy may be an essential phase in adaptation to reality' (*SMSM* 85). In such states the artist, like the infant, seeks to re-find

---

[28] *Developments in Psycho-Analysis*, 109.

[29] For Milner's theoretical intervention, see Turner, 'A Brief History of Illusion: Milner, Winnicott and Rycroft', *International Journal of Psycho-Analysis*, 83 (2002), 1063–82.

[30] Citations of the revised 1955 paper refer to the expanded version rpr. in Milner's collection, *The Suppressed Madness of Sane Men* (London and New York: Routledge, 1987), 83–113 (*SMSM*); Milner also includes Klein's letter commenting on the case-history. Originally titled 'Aspects of Symbolism in Comprehension of the Not-Self', the paper was first published in the special issue of the *International Journal of Psycho-Analysis* celebrating Melanie Klein's seventieth birthday; see *International Journal of Psycho-Analysis*, 33 (1952), 81–95. It was republished in Melanie Klein, Paula Heimann, and R. E. Money-Kyrle (eds.), *New Directions in Psycho-Analysis* (1955; rpr. London: Karnac, 1985), alongside other papers on literary and aesthetic topics that included Klein's 'On Identification' (1955). For its context in the larger framework of Milner's thought and writings, see Naomi Rader Dragstedt, 'Creative Illusions: The Theoretical and Clinical Work of Marion Milner', *Journal of Melanie Klein and Object Relations*, 16/3 (1998), 429–536.

[31] See Ernest Jones, 'The Theory of Symbolism' (1916), in *Papers on Psycho-Analysis* (1948; rpr. London: Karnac Books, 1977), 87–144, and Melanie Klein, 'The Importance of Symbol-Formation in the Development of the Ego' (1930); *LGR* 219–32.

'a fusion of self and object' (*SMSM* 87, 88). Milner's view of symbolization draws on a distinction that Herbert Read had made in a lecture on psychoanalysis and aesthetic value. Read contrasts the 'throwing together of tangible, visible objects' (whether with each other or with abstract ideas) with uses which 'treat the symbol as an integral or original form of expression. A word itself may be a symbol in this sense' (*SMSM* 86).[32] The word as symbol provides a model for the privileging of pre-logical fusion that underpins Milner's entire approach to aesthetics—a position implicitly at odds with Klein's view that recognizing the object as separate and whole was the precondition for symbolization.

The clinical case in Milner's paper made an appropriate birthday offering to Klein, since the patient she calls Simon was Klein's 11-year-old grandson (Michael Clyne)—a bright boy who had lost all interest in his schoolwork and turned into a school-refuser. Milner was at first supervised by Klein herself. But she came to feel that the Kleinian concept of phantasy was not specific enough to cover the forms of artistic fusion that she saw in Simon.[33] She needed the concept of 'illusion', which she links in her paper to the temporal or spatial frame marking off a special kind of reality for art. The terms she uses—'ecstasy', 'concentration', and 'absorption'—derive not only from her observation of children's play but from her own creative thought-experiments. In the 'poetry' of imaginative play, when the outside world is both created and re-found in the familiar, she glimpses 'moments when the original poet in each of us created the outside world for us' (*SMSM* 88).[34] Memories of such 'visitations of the gods', she writes, are 'guarded in some secret place of memory', or else told in autobiography or poetry. Milner's prototypical scene of divine visitation takes place in a circle of stage fire, when 'imagination catches fire and a whole subject or skill lights up with significance' (*SMSM* 88). Simon has lived through part of the Blitz during which his analyst's own house was damaged. He has the habit of setting out the toys in her playroom in the form of a village full of people and animals and deliberately setting light to them: 'the boy would then bomb the village by dropping balls of burning paper upon it' (*SMSM* 89). Milner's imagination catches fire, along with the toys, in the dramatic light of wartime incendiary bombs.[35]

---

[32] Herbert Read, 'Psycho-analysis and the Problem of Aesthetic Value', *International Journal of Psycho-Analysis*, 32 (1951), 73–82.

[33] See Phyllis Grosskurth, *Melanie Klein: Her World and her Work* (Cambridge, Mass.: Harvard University Press, 1986), 395–6. Milner herself records: 'Soon after I was considered qualified as a child analyst I told Melanie Klein that, although very grateful for her supervision, I now wanted to work on my own with Simon. Thus the work I did with him when I had to be his "lovely stuff" that he made and also the solemn ritual kind of play were all unsupervised' (*SMSM* 292).

[34] Milner's phrase is later quoted by Winnicott in *Playing and Reality* (1971); rpr. London and New York: Routledge, 1991), 39 (*P&R*). These were experiences that Milner herself saw as the starting-point for her first book; see 'Winnicott and the Two-Way Journey' (1972), her memorial tribute to Winnicott (*SMSM* 249).

[35] For 'how the Blitz got into the poem that is psychoanalysis', and the importance of war in psychoanalysis (including Kleinian theory), see Adam Phillips, 'Bombs Away', *History Workshop Journal*, 45 (1998), 183–98.

Milner's peace-keeping role is to play the part of the hapless villagers and try to save the toys from going up in flames. But, as she relates, 'The rules of the game were such that this was often very difficult, so that gradually more and more of the toys were burnt' (*SMSM* 89). Simon has the upper hand, playing dictator to a subjugated people, unleashing shock and awe with his superior air power. Milner describes a session in which there are two villages, but 'the war is not to begin at once'. Her village is to be made up of the people, animals, and houses; his of the toy trucks, cars, and 'lots of junk and oddments to exchange'— entrepreneurial imperialism in action. The war starts with an exchange of goods: a truck delivers half a gun, then a test-tube, and takes various small objects back in return. When Milner comments that the exchange seems unequal, Simon responds with a plan for reprisals and unleashes his stockpiled weapons of mass destruction: ' "I think those people were a bit odd, I don't think I like those people much, I think I will give them just a little time-bomb." ' Her village promptly capitulates and he celebrates his victory by setting light to a stack of matchboxes:

So he takes back his test-tube, sticks some matches in it, and drops it over my village. He then drops a whole box of matches on my village and says the villagers have to find it and put it out before it explodes. But then I have to come and bomb his village, and when I drop a flare, instead of putting it out he adds fuel to it. Then he says, 'You have got to bring all your people over to my village, the war is over.' I have to bring the animals and people over in trucks, but at once he says they must go back because they all have to watch the burning of the whole stack of match boxes (which he has bought with his own money). He makes me stand back from the blaze, and shows great pleasure.   (*SMSM* 89)

Where have we seen this phantasy played in real life? Simon's war-game enacts the transfer of goods and power to an overwhelming military aggressor under the familiar guise of 'exchange' and 'liberation', with no pretence at symbolic exchange.

Combining overwhelming fire-power and neo-imperialist condescension, Simon instructs Milner that his 'people' (in the forms of empty trucks) are not really aggressors but explorers; they are to call on her people, who have to be frightened and mistake them for gods. The Mrs Noah figure is made to broadcast a command to prepare food 'in a god-like voice'. The subjugated people are to be grateful and welcome their 'liberators'. Milner at first tries to interpret Simon's war-game in terms of bisexual conflict (the maternal is identified with human values, whereas he only has mechanical ones). Earlier, this budding New Prometheus was unable to make a Meccano model of a mechanical man who could move—'a live baby'. Now (according to Milner) he tries to give her some of his phallic maleness in the form of guns and test-tubes, while he is to acquire some femaleness in the form of the Mrs Noah figure. In a similar vein, Milner suggests that 'by burning his own village he was not only punishing himself, but at the same time expressing (externalizing) the sense of anxiety in which he felt full of explosive faeces'— giving a new twist to the idea of destroying a village in order to save it. Unable to stand 'the empty, depersonalized gods' (i.e., trucks), he has tried to create a compromise 'by borrowing the good mother figure to fill the empty truck' (*SMSM* 90). But Milner finds herself dissatisfied with this orthodox interpretation. Even if Simon is working out his Oedipal conflicts, another strand of meaning surfaces—that of the empty desert represented by his school, and symbolizing the mother's forbidden body. This would help to explain his lack of academic progress. Re-enacting Simon's school phobia, Milner is made to play the part of the persecuted schoolboy while he plays the sadistic schoolmaster: 'I was set long monotonous tasks, my efforts were treated with scorn, I was forbidden to talk and made to write out "lines" if I did'.

Milner dutifully resists interpreting Simon's severity in terms of actual conditions in contemporary British private schools, where scorn and the repetition of useless tasks might well have been everyday forms of discipline. Instead, she evades both the orthodoxy of Kleinian unconscious phantasy and the realities of Simon's school life to explore a more elusive problem. What is going on between herself and Simon, she speculates, has 'something to do with difficulties in establishing the relation to external reality as such' (*SMSM* 92). She notices that Simon drops his bullying and his hectoring tone as soon as he begins to play freely and imaginatively. Once he has 'settled down to using the toys as a pliable medium', he becomes friendly and considerate. Milner begins to wonder whether Simon's fiery drama with the toys—as opposed to either formless day-dreaming or purposive instinctual activity—represents a kind of half-way house. Simon's 'war-of-the-villages play' makes him an improvisatory artist, 'just as in free imaginative drawing, the sight of a mark made on the paper provokes new associations, the line as it were answers back' (*SMSM* 92). A few months later, a change for the better in Simon's 'dictatorship' attitude occurs when he is allowed to incorporate his enthusiasm for photography into a club at school, modifying its 'mechanized, soulless world' and its 'unmitigated not-me-ness'. Milner recalls that Simon's father had gone to war just when his baby brother had been born at the time of the Blitz, which had also coincided with the loss of a valued toy, Simon's woolly rabbit. She comes to see her role in the transference as that of the lost rabbit. In his bullying treatment of her, 'he did need to have the illusion that [she] was part of himself' so that he could do what he liked with her (*SMSM* 93, 94). The Kleinian repertoire—splitting as a defence, idealization, omnipotent control—falls short of the way Simon makes use of her, 'for all of them take for granted the idea of a clear boundary'. Treating Milner like his toy rabbit blurs the line between illusion and reality. In her, he recovers his transitional object, at once found and created, loved and maltreated.

For Milner, Simon's need to obliterate boundaries is also expressed in the violent activities of 'burning, boiling down, and melting' that occupy him in the playroom. Milner cites Clifford Scott (by now her analyst) and Winnicott (her friend, colleague, and ex-analyst), to the effect that the good mother allows the child to fuse its hallucination of the breast with its actual sensation of a good breast.[36] The oscillation between illusory union and actual contact represents, according to Scott, 'the discovery of an interface, a boundary, or a place of contact' that also allows for a discovery of 'the me' and 'the you'. Illusion paradoxically allows for the discovery of otherness (for 'the you' or not-me). The destruction of boundaries leads simultaneously to what Scott calls 'cosmic bliss' and 'catastrophic chaos'—contrary states which Milner sees in the seraphic face of a 6-year-old patient concentrating on painting outlines, or in her schizophrenic patient (Susan in *The Hands of the Living God*) 'who would at times have moments of startling physical beauty counterbalanced by moments of something startlingly repellent' (*SMSM* 95).[37] These states can be seen in terms of fusion with an inner object (whether good or monstrous), but they also involve bodily boundaries. Importantly, the aesthetic perception of beauty or ugliness implicates the analyst's own counter-transference. Milner notes that the quality in the boy's play that she responds to as 'beautiful' is associated with 'occasions when it was he who did the stage managing and it was [her] imagination which caught fire. It was in fact play with light and fire' (*SMSM* 96). As Susanne Langer writes in *Philosophy in a New Key* (1942)—a book that came to influence Milner's thinking about symbolism—fire is a natural symbol of life and passion: 'Its mobility and flare, its heat and color, make it an irresistible symbol of all that is living, feeling, and active.'[38] Simon lights up when he plays, and Milner glows with him.

Rather than focusing on Simon's violence and aggression, Milner celebrates the qualities of life and feeling that characterize his fire-play. She comes to see the battle between the villages as 'a genuine work of dramatic art in which the actual process by which the world is created, for all of us, is poetically represented' (*SMSM* 107). Not content with fire-bombing the toy village, Simon practises fiery fertility rituals which resemble those described by James Frazer in *The Golden Bough*:

He would close the shutters of the room and insist that it be lit only by candle light, sometimes a dozen candles arranged in patterns, or all grouped together in a solid block. And then he would make what he called furnaces, with a very careful choice of what ingredients should make the fire, including dried leaves from special plants in my garden; and sometimes all the ingredients had to be put in a metal cup on the electric fire and stirred continuously, all this carried out in the half darkness of candle light. And often there had to be a sacrifice, a lead soldier had to be added to the fire, and this figure was spoken of either

---

[36] See W. C. M. Scott, 'The Body Scheme in Psychotherapy', *British Journal of Medical Psychology* 22 (1949), 137–43, and D. W. Winnicott, 'Primitive Emotional Development' (1948), in *Through Pediatrics to Psycho-Analysis* (1958; rpr. New York: Bruner/Mazel, 1992), 145–56. In a private communication, however, Winnicott disagrees with aspects of Scott views about regression (see *SMSM* 112 n. 13).

[37] For Susan and her drawings, see Marion Milner, *The Hands of the Living God* (New York: International Universities Press,1969), discussed in Ch. 5 below.

[38] Suzanne Langer, *Philosophy in a New Key: A Study in the Symbolism of Reason, Rite, and Art* (Cambridge, Mass.: Harvard University Press, 1942), 145. Langer's views on language, symbolism, myth, and ritual are relevant to Milner's thinking, although Milner's note suggests that she was not able to read her book before writing her original paper (see *SMSM* 113 n. 19). Milner also refers to Langer's view on unconscious thinking in a footnote to *The Hands of the Living God*, p. xx.

as the victim or the sacrifice. In fact, all this type of play had a dramatic ritual quality comparable to the fertility rites described by Frazer in primitive societies.   (*SMSM* 96)

Milner elsewhere records her own fascination with the third part of *The Golden Bough* (*The Dying God*), where Frazer writes that 'magical ceremonies are nothing but experiments which have failed and which continue to be repeated merely because . . . the operator is unaware of their failure'.[39] This is the proto-scientific hypothesis. Frazer himself had put forward two theories about fire festivals: the solar theory and the purificatory theory; either they are magical ceremonies intended to ensure sun and fertility, or they are ceremonial fires designed to destroy harmful influences (i.e., incendiary rituals that ward off witchcraft). But Milner has other ideas. The theme of the Dying God that had long haunted her imaginings also colours her view of Simon's fire-play.

In *An Experiment in Leisure* (1937), Milner records disarmingly that she 'was always borrowing Frazer's Golden Bough, but daunted perhaps by its size, [she] never managed to read it'.[40] She finally bought a shilling reprint of the Adonis chapter, which deals with the custom of putting a king or his son to death by fire. Milner even thought of becoming an anthropologist and studying primitive religions. But increasingly she came to view her 'preoccupation with the ritual of the killing of the god' as a symbolic way to think about unresolved problems of her own. These had to do with giving up her anxious strivings and morbid desire for failure. The realization that this was the case, she says, freed her from her long-standing interest in witchcraft as well as from her fantasies of sexual submission.[41] Milner depicts herself as grappling with the rationalist tradition that told her that magical beliefs and practices were rooted in a misunderstanding of the laws of cause and effect, or else sprang from mere wish-fulfilment: 'I had gathered that myths and fairy tales and magic rituals were all roundabout ways of pretending you could get what you wanted without the trouble of common-sense working for it'. Yet these images retained a compelling aura: 'The still glow that surrounded some of these images in my mind, images of the burning god . . . did it come because they satisfied surreptitiously some crude infantile desire that I ought to have left behind long ago?' Or were they imaginative ways of 'thinking about hard facts'? The image of the Dying God might not only satisfy primitive desires to give or inflict pain but also, she thought, 'dimly foreshadow the truth of a purely psychic process for which no more direct language was available'.[42] Even if the image came from infancy, it could presage psychic transformation.

---

[39] J. G. Frazer, *The Golden Bough: A Study in Magic and Religion*, Part III: *The Dying God* (London: Macmillan, 1911), 269. Milner refers to her interest in Frazer in her 1967 memorial tribute to Anton Ehrenzweig, whose paper 'The Creative Surrender' (1957) had reinterpreted the theme of the Dying God that recurs in Milner's *An Experiment in Leisure* (1937) in terms of the ego-rhythms of creative work (see *SMSM* 242–3).

[40] Joanna Field [Marion Milner], *An Experiment in Leisure* (London: Chatto & Windus, 1937), 36.   [41] See ibid., 32–5, 38–44.

[42] Ibid., 49, 51.

An Experiment in Leisure realigns magical thinking with the reality principle. Magic may appear childish from a modern scientific point of view, 'But was that the only point of magic?' What if magic was practised 'not only because of its imagined effect on the outside world, but because of its real constructive effect on the inner world'? Magic, Milner speculates, may have 'played a very definite part in the growth of the mind, by giving dramatic expression to internal processes of vital importance'.[43] It may even have provided the only available access to inner reality. No wonder, then, that she is fascinated by the ritual quality of Simon's play, reading its sense of pattern as a literal 'play' or dramatic performance with its own form and meaning: 'Thus the fire seemed to be here not only a destructive fire but also the fire of Eros'—and not only an expression of passionate bodily and erotic feeling 'but also a way of representing the inner fire of concentration' (*SMSM* 96). Simon's boiling and melting down of ingredients in 'the fire cup' corresponds to her own haunting by 'images of fiery vessels' as images of concentrated thought: 'I had felt my thought to be a glowing crucible and the process of becoming con-centrated in order to find forms of expression had seemed like a gradual raising of inner fires'.[44] Simon's sacrifice of a toy soldier, melted down on her electric fire, allows him to be 'good at art' despite his common-sense scientific orientation and his love of Meccano.[45]

Milner's view of 'artistic ecstasy' is informed by Bernard Berenson's account of the 'aesthetic moment'—'so brief as to be almost timeless, when the spectator is at one with the work of art he is looking at'. Fused with the aesthetic object, the spectator returns to ordinary consciousness 'as if he had been initiated into illumi-nating, exalting, formative mysteries' (*SMSM* 97). In the clinching sentence (not quoted by Milner), Berenson restates 'the aesthetic moment' as 'a moment of mystic vision'.[46] Aesthetic response for Milner recapitulates an earlier form of object relations in which a temporary merging with the object takes place. Simon's imaginative activity has its parallel in the artist's recovery of an infantile state. Traherne and Wordsworth, Milner believed, express in their poetry what Simon tries to express with candles and matches. Art and play fuse (without confusing) the edges of what Otto Rank calls 'subjective unreality' and 'objective reality' so as to permit illusion to occur.[47] For Milner, 'the enclosed space-time of the drama or

---

[43] Joanna Field [Marion Milner], *An Experiment in Leisure* (London: Chatto & Windus, 1937), 138, 139.   [44] Ibid., 157.

[45] Milner's brother, Patrick Blackett, won the Nobel prize for his discoveries in physics; the recon-ciliation between science and art that Milner sees in Simon may replicate tensions within her family and herself (trained as an industrial psychologist), as well as rehearse her awareness of creative processes common to scientific and artistic work.

[46] See Bernard Berenson, 'The Aesthetic Moment', *Aesthetics and History* (London: Constable, 1950), 80; Milner's quotation omits a phrase. For an account of Milner's leanings towards mysticism, see Janet Sayers, *Divine Therapy: Love, Mysticism and Psychoanalysis* (Oxford: Oxford University Press, 2003), 162–83.

[47] See Otto Rank, *Art and Artist* (New York: Knopf, 1932), 104. As Rudnytsky points out, Rank's account of 'the play instinct' and an 'intermediate quality of the work of art, which links the world of subjective unreality with that of objective reality—harmoniously fusing the edges of each without

the picture or the story' includes the analytic space-time of her playroom, where ordinary perception is transcended and illusion flourishes. Simon becomes a proto-poet who does with his environment 'what Caudwell says the poet does with words, when . . . he makes the earth become charged with affective colouring and glow with a strange emotional fire' (SMSM 99).[48] Milner's reference to Caudwell's Marxist-materialist defence of art suggests her debt to his aphorism: 'Illusion . . . plays into the hands of reality'.[49] Caudwell proposes that the literary reader 'accepts the phantasy as expressing objective reality while immersed in the phantasy, but, once the phantasy is over, he does not demand that it be still treated as part of the real world'. Simon is a progressive artist-scientist in the Caudwell mould, refashioning his world and rendering his ideas in experimental ways: 'Art is . . . affective experimenting with selected pieces of external reality.'[50] Both Simon and Milner are graduates of this experimental school.

Milner ends by wondering if Simon had been made aware of his separateness too soon, or too often; perhaps his play contains the memory of a traumatic impingement, 'a too sudden breaking in on the illusion of oneness' (SMSM 102). Necessity, like his school, becomes a prison when it refuses his need to shape his world. Perhaps he has also been forced to distinguish prematurely between internal and external reality in order to survive the traumas of separation and war. The environment of Milner's playroom provides 'a framed space and time and a pliable medium' (SMSM 101)—an art room—where he no longer needs to maintain such a sharp division between inner and outer, self and not-self. This, she concludes, was what Simon had been trying to communicate by the moment of deferral in his 'village play'—'there was to be a war, "but not yet" '. The battle had to be postponed until he had 'established his right to a recurrent merging of the opposites' (me and not-me). When she tried to interpret Simon's aggression along Kleinian lines, Milner discovered that her interpretations made him all the more

---

confusing them', anticipates Winnicott's theory of play; see Peter Rudnytsky, *The Psychoanalytic Vocation: Rank, Winnicott, and the Legacy of Freud* (New Haven, Conn.: Yale University Press, 1991), 65–6.

[48] Caudwell defines poetry as 'concerned with the emotions struck from the instincts—like sparks from flint'; see Christopher Caudwell, *Illusion and Reality: A Study of the Sources of Poetry* (London: Macmillan, 1937), 18. Caudwell's psychoanalytic account of poetry consistently emphasizes the affective 'glow' or emotional colouring of words; for instance, 'The affective colouring of one word takes reflected shadow and light from the colours of the other words'; 'Poetry colours the world of reality with affective tones'; 'Poetry grasps a piece of external reality, colours it with affect tone and makes it distil a new emotional attitude' (ibid., 242, 244, 271).

[49] For the pervasive, if depoliticized, influence of Caudwell's Marxist legacy on Milner and Winnicott, see Turner's discussion of the dualistic aspects of Milner's concept of illusion ('A Brief History of Illusion', *International Journal of Psycho-Analysis*, 83 (2002) 1069–71).

[50] Caudwell, *Illusion and Reality*, 28, 29. Caudwell emphasizes the social and communal aspects of poetry and ritual: 'In the dance and the chant man retires into a half-sleep by dismissing the world of immediate reality . . . the items of the common perceptual world are selected, organized, blended and reoriented round the social ego, the "god" of early Greek ritual who descended into his worshippers and who was nothing but the symbol of the heightened common ego formed by the dance' (ibid., 207).

implacable and 'he went on attacking me with almost the fervour of a holy war' (*SMSM* 102). By contrast, acknowledging his own reality lessened his furious jihad against her. When Simon promises to give her a specially invented papier-mâché clock, Milner interprets it as his way of saying that 'he had been able to find a bit of the external world that was malleable . . . and so had let it serve as a bridge between inner and outer' (*SMSM* 103). Milner gets heartily sick of being maltreated by Simon 'as his gas, his breath, his faeces'. But she sees that if he can feel 'that he had "made [her]," that [she] was his lovely stuff' (*SMSM* 103), he can tolerate her possessing good qualities of her own. She is his 'lovely stuff', something he can make a mess with, and treat as part of himself, yet recognize as other.

Just as Milner allows Simon to remould both his world and her, she refashions her own analytic ideas. A postscript added to the 1955 version of her paper refers to an 11-year-old patient who had scribbled furiously rather than talking.[51] Covering every available surface, her scribbles show her 'struggling with the problem of the identity of the symbol and the thing symbolized'. As she tries to make the world her own through proto-writing, she begins to discriminate between symbolic reality and the libidinal pleasure of making a mess as a gift of love. The mess Simon makes is an aspect of 'the actual process by which the world is created, for all of us' (*SMSM* 107). Even mess has symbolic meaning—it is at once a gift and an art form. An affectionate letter from Klein strongly implies that Milner had idealized the state of primary fusion or 'illusion'.[52] Along with Milner's failure to analyse Simon's violence and aggression, Klein identifies the dangers of uncontrollable omnipotent impulses involved in regression (disintegration, falling to bits, the introjection of dangerous objects, and so on).[53] But, for Milner, this was the point. The analytic medium had to be made sufficiently pliable to become hers. Her loving defacement of Klein's legacy—the paper that is her birthday gift—must (as she had once tentatively suggested to Klein) 'go back in order to come forward' (*SMSM* 111). Her 'lovely stuff' is the gift forged in the crucible of Simon's dramatic fire-play.

THE MAGIC BLANKET

Winnicott's theory of the transitional object starts and ends with a blanket. In 'Playing: A Theoretical Statement', included in *Playing and Reality* (1971), he refers not only to Anna Freud on the child's use of the 'talisman' but to a paper by Wulff, 'Fetishism and Object Choice in Early Childhood' (1946). This was the paper he had discussed twenty years before, in the original 1951 version of

---

[51] See *New Directions in Psycho-Analysis*, 106–8.

[52] Milner includes Klein's letter at the end of her reprinted paper (*SMSM* 110–11).

[53] For a recent discussion of Klein's ideas about the processes of splitting that also takes into account the influence of Winnicott's ideas about un-integrated states, see Likierman, *Melanie Klein: Her Work in Context*, 156–71.

'Transitional Objects and Transitional Phenomena'.[54] Wulff's paper—taking issue with Freud's theory of the fetish as a defence against castration anxiety—is rich in material illustrating the magical effects of children's fetish-objects. Wulff sees the fetish as a substitute not for the absent penis but for the mother's body, and particularly her breast. His clinical material includes a 4-year-old who screams and is unable to settle to sleep until his mother gives him what she calls his 'magic blanket', which soon works its customary 'magic spell' (much to his parents' relief). The young mother confides: 'ever since he fed at the breast he has had a small, warm and very soft woollen coverlet which he prizes more than anything else in the world—more than me and his father. If only he can have this coverlet—we call it the "magic blanket"—he is so happy that nothing else matters.'[55] Wulff fancifully refers to the coverlet as a 'magic carpet' that wafts the child to sleep. The objects his paper describes (a bib, a drooling cloth, handkerchiefs, stockings, or bras) are all intimately associated with nursing and with the mother's smell. These pieces of cloth are vividly alive for their owners. One 15-month-old boy calls his bib a 'Hoppa', the name of a dance he performs in his bed, singing 'hoppa, hoppa, hoppa'. True to form, the bib loses its magic if washed.

Wulff cites Edith Sterba's account of a 20-month-old girl who is tenderly attached to her drooling cloth. She calls it her 'my-my' ('her first distinct syllable') and 'if one in fun tried to pull it away, she would protest "my-my"—meaning "mine, mine, it belongs to me." This became a favorite game in which one could plainly observe the development of the feeling of possession'.[56] Winnicott's original subtitle for the 1951 version of 'Transitional Objects and Transitional Phenomena' ('A Study of the First Not-Me Possession') riffs on this first game. Borrowing Fairbairn's phrase 'transitional states', Winnicott reminds us that, properly speaking, it is not the *object* but the *infant* who is in transition. The transitional object marks 'the intermediate area between the subjective and that which is objectively perceived' (*P&R* 3); its function is to keep the two separate yet interrelated. Mauss's definition of *mana* parallels Winnicott's slide between transitional subject and transitional object when he writes that '*Mana* is not simply a force, a being, it is also an action, a quality, a state. In other terms the word [*mana*] is a noun, an adjective, and a verb'. For Mauss, this merging of concepts, functions, and verbal forms reveals 'a fundamental feature of magic—the confusion between

[54] As Green points out in his careful reading of the different versions of 'Transitional Objects and Transitional Phenomena', the original paper of 1951 has a longer discussion of Wulff's paper and the relation between fetishism and transitional object. Winnicott notes the potential for the transitional object to become a fetish object in adult sexual life, but criticizes Wulff for 'working backwards from the psychopathology of fetishism to the transitional phenomena . . . which are inherent in healthy emotional development'; Winnicott want to distinguish between 'a *delusion* of a maternal phallus' and 'the concept of illusion' (see Winnicott, *Through Pediatrics to Psycho-Analysis*, 236–7, 241–2).

[55] M. Wulff, 'Fetishism and Object Choice in Early Childhood', *Psychoanalytical Quarterly*, 15 (1946), 455.

[56] Ibid., 454. See Edith Sterba, 'An Important Factor in Eating Disturbances in Childhood', *Psychoanalytical Quarterly*, 10 (1941), 365–72. For Sterba the 'my-my' is 'an oral fetish from the nursing period' (ibid., 372).

actor, rite and object' that is not to be accounted for by mere animism.[57] Winnicott's definition of illusion points to the same magical confusion: 'that which is allowed to the infant, and which in adult life is inherent in art and religion ... yet becomes the hallmark of madness when an adult puts too powerful a claim on the credulity of others' (*P&R* 3). When 'The Location of Cultural Experience' (1971) asserts that 'Cultural experience begins with creative living first manifested in play' (*P&R* 100), Winnicott extends transitional phenomena across the cultural field much as Mauss had extended *mana* across the social field as what 'gives things and people value, not only magical religious values, but social value as well'. For Mauss, 'Magic is everywhere in a diffuse state'.[58] Winnicott's theory of the transitional object verges on being a theory of magical cultural diffusion.

Like *mana*, the meaning of the infant's transitional object—sheet, blanket, nappy, handkerchief, maternal lingerie—is both abstract and concrete, primitive and, therefore, culturally complex and confused; above all, it is resistant to logical analysis. When Winnicott sets out the rules for the use of the transitional object, he endows both infant and object equally with life and meaning-making capacity. The infant assumes rights over the transitional object, and affectionately cuddles it; the transitional object must never change, it must survive loving and hating; it must appear to have warmth and life of its own; it comes neither from without nor from within; it gradually fades away; its meaning spreads out over the entire cultural field; and so on. The transitional object becomes the root of all symbolism. Winnicott adduces the *locus classicus* of religious symbolism to explain its symbolic function. The wafer in the Blessed Sacrament (to a Roman Catholic, the body of Christ; to a Protestant, its symbolic substitute) is simultaneously incarnation and symbol—just as the transitional object is both representative of the breast and not the breast, while at the same time being a substitute for it. In 'The Fate of the Transitional Object' (1959), Winnicott calls this the first symbol, at once hallucinatory and representative of psychic reality: 'The transitional object is for us a bit of the blanket but for the infant a representative both of the mother's breast, say, and of the internalised mother's breast.'[59] Winnicott compares the mother's 'making real of the hallucination' with Mme Sechehaye's technique of 'symbolic realization'—the making real of the symbol, or rather 'the making real of the hallucination' which enables the illusion that objects in external reality are indeed real (since only hallucinations feel real to the infant).[60] Because the trauma

[57] Mauss, *A General Theory of Magic*, 108.

[58] Ibid., 109, 88. According to Mauss: '[*Mana*] is obscure and vague, yet the use to which it is put is curiously definite. It is abstract and general, yet quite concrete. Its primitive nature—that is its complexity and confusion—resists any attempt at a logical analysis, and we must remain content to describe the phenomenon' (ibid., 108).

[59] D. W. Winnicott, *Psycho-Analytic Explorations*, ed. Clare Winnicott, Ray Shepherd, and Madeleine Davis (Cambridge, Mass.: Harvard University Press, 1989), 58.

[60] Ibid., 53. Sechehaye's home-based, mother-focused, regression therapy had been used to treat a severely schizophrenic girl during the 1930s—'a cure of [i.e., by] the magic associations' that involved repeated, concrete representations of pre-symbolic infantile desires in the form of non-verbal

preceded language (so Mme Sechehaye believed), it could not be dealt with by verbal means, but only by means of symbolic language.[61]

Winnicott is at pains to distinguish his theory of the transitional object from Klein's reigning concept of the internal object: 'The transitional object is *not an internal object* (which is a mental concept)—It is a possession. Yet it is not (for the infant) an external object either' (*P&R* 9).[62] As the problems of defining the transitional object becomes more intractable, Winnicott's style grows more convoluted and his syntax more tortured ('The following complex statement has to be made . . .'). The life of the transitional object depends on the health of both internal and external object. A failure in the external object leads to a loss of meaning in the internal object, which in turn leaches the transitional object of symbolic meaning: 'The transitional object may therefore stand for the "external breast," but *indirectly*, through standing for an "internal" breast. The transitional object is never under magical control like the internal object, nor is it outside control as the real mother is' (*P&R* 10)—not magical, then, yet not beyond the reach of infantile omnipotence. Winnicott's paradoxical definition emerges from a sequence of theoretical propositions, another version of the rules for the proper use of the transitional object. The fiction is that the infant is capable of negotiating the terms of the transitional object's meanings and uses, in tacit agreement with the adult. Just as the transitional object mediates between internal and external breast, 'but *indirectly*', so (one might argue) Winnicott's theory of the transitional object mediates ('but *indirectly*') between internal object and what it 'stands for', the maternal environment for which Winnicott tried to make room in Kleinian theory.[63] For Winnicott, the actual mother can be either good-enough, or non-present, or traumatically impinging—differences precisely registered in the uses and life-expectancy of the transitional object, but comparatively absent from Kleinian theory where, for all the disparity between internal and external mother, it is the breast that is good or bad, not the mother (and objects 'stand for' what they symbolize in a less indirect way). To Winnicott, trained as a paediatrician, this was the problem.

The transitional object has to exhibit certain qualities (blankness or aliveness). It must be capable of standing up to cuddling and destruction. In the same way, the good-enough mother's adaptation to the baby must not be too complete, 'since exact adaptation resembles magic and the object that behaves

symbolic substitutes (apples, balloons, etc.); see M. A. Sechehaye, *Symbolic Realization: A New Method of Psychotherapy Applied to a Case of Schizophrenia*, trans. Brabrö Würsten and Helmut Würston (New York: International Universities Press, 1951), 137.

[61] Compare Suzanne Langer, for whom 'Magic . . . is not a method but a language'; see Langer, *Philosophy in a New Key*, 44.

[62] For the theory of the internal object, see R. D. Hinshelwood, *A Dictionary of Kleinian Thought* (London: Free Association Books, 1991), 68–83.

[63] For Winnicott's wish to write a book on the environment, and his report of Riviere's adverse reaction to the idea during his analysis with her, see Brett Kahr, *D. W. Winnicott: A Biographical Portrait* (London: Karnac Books, 1996), 64.

perfectly becomes no better than a hallucination'. But the mother must also allow the baby to experience 'the *illusion* that her breast is part of the infant. It is, as it were, under the baby's magical control' (*P&R* 11); only then should she permit the inevitable process of disillusion to set in, so that reality can come to occupy the place previously held by hallucination. If reality is to have meaning, the infant must create the breast by finding it, repeatedly, and at just the right moment. The 'found' breast resembles the transitional object, eliciting another ventriloquistic sleight of hand on behalf of the Winnicottian baby: 'I hallucinated that [i.e., the breast] and it is part of mother who was there before I came along'.[64] Hallucination makes possible the 'primary creativity' that includes Winnicott's own anthropomorphism when he endows the speechless *infans* with speech. He enunciates his rules for play in the context of an imaginary dialogue that issues in a symptomatic flurry of italics, negatives, and a final blanket prohibition: '*Of the transitional object it can be said that it is a matter of agreement between us and the baby that we will never ask the question: "Did you conceive of this or was it presented to you from without?" The important point is that no decision on this point is expected. The question is not to be formulated*' (*P&R* 12; Winnicott's emphasis). To reach an imaginary agreement with a baby about a blanket is one thing. But it is a feat of linguistic imagination to ventriloquize an unasked question, and then refuse either to answer it or to allow it to be asked. Yet this paradox is the transitional object's self-declared condition of (im)possibility.[65]

Winnicott alludes to the strain involved in reality-acceptance when he writes that 'no human being is free from the strain of relating inner and outer reality, and ... relief from this strain is provided by an intermediate area of experience' (*P&R* 13).[66] Art and religious belief provide culturally accepted forms of relief from the strained relations between inner and outer reality. But only if the adult can enjoy 'the personal intermediate area without making claims' can we allow another's intermediate area to overlap with our own—'that is to say common experience between members of a group in art or religion or philosophy' (*P&R* 14), or indeed psychoanalysis itself. Winnicott's theory of culture is hedged around with caveats: 'Should an adult make claims on us for our acceptance of the objectivity of his subjective phenomena we discern or diagnose madness'

---

[64] Winnicott, *Psycho-Analytic Explorations*, 58. See Barbara Johnson, 'Using People: Kant with Winnicott', in Marjorie Garber, Beatrice Hanssen, and Rebecca L. Walkowitz (eds.), *The Turn to Ethics* (London and New York: Routledge, 2000), 47–64, for a succinct but brilliant discussion of Winnicott's ventriloquization of the baby in the context of the transitional object and object-usage.

[65] For the 'communicative paradox' that inflects both Winnicott's theory of play and his theoretical statements, see also Gregory Bateson, 'A Theory of Play and Phantasy', *Psychiatric Research Reports* 2 (1955), 39–51.

[66] Winnicott invokes the paper by his former analyst, Joan Riviere, 'On the Genesis of Psychical Conflict in Earliest Infancy' (1936), conceding that 'phantasy-life is never "pure fantasy." It consists of true perceptions and of false interpretations; all phantasies are thus *mixtures* of external and internal reality'; see Athol Hughes (ed.), *The Inner World and Joan Riviere: Collected Papers 1920–1958* (London: Karnac Books, 1991), 277. For Riviere, however, phantasy functions as a means to separate not confuse the positive and negative qualities of the internal and external object.

(*P&R* 14). In 'The Fate of the Transitional Object', he offers the example of simultaneously hallucinating and creating a late Beethoven quartet ('you see I'm highbrow') heard at a concert: 'I enjoy it because I say I created it, I hallucinated it, and it is real and would have been there even if I had been neither conceived of nor conceived. This is mad. But in our cultural life we accept the madness.' Such a 'third area of existing', he acknowledges, is hard to fit into psychoanalytic theory, 'which has had to build up gradually by the stone-by-stone method of a science'.[67] Elsewhere, Winnicott remarks casually that a good-enough environment 'enables the baby to be mad in one particular way that is conceded to babies' (*P&R* 71). In a talk called 'Playing and Culture' (1968), he reflects that the most important part of his paper on transitional phenomena was his claim 'that we need to *accept the paradox*, not to resolve it'.[68] By contrast, philosophy operates by 'non-acceptance of the inherent paradox' between realism and idealism. This was the paradox maintained by Winnicott's hallucinatory definition of both illusion and perception.[69] Located in the intermediate or third area between paediatric observation and magic, psychoanalytic inquiry and paradox, the theory of the transitional object—Winnicott's best-known and most widely accepted concept—mutates into a form of mutually acknowledged, generally diffused cultural madness found in concert-goers and babies alike. On this madness (shared or private) hangs his entire theory of play.

In 'Playing: A Theoretical Statement' (1971), psychoanalysis becomes the paradigmatic form of play, with its own poetics and logical paradoxes, its peculiar shared madness: 'The natural thing is playing, and the highly sophisticated twentieth-century phenomenon is psychoanalysis' (*P&R* 41). Winnicott defines play both as universal and as leading to growth, socialization, communication—and psychoanalysis. He invokes Milner's 'Moments when the original poet in each of us created the outside world for us' (*P&R* 39; *SMSM* 88). Linking magic to the expansive playground provided by the mother ('where the idea of magic originates'), he invokes the developmental choreography that leads from Rank's 'subjective unreality' to 'objective reality' (from subjective object to object realistically perceived). Tellingly, he does so by means of an allusion to Shakespeare's Sonnet XXX: 'If the mother can play this part over a length of time without admitting impediment (so to speak) then the baby has some *experience* of magical control' (*P&R* 47).[70] In case we should miss the Shakespearean allusion, Winnicott repeats

---

[67] *Psycho-Analytic Explorations*, 57–8.   [68] Ibid., 204.

[69] Winnicott cites the limerick by John Knox to make this point in 'The Fate of the Transitional Object': ' "Do the stone and the tree | Continue to be | When there's no-one about in the quad? | The stone and the tree | Do continue to be | As observed by yours faithfully…" '. Winnicott casually glosses 'observation' as 'hallucinating where we know what to see' (ibid., 54).

[70] Winnicott cites his paper 'Ego Integration in Child Development' (1962); see *The Maturational Processes and the Facilitating Environment* (1965; rpr. London: Karnac Books, 1990), 55–63, in which he emphasizes the mother's provision of the '*experience of omnipotence*' (ibid., 57). He also refers to what Sechehaye had done when she gave her schizophrenic patient an apple at the right moment: 'The important thing was that the patient was able to create an object, and Sechehaye did no more than enable the object to take the apple-shape, so that the girl had created an actual part of the world, an apple' (ibid., 60).

it, referring to the baby's enjoyment of 'experiences based on a "marriage" of the omnipotence of intra-psychic process with the baby's control of the actual' (*P&R* 47). The opening lines of Shakespeare's sonnet refer not just to a marriage of true minds but to constancy in the face of the lover's alteration: 'Let me not to the marriage of true minds | Admit impediments. Love is not love | Which alters when it alteration finds . . .'. The excitement of playing lies in the precarious interplay between psychic reality and control of a constant object: 'This is the precariousness of magic itself, magic that arises in intimacy, in a relationship that is being found to be reliable' (*P&R* 47). Such magical constancy (finding no alteration when it alteration finds) remains permanently available, whether remembered or forgotten: 'Thus the way is paved for a playing together in a relationship' (*P&R* 48). Transitional phenomena lead to playing, and playing to the intimacies of mature object-relating.

'Playing: A Theoretical Statement' alludes to Arthur Miller's contemporary children's book, *Jane's Blanket* (1963). Illustrated by Al Parker and belonging to a series commissioned from well-known writers, Miller's robust developmental fable depicts the tug-of-war between growing up and clinging to 1950s-style babyhood. Surrendering the comfort-object ('my bata') is the price paid for playing with Daddy, helping her mother with the chores, going to the shop on her own, and starting school. As the little girl gets bigger, the blanket gets smaller and more ragged, until it provides nesting materials for a foraging bluebird (another tribute to bygone times).[71] Winnicott notes the falling off from observation into sentimentality; for him, the fate of the transitional object is to fade away rather than be recycled into the eco-system. Indeed, the fate of the magic blanket as he himself retells it involves an altogether less reassuring developmental fable. As André Green points out in 'The Intuition of the Negative in *Playing and Reality*' (1997), Winnicott expanded the original 1951 version of 'Transitional Objects and Transitional Phenomena' by illustrating not just its pathologies but the poignant failure of the transitional object in the face of the fading of both internal and external objects. The new clinical material added for the revised first chapter of *Playing and Reality* involves a woman patient who had been evacuated as a child during the Second World War, and who later became Green's patient, having sought him out during a visit to London as 'a kind of French Winnicott'.[72] During her prolonged wartime separation from her parents, she had survived by forgetting them, reaching the position that 'the only real thing is the gap; that is to say the death or absence or the amnesia'. What was real to her was the blotting out: 'this blank could be the only fact and the only thing that is real' (*P&R* 22). Loss could be mourned and let go, but non-existence (absence or amnesia) could not, since it had become her psychic reality. And although the object could never

[71] See Arthur Miller, *Jane's Blanket*, illustrated by Al Parker (New York: Crowell-Collier Press, 1963).
[72] See André Green, 'The Intuition of the Negative in *Playing and Reality*', in Gregorio Kohon (ed.), *The Dead Mother* (London and New York: Routledge, 1999), 211–12.

be let go, there was no hope that it would ever return. This is the bleak fable that unexpectedly concludes Winnicott's thinking about the cuddly transitional object.

Green writes that 'Winnicott's contribution is to show how this negative, the non-existence, will become, at some point, the only thing that is real'.[73] Winnicott did not accept the Kleinian view of the death instinct. But linking Winnicott's 'intuition of the negative' to his own interest in blank psychosis, Green redefines it in terms of 'a *disobjectualizing function*'—the process by which the object becomes 'any object, or no object at all' (the end of object relations as such). What the death-drive means for Green is 'an inclination to self-disappearance', linked less to aggression or destructiveness than to nothingness.[74] The disappearance (rather than fading) of the transitional object disables object-relating. The patient whose clinical session forms the added coda to Winnicott's original paper still hankers after her former analyst (just as Green can only ever be a French Winnicott). She tells Winnicott: 'The negative of him is more real than the positive of you' and 'the real thing is the thing that is not there' (*P&R* 23). During the pre-adolescent years of her evacuation, she had managed never to call her surrogate parents anything at all, even though she had forgotten her real parents. This was when she reached the position 'that the only real thing is the gap' (*P&R* 22). Her relation to reality is not a matter of nostalgia or loss. Rather, what is most real to her remains negative; the negative is installed as her last-ditch defence against loss. The formula that she and Winnicott arrive at together—'the real thing is the thing that is not there'—has profound implications, not just for reality but for symbolization. The failure of transitional phenomena meant that 'she had to *doubt the reality of the thing that they were symbolizing*' (*P&R* 24). This is the haunting doubt that surfaces in the mantra to which she clings for comfort, in place of a transitional object: 'All I have got is what I have not got'.

Winnicott ends his account of their session with a bit of play involving an actual blanket in his consulting room. His patient has used the blanket once before for a regressive episode, but she prefers not to rely on it now. Winnicott explains: 'The reason is that the rug that is not there (because she does not go for it) is more real than the rug that the analyst might bring' (*P&R* 22). She ends by saying about 'the rug that she did not use: "you know, don't you, that the rug might be very comfortable, but reality is more important than comfort and *no rug* can therefore be more important than *a rug*"' (*P&R* 25). The first not-me posses-sion becomes a negative '*no rug*'—the final self-disappearance (the disobjectual-ization) of the magic blanket. Clinging to the threads of a lost (not merely faded) transitional object, Winnicott's patient remains forever in transit. The train jour-neys that feature in her phantasies and associations surface once more in Green's account of his own analysis of the same woman, still in search of her former analyst. In an unmistakably Winnicottian formulation, his patient—a modern

---

[73] Ibid., 218.
[74] Ibid., 220; Green compares Bion's pregnant distinction between the 'no-thing' and 'the nothing'.

Alice, on board the London–Paris shuttle—describes 'a space in which something happens like travelling, going there and coming back. What can I do to go from here to there? Who is here and who is there? And above all, how do I come back?'[75] As Green understandably remarks, 'you will easily recall how these words remind us of what Winnicott said . . .' (and of what he makes the Winnicottian baby say). Blanketless, the transitional patient clings instead to the fragile verbal signifiers that link her to an uprooted past as an evacuee: 'Who is here and who is there?' Her childhood journeys and wartime evacuation, her holiday breaks from analysis with Winnicott, her shuttling between the 'here' and 'there' of past and present, and now her unsatisfactory commute between London and Paris—all these render her, so to speak, lost in transition.

Green's analysis of 'Transitional Objects and Transitional Phenomena' and of Winnicott's former patient attempts to relocate the drives in relation both to the object and to space, mapping his own movement between London and Paris (theoretically, between Winnicott's *no rug* and his own Hegelian intuition of the negative). Green reports: 'I warned her that I didn't feel I was omnipotent enough to cure her with that kind of magic therapy.'[76] Magic surfaces again at the very moment when his signature is superimposed on Winnicott's, in what turns out to be the earliest 'not-me' signature ever inscribed. This is the sign of the *negative hand*, or 'non-drawn hand' ('what prehistorians call *negative hands*')—the representation of a hand by means of its negative outline that has been found in pre-historic cave-paintings. Klein's 'magic gesture' of painting produces a hallucinatory sign of absence (the negative handwriting on the wall). Green's Magian allusion to cave painting, the first form of artistic production, extends his intuition of the negative into the aesthetic realm, which is also the scene of proto-writing. Playing with (and on) the traces of writing—our last-ditch defence against absence—allows aesthetics to function as an 'intermediate area of experience' when it comes to the difficult task of reconciling inner and outer in psychoanalytic theory. But perhaps the last word should go to Marcel Mauss, who suggests that 'a good part of all those non-positive mystical and poetical elements in our notions of force, causation, effect and substance could be traced back to the old habits of mind in which magic was born'.[77] The magical pre-history of play can be read as a history of aesthetics lost and found in the course of its own psychoanalytic transit. Tracing the non-positivistic mystical and poetical elements in British Object Relations reveals the extent to which the poetics of play is the poetics of psychoanalysis writ large.

[75] See Green, 'The Intuition of the Negative', 213.   [76] Ibid., 216.
[77] Mauss, *A General Theory of Magic*, 144.

5

Flaying the Mind: *Milner and the Myth of Marsyas*

Skin is the moment that separates a thing from its environment, it is also the surface on which or through which we read an object, it's the moment in which the two-dimensional world meets the three-dimensional world.

Anish Kapoor, *Marsyas*[1]

THE BLANK CANVAS

Marion Milner's *The Hands of the Living God* (1969) recounts her extraordinary sixteen-year analysis of a schizophrenic woman named Susan. Starting in 1943, towards the end of the war, the analysis continued throughout the 1950s until Susan eventually married.[2] Milner's book focuses on the prolific drawings (over 4,000 in nine months) which Susan began to bring to her part-way through the analysis.[3] Susan's drawings provide the basis for a complex creative and speculative interchange between patient and analyst that is unique not only because of its length but also because of the extent of its dependence on a visual medium. This is the surface on, or through, which Milner reads Susan, and by which Susan herself is enabled to enter a three-dimensional psychic world. Inspired by Milner's earlier book, *On Not Being Able to Paint* (1950), an account of her own struggles to overcome artistic blockage, and encouraged by Milner herself, Susan discovers

[1] Anish Kapoor, *Marsyas* (London: Tate Publishing, 2002), 64.
[2] *The Hands of the Living God: An Account of a Psycho-Analytic Treatment* (London: Hogarth, 1969), 417 (*HLG*). For an account of Milner's analysis of Susan, see Naome Rader Dragstedt, 'Creative Illusions: The Theoretical and Clinical Work of Marion Milner', *Journal of Melanie Klein and Object Relations*, 16 (1998), 485–501; and for a discussion of Susan's analysis in the context of Milner's interest in artistic and mystical experience, see Janet Sayers, *Divine Therapy: Love, Mysticism and Psychoanalysis* (Oxford: Oxford University Press, 2003), 162–83.
[3] Begun in November 1943, the analysis proceeded slowly until 1950, when the burst of drawings during the seventh year of the analysis provided a new means of communication between Milner and Susan. Between 1951 and 1957, Susan's drawings continued to evolve in new directions. The analysis apparently ended around the time of her marriage to a man who had renounced the priesthood, but Milner and others continued to provide support; see Dragstedt, *Journal of Melanie Klein and Object Relations*, 16, 500.

Figure 3
Drawing
by Susan (*HLG*
fig. 32).

that spontaneous doodling frees up her unconscious.[4] Her drawings allow her to explore aspects of what Freud called the bodily ego—archaic mental processes that reflect infantile bodily experiences and precede clear boundaries between outside and inside. Susan, in fact, creates her own language for psychoanalysis: the drawing cure.[5]

Susan's first drawing is a shape like an ear, the organ that links her to the analytic process. Later she draws a shouting mouth, 'wide open to form an empty circle'—a figure of voice, or forbidden anal trumpeting (Figure 3: *HLG* fig. 32). Milner

[4] See Marion Milner, *On Not Being Able to Paint* (London: Heinemann, 1950), originally published—like Milner's earlier books, *A Life of One's Own* (London: Chatto & Windus, 1934) and *An Experiment in Leisure* (London: Chatto & Windus, 1937)—under the name Joanna Field; later republished under her own name with a preface by Anna Freud (2nd edn., London: Heinemann, 1957).

[5] Klein had made extensive use of drawings in her work with children (but not with adults), for instance her wartime analysis of Richard; see Melanie Klein, *Narrative of a Child Analysis* (1961; rpr. London, Hogarth Press, 1975). In Richard's case, Klein emphasizes the role of his drawings in relation to her, as well as the wars being waged in him and in Europe; see Mary Jacobus, 'Portrait of the Artist as a Young Dog', *First Things: The Maternal Imaginary in Literature, Art, and Psychoanalysis* (London and New York: Routledge, 1995), 173–204.

links the shouting mouth to music via the emblem of a musical stave. Music imposes order on the frightening or unruly noises (screaming or bursting) emitted by the infant at either end:

> This is the first open mouth that she has drawn and it is interesting that she has also drawn a musical stave with a series of notes and linked this by a line down from the treble clef sign to another head . . . This theme of music being introduced into the drawing in conjunction with what looks like a shouting mouth also suggested the aspect of music which is to do with the need to impose an order on frightening or disorderly noise, whether it is the noise from a screaming mouth shouting for a mother who has gone out, or the forbidden noise of bursting flatus. (*HLG* 124)

An encircling face contains the shouting mouth (circles will later form a recurrent motif, standing both for an empty mouth and for the emptiness of non-being).[6] The chrysalis-like body of a second hooded figure is 'made up of a maze of wavy lines' like an acoustic field. In another drawing, that of a cello-woman, or a woman playing herself as a musical instrument, Susan picks up the theme of the body as a container, cocooned by a series of wavy lines to form a kind of acoustic nest (Figure 4: *HLG* fig. 56). Milner speculates that these are desperate, self-made attempts to create permanent 'nests' for Susan's incomplete separateness. She comments: '[Susan] looks quite happy about being held . . . The theme of music suggests that the picture is also to do with infantile experiences of making music from her bottom with flatus' (*HLG* 162).[7] Susan is a body artist—a rude musician.

For Milner, the singing mouth, the instrumental body, and the musical bottom are phantasized aspects of the undifferentiated infant body. Unable to tell the difference between the winds of her spirit and the 'rude' winds of her body, Susan cannot (in Milner's view) 'make contact with the true winds of her spirit'. In 1943, aged 23, she had been persuaded by a woman psychiatrist to undergo Electro Convulsive Therapy (ECT, or electric shock treatment) after a breakdown led to her admission to a mental hospital.[8] Among the traumatic after-effects of the ECT was the loss of her ability to enjoy music, along with the sense that she had no back to her head, had been 'shot forward', and 'lost her background' (*HLG* 45). Since the ECT, she told Milner, music had become just a meaningless 'jingle of

---

[6] See Milner's 1975 discussion of Masud Khan's 'In Search of the Dreaming Experience', *The Suppressed Madness of Sane Men* (London and New York: Routledge, 1987), 277 (*SMSM*).

[7] Cf. 'The Communication of Primary Sensual Experience' (1955), where Milner comments on Susan's cello-woman drawing in terms of the link between musical sound and genital sexuality: 'the multiple boundary suggests the orgastic oceanic state, but the shape of it suggests a female genital' (*SMSM* 123).

[8] After a chaotic childhood, Susan left school early and then worked on a farm for four years during the war, until her first breakdown occurred. Winnicott asked Milner to take on the analysis, but not before she had undergone two episodes of ECT, persuaded by her psychiatrist. Milner later wrote to Robert Rodman, Winnicott's biographer: 'The tragedy was that, when Alice brought Susan to see them both and the house being offered her, Donald [Winnicott] said nothing, did not say "*Don't* have the ECT" '; see F. Robert Rodman, *Winnicott: Life and Work* (Cambridge, Mass.: Perseus Publishing, 2003), 135.

Figure 4 Drawing by
Susan (*HLG* fig. 56).

sound' (*HLG* 17).⁹ She only gradually comes to hear it again, whether in her head
as background music, or connected with her feelings. Eventually she takes up piano
lessons and learns to play her body again, although she is still prone to loss of feeling when she is using her hands (or feels that she is losing her hands altogether).¹⁰
But for many years, she confesses, she was frightened to go to concerts in case she
screamed out loud. 'This was interesting', Milner writes, 'because later she told me
how music used to join up inside her and cause a lovely but painful feeling, and also
that it touched a nerve at the back of her hips somewhere' (*HLG* 30). The cello-
woman's body, re-strung by music, vibrates in an inside space, causing a 'lovely but
painful feeling' that comes from the feeling of being joined up again.

In the face of its increasing use in mental hospitals at the time, Milner argues
that ECT had destructive effects, and that hostels were needed instead of hospitals
to support high-strung patients like Susan in the long term. Susan experienced a

⁹ Cf. Milner's later paraphrase: 'She said she had lost her background as well as her feelings but also
her appreciation of music, which before had been the centre of her life but now was nothing but a jan-
gle of sound' (*SMSM* 277).
¹⁰ 'She cannot put feeling into them, but notes that she made a slip of the tongue and said 'losing'
instead of 'using' her hands' (*HLG* 315).

succession of temporary homes in which she was an unpaid worker, before eventually achieving a limited emotional and economic independence. Along with Winnicott, who also campaigned publicly against the use of ECT at the same period, Milner accepted Susan's need to regress to extreme dependence on her analyst.[11] But *The Hands of the Living God* resembles Milner's other books in recording a psychoanalytic experiment of her own. It charts the growth of Milner's ideas about the body and about creativity in tandem with Susan's gradual movement towards independence. Milner began by working within a Kleinian frame, analysing Klein's grandson under her supervision and in close contact with Klein as a supervisor.[12] During her early years with Susan, she was having weekly discussions with Klein, and at first approached the analysis in terms of Klein's well-defined theories about infantile phantasy.[13] But she soon discovered that Susan was unenlightened by her attempts at Kleinian interpretation. When Milner tried to use the concept of fragmentation or projective identification of parts of herself into others, for instance, Susan bafflingly 'continued to maintain that neither she nor I was there' (*HLG* 24). This brought Kleinian interpretation to a halt. Only gradually did Susan's own evolving drawings prove able to unlock her previously inaccessible bodily phantasies, while allowing Milner to develop her psychoanalytically based theories of creativity.[14]

As the years went by, Susan's analysis was shaped less by Kleinian theory than by Milner's close professional and personal collaboration with Winnicott—who (to complicate matters) was analysing Milner herself in the immediate post-war years, while Susan lived under his roof.[15] Milner ends by offering Susan (and herself) a

[11] For Winnicott's campaign against the use of physical treatments such as leucotomy and ECT, see his letters to the *Lancet* in April 1943 and the *British Medical Journal* in December 1943, which provoked a sustained discussion; Winnicott also organized a symposium on shock treatment at the British Psycho-Analytical Society in 1944. His letters and papers opposing the use of ECT are included in D. W. Winnicott, *Psycho-Analytic Explorations*, ed. Clare Winnicott, Ray Shepherd, and Madeleine Davis (Cambridge, Mass.: Harvard University Press, 1989), 515–41.

[12] See 'The Role of Illusion in Symbol Formation' (1952), *SMSM* 83–113, and see also Phyllis Grosskurth, *Melanie Klein: Her World and her Work* (Cambridge, Mass.: Harvard University Press, 1986), 395–6; the child whose case Klein supervised was Michael Clyne (see Ch. 4).

[13] See *HLG* 24. Milner was drawn initially to psychoanalysis after reading Susan Isaacs's books on children and hearing lectures in 1938 by Winnicott, who became her husband's analyst; her own (first) analyst was Sylvia Payne (*HLG* xxvii), although she later entered analysis with Clifford Scott after a brief interlude with Winnicott.

[14] Among other influences on her thinking, Milner pays tribute to that of Anton Ehrenzweig, whose critique of *An Experiment in Leisure* prompted his phrase, 'creative surrender' (*HLG* 262). Milner acknowledges both Ehrenzweig's earlier *The Psycho-Analysis of Aesthetic Hearing and Perception* (London: Routledge, 1953), and *The Hidden Order of Art* (London: Weidenfeld & Nicolson, 1967) which she read while writing the last chapters of her own book (see *HLG* 410). She also refers to (and takes issue with) Kris's co-authored study of a schizophrenic artist; 'The Function of Drawings and the Meaning of the "Creative Spell" in a Schizophrenic Artist', in Ernst Kris, *Psychoanalytic Explorations in Art* (London: George Allen & Unwin, 1953), 151–69.

[15] For an account of Milner's relationship with Winnicott, including their analytic relationship during the early period of Susan's analysis, see Rodman, *Winnicott: Life and Work*, 132–41. Susan's living arrangement with the Winnicotts continued until their marriage ended in 1949, precipitating another breakdown and a move to a different home.

combined Kleinian and Winnicottian life-myth: Susan had never been able to accept in herself the ruthless love and greed of infancy in relation to a confused and confusing mother; hence 'her basic myth of feeling she had ruined her mother' (*HLG* 411).[16] Meanwhile, Milner herself had developed new ways of working based on her own bodily perceptions and experiences. Her approach included an emphasis on self-surrender, reverie, or what she called 'contemplative action' (*HLG* 263), and even an element of mysticism (by which she meant, as she later explained, 'just living').[17] *The Hands of the Living God* puts bodily experience at the centre of psychoanalytic and creative experience, making the body at once the founding site and the dominant trope of psychic life. Throughout, Milner's emphasis on skin and sound articulates the action of the psyche in terms of surfaces, interiors, and orifices. Her model of psychic interiority superficially resembles Klein's, at least in taking for granted the defining relation of inside and outside. But she departs from Klein in important ways. Whereas the Kleinian inner world is built up through complex processes of introjection, jostling with primitive object relations, phantasies, and anxieties, for Milner the space has first to be empty before it can be filled.[18] Emptiness and un-integration represent crucial stages in creativity and psychic development.

Kristeva (the pre-eminent theorist of the feminine *chora*) hypes up the Kleinian maternal space as 'a sublimation of the cavity, a metamorphosis of the womb, and a variation on female receptivity'.[19] By contrast, Lacan evokes a monster-filled void when he refers to Klein backhandedly as 'an inspired gut-butcher' ('*la tripière*', or tripe-monger), an operator who goes for the guts.[20] Milner's metamorphosis of the womb simply empties it, rather than either sublimating it or making it

---

[16] See *HLG* 398, and cf. Klein on the depressive position in 'Mourning and its Relation to Manic Depressive States' (1940): 'The object which is being mourned is the mother's breast and all that the breast and the milk have come to stand for in the infant's mind . . . these are felt by the baby to be lost, and lost as a result of his own uncontrollably greedy and destructive phantasies and impulses against his mother's breasts' (*LGR* 345), and cf. D. W. Winnicott's account of the infant's primitive ruthlessness, 'Primitive Emotional Development' (1945), *Through Pediatrics to Psychoanalysis: Collected Papers* (1958; rpr. New York: Bruner/Mazel, 1992), 154–5.

[17] See Milner, 'The Sense in Nonsense: Freud and Blake's *Job*' (1956), *SMSM* 168–91, and 'Psychoanalysis and Art' (1956), *SMSM* 192–215. For Milner's dislike of being called a mystic, see Dragstedt, *Journal of Melanie Klein and Object Relations*, 16, 522.

[18] See Klein's definition of the internal world and internal objects in 'Mourning and its Relation to Manic Depressive States' (1940): 'The baby, having incorporated his parents, feels them to be live people inside his body in the concrete way in which deep unconscious phantasies are experienced—they are, in his mind, "internal" or "inner" objects, as I have termed them. Thus an inner world is being built up in the child's unconscious mind, corresponding to his actual experiences and the impressions he gains from people and the external world, and yet altered by his own phantasies and impulses' (*LGR* 345).

[19] Julia Kristeva, *Melanie Klein*, trans. Ross Guberman (New York: Columbia University Press, 2001), 246.

[20] 'Indeed, the child filled this void with monsters—a crowd of monsters known to us, since a diviner with a child's eyes, an inspired gut-butcher, has catalogued them for us—projecting those monsters into the womb of the nursing mother'; see Kristeva, *Melanie Klein*, 230, and Lacan, *Écrits* (Paris: Editions du Seuil, 1966), 750–1.

monstrous. As if she needs to regress to a time and space that precede thought in order to make contact with Susan, she finds that she is unable to express herself in the psychoanalytic terms available to her. Adrian Stokes writes of an all-embracing element—'the stage, silence, the blank canvas'— waiting to be cathected as the artist's medium.[21] For Milner, emptiness, blankness, and silence, 'whether empty unstructured space or the empty unstructured time that is silence', exist prior to conceptualization. This is also the threshold that provides the 'growing point of psycho-analytic theory and practice' (*HLG* 411). Milner advocates a 'syncretistic vision' or Piagetian breadth and comprehensiveness which she wishfully attributes to both child and artist, and attempts to emulate in her own work. Combining 'the ambiguity of dreaming with the tension of being fully awake' (*HLG* 420), syncretic vision implies both tolerance of paradox and freedom from analytic preconceptions.[22] Milner's home-made, wondering way of expressing herself gives form to Susan's inchoate states of mind. But it also introduces a new strand into Klein's theoretical legacy.[23]

Whereas the content of bodily phantasy and mental anxiety forms the basic narrative of Kleinian psychic life, Milner imagines a psychic container that is brought into being by skin and sound.[24] The introjection of a skin-container becomes the necessary step preceding unconscious phantasy and ego-functioning. Without something to hold internal objects, there can be no inner world for the fragile, unintegrated neonate. The psychic container has to be imagined retrospectively, prior to being filled—emptiness imagined in positive rather than negative terms.[25] In an essay called 'Primitive Emotional Development' (1945), belonging to the same period during which Milner was embarking on her analysis of Susan, Winnicott posits the existence of a 'primary unintegrated state', and insists on the caretaker's vital role in providing 'repeated quiet experiences of body-care'—feeding,

---

[21] 'Now the artist or would-be artist may be distinguished by the extent to which he cathects a medium . . . In art an all-embracing element, the stage, silence, the blank canvas, can serve as the sleep of which dreams, though wakeful and rapid, are the guardians'; quoted in Milner's 'Glossary' (*HLG* 417), from Adrian Stokes, 'Form in Art' (1952); see Melanie Klein, Paula Heimann, and R. E. Money-Kyrle (eds.), *New Directions in Psychoanalyis* (London: Tavistock Publications, 1955), 408.

[22] Definitions drawn from Milner's 'Glossary' at the end of *HLG*; her sources, besides Jean Piaget, are aesthetic (Ehrenzweig, *The Hidden Order of Art* and *The Psychology of Aesthetic Hearing and Perception*).

[23] In a letter to John O. Wisdom of 26 October 1964, Winnicott called Milner 'the one who has reverie in her presentation of her ideas' (adding that 'although she is modest she is one of the ones we have who has brains'); see F. Robert Rodman, *The Spontaneous Gesture: Selected Letters of D. W. Winnicott* (Cambridge, Mass.: Harvard University Press, 1987), 144. Contemporary psychoanalytic writers influenced by Milner's ideas include André Green and Christopher Bollas.

[24] For the prolonged struggle waged over 'internal objects' that became the hallmark of Kleinian thinking and vocabulary, see Pearl King and Riccardo Steiner (eds.), *The Freud–Klein Controversies 1941–45* (London and New York: Routledge, 1991), *passim*, and especially Paula Heimann, 'Some Aspects of the Role of Introjection and Projection in Early Development' (1943), ibid., 515–25.

[25] Cf. Milner's comment on the empty undifferentiated space of dreaming: 'So here what seemed to be emerging was the possibility of there being something positive about emptiness, nothingness, whether empty unstructured space or the empty unstructured time that is silence' (*SMSM* 277).

cleaning, holding, caressing. The experience of loving care (what Winnicott calls the maternal environment) coincides with instinctual experiences, building up 'the feeling that one's person is in one's body'.[26] Migrating into Continental psychoanalysis, the idea of the skin-container takes on a life of its own. For instance, it shapes Didier Anzieu's influential concept of the psychic envelope in *The Skin-Ego* (*Le Moi-peau*).[27] Among his case-histories is the patient he names 'Marsyas'—a reference to Ovid's account in the *Metamorphoses* of the flaying of Marsyas, a rude country-style musician who had the temerity to challenge Apollo to a musical competition: his crude pipes, discarded by Athena, versus Apollo's lyre (wind versus strings; lungs versus guts). Marsyas's hideous punishment for losing the competition was to be hung up and flayed like an animal—'his body . . . was all one raw wound. Blood flowed everywhere.' The sympathetic tears shed by the satyrs, nymphs, and shepherds of Olympus became the river that bears his name.[28] From antiquity to the present, the myth has inspired accounts that emphasize aesthetic judgement. Tony Harrison's vigorously demotic retelling of the Marsyas myth in *The Trackers of Oxyrhynchus* (1990) recasts Ovid's story as a political satire played out in terms of high versus low art, the aesthetic class-transgression of a half-animal pitted against ruthless Apollonian cultural supremacy: 'Marsyas suffered his terrible flaying | For a bit of innocent *aulos* playing . . . . He'd crossed the bounds. | Half-brutes aren't allowed to make beautiful sounds.'[29]

Harrison makes Apollonian aesthetics a mask for cruelty. Like Marsyas, Susan (a working-class woman) has been turned inside out by her electric flaying and lacks a protective skin; as Milner puts it, 'the world is no longer outside her' (*HLG* 15). Hers is both a skin-problem and a space-problem. The Marsyas myth has recently been re-examined in terms of the relation between inside and out, as an exploration of sculpted space. Anish Kapoor's Tate Modern installation, *Marsyas* (2002) uses the capaciousness of skin to probe the boundaries and limits of spatial

---

[26] See Winnicott, *Through Pediatrics to Psychoanalysis*, 150–1.

[27] Didier Anzieu, *The Skin-Ego*, trans. Chris Turner (1985; New Haven: Yale University Press, 1989). For a critique of Anzieu's 'interpretatively versatile' pan-pellicularism and his therapeutically oriented model of the skin-container, see Steven Connor, *The Book of Skin* (London: Reaktion Books, 2004), 38–9, 49–50, 91–2. Connor's wide-ranging cultural study of the modern meanings of skin includes visual representations of flaying, such as Titian's *The Flaying of Marsyas*, among the many forms of skin's scarification and decoration; see ibid., 65–6.

[28] *The Metamorphoses of Ovid*, trans. Mary M. Innes (Harmondsworth: Penguin, 1955), 145. Ovid's narrative continues: 'his nerves were exposed, unprotected, his veins pulsed with no skin to cover them. It was possible to count his throbbing organs, and the chambers of his lungs, clearly visible within his breast.'

[29] Tony Harrison, *The Trackers of Oxyrhynchus* (London: Faber & Faber, 1990), 124 (National Theatre text). For the relation between satyr play and tragedy (Harrison also wrote the text for the National Theatre's *Oresteia*), see John Kerrigan, *Revenge Tragedy: Aeschylus to Armageddon* (Oxford: Clarendon Press, 1996), 67–70, and, for the ironies (intended and unintended) of Harrison's protest against the inequities of 'culture', see Adrian Poole's 1999 Open University paper, 'Harrison and Marsyas' (http://www.open.ac.uk/Arts/Colq99/Poole.htm).

form (Figures 5a, 5b).[30] His vast pellicular construction creates new volumes, new forms of enclosure and opening; a new kind of interiority linked to subjectivity and surface. Along with other references to skinning, Kapoor invokes Titian's late painting, *The Flaying of Marsyas* (*c.*1570–6)—at once a graphic display of the body in pain and a strangely composed (in every sense) meditation on the disturbing relation between Apollonian beauty and cruelty (Figure 6).[31] Behind Titian's painting lies a complex tissue of interwoven Classical and Renaissance traditions involving aesthetic judgements about high and low art, Christianized allegories of cleansing through suffering and healing, not to mention the Classical competition between chaotic wind instrument and harmonious strings.[32] But *The Flaying of Marsyas* can also be read as an anatomy of artistic subjectivity, as well as the brutality or panic aroused in the artist when confronted by space. Pointing to its 'florid sadism' and 'uncontestable gruesomeness', Frank Stella has written that it 'reveals the blood-filled sinew and bone of pictorial technique, showing us how difficult it is for the artist to nurture and manipulate the body of his creation without mutilating it.'[33] The body becomes the focus for a problem about space. Stella argues that, confronted by the horror of emptiness (*horror vacui*), surface and space combine to engender the terrifying image of flaying.

The visceral cruelty in Titian's representation of the Marsyas myth constitutes an unsolved psychoanalytic enigma. But it also provides a touchstone for the convergence of psychoanalytic and aesthetic theory around the trope of the body

---

[30] For 'texturology' (a theory or philosophy of the surface as skin), see Gilles Deleuze, *The Fold: Leibnitz and the Baroque*, trans. Tom Conley (1988; Minneapolis: University of Minneapolis Press, 1993). Drawing on Deleuze, Mieke Bal writes that the fold 'insists on surface and materiality, a materialism that promotes a realistic visual rhetoric in its wake', serving to implicate the subject via its relation to a surface viewed as skin; see Mieke Bal, *Quoting Caravaggio: Contemporary Art, Preposterous History* (Chicago: University of Chicago Press, 1999), 30.

[31] See Kapoor, *Marsyas*, 61. In her evocative account of the relation between Kapoor's *Marsyas* and Titian's, Marina Warner writes of the way in which the Marsyas myth resonates with Kapoor's sculptural concern with 'the translation of forms from plane to volume, from line to surface, the tension between contour and space, the boundary of inner and outer bodies, [and] the interdependency of bulk and membrane'; see Marina Warner, 'Anish Kapoor: The Perforate Self, or Nought is Not Nought', *Parkett*, 69 (Spring 2004), 126–39.

[32] See Philipp Fehl, 'The Punishment of Marsyas', *Decorum and Wit: The Poetry of Venetian Painting* (Vienna: IRSA, 1992), 130–49. The painting belongs to a long tradition involving the reconciliation of music in its various forms, including the chaos of wind or pipe versus the harmony of strings or lyre. For a comprehensive illustrated account of the changing representations, iconography, and allegorical meanings of the Marsyas myth from classical antiquity to Titian, including the role of Midas as erroneous judge of the competition, see also Edith Wyss, *The Myth of Apollo and Marsyas in the Art of the Italian Renaissance* (Newark, NJ: University of Delaware Press, 1996), esp. 133–41. Wyss's reading spans the cosmic harmony of the exalted musician and the melancholic figure of Midas (Titian himself?), wrestling with the problems of suffering and death; Marsyas (silene rather than satyr) will be raised to the celestial realm—cleansed through his ordeal—via Apollo's cruel sacrifice, while the despondent mind of Midas/Titian is healed by the strains of celestial music: 'harnonia est discordia concors' (ibid., 139).

[33] Frank Stella, *Working Space* (Cambridge, Mass.: Harvard University Press, 1986), 100. Stella's reflection on the role of brutality in Titian's *The Flaying of Marsyas* relates it specifically to the artist's panic in the face of pictorial surface and space.

(a)

(b)

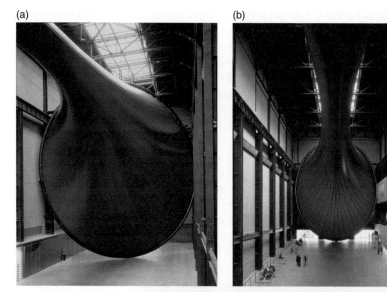

Figures 5a and 5b
Anish Kapoor, *Marsyas*
(2002); Tate Modern.

Figure 6 Titian, *The
Flaying of Marsyas*
(*c.*1570–6); State
Museum, Kromeriz,
Czech Republic.

turned inside out—half-human, brutalized, poised between animality and
transcendence. The myth of the flaying of Marsyas can be read as an inverted figure
for the forcible (de)humanization of the embodied subject that is among the
penalties paid for the acquisition of psychic interiority, if not also for aesthetics,

morality, and language.[34] Perhaps there can be no human subjectivity without the cut that demarcates the boundaries of the non-human and severs the mind from the body, just as there can be no art without an element of the destructiveness evoked by Stella. Equally, torture and therapy converge on the body. This ambiguity haunts *The Hands of the Living God*, which inserts Susan into an institutional formation—psychoanalysis—where the schizophrenic is supposedly humanized by the discipline of speech.

THE MUSICAL ENVELOPE

Current theories of psychic space tend to be derived from structuralist or linguistic models, or, more recently (in Klein-derived accounts), from melancholia.[35] But one strand of thinking about psychic space within British Object Relations psychoanalysis is distinguished by its attempt to theorize the relations between body and mind in terms of primary skin sensation, and even in terms of sound. Esther Bick's foundational ideas, along with the infant observation training which she developed at the Tavistock Clinic from the late 1940s onwards, in tandem with John Bowlby, shaped generations of clinical practitioners with its emphasis on understanding the infant's state of mind through its impact on the mother and, indirectly, on the observer. Like Milner, Bick had been supervised by Melanie Klein (who was also her analyst).[36] Although hampered by difficulties in committing her intuitions to paper—she found no words adequate to describe what she sensed

[34] For a persuasive analysis of *The Flaying of Marsyas* as cultural representation, see David Richards, 'The Satyr Anatomised: Venice 1570', *Masks of Difference: Cultural Representations in Literature, Anthropology and Art* (Cambridge: Cambridge University Press, 1995), 9–36. Connecting flaying to the discourse of musical bands, Richards concludes: 'The image presents us with a construction, a making of the world of the other which forms around the body of the wild creature. The body is subjected to a violence which creates art, music, rapture, aggrandizement, sacrifice, triumph, moral order, evolutionary schemes and knowledge, all of which are produced by the Apollonian designation of difference' (ibid., 36).

[35] '[T]hought is what allows *psychic interiority* to take shape, a depth that is at first grieving, then relieving or joyful' (Kristeva, *Melanie Klein*, 246). For a post-Kleinian emphasis on the centrality of melancholia in creating psychic interiority, see also Judith Butler, 'Psychic Inceptions', *The Psychic Life of Power* (Stanford, Calif.: Stanford University Press, 1997), 167–98, and 'Moral Sadism and Doubting One's Own Love: Kleinian Reflections on Melancholia', in John Phillips and Lyndsey Stonebridge (eds.), *Reading Melanie Klein* (London and New York: Routledge, 1998), 178–89.

[36] Bick had studied behavioural child psychology in Vienna under Charlotte Bühler before her arrival in England as a refugee from Nazi Germany. She became an analyst after the Second World War, having entered analysis first with Michael Balint and then with Melanie Klein; see Andrew Briggs, 'The Life and Work of Esther Bick', in Briggs (ed.), *Surviving Space: Papers on Infant Observation* (London: Karnac Books, 2002), pp. xix–xxx. For a first-hand account of Bick, see Joan Symington, 'Mrs Bick and infant observation', ibid., 105–16, and, for an overview of Bick's work, see Janet Sayers, *Kleinians: Psychoanalysis Inside Out* (Cambridge: Polity, 2000), 135–46. Sayers (ibid., 88) notes that Bick analysed Adrian Stokes's daughter, Ariadne, of whom Stokes wrote in his poem, 'Schizophrenic Girl': 'Hugging yourself to preserve a skin | That barely separates | Barely resists the air . . .'; Peter Robinson (ed.), *With All the Views: The Collected Poems of Adrian Stokes* (Manchester: Carcanet, 1981), 124.

in infants—Bick extended Klein's ideas to rethink the very earliest period of
infancy. Slender as her written output is, her work provides the conceptual basis
for viewing internal space as the primary locus of psychic life. In Bick's words, the
neonate's introjection of its skin (rather than the *content* of infantile anxieties, as
Klein had emphasized) 'gives rise to the fantasy of internal and external spaces'.[37]
This initial introjection is needed in order to defend the fragile infant personality
against the ever-present threat of falling to pieces. Bick speculates that the skin
functions (or fails to function) as a container from the very earliest stages of
infancy, creating the passive experience of being held together. Her ideas offer a
model for the primitive process by which the very first object is introjected, creating
the space in which subsequent introjections may be lodged, and making room for
the teeming complexities of the Kleinian cavity.

In Bick's account, the containing function of the skin is matched by catastrophic anxieties about disintegration. The process she describes not only precedes the rudimentary structures of the ego presupposed by Kleinian theory but
also (in its passivity) differs from the destructive mental processes analysed by
Klein herself, and later by Bion and Rosenfeld in their work with schizophrenics.
Nor is Bick's passive model identical to the Winnicottian infant's active gathering
of instinctual experience in the context of maternal care and the need for a 'holding' environment. In 'The Experience of the Skin in Early Object Relations'
(1968), Bick describes the unintegrated infant's need for a focus in order to bind
its inchoate personality together. The nipple closes the hole represented by the
mouth, creating a space which can be thought of as capable of holding things. The
function of the skin is to provide a boundary that makes it possible for the infant
to experience itself as integrated. Bick writes that 'in its most primitive form the
parts of the personality are felt to have no binding force among themselves and
must therefore be held together in a way that is experienced by them passively, by
the skin functioning as a boundary'. In the absence of the boundary provided by a
containing object, the infant searches for a substitute:

> The need for a containing object would seem, in the infantile unintegrated state, to pro-
> duce a frantic search for an object—a light, a voice, a smell, or other sensual object—which
> can hold the attention and thereby be experienced, momentarily at least, as holding the
> parts of the personality together. The optimal object is the nipple in the mouth, together
> with the holding and talking and familiar smelling mother.[38]

For the infant, this psychic skin—at once a border and an object created by the
caretaker in the process of handling, feeding, and vocalizing—is felt to hold the
body together. Only then can the concept of space within the self arise, and with it
the introjection of internal objects.

Using the counter-transferential experience of the observer, infant observation
provides a way to account for primitive experiences which are, strictly speaking,

[37] 'The Experience of the Skin in Early Object Relations' (1968), in Briggs (ed.), *Surviving Space*, 55–6.
[38] Ibid., 55, 56.

unobservable. Descriptions of mother–infant interactions based on Bick's theories often refer to the coruscating aspects of babies' skin experience. Infants scrunch and attack their own skin, redden with rage and distress at frustration, stiffen or go limp in response to insensitive handling.[39] In the absence of an external object capable of binding it together, Bick's half-flayed infants resort to increasingly frantic and confused projective identifications, or else strive desperately to create a so-called 'second skin', a secondary carapace or body armour. Object-dependence is replaced with 'pseudo-dependence' on 'the inappropriate use of certain mental functions, or perhaps innate talents, for the purpose of creating a substitute for this skin container function'.[40] Bick suggests that continuous sensuous experience—a light or a sound (for instance, a washing machine)—may be clung to as a kind of supplement, by eyes or ears used as suction pads, on the model of a baby's mouth adhering to the nipple. She coins the phrase 'adhesive identification' to describe the peculiar 'stickiness' of adhesion to maternal object, caretaker, or analyst. Sticking to the object becomes a defence against what she calls 'the catastrophic anxiety of falling-into-space'—a vertiginous free-fall associated with the trauma of separateness and discontinuity, sickening 'anxieties of the dead-end, falling through space, life-spilling-out variety'.[41] Bick's observations of babies trembling, quivering, and sneezing at the loss of the nipple, or clinging with eyes, mouth, and ears to caretaker or analyst, provide poignant testimony to the need for what Winnicott (in a different theoretical register) calls a 'holding' environment.[42]

Bick's work with infants both underpins and anticipates Didier Anzieu's later account of the psychic skin envelope in *The Skin Ego*, along with his development of a related concept, the 'sound envelope'.[43] Anzieu articulates the bodily ego's relation to psychic space in terms of breath. Breathing, he argues, is one of the

[39] For an infant's use and abuse of its skin, see, for instance, the infant observation recorded in Judith Jackson and Eleanor Nowers, 'The Skin in Early Object Relations Revisited', ibid., 208–26.

[40] Ibid., 56.

[41] Esther Bick, 'Further Considerations on the Function of the Skin in Early Object Relations' (1986), ibid., 71, 70. Compare the vertiginous sensation of 'falling for ever' included by Winnicott in the phenomenology of an unremembered primitive breakdown.

[42] Winnicott uses the concept of 'holding' from the late 1950s onwards with reference both to the baby's individual handling (the mother's arms) and to the 'holding environment' (maternal, familial, analytic); see Jan Abram, *The Language of Winnicott: A Dictionary of Winnicott's Use of Words* (London: Karnac Books, 1996), 183–9. Bick counteracts the tendency to see Kleinians as giving insufficient weight to individual variations in maternal care, as well as emphasizing the infant's conservatism and its need for stabilizing support from the outside world in the face of catastrophic anxiety; see *Surviving Space*, 71.

[43] Kaja Silverman argues that the emphasis by Anzieu and others (including Kristeva) on the maternal voice as sound envelope 'grows out of a powerful cultural fantasy' which psychoanalytic theory shares with classic cinema, the retroactive fantasy of infantile containment: 'the image of a child held within the environment or sphere of the mother's voice'. For Silverman, this ambivalent fantasy 'attests to the divided nature of subjectivity, and . . . underscores the fact that pleasure for one psychic system almost invariably means unpleasure for another psychic system'; see *The Acoustic Mirror: The Female Voice in Psychoanalysis and Cinema* (Bloomington, Ind.: Indiana University Press, 1988), 72–3. Compare the ambivalent fantasy in Titian's *The Flaying of Marsyas*, where one man's music is another man's torture.

primary ways in which the nascent self acquires interiority: 'The auditory sensations produced when sounds are made are associated with the respiratory sensations which give the Self a sense of being a volume which empties and re-fills itself, and prepare that Self for its structuring in relation to the third dimension of space (orientation and distance) and to the temporal dimensions.'[44] Without breathing, one would not acquire the sensation of inhabiting the dimensionality of either space or time. For Anzieu, breath structures the third dimension, orienting the body and giving it a sense of volume, along with a psychical sound-space 'within which there are rumblings, echoes, and resonances'.[45] The body becomes an acoustic container that empties and refills—the wind-making, voice-producing lungs, an air-cavity that constantly collapses and refills like a bellows, resonating with potential sound. What Anzieu inclusively terms 'the bucco-pharyngeal cavity' plays an essential role in the expression of emotion. The gasps, gurgles, wails, and howls of infancy are the prototypes of affective expression; the infant comes crying into a world where its earliest vocalizations are those of hunger, anger, pain, or frustration. As Anzieu memorably describes it, alimentary and digestive spaces 'turn the body into a resonant cavern whose noises are all the more disquieting for the baby since they cannot be localized'.[46] Anzieu's baby is haunted by the sounds it makes.

Bathed in a sound bath prior even to birth (the gurglings and rhythmic pulsations of the mother's insides), the infant is most effectively soothed by the mother's voice. With luck, and love, an initially disorganized cacophony shapes itself into a lulling musical continuity, 'music made up of sounds rich in harmonics, music properly so-called—the human voice speaking or singing'.[47] From the very earliest phase, Anzieu writes, 'the Self forms as a sound envelope through the experience of a bath of sounds (concomitant with the experience of nursing)'.[48] As the cries of basic need give way in the early weeks to wails designed to capture the mother's attention, the first intentional sounds—the first communication—establish the context for acoustic interaction with the mother's voice. Babbling, playing with sounds, differentiating and elaborating them, passing them back and forth between baby and mother, all pave the way for vocalizations that are imitative and reciprocal. Like the skin-ego, the sound bath has two surfaces (two 'ears'), one turned towards the outer world and the other towards the inner—'creator and receiver both', like the Wordsworthian infant of *The Prelude* (1805, *Prelude*, ii. 273). For Anzieu, this two-way exchange creates the first spatio-auditory image of the body and enables the fusional relationship with the mother which paves the way for later, imaginary forms of fusion and the emergence of object-relating. Alluding to Winnicott's idea of the mother's mirroring face, Anzieu calls this 'the sound mirror', the sounding-board that is provided by the mother's song-like vocal accompaniment.[49]

[44] Anzieu, *The Skin-Ego*, 157.   [45] Ibid., 171.   [46] Ibid., 162–3.
[47] Ibid., 170–1.   [48] Ibid., 167.
[49] See D. W. Winnicott, 'Mirror-role of Mother and Family in Child Development' (1967), *Playing and Reality* (1971; rpr. London and New York: Routledge, 1991), 111–18. Anzieu's account of the sound envelope ends with a story set on Mars, 'La Vallée des échos' by Gérard Klein (1966),

Anzieu interweaves the myth of Marsyas with the myth of Narcissus and Echo, invoking the deadly defusion of drives when the image or voice returned to the subject is only that of its own anxiety, disintegration, or unutterable distress. The voice of the schizophrenic child's mother, Anzieu suggests, is typically monotonous or invasive in tone—not mirroring or enveloping, but impersonal, discordant, and rupturing. A meaningless wall of words or silence reduces the child to nothingness. Instead of finding himself in his mother's voice, the patient Anzieu names 'Marsyas' feels irrelevant, ignored, or invaded, lost in an echo-chamber of meaningless sound and condemned to chaotic and undifferentiated noise. What would it be like to lose the auditory and tactile connection between inner and outer? Perhaps this is the plight of Titian's Marsyas, suspended from his tree, reduced to the level of an animal, lacking proper boundaries to the self—just raw meat. Yet Titian's dead, dangling Marsyas appears drugged into passive quiescence, as if anaesthetized by exquisite music beyond our hearing. The bloody activity focused on his strung-up body takes place to a string accompaniment performed by an angelic musician on the then-fashionable 'lira da braccio'. The sound envelope— Titian's consolatory fiction—takes the edge off the flayer's knife. Tony Harrison comments satirically on this (an)aestheticization of pain, when he insists on the politics of cruelty that accompany Apollo's virtuoso performance: 'Whenever the racked and the anguished cry | There's always a lyre-player standing by.'[50] We should resist aesthetic palliation.

But the same myth can have different meanings folded into it. The idea of the musical envelope developed by Edith Lecourt, an Anzieu-inspired music therapist, does not imply that cover-up and music occupy the same ambiguous domain. Instead, she suggests that the absence of boundaries inherent in sound can become a spur to mental activity. Lecourt writes that 'sound reaches us from everywhere, it surrounds us, goes through us, and, in addition to our voluntary sonorous productions, sounds even escape surreptitiously from our own bodies'.[51] Sonorous perception and sound-making are characterized not only by their omnipresent simultaneity but, importantly, by their *lack of concreteness* (her emphasis). This makes the sound envelope, since it lacks physical support, 'the very type of psychic construction'.[52] What is 'typical' about sonorous experience, so defined, is the requirement it imposes for mental elaboration. Sonorousness functions for Lecourt as 'a veritable acoustic womb', and even as the memory of an imaginary choreography of weightlessness that is involved in being carried as an

---

which invents the idea of audio-phonic sound fossils: 'a voice, or rather the murmur of a million voices. The uproar of a whole people speaking incredible, incomprehensible words'; see Anzieu, *The Skin-Ego*, 173.

[50] Harrison, *The Trackers of Oxyrhynchus*, 65. For the conversion of pain into a fiction of absolute power, see Elaine Scarry, *The Body in Pain: The Making and Unmaking of the World* (New York: Oxford University Press, 1985), 27–59.

[51] Edith Lecourt, 'The Musical Envelope', in Didier Anzieu (ed.), *Psychic Envelopes*, trans. Daphne Briggs (London: Karnac Books, 1990), 211.   [52] Ibid., 211, 212.

infant.[53] The musical mother contains or dreams the baby's unruly affects, its uncontrolled projections and tendency to disintegrate. For Daniel Stern, the rhythmic vocal exchange between infant and mother—cognitive and affective cue and response—has a regulatory function.[54] For Lecourt, the interchange gives rise not only to the earliest forms of mental organization but to the fragile yet persistent aural memories connecting us to the past. As Anzieu had done, Lecourt stresses that the first cries are heard both inside and outside, doubling and distancing vocal production at its source. The 'bucco-pharyngeal cavity' becomes an omni-sonorous cavity that now includes nose and ears as well as the primitive cavity of the mouth, the baby's original cradle of perception.

The capacity of this enlarged vocal cavity to vibrate with something other than speech—with pure, wordless songs and cries—identifies it as 'an altogether privi-leged zone within the sonorous bath, a zone that has the advantage of offering a pre-form for sonorous experience'.[55] Lecourt argues that this pre-form provides the basis for a psychic container. The mythic prototype or pre-form is the cave of Pan, resounding and echoing with the sounds of the so-called 'noisy' god (aban-doned by his mother at birth, like Apollo). Pan creates the sound illusions that create panic in individuals and groups, inducing confusion, the sense of invasion by persecutory noise, loss or disintegration of the self. Rough music has its down-side (an aspect acted out by Harrison's ghetto-blasting satyrs in *The Trackers of Oxyrhynchus*). In Ovid's *Metamorphoses*, Marsyas clamours indignantly, 'Why are you stripping me from myself? Never again, I promise! Playing a pipe is not worth this!'[56] Lecourt's deployment of the Pan myth homes in on the destructive potential of sheer noise or pandemonium. Hollow pipes—like skin and guts that are struck, plucked, or scraped to make music—allude to the scene of musical expression in its earliest forms. Milner's cello-woman is also a sound-box, her strings made of her own guts, shouting and farting in infant phantasy. Can a rude musician become a polite one? Lecourt describes an autistic child, David, magically trans-ported by the sound of low G on the piano. He invents a game of communicating with the therapist by means of imitation farts, which she playfully returns. David, she says, feels half-flayed. The backside of his body is vulnerable, because this reverse 'face' is subjected to uncontrollable noises or enforced silence. Eventually his mouth, at first 'an opening that did not seem to belong to him', begins to close around musical instruments and toys, and then around sounds and words. Transferring sound from behind to mentalized mouth enables other kinds of control and co-ordination. Like Marsyas (whom Apollo forces to invert his instrument so

[53] Edith Lecourt, 'The Musical Envelope', in Didier Anzieu (ed.), *Psychic Envelopes*, trans. Daphne Briggs (London: Karnac Books, 1990), 213. Lecourt refers to the experience of feeling 'borne, transported, lulled or dancing, in a movement that has no grip on reality, is "for free" and for pleasure', relating it to the gesticulations of a baby being carried and held.

[54] For the debate between psychoanalytic and behaviouristic accounts of mother–infant relating, and a range of responses to their theoretical differences, see the argument between André Green and Daniel Stern, *Clinical and Observational Psychoanalytic Research: Roots of a Controversy* (London: Karnac Books, 2000).   [55] *Psychic Envelopes*, 216.

[56] *The Metamorphoses of Ovid*, 145.

that he can only produce breathy wind sounds), David has tried to play his instrument upside down.[57]

Lecourt's account of aural hallucination suggests how internal sounds are progressively built on and perfected as a form of music. She quotes work on the auditory hallucinations of the deaf, 'subjective ear noises' which 'follow an ascending scale, from simple droning to songs' and voices 'formed from it like a sort of transformation or perfection'.[58] Some of these hallucinating patients report hearing a distant choir, or an isolated voice, just as Susan reports hearing music in her head. Lecourt interprets these aural hallucinations in terms of the need, even in deafness, to recreate the infant's original audiophonic sound bath. When the deaf hear voices, they are experiencing a form of aesthetic pleasure rather than paranoia. What unheard melody, then, might Marsyas be hearing as he hangs slack-jawed from his tree, released from the undifferentiated droning of his own disastrous concert? The hallucinatory sound bath—so Lecourt argues—recapitulates our pleasurable immersion in the musico-verbal environment in which we first begin to shape our mental experiences through the interchange of inside and out. Titian's *The Flaying of Marsyas* could be read as an allegory of the flaying of the senses set to music, bandaging the visual wound created by the hideous outing of the inside body and its lungs (Ovid specifically mentions 'the chambers of the lungs, clearly visible within his breast').[59] Titian's visual anatomy of cruelty is anaesthetized and rendered bearable by transcendent harmony—an unheard musical envelope which surrounds both victim and viewer.

'SHE DOES NOT KNOW WHERE HER SKIN IS'

The myth of the flaying of Marsyas implicates a cruelty that surfaces even within comparatively recent psycho-therapeutic régimes. Susan, we are told, 'came to her first session saying three things: that she had lost her soul; that the world was no longer outside her, and that all this had happened since she received ECT in hospital three weeks before' (*HLG* xix). Winnicott's foreword to the book writes appreciatively of 'some miracle of detachment' made possible by Milner's 'special reflective capacity' (*HLG* ix). Titian's figure of aesthetic and contemplative reverie, Midas (or perhaps the artist himself), is often seen as reflecting on the sorry spectacle of Marsyas's hubris, abasement, and pain. What, one wonders, is the basis for Milner's miraculous detachment in the face of Susan's psychic flaying? Coming to psychoanalysis from social psychology, Milner was influenced by the concepts of reverie that she had learned from Elton Mayo, a Harvard industrial

[57] *Psychic Envelopes*, 218–22, 226–7. Lecourt notes that Apollo's counter-challenge to Marsyas involves '*taking the reverse for the right side up*'; instead of using language to reply, Marsyas 'only produced a body noise, of blowing, or wind. He lost his skin for this' (ibid., 222).

[58] Ibid., 233.   [59] *The Metamorphoses of Ovid*, 145.

psychologist. Mayo suggested that a disturbance in the capacity for reflective thought might have to do with the dislocation between reverie and directed thinking, a dislocation which Milner identified and tried to overcome in herself.[60] Milner's capacity for reverie (what Winnicott described as her 'special reflective capacity') interposes a mediating layer between the reader and a patient already damaged in childhood by her dysfunctional family and her psychotic mother, even before undergoing the trauma of primitive ECT in the 1940s.

As well as campaigning against the use of ECT Milner brought to Susan's analysis her pre-existing interest in the nature of creative processes. Susan already came pre-packaged in the guise of an aesthetic object. When Winnicott's first wife, Alice, spotted her in hospital, Susan struck her as exceptionally beautiful: ' "She looked like the Botticelli Venus rising from the waves." ' A combination of film star and Madonna, Susan (according to Milner) 'was a tall and slim girl with a walk like Garbo in *Queen Christina* and a remotely withdrawn Madonna-like face' (*HLG* 3). Along with her shimmering beauty, she possessed a mysterious quality that made others (including Milner and Winnicott) want to save her. Milner undertook Susan's analysis at Winnicott's request after he and his first wife had invited her to live with them (an arrangement that ended traumatically when their marriage broke up in the late 1940s).[61] Susan described herself during her first spell in a mental hospital, aged 22, as having '*broken down into reality*' (*HLG* xxviii): 'For the first time in her life, she felt she was "in the world": she discovered that she was in her body, that space existed, that if she walked away from things they got farther away.' This felt 'terrific', she said, because she now felt that 'her emotions were inside her' (*HLG* 9). But the experience of ECT destroyed this precarious sense of being in the world and in her body for the first time. Susan complained that since undergoing ECT, 'she had no inner world nor inner perceptions' (*HLG* xxix). Milner was challenged to respond, counter-transferentially, to her patient's 'body-ego perceptions' by using her own bodily perceptions as a means of understanding and communication.

During the formative period of her work with Susan, Milner was preoccupied with 'the concept of the internal object and its relation to internal perception'. The concept of the internal object and the internal world had been a major intellectual focus for Kleinian discussion. But she also wanted to clarify, in recognizably Winnicottian terms, 'the problem of how the external world does come to be felt

[60] See *HLG* xxiv–xxvii, where Milner describes her immersion in industrial psychology while working with Mayo in Boston. She began analysis with Sylvia Payne after her adventures in writing as 'Joanna Field' in *A Life of One's Own* (1934) and *An Experiment in Leisure* (1937), her pioneering work with girls in secondary education in *The Human Problem in Schools* (1938), and her own experiences as a mother, partly inspired by her reading of Susan Isaacs, Melanie Klein, and D. W. Winnicott. Milner's psychoanalytic training included supervisions with Joan Riviere and Ella Sharpe, as well as Klein (see *HLG* xxvi–xxviii).

[61] See Rodman, *Winnicott: Life and Work*, 133–5. Susan's living arrangements were a recurrent problem. Before she eventually married, she was able to move into relative independence (encouraged by Milner) after years of unpaid domestic work.

to be real, separate, and "out there" for any of us' (*IILG* xxviii). This tension—between the complex relation of internal object world and internal perception, on the one hand, and the separation and 'out thereness' of the external world, on the other—runs through Susan's entire analysis. But Milner had another, aesthetic agenda. Susan believed that her doodles were inseparable from her mental condition and that she might lose her ability to draw if she got well. Milner saw this as confirmation of her thesis in *On Not Being Able to Paint* that creative vision is inhibited by fear of madness. Susan was to be saved by rediscovering her capacity for self-surrender—the capacity that Milner herself had struggled to achieve in her artistic experiments. Milner asks her readers to accept not only 'the archaic way of wanting to relate herself to the world that this patient revealed' but also the value of 'pre-logical, non-discursive modes of thinking' (*HLG* xx), including thinking in visual forms.[62] What started as 'the story of an attempted therapy', she wrote, 'had also become the study of what happened to my own way of seeing the experience when I tried to write about it' (*HLG* xxi). Susan describes her state in hospital prior to undergoing ECT as a period of intense, sometimes agonizing, sometimes wonderful feeling: ' "I had so much, I felt so many things, I felt in my heart and in my stomach." ' During periods of intense ecstasy that coincided with 'an inner gesture of total surrender', she appeared to the other patients as 'extremely beautiful, with a kind of shimmer' (*HLG* 11).[63] Transformed by her surrender, she became a star.

The ambiguous aesthetics of surrender and aesthetic transformation preoccupied Susan herself. In occupational therapy she made a clay copy of a photograph of Michelangelo's *Dying Slave* (Figure 7: *HLG* fig. 12), whose look of deathly peace she associated with the appearance of post-ECT patients. Eyes wide shut, strangely androgynous, the bas-relief was later mutilated by Susan herself when she rebelliously cut out and then restored the mouth—once so resigned—as sensual. By contrast, a drawing which Susan made immediately after the ECT, but which she only showed Milner nine years later (Figure 8: *HLG* fig. 100), depicts a hunched, shrouded, figure expressive of terrible anguish and despair, nursing its own sore head after the ECT, while encircling itself with its arms, as if holding an infant self. Milner suggests that Susan could bring her this drawing because she had at last rediscovered what it means to be held by 'the hands of the living god', an allusion to the D. H. Lawrence poem from which Milner took her title: 'It is a fearful thing to fall into the hands of the living God. | But it is a much more fearful

---

[62] Milner notes that she is drawing on Suzanne Langer's distinction between discursive and non-discursive thought processes, which emphasized the non-discursive character of visual forms and symbolism; see Suzanne Langer, *Philosophy in a New Key* (Cambridge, Mass.: Harvard University Press, 1942), 93–5.

[63] Milner refers to this aesthetic transformation in 'The Role of Illusion in Symbol Formation' (1952)—'a schizophrenic patient (adult) who would have moments of startling physical beauty counterbalanced by moments of something startlingly repellent'. The transformation is seen in terms of 'union with a marvellous or atrocious inner object' but also as a counter-transferential phenomenon (see *SMSM* 95).

Figure 7 Susan's copy of
Michelangelo, *Dying
Slave*, photograph
(*HLG* 12).

Figure 8 Drawing by
Susan (*HLG* fig. 100).

thing to fall out of them' (*HLG* 52).[64] Susan's experience of ECT had destroyed all
sense of ever having been held as an infant: 'the feeling of tragedy in the picture
expressed the terrible knowledge that this was what she had lost, she had fallen out
of the hands of the living god' (*HLG* 411). Susan has no holding environment.

Milner pays particular attention to the meaning of Susan's feelings about her
body, since she thought that the problem lay in her confusion between inner and
outer. Could it even be safe to be 'born'? And 'if she was not born yet, was still
inside, what was she inside?'(*HLG* 25) Susan exists in a state of fusion with her
psychotic mother: 'she could never find a separate image of herself in her mother's
preoccupations, since it seemed that in her mother's mind her daughter had never
had any separate existence at all' (*HLG* 41).[65] As a result, the concepts of inside and
outside are meaningless to her. 'In short,' Milner concludes, 'she does not know
where her skin is' (*HLG* 164).[66] Post-ECT, Susan feels she lacks any boundary: 'the
world is no longer outside her' as it had been after her 'breakdown into reality'
(*HLG* 15). Milner associates this lack of boundary with an undifferentiated anal
world, as opposed to the sensitive perceptions of the tongue in the cavity of the

---

[64] From 'The Hands of God', in *Last Poems*; see Vivian de Sola Pinto and Warren Roberts (eds.),
The Complete Poems of D. H. Lawrence, 2 vols. (London: Heinemann, 1972), ii. 699.

[65] Milner speculates that Susan's drawings were a means of unloading onto her both her own
' "craziness" ' and her mother's: 'the flood of drawings was partly intended to drive me mad as she felt
she had been driven mad' (*HLG* 242). For Milner, Susan had been driven mad by the 'opposites in her
mother's attitude to her, on the one hand writing to her "O moon of my delight", and on the other,
saying that everything was Susan's fault' (*HLG* 242 n.).

[66] Cf. Giles Deleuze's formulation of the schizophrenic body-sieve: 'Things and propositions have
no longer any frontier between them, precisely because bodies have no surface. The primary aspect of
the schizophrenic body is that it is a sort of body-sieve ... In this collapse of the surface, the entire
world loses its meaning'; see Constantin V. Boundas (ed.), Giles Deleuze, *The Logic of Sense*, trans.
Mark Lester and Charles Stivale (1969; London: Athlone Press, 1990), 86–7.

mouth.[67] Like Lecourt's piano-playing child, Susan inhabits an upside-down world, demanding of Milner too 'that [she] should turn [herself] upside-down' and experience the world 'from the "bottom's eye" point of view' (*HLG* 88). Having lost the back of her head to ECT, as if trepanned, she feels that her front and back no longer join up. She lives with a rigid muscular contraction of her neck which makes her turn her head aside, a seemingly incurable nervous tic or aversion of her face like that of the unlucky 'Jynx', the wry-necked bird of Greek myth.[68] In one Mattisse-like drawing of a female nude, her head is swathed in a 1950s headscarf as if to hold it together (Figure 9: *HLG* fig. 85).

Like Anzieu later, Milner speculates on the ways in which an internal awareness of one's body as a three-dimensional inner space depends on the sense of a maternal background provided by the rhythmic sounds of the mother's heart and breathing, 'a slow creating of a concept of an inner containing space' (*HLG* 122). Susan's attempts to create a cocoon of her own in her drawings are entangled with phantasies about internal organs and excretion. She represents herself as a coiled creature so primitive as to be sheer organism, all digestive tube (Figures 10a and 10b: *HLG* figs. 52, 53). Later, Milner herself thinks of Susan in terms of the image derived from biology of a caterpillar's metamorphosis into a chrysalis: 'all its internal organs dissolve into a fluid and . . . it is from this that the new organs and shape of the butterfly somehow emerge' (*HLG* 409).[69] The intestinal coil morphs into the interior of a shell, then forms the basis for a comical bird-like creature, an ugly duckling about to turn into a swan, or perhaps the 'little duck' that Susan's mother used to call her (Figure 11: *HLG* fig. 77). Along with the coil (intestine, snake, nest, or bird), the empty circle becomes the focus of Milner's attention. At first she thinks of it negatively, simply as 'a gap, a naught, whether the gap is in knowledge, the experience of not-knowing; or a physical gap, an empty stomach, or mouth or womb; or an emotional gap, the feeling of someone or something missing, leaving a blank, an emptiness' (*HLG* 246). Perhaps this is the blankness of the infant's satisfied sleep after a feed, 'the so-called dream screen'.[70] Milner senses that if she is to heal Susan's mind–body split, she too must find in herself the capacity 'to achieve, knowingly, a partially undifferentiated and indeterminate

---

[67] For Milner the bowel is a place 'where there is no discriminating tongue and therefore, in the "bottom's eye" view there are no distinct boundaries and perception is far more primitive and undifferentiated' (*HLG* 403).

[68] The Jynx is 'the wryneck, a bird made use of in witchcraft; hence a charm or spell' (*OED*); I owe this information to Marina Warner.

[69] Milner may have in mind the morphogenesis in natural forms which occupies a central place in Lancelot Law Whyte (ed.), *Aspects of Form* (London: Humphries, 1951), which contains essays by biologists, astronomers, and embryologists, as well as art historians; see also Milner's allusion to Whyte in connection with her preoccupation with 'the spontaneous urge to pattern inherent in the living organism' (*HLG* 263 and n.), as well as Whyte's 'formative principle' or 'organizing pattern-making aspect of instinct, something that is shown in a person's own particular and individual rhythms and style' (*HLG* 384).

[70] See the classic paper by Bertram Lewin, 'Sleep, the Mouth, and the Dream Screen', *Psychoanalytic Quarterly*, 15 (1946), 419–34.

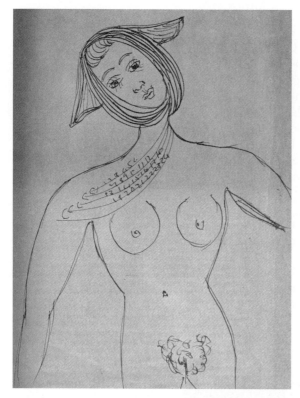

Figure 9 Drawing by
Susan (*HLG* fig. 85).

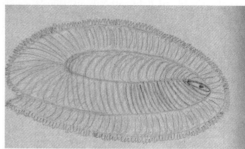

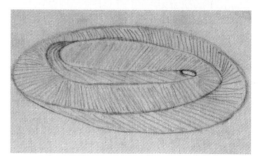

Figures 10a and 10b Drawings
by Susan (*HLG* figs. 52, 53).

Figure 11 Drawing by Susan (*HLG* fig. 77).

state . . . to hold in [herself] a blankness, an empty circle, emptiness of ideas' (*HLG* 253). But this state of emptiness can also manifest itself as a deathly, narcissistic state of non-differentiation.

Milner recognizes that Susan holds 'grimly onto the fused state of no-difference, so that she could still go on saying that the world was not really outside her' (*HLG* 258). Hence the erasure of boundaries symbolized in Susan's 'many drawings of figures or faces showing multiple or indeterminate boundaries of the skin' (*HLG* 259 n.). The circle can also take three-dimensional form, like an egg, or a sound cocoon. Susan claims 'that she constantly heard music in her head, some piece she knew, usually played by an orchestra, and how she thought she had had it as long as she could remember', although she temporarily lost it after the ECT (*HLG* 270). Milner wonders if this inner music or 'self-created cocoon of sound' was intended to insulate her from the frightening noises of familial and internal conflict, or as a substitute for her lost unity with her mother—perhaps 'a self-created womb of sound which encloses her as a halo encloses a head?' (*HLG* 270). Alert though she is to the possibilities of malign or delusory cocoons, Milner also speculates that a different, non-delusory aspect of the cocoon symbol might provide the basis for 'a new kind of womb', a form of separation 'affirming and claiming [Susan's] own privacy within her skin' along with the right to 'her own private inner space' (*HLG* 272). The paradox of the circle (at once fusion and separation, both a way of getting back into the mother and of getting into one's self) prompts

Milner to wonder whether inner body awareness could take over the role of the internal mother, 'fashioning a kind of psychic sphere or new womb out of one's own body image, as being the only secure place to inhabit, from which to put out feelers to the world' (*HLG* 273).

Listening throughout this period to Kleinian papers by Bion and Rosenfeld that placed the emphasis on defensive splitting in the analysis of schizophrenics, Milner (by her own account) had begun to feel her way towards an approach that emphasized the provision of a supporting medium or container. Rather than offering Kleinian interpretations to do with breasts and milk, which entirely failed to ease Susan's phobias, she offers her the missing background for a figure that has lost its ground. Meanwhile, she had been exploring a new motif in Susan's draw-ings, that of the diagonal line dividing the page, which she interprets in terms of 'the boundary that is the skin' and the permeable 'inner surface or threshold between consciousness and unconsciousness' (*HLG* 335–6).[71] Then, sometime late in the 1950s, Susan brought her what she immediately recognized as 'a remarkable drawing' (Figure 12: *HLG* fig. 141). Susan's 'The Sleeping Head and the Egg' depicts a haloed egg or stylized Madonna composed of circular interlocking forms and string-like shading and cross-hatching, accompanied by the flying part-objects that routinely pepper her drawings. The curvilinear allusion to the relation of mother and child perhaps reflects Susan's flirtation with religion during this period (she eventually married an ex-priest). But Milner chooses to interpret the drawing in terms of Susan's potential for differentiation and rebirth, and the possibility of her emergence from the flat two-dimensional world where she can remain in a state of blissful but delusional fusion:

It begins as a large and beautifully drawn egg; and emerging from one side is a haloed face, deeply asleep, and shaded across with stripes like a zebra. She says this face represents retreat from the world. There is also a shaded-in flat shape, on which the chin of the sleeping head is resting; she says this flat thing is the world.

I notice that the sleeping, haloed head is not entirely cut off from the inside of the large egg on which it rests, for the line of its left cheek is continued right down into the big egg, where it is echoed by a second head shape, this time upside down, so that its chin is towards the chin of the sleeping, haloed head which is outside the egg; but this second head is quite featureless, except that what would be its top and its forehead area is shaded in with regular black lines, which is the way she so often draws hair.

At first I found the drawing very puzzling; but then I began to try looking on the big egg as her own body, which she cannot truly inhabit as long as part of her wants to remain asleep, unborn, in a delusion of perpetual blissful unity; for this means, of course, that the world is flat, since all her body memories to do with solidity, whether of sucking the nipple in her mouth, of grasping with her hands, of swallowing, of feeling full, satisfied, or empty, of holding or letting go the faeces in her bowel—all these are obliterated. So also, the undifferentiated face within the egg is perhaps her own undeveloped potentiality; or, to

---

[71] See also *HLG* 335 n., where Milner makes the connection between Susan's use of the diagonal in her drawings and Bion's idea of the 'contact barrier' and 'alpha functioning'.

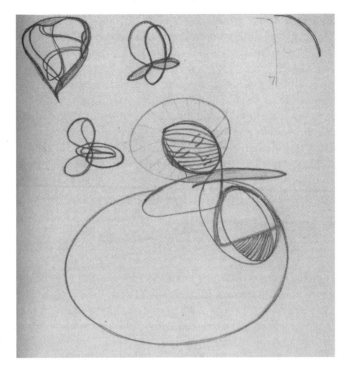

Figure 12
Drawing by Susan
(*HLG* fig. 141).

put it in another way, it is yet another symbol of the undifferentiated source from which what she is capable of being can emerge.   (*HLG* 345–7)

Three-dimensionality emerges from undifferentiation, along with bodily memories of solidity (sucking, feeling full or empty, holding in or letting go). Milner sees this as 'a picture of a new kind of womb that Susan knew she must create within herself, a task she knew about when she drew it'. The drawing 'seems to be about her struggles to reach that higher level of psychic containment from which her new self can grow' (*HLG* 409–10).

The 'higher level of psychic containment' glimpsed in Susan's drawing is associated with the experience of being contained within a bounded body. Milner's wished-for telos for Susan's analysis is that she can become 'a whole person existing in a body and rooted in its own ground, having a clear boundary, yet also having a way in and a way out, and creativeness going on' (*HLG* 349). Milner associates this rootedness with the tree that appears in her drawings, symbolizing 'Susan's growing sense of her own separate and rooted existence, upright, in a body, with her feet upon the ground' (*HLG* 383). In contrast with this language of visual symbols, Milner realizes that the Kleinian 'language of "internal objects" had meant nothing to Susan' (*HLG* 400). What matters is her discovery of three-dimensional oral space, as she uses her tongue to explore 'the difference between what was in her mouth that was part of her and what was not' (*HLG* 403–4). Shifting from the mouth space to inner space, Susan (she hopes) will have 'installed within herself the womb-like crucible of the analytic room' (*HLG* 411). For Milner herself, this analytic space has been the crucible for the emergence of ideas which elude 'the language of psycho-analysis' (*HLG* 411). Her glossary defines the circle not only as a negative space or an absence—'a hole, an empty orifice, a gap, a wound, something not there'—but also as a positive sign, 'symbolizing the de-differentiation of the ego in creative process' (*HLG* 414). Understood as an 'undifferentiated state of the ego, as one phase of the creative process' (*HLG* 420), the analytic space becomes the womb-like crucible from which thought emerges. Susan's innate capacity for self-surrender makes her the bearer of Milner's highly personal myth of the creative process in psychoanalysis.

BETWEEN OBJECT AND NON-OBJECT

In *The Flaying of Marsyas*, Titian's depiction of the bestialization and torture of a young, quasi-human, androgynous satyr takes the eye and mind in two directions. One leads from the flap of skin lifted by Apollo's knife to the impertinent, blood-lapping little dog, or to the restrained hunting dog held back as he slavers for a taste of the action. Here the emphasis is on physicality of texture, flesh, and surface—the figure of Marsyas up-ended like an animal in a hunting scene, the ugly anatomical matter-of-factness of his flaying, the attendants at their gruesome task. In this grotesque yet businesslike scene, with its knife-wielding, bucket-bearing workers, the tactile beauty of fur, foliage, drapery, clouds, and rushing water is inextricably intertwined with blood and cruelty. It is as if Titian means to remind us that aesthetic enjoyment and the most primitive libidinal pleasures meet at the level of the body—or, as Stella suggests, at the level of a violated surface: 'He showed that the articulation of surface can be as destructive as it is creative, that a blurred, pulsating surface often announces the exhaustion of space.'[72] Viewing Marsyas himself right-side up brings a further surprise: a snub-nosed, open-eyed adolescent, mouth agape, he lies in a posture of supreme abandonment, seemingly beyond enjoyment or pain, as if doped. But in the serene gaze and melancholy pose of an onlooker who has been identified with the artist reflecting on the perils of art, in Apollo's concentration, and in the rapt face of the viol-playing musician, we glimpse something else—an allegory of aesthetic production, with its contemplative absorption and idealization, but also its ruthlessness in the pursuit of aesthetic effects (Stella's 'blood-filled sinew and bone of pictorial technique').

In the production of beauty, whether in painting or music, something visceral is demanded, a toll of flesh exacted. The knife that scrapes Marsyas's skin works the thick impasto of the canvas. Spilled blood is like paint; stretched skin resembles

[72] Stella, *Working Space*, 102.

taut canvas; the loosened air that surrounds Marsyas suggests the exhalation of breath as well as the pulsation and flux of the river-tumbling atmosphere. Titian's *The Flaying of Marsyas* allows us to look both at, and beneath, the surface of a complex and painful art. A profound disturbance at the level of the surface compels us to probe beneath the skin. For Stella, the flaying is Titian's own: 'The skin of a defeated artist is scored and peeled away, his body is openly violated to reveal the anatomy of pictorial creation.'[73] The structural engineer who worked with Anish Kapoor to realize the Tate Modern installation writes in a similar vein that 'The imagination is exposed—raw, vibrant... Preconceptions are stretched and warped.'[74] The blood-red, throat-like orifices of Kapoor's *Marsyas* draw the viewer's eye into an intimate, visceral close-up of the body—skin, ear, lungs, entrails—whose swelling openings vanish into an internal void. Multiple viewpoints invite reverie and wandering, as if we could enter the labyrinth of the body, hear the intake and exhalation of breath, catch its echoing trumpetings and its amplification of our own sounds: 'Like a giant ear the construction is open to our whispers.'[75] Filling the six-storey turbine room, *Marsyas* encouraged the viewer to move around under its capacious, suspended form, as if searching for a possible point of entry. Kapoor explicitly invokes the stretched membranes in Soutine's paintings of flayed meat ('the skin that is stretched'), along with Titian's anatomy of flaying.[76]

This modern *Marsyas* simultaneously represents a kind of technological Sublime, engineered by the tension between huge steel rings and swathes of taut, touchable, industrial fabric. A sculptor of potential space, Kapoor asks, 'What happens in the moment when form ceases to be form and becomes space?' He starts from abstract concepts involving complex, irregular, three-dimensional, computer-generated geometrical shapes. Yet the forms that emerge are not so much constructed as revealed—'not that they were made but that they were always there'. *Marsyas* is dedicated to 'the idea that the space within is bigger than the space as seemingly defined by the outside'.[77] The same could be said of the metaphor of psychic space. Countering the rigorous predictive logic of structural engineering, Kapoor insists: 'I am really interested in the things that we know, but somehow didn't know we knew.' And, again, he insists on organic transformation and emotive colour: 'The form, I insist, made itself. I wanted to hold onto my ponderings on Soutine and on this late Titian. And this rather difficult area of some kind of transformational event—for ever I've been trying to turn the red of earth and body into sky' (compare Titian's transformation of corporeality into transcendence, blood into air). Kapoor uses abstraction, along with vast scale and

---

[73] Ibid., 103.   [74] Cecil Balmond, 'Skinning the Imagination', in Anish Kapoor, *Marsyas*, 69.

[75] Ibid., 68.

[76] 'I've been looking a lot at Soutine, those flayed pictures of the meat, the skin that is stretched... And then this Titian, which is the most incredible painting, *The Flaying of Marsyas*. There are obvious references in the Turbine Hall piece to skinning' (Anish Kapoor in conversation with Donna de Salvo, ibid., 61).   [77] Ibid., 60, 61, 62.

industrial techniques, to create effects that paradoxically implicate human subjectivity: 'I work with non-figurative form to talk about the human subject'. What interests him is the vertiginous leap into the void, 'the body in a kind of free fall, the body given over to our dream of the angels'—falling upwards, like Titian's half-flayed Marsyas.[78]

Skin, Kapoor reminds us, is 'the moment that separates a thing from its environment', what allows a thing to become legible ('the surface on which or through which we read an object').[79] Kapoor writes of the compulsion to get inside objects and plumb their depths ('you don't see the internal until you get inside it'). By this, I think, he means not only the relocation of the viewer's perceptual experience from outside to inside but an aesthetic stance towards the object on the part of the artist. The same goes for the analyst, as we see from Milner's analysis of Susan (and perhaps for the critic, too). Apropos of his work, Kapoor uses the haunting phrase 'this strange place between object and non-object'. This strange place between object and non-object, human and non-human—the space that creates the surface tension in Titian's spectacle of pain—also emerges from the ambiguities in Milner's long analysis of Susan. Just as Titian's painting probes the dehumanizing of human form, Milner gets beneath a woman's skin to recover the experience of the undifferentiated infant. The lurking question is why pain and aesthetic beauty, sacrifice, suffering, and surrender, should converge, seemingly ineluctably, in these very different inscriptions of the body, from different periods and differing perspectives—and why Milner should respond to the shimmering effects of Susan's self-surrender with such counter-transferential raptness, as if envying her abjection.

Tony Harrison offers a disquieting answer when he invokes the recalcitrant politics of transcendence:

> Wherever the losers and the tortured scream
> the lyres will be playing the Marsyas theme.
> You'll hear the lyres playing behind locked doors
> when men flay their fellows for some abstract cause.[80]

In *The Trackers of Oxyrhynchus*, aestheticization is the definitive cover-up: 'Wherever in the world there is torture and pain | the powerful are playing the Marsyas refrain.' His rendering of the Marsyas myth exposes torture for what it is, even when it masquerades as the supposedly therapeutic ECT administered to social losers like Susan. The Foucauldian account of psychoanalysis would be its conversion of punishment not into flaying or electrical assault but into the discursive discipline of the analytic consulting room, where pleasure and pain are forced into speech.[81] As Milner's glossary defines it, 'the self is a discovery made in

---

[78] Kapoor, *Marsyas*, 61, 62.   [79] Ibid., 64.
[80] Harrison, *The Trackers of Oxyrhynchus*, 126.
[81] See Scarry, *The Body in Pain*, 27–59, for the argument that the transformation of body into voice is implicit in the infliction of torture.

communication' (*HLG* 419). The price paid for becoming human is the subject's insertion into the communicative relations demanded by psychoanalysis: the mind laid open, not to the knife but to language. Derrida, however, arguing that psychical cruelty is the proper concern of psychoanalysis, writes of impersonal cruelty—suffering without the exercise of cruelty: 'Cruelty there will have been, before any personal figure, before "cruel" will have become an attribute, still less anyone's fault.'[82] Psychoanalysis provides a means of interrogating the suffering that lies beyond the pleasure principle.

[82] Jacques Derrida, 'Psychoanalysis Searches the States of its Soul: The Impossible Beyond of a Sovereign Cruelty', *Without Alibi*, trans. Peggy Kamuf (Stanford, Calif.: Stanford University Press, 2002), 280.

6

Communicating and Not Communicating: *Wordsworth and Winnicott*

*Lei-gha—Lei-gha—*Then did he cry
*Lei-gha—Lei-gha—*most eagerly....
William Wordsworth, 'The Blind
Highland Boy', ll. 161–2

The work is itself communication...
Maurice Blanchot,
'Communication'[1]

When it was pointed out to Winnicott that his view of the relations between infants and their mothers resembled Wordsworth's in *The Prelude*, Winnicott replied cheerfully: 'He seems to have read my books!'[2] The comparison with Wordsworth has become a staple of Winnicottian approaches to literary criticism, as if their distinctive visions and idiolects are reassuringly mirrored in each other. But reading these two Cambridge-educated writers together—one a Romantic poet, the other a twentieth-century psychoanalyst—often produces an uncanny sense of reversed priority across the two hundred years that separate them. This may well be because the cultural context of the British Object Relations tradition is rooted in the values of British Romanticism; both privilege childhood, literature, and the imagination. One need not look far for reasons why psychoanalysts (or poets, for that matter) might want to make space for their own work by turning the tables on their predecessors, even as they draw on the legacy of Romanticism

---

[1] Maurice Blanchot, *The Space of Literature*, trans. Ann Smock (1955; Lincoln, Nebr.: University of Nebraska Press, 1982), 198.

[2] See Rosemary Dinnage, 'A Bit of Light', in Simon A. Grolnick and Leonard Barkin (eds.), *Between Reality and Fantasy: Transitional Objects and Phenomena* (New York and London: Aronson, 1978), 371: 'Winnicott caught the somewhat uncanny similarity between the passage and his own ideas about the infant–mother relationship by responding playfully, "He seems to have read my books" '; see also Brooke Hopkins, 'Wordsworth, Winnicott, and the Claims of the "Real" ', *Studies in Romanticism*, 37 (Summer 1998), 185 n. In an unpublished paper, 'Isolation and Communication in Wordsworth and Winnicott', written in the wake of reading this chapter, Brooke Hopkins argues within a Winnicottian frame for the role of cultural communication in Wordsworth and Winnicott.

in their writing. But the peculiar form this impulse takes in Winnicott and Wordsworth is not so much a resistance to reading, or to being read, as an emphasis on not communicating. They both insist on an area of experience that is resistant to being shared. This appears particularly strange when one considers how Wordsworth championed the language and experience of ordinary men in his poetry, while Winnicott went out of his way to speak directly and informally to parents and children in his clinical writing and broadcasts.[3]

But perhaps it is not so strange after all. Wordlessness has a perennial appeal. In a poignant and personal paper that was published only after her death, Melanie Klein defined what she called 'the sense of loneliness' as 'an unsatisfied longing for an understanding without words' (*E&G* 301).[4] She saw this as a yearning for the pre-linguistic communication which had once existed between nursing infant and mother—now irretrievably lost, and always liable to be disturbed by the fearsome persecutory anxieties and insecurities that darken her view of unconscious infant phantasy. Klein's paper goes on to make two intriguing connections. One is to the work of her former analysand, Wilfred Bion, whose own best-known patient from the 1930s, Samuel Beckett, later made an art form out of not communicating. The other is to an unnamed analysand who is characterized by his 'Love of nature'—Klein's own Wordsworthian phrase. Let's call him William; I shall come back to him in a moment. But first I want to follow up Klein's reference to Bion's 'The Imaginary Twin', read to the British Psycho-Analytical Society in 1953.[5] Klein understands twinning wistfully, in terms of a dialogue between 'those un-understood and split off parts which the individual is longing to regain, in the hope of achieving wholeness and complete understanding' (*E&G* 302)—the never-to-be-completed process of integration that preoccupies her later work. But Bion's stance is altogether less benign.

His paper starts with an observation about rhythm. During his analysis of a drearily monotonous and indifferent patient, he becomes aware of two alternative 'scansions' (his word) of his patient's attempts at communicating. One imparts 'an overwhelming sense of boredom and depression'. The other produces

---

[3] For Winnicott talking directly to children and parents, see, for instance, Ishak Ramszy (ed.), D. W. Winnicott, *The Piggle: An Account of the Psychoanalytic Treatment of a Little Girl* (London: Hogarth Press, 1977) and Clare Winnicott *et al.* (eds.), D. W. Winnicott, *Talking to Parents* (Reading, Mass.: Addison-Wesley, 1993).

[4] Cf. Winnicott's paper, 'The Capacity to Be Alone' (1958), *The Maturational Process and the Facilitating Environment* (1965; rpr. London: Karnac Books, 1990), 29–36 (*MPFE*). Winnicott defines the capacity to be alone as 'the experience of being alone while someone else is present' (ibid., 30), parsing the sentence 'I am alone' in terms of the individual's development. For a helpful discussion of Klein's posthumously published paper, see Meira Likierman, *Melanie Klein: Her Work in Context* (London: Continuum, 2001), 192–7.

[5] 'The Imaginary Twin' was Bion's membership paper for the British Psycho-Analytical Society. For a speculative identification of Beckett as Bion's 'imaginary twin', see Didier Anzieu, 'Beckett and Bion', *International Journal of Psycho-Analysis*, 16 (1989), 193–9. Bion's reticent commentary on his own essay, however, suggests that his clinical narratives should be regarded as fiction; see *Second Thoughts* (1967; rpr. London: Karnac Books, 1987), 120.

'an almost jocular effect', which depends on the rhythm of the patient's associations—regularly spaced pauses that seem to invite a response from the analyst, as
if to say ' "Go on; it's your turn." ' Bion suggests that this rhythm 'indicated that
I [the analyst] was the twin of himself'.[6] Twinning corresponds to the patient's
earliest relationships, when his internal objects (the people he loved, feared, or
depended on) were felt to be harmoniously under his control, just as the jocund
owls hoot back at the Boy of Winander in *The Prelude*, 'responsive to his call'
(*Prelude*, v. 401)—and then fall shockingly silent.[7] The episode of call and
response, call and silence, is end-stopped by death: 'This boy was taken from his
mates, and died | In childhood . . .' (*Prelude*, v. 414–15). A second (Oedipal)
motif emerges from Bion's paper, however: that of 'eye men' (eye-doctors)—in
fact '*two* eye men' (a pair of them), or perhaps they are '*two-eye*' men (men with
two eyes)—who may be able to help the patient see better. The eye-motif culminates in a deliciously 'all-embracing pun, I am unreliable'.[8] Bion is clearly enjoying himself.

Oedipal jokes apart, so far, so Kleinian; Bion, after all, was negotiating his own
mid-life analysis with Klein at the time.[9] But what intrigues me in Bion's paper is
the constellation of ideas: the wish to understand and be understood; the rhythm
of pause and response; the imaginary twin; the unreliable, autobiographical 'I' or
ocular eye—a problem that concerns blindness and insight.[10] To return to Klein's
nature-loving patient, William: neither unhappy nor ill, he is aware of having
been lonely as a child, and he remains so: 'Even from earliest childhood he found
comfort and satisfaction in being out of doors' (*E&G* 307). A hill-walker who dis-
likes cities, 'he was supposed to have been a happy baby, well fed by his mother'.
Still, writes Klein, 'he felt himself hemmed in at home and was aware of an urgent
longing to be out of doors' (*E&G* 308). His greatest pleasure was to wander the
woods and fields with other boys, committing minor acts of vandalism such as
robbing nests and damaging hedges, and perhaps a bit of nocturnal boat-stealing.
But, whatever his depredations, he remains confident that 'nature always repaired
itself'. Klein links his 'obsessional need to be out of doors' with claustrophobic
anxieties about imprisonment within the mother. For her, the freedom and
aesthetic pleasure he derives from nature counteract his underlying sense of
loneliness.

---

[6] *Second Thoughts*, 5, 7.
[7] Unless otherwise specified, references are to the 1805 text in Jonathan Wordsworth (ed.), *The
Prelude 1799, 1805, 1850* (New York: W. W. Norton, 1979). For drafts and revisions to the 1805
text, see also Mark L. Reed (ed.), *The Thirteen-Book Prelude*, 2 vols. (Ithaca, NY: Cornell University
Press, 1991).   [8] *Second Thoughts*, 17.
[9] See Gérard Bléandonu, *Wilfred Bion: His life and Works 1897–1979* (London: Free Association
Books, 1994), 93–101, for an account of the tensions and difficulties involved in Bion's post-war
analysis with Klein.
[10] For the negative manifestations of this wish to understand in a clinical context, see Betty Joseph,
'On Understanding and Not Understanding: Some Technical Issues' (1983), *Psychic Equilibrium and
Psychic Change: Selected Papers of Betty Joseph* (London and New York: Routledge, 1989), 139–50.

Could this, one wonders, be Klein's matri-fugal reading of *The Prelude*? 'Oh there is a blessing in this gentle breeze...A captive greets thee, coming from a house | Of bondage...Now I am free, enfranchised and at large . . .' (*Prelude*, i. 1–9). Wordsworth's opening lines can certainly be read as an urban claustrophobic's hymn to the great outdoors. But no reader will fail to be struck by the terrors and traumas, the anxieties and perplexities, encountered along the way. These terrifying childhood experiences form the nucleus of the earliest versions of *The Prelude*. Later, the road will be mistaken, the 'I' lost as in a mist, the Alps crossed without realizing it. Even the poetical open road brings disquieting encounters. Think of the 'uncouth shape' of the Discharged Soldier—a monotonous complainer, indifferent to his story, groaning by the roadside: '. . . and still from time to time | Sent forth a murmuring voice of dead complaint, | Groans scarcely audible' (*Prelude*, iv. 430–2). His voice interrupts the contented self-communing of the poet as he 'sauntered, like a river murmuring, | And talking to itself' (*Prelude*, iv. 110–11). This walking wound ('his bones wounded him') breaks the rhythm of ambulatory composition with his dead complaint. He erupts into the landscape from another scene, bringing with him a history of colonial wars and tropical sickness. And yet the poet assumes a special responsibility for him, as if recognizing their twinned relation along with the impossibility of communicating with him.[11]

One might speculate that Wordsworth—who tells us that he had a good nursing experience ('Blest the babe | Nursed in his mother's arms', *Prelude*, ii. 239–40)— was inevitably subject to Klein's lifelong struggle to recover his own lost and un-understood parts. The ever-expanding *Prelude* testifies to this interminable project. But reading Wordsworth's autobiographical poem literally, through a Kleinian lens, is bound to strike the two-eyed critic as monocular. I want to take Klein as my point of departure for a bifocal reading that puts Wordsworth alongside Winnicott in order to say something about both. My aim in doing so is to explore questions that bear on both literary priority and psychoanalytic criticism. I shall be focusing on their common turn to wordlessness and self-isolation, and on the figuration of emptiness and voice in their writing, as well as forms of blankness that are quite distinct from either repression or forgetting. The harmonious music of *The Prelude* is, after all, predicated on the mute dialogue of infant and mother; the mind's dialogue with itself; the murmurings of streams, rivers, and waterfalls; even the subtle auditory rhythms and semiotic breath of blank verse composed on foot or aloud on the public road.

But from time to time something surfaces in *The Prelude* that is designated as unreachable, secret, or undisclosed: 'The hiding places of my power | Seem open, I approach, and then they close . . .' (*Prelude*, xi. 335–6). Wordsworth's complaint— 'I

---

[11] 'You might almost think | That his bones wounded him'; MS draft for the 'Discharged Soldier' (see *The Prelude*, 146 n.). Cf. the function of those other imaginary twins in *The Prelude*—Coleridge, the 'most precious friend [who] didst lend a living help | To regulate my soul' (*Prelude*, x. 905–7), and Dorothy Wordsworth, who 'maintained for me a saving intercourse | With my true self' (*Prelude*, x. 914–15).

see by glimpses now'—is first and foremost an elegy for the fugitive sources of his imagination and the waning of vision.[12] But one could hear it as a deliberate game of hide and seek ('I *am seen* by glimpses now . . .') as well as the fear of having lost one's way. It may even involve a wish not to be found. This paradox is at odds with *The Prelude*'s ostensible emphasis on two-way communication—between mother and infant, nature and boy, landscape and poet, past and present. *Not* communicating puts negativity at the heart of Wordsworth's autobiographical poem. What kind of poetry—what kind of poetics—is bound up with this peculiarly Wordsworthian and (I shall argue) Winnicottian form of negativity?

If we ask in what sense Wordsworth and Winnicott can be considered thinkers, it may help to recall the Hegelian roots of 'negativity'. In *The Restlessness of the Negative* (1997), Jean-Luc Nancy's philosophically probing meta-reading of Hegel ('the philosopher who wants to enunciate the unenunciable'), negativity is redefined as the language of thought. This language requires for its penetration 'another language' than that of representation:

> To penetrate negativity demands 'another language' than the language of representation. The latter is the language of separation, the language of concepts in their fixity, of propositions and their copulas; it is the language of signification. This language is quite simply language itself, and there are no others—or there are only many of them. To speak the other language—that of thought—is not to speak a mysterious extra language. But it is above all not to enter the ineffable. It is to *think*: to say within language what language does not say . . .[13]

Thinking, in this sense, places extraordinary pressure on 'language itself', given the exhaustion over time of its signifying potential and its alteration by use. Passages of visionary obscurity in Wordsworth's poetry, or of psychoanalytic opacity in Winnicott's prose, register both the exhaustion and the alteration of language under the pressure of intense thought. What links Wordsworth and Winnicott is not so much their views on the nursing couple as their attempt to say within language what language does not say. Not communicating is the form their work takes when the work is itself communication.

MY PRIVATE BOOK

I have already suggested that Wordsworth is liable to be read as Winnicott's imaginary twin—a comforting affirmation of his emphasis on the active and reciprocal creativity of infant and environment, or the concept of transitional space, where

---

[12] For a relevant discussion of loss in Wordsworth's poetry, especially *The Prelude*, see Ronald Britton, *Belief and Imagination: Explorations in Psychoanalysis* (London and New York: Routledge, 1998), 120–45; Britton includes a discussion of the 'infant babe' passage from a contemporary Kleinian rather than Winnicottian perspective (ibid., 134–6).

[13] Jean-Luc Nancy, *The Restlessness of the Negative*, trans. Jason Smith and Steven Miller (1997; Minneapolis: University of Minnesota Press, 2002), 35; see also 116 n. Nancy offers a particularly succinct and suggestive contemporary reading of the concept of the negative in Hegel.

the external world has to be omnipotently created rather than simply found, and only the swerve via illusion makes it possible to apprehend reality.[14] All this, and more, one can certainly find in *The Prelude*: 'The infant experiencing omnipotence ... *creates and re-creates the object*, and the process gradually becomes built in, and gathers a memory backing' (*MPFE* 180). Not Wordsworth, as it happens, but Winnicott—who wrote self-deprecatingly to Anna Freud: 'I have an irritating way of saying things in my own language'. At the time, he was struggling to express himself in his own words in the face of what he saw as the orthodoxies of Kleinian terminology.[15] Compare his description of the infant to Wordsworth's Infant Babe, 'creator and receiver both' who 'gather[s] passion from his mother's eye' (*Prelude*, ii. 273, 243)—the very passage describing the nursing couple that prompted Winnicott's quip about Wordsworth having read his books. But not communicating is a much more charged area than even the paradoxes of those much-travelled Winnicottian concepts: the transitional object, potential space, and playing.

My title comes from Winnicott's strangest and most personal essay: 'Communicating and Not Communicating Leading to a Study of Certain Opposites' (1963).[16] Winnicott's 'certain opposites' do not refer to not speaking, or even to a speaking silence, but to a different order of not communicating altogether, one that includes both the inevitability and the necessity of failed communication. One could think of this as the degree-zero of aloneness figured by the Discharged Soldier, in whom the poet sees 'A desolation ... | That seemed akin to solitude' (*Prelude*, iv. 418–19), and with whom two-way communication seems to be precluded despite the soldier's tale of distress. Winnicott, however, finds greatest assurance of the existence of a solitary self in the figure that he calls the 'isolate'. The isolate represents the negation and repudiation of any form of communication with another. It thus puts dramatically at risk the founding tenets of British Object Relations psychoanalysis: that the subject is constituted in, and via, its relations, and that object-relating—however primitive, rudimentary, and unconscious—is present from the very beginnings of life. Winnicott's

[14] See, for instance, John Turner, 'Wordsworth and Winnicott in the Area of Play', Peter Rudnytsky (ed.), *Transitional Objects and Potential Space: Literary Uses of D. W. Winnicott* (New York: Columbia University Press, 1993), 161–88; for illusion, see also John Turner, 'A Brief History of Illusion: Milner, Winnicott and Rycroft', *International Journal of Psychoanalysis*, 83 (October 2002), 1063–82.

[15] 18 March 1954. Winnicott's letter continues, '... instead of learning how to use the terms of psycho-analytic metapsychology'; see F. Robert Rodman (ed.), *The Spontaneous Gesture: Selected Letters of D. W. Winnicott* (London: Karnac, 1999), 58. Cf. Winnicott's protest in a letter to Klein: 'I want to put it in my own language. This is annoying because ... in a scientific society one of our aims is to find a common language. This language must, however, be kept alive as there is nothing worse than a dead language' (17 November 1952; ibid., 34).

[16] For an essay preparatory to Winnicott's theme, see also 'The Theory of the Parent–Infant Relationship' (1960), *MPFE* 37–55. Winnicott's letter to Bion of 7 October 1955 shows that he was already thinking about the themes of communication and isolation; see *The Spontaneous Gesture*, 9. For an eloquent account of 'Communicating and Not Communicating', see Adam Phillips, *Winnicott* (Cambridge, Mass.: Harvard University Press, 1988), 144–52.

alarmed rejection of any form of impingement and his impassioned defence of an incommunicado core, as he told Klein, 'touches on the very root of my own personal difficulty'. In his letter to her, he defined this difficulty as an illness peculiar to himself while refusing to allow it to be dismissed on these grounds. His own illness, he pointed out, was 'not far from the inherent difficulty in regard to human contact with external reality'—the inherent difficulty that Freud had addressed in his seminal essay on 'Negation' (1925) when he asserted that 'What is bad, what is alien to the ego and what is external are, to begin with, identical' (*SE* xix. 237).[17]

Winnicott's 'Communicating and Not Communicating' alludes to a sophisticated form of hide-and-seek played by the poet and the artist, in whom Winnicott sees 'the urgent need to communicate and the still more urgent need not to be found' (*MPFE* 185). He gives two everyday examples from his clinical practice. The first is an adolescent girl who uses a stolen school book to collect poems and sayings: 'she wrote in it "My private book". On the front page she wrote: "What a man thinketh in his heart, so is he." '[18] Mothers and daughters may feel a frisson of familiarity about what comes next: 'In fact her mother had asked her, "Where did you get this saying from?" This was bad because it meant that the mother must have read her book. It would have been all right if the mother had read the book but had said nothing' (*MPFE* 186). Winnicott makes no comment on either the intrusiveness of mothers or the indirectness of adolescent communication—let alone on a private self that advertises its innermost thoughts with an epigraph from the Book of Proverbs. Instead, he turns it into a sophisticated game: 'Here is a picture of a child establishing a private self that is not communicating, and at the same time wanting to communicate and to be found. It is a sophisticated game of hide-and-seek in which *it is joy to be hidden but disaster not to be found*' (*MPFE* 86).

But the game can take a different and more disturbing turn, away from wanting to be found. It may also be a disaster to be found. Winnicott's counter-example is another, more precariously poised adolescent girl who writes poems in secret (rather than writing her autobiography) when 'she needs to form a bridge with childhood imagination' or keep open the traffic between imaginative life and everyday existence. She does not publish her poems or show them to anyone; they are private. Winnicott speculates that there is a core in even the healthiest person that corresponds to the hidden self of the pathologically split personality:

I suggest that this core never communicates with the world of perceived objects, and that the individual person knows that it must never be communicated with or be influenced by external reality. This is my main point, the point of thought which is the centre of an

[17] 17 November 1952: 'The matter which I am discussing touches the very root of my personal difficulty so that what you see can always be dismissed as Winnicott's illness, but if you dismiss it in this way you may miss something which is in the end a positive contribution. My illness is something which I can deal with in my own way and it is not far away from being the inherent difficulty in regard to human contact with external reality' (*The Spontaneous Gesture*, 37).
[18] The quotation is from Proverbs 23: 7.

intellectual world and of my paper. Although healthy persons communicate and enjoy communicating, the other fact is equally true, that *each individual is an isolate, permanently non-communicating, permanently unknown, in fact unfound.*   (*MPFE* 187)

With this 'point of thought', Winnicott defines the inner isolate as a fundamentally negative (and possibly feminine) entity. Its first requirement is simply not to be found at all. The traumatic nature of any impingement on this inviolate core— 'the threat of its being found, altered, communicated with' (*MPFE* 187)—makes hiding the secret self the first line of defence against otherness. Startlingly, Winnicott asserts that 'Rape, and being eaten by cannibals, these are mere bagatelles as compared with the violation of the self's core, the alteration of the self's central elements by communication seeping through the defences' (*MPFE* 187). Hence the adolescent's wariness 'of being found before being there to be found' (*MPFE* 190)—and hence, Winnicott adds, people's hatred of psychoanalysis as an invasion of the central privacy of the self. No man is an island—but what if the island were to be colonized before it even existed as such?

For Winnicott, communication from outside is always both premature and potentially traumatic. The first primitive defences are energetically mobilized against the threat of being found. His lurid language (rape and cannibalism) is charged with 'a protest from the core of [himself] to the frightening fantasy of being infinitely exploited' (*MPFE* 179). A self-confessed claustrophobe, he often found himself resisting Klein's language and ideas and holding out for his own: 'I am one of those people who feel compelled to work in my own way and to express myself in my own language first', he wrote, announcing himself as both iconoclastic and claustrophobic.[19] His defence of this personal core anticipates Kristeva's view of a subject similarly constituted by a defensive repudiation of what threatens its not-yet-individuation. What she calls an abject, Winnicott calls an isolate.[20] This odd term is not quite his own invented neologism. Reminding us of the etymological link between isolation and *insula* (island), the dictionary yields a quasi-scientific citation: 'We may call the process . . . isolation, and the products of the process we may term isolates' (*OED*). The isolate, then, is the product of a process—a defensive structure, as opposed to an essence. The isolate is retrospectively produced by the threat of invasion. There is no core prior to its having already been defended against the threat or actuality of otherness.

The cognate meanings of 'isolated'—'placed or standing apart or alone; detached or separate from other things or persons; unconnected with anything else; solitary' (*OED*)—have far-reaching implications for any psychoanalytic

---

[19] To David Rapaport, 9 October 1953 (*The Spontaneous Gesture*, 53). In a letter written jointly to Klein and Anna Freud, Winnicott wrote: 'if we in the present try to set up rigid patterns we thereby create iconoclasts or claustrophobics (perhaps I am one of them) who can no more stand the falsity of a rigid system in psychology than they can tolerate it in religion'; 3 June 1954 (ibid., 72).

[20] For the concept of the 'abject' (a not-yet object whose casting-out defines its boundaries of a not-yet subject), see Julia Kristeva, *Powers of Horror: An Essay on Abjection*, trans. Leon S. Roudiez (New York: Columbia University Press, 1982), 1–31.

theory predicated on the organism's interaction with its surroundings.[21] After all, it was Winnicott the paediatrician who famously insisted that no baby is an island, but always forms part of a nursing couple.[22] 'Communicating and Not Communicating' comes close to saying that negativity defines the core, and that negativity is constitutive of the self. The 'core of the self, that which could be called a true self' (*MPFE* 184), exists on the cusp of the point that he announces as the centre of his intellectual world and his paper. The reference is to his epigraph, which he takes from Keats's letter of 1818 to Benjamin Bailey: 'Every point of thought is the centre of an intellectual world.'[23] The origins of the voluminously defined word 'point' are bound up with the idea of pricking or piercing, and hence with both printing and writing.[24] But the *punctum* is a kind of wounding as well as a mark. Roland Barthes writes of the photograph's *punctum* as an arrow that pierces the viewer—'*c'est ce hasard qui...me point (mais aussi me meurtrit, me poigne)*'. This accident, whether danger or chance, marks, wounds, and penetrates.[25] The isolate forms as the result of its defences having been pierced and a wound created. Like Wordsworth's Discharged Soldier, the isolate is the survivor of a previous, unrecorded trauma.

Winnicott's profoundly negative definition of 'the isolated core' (non-communicating, unknown, unfound) takes on an almost mystical, quasi-Jungian aura towards the end of his paper: 'at the core of the individual there is no communication with the not-me world either way. Here quietude is linked with stillness' (*MPFE* 189–90).[26] This is 'the central still and silent spot' (*MPFE* 189) of the patient's psyche, which even the analyst should avoid disturbing. Winnicott's respect for 'the idea of primordial experience occurring in solitude'

---

[21] For a succinct account of the theoretical approaches included under the heading of 'Object Relations' since Freud's 'one-body' psychology, see Robert Hinshelwood, *A Dictionary of Kleinian Thought* (London: Free Association Books, 1991), 367–73.

[22] Winnicott's formulation is often cited: 'I said it rather excitedly and with heat: "There's no such thing as a baby!" I was alarmed to hear myself utter these words.... One sees a "nursing couple"'; see 'Anxiety Associated with Insecurity' (1952), *Through Paediatrics to Psycho-Analysis* (1958; rpr. New York: Brunner/Mazel, 1992), 99.

[23] Keats's letter to Benjamin Bailey, 13 March 1818: 'it is an old maxim of mine and of course must be well known that evey [*sic*] point of thought is the centre of an intellectual world—the two uppermost thoughts in a Man's mind are the two poles of his World he revolves on them and every thing is southward or northward to him through their means'; see Hyder E. Rollins (ed.), *The Letters of John Keats*, 2 vols. (Cambridge: Cambridge University Press, 1958), i. 243.

[24] From *pungere* (to prick or pierce); the primary meaning of 'point' is a prick, dot, or mark used in printing or writing, hence 'punctuation mark' (*OED*).

[25] *La Chambre claire: note sur la photographie* (Paris: Gallimard Seuil, 1980), 49. 'A photograph's *punctum* is that accident which pricks me (but also bruises me, is poignant to me)'; see Roland Barthes, *Camera Lucida: Reflections on Photography*, trans. Richard Howard (1980; London: Vintage, 1993), 27. The *punctum* is also said to be '*comme une flèche et vient me percer*'. The word '*poigne*' suggests both '*percer*' and '*poignarder*' (to stab).

[26] 'I can refer to Michael Fordham's very interesting view of the concept of the Self as it has appeared in Jung's writings. Fordham writes: "The over-all fact remains that the primordial experience occurs in solitude"' (*MPFE* 190). For Winnicott's letter about the word 'self' to the Jungian Fordham during the mid-1950s, see *The Spontaneous Gesture*, 88.

(*MPFE* 190) sounds innocuous. No hill-walker or mystic would disagree that important things happen to us when we are alone, or that an eye made quiet is apt to be looking inward. But Winnicott has something else in mind. When do stillness and peace become cognate with death? Notoriously, Winnicott could not swallow the Kleinian idea of the death-drive, preferring the concept of aggression to that of primal destructiveness just as he preferred the words 'concern' or 'ruth' to Kleinian 'reparation'.[27] But for the Freud of *Beyond the Pleasure Principle* (1920), the inertia of the organism was the sign of the deathward *telos* of all life; among the associations of 'quietude' are both 'quietism' and '*quietus*'. When does primordial solitude turn into something more malignant—active hostility to the link of language, thought, and emotion?[28]

Leaving aside the vexed question of the death-drive, I want to return to *The Prelude*, and specifically to the Cambridge book where we see Wordsworth himself as a late adolescent. His account of himself as a newly arrived student in the small-town bustle of late eighteenth-century Cambridge is restless, disoriented, unreal: 'I was the dreamer, they the dream' (*Prelude*, iii. 28).[29] He expresses his sense of dislocation in temporal and spatial terms as 'A feeling that I was not for that hour | Nor for that place' (*Prelude*, iii. 80). If he was 'a chosen son', just what he had been chosen for remained to be seen (his family envisaged a college fellowship, the law, or the church). Wordsworth conveys the tensions between an exceptionally well-educated north country grammar-school boy and the aristocracy-aping milieu into which he had been transported, as if by magic. The wayward student stays in touch with his boyhood self by walking out into the flat fen landscape with its huge sky—'the fields, the level fields, | With heaven's blue concave reared above [his] head' (*Prelude*, iii. 99–100)—or by 'turning the mind in upon itself', an old solipsistic habit from his younger Lake District days (*Prelude*, iii. 112).[30] Beneath the restless pleasure-seeker is a resistant isolate: 'I had a world about me—'twas my own, I made it' (*Prelude*, iii. 142–3). At times, he might even have been mistaken for a madman with a sight-disorder—a form of

[27] See Winnicott's letter to Roger Money-Kyrle on 27 November 1952: 'I am sorry that you bring in the death instinct here because it muddles everything up.... the term death instinct is abused in our Society more than any other term and used instead of the word aggression or destructive urge or hate in a way that would have horrified Freud' (ibid., 40, 42). For Winnicott's use of the term 'concern' and its cognate 'ruth' (as opposed to the infant's ruthlessness), see, for instance, Winnicott's development of Klein's views in 'Psycho-Analysis and the Sense of Guilt' (1958), *MPFE* 15–28, and 'The Development of the Capacity for Concern' (1963), *MPFE* 73–82.

[28] See Bion's post-Kleinian development of the concept of the death instinct in 'Attacks on Linking' (1959), *Second Thoughts*, 93–109.

[29] For Wordsworth's Cambridge years, see Stephen Gill, *William Wordsworth: A Life* (Oxford: Clarendon Press, 1989), 38–49; and, for a more colourful account of the political and sexual climate of late eighteenth-century Cambridge, see also Kenneth Johnston, *The Hidden Wordsworth: Poet, Lover, Rebel, Spy* (New York: W. W. Norton, 1998), 111–34, 155–87.

[30] To fill the gap here, Wordsworth imports a passage from 'The Pedlar', transferring it from the third person to the first, and backdating his apprehension of a moral and imaginative universe linking all natural phenomena: 'I saw them feel, | Or linked them to some feeling' (*Prelude*, iii. 126–7).

madness shared 'By poets of old time' (*Prelude*, iii. 152) such as the blind Homer and Milton.

But, he insists, 'It was no madness.' The visible realm of words and signs was less important than 'what passed within [him]':

> Not of outward things
> Done visibly for other minds—words, signs,
> Symbols, or actions—but of my own heart
> Have I been speaking...
>
> (*Prelude*, iii. 174–7)

And at a stroke, this non-verbal reserve—'far hidden from the reach of words'—becomes the heroic argument of *The Prelude*, now a philosophic poem as well as an autobiographical poem, and struggling with the language of thought:

> Points have we all of us within our souls
> Where all stand single; this I feel, and make
> Breathings for incommunicable powers.
>
> (*Prelude*, iii. 186–8)

Winnicott's epigraph to 'Communicating and Not Communicating' ('Every point of thought is the centre of an intellectual world') suggests the sense in which a point 'Where all stand single' may be at once centre and turning-point. It implies both fixity and movement, simultaneously serving as a pivot and as a point of leverage. In his well-known note on 'The Immortality Ode', Wordsworth equates this fulcrum with his own mind ('Archimedes said that he could move the world if he had a point whereon to rest his machine').[31] For Hegel, the fulcrum is negativity itself: 'negativity... constitutes the *turning point* of the movement of the concept'.[32]

What conceptual point turns the world of *The Prelude*? Perhaps a fixation-point—not so much a location, as an isolocation. In the London book of *The Prelude*, the fixed and sightless eyes of a blind beggar make the mind turn round 'As with the might of waters' (*Prelude*, vii. 617). An unsightly sight attacks the eye. The Cambridge book is presided over by the obduracy of another local poet, the blind isolate, Milton, 'who, in his later day | Stood almost single' (*Prelude*, iii. 284–5). This was a time of apparent pointlessness and superficial sociability for Wordsworth himself. His distinction as a student declined and he lost direction. But the spatial geography of undirected student life, lived idly and on the surface ('my life became | A floating island, an amphibious thing'), also embraces

[31] See Jared Curtis (ed.), William Wordsworth, *Poems, in Two Volumes, and Other Poems, 1800–1807* (Ithaca, NY: Cornell University Press, 1987), 428.

[32] Jean-Luc Nancy cites this passage, a reminder that the form of the circle privileged by Hegel is 'the pure movement of the point that turns'; see *The Restlessness of the Negative*, 17–18. The reference is to 'The Absolute Idea' in *Hegel's Science of Logic*, trans. A. V. Miller (New York: Humanities Press, 1989), 835.

impenetrable darkness and vacancy: 'Caverns there were within my mind which sun | Could never penetrate' (*Prelude*, iii. 339–40, 246–7). What was going on?

Playing on university Terms, Wordsworth describes his state as 'this deep vacation' (*Prelude*, iii. 542)—not just a pause or interval, or an extended playtime, but a complete suspension of activity:

> Hushed meanwhile
> Was the undersoul, locked up in such a calm,
> That not a leaf of the great nature stirred.
> Yet was this deep vacation not given up
> To utter waste.
>
> (*Prelude*, iii. 539–43)

'Utter'—a word commonly used to intensify destruction or negation—is itself negated here: *not* given up to waste, or at any rate, not to *utter* waste; a void rather than total devastation. In an essay called 'Fear of Breakdown', which was probably written in the same year as 'Communicating and Not Communicating', Winnicott writes of the importance of experiencing emptiness and un-integration: 'Primary emptiness simply means: before starting to fill up.' Emptiness is a prerequisite for taking in anything at all, even food. It is also the state of nothing-yet-having-happened that the adolescent must defend so fiercely against the threat of impingement. But, by the same token, one needs 'to think, not of trauma but of nothing happening when something might profitably have happened'.[33] With hindsight, Wordsworth writes that in Cambridge, 'Imagination slept, | And yet, *not utterly*' (*Prelude*, iii. 259–60; my emphasis). '*And yet*'—Wordsworth's saving qualification risks being undone. As Freud reminds us, negation ('not utterly') allows the unconscious to communicate what would otherwise be unacceptable ideas. Potential space can be utterly wasted; something might profitably have happened rather than nothing much happening at all. Or perhaps—and Wordsworth hints as much—this was the defensive sleep of the isolate.

BLANK DESERTION

In the essay that paves the way for 'On Communicating and Not Communicating', 'Ego Distortion in Terms of True and False Self' (1960), Winnicott makes what appears to be a problematic distinction between 'true' and 'false' selves. For Winnicott, the self turned outward and relating to the world is the socially adaptive self. It exists to protect and defend the existence of a secret self against

---

[33] D. W. Winnicott, *Psycho-Analytic Explorations*, ed. Clare Winnicott, Ray Shepherd, and Madeleine Davis (London: Karnac Books, 1989), 94, 93 (*PAE*). Winnicott is speculating that a complete breakdown may not be capable of being experienced. For the influence on Klein of Winnicott's ideas about disintegration and 'primary unintegration', see Likierman, *Melanie Klein: Her Work in Context*, 163–8.

discovery. The False Self hides the True Self; it may provide the only way to communicate with the hidden self and bring it to life. The False Self in its patho-logical guise prevents and inhibits what Winnicott calls the 'spontaneous gesture' of the True Self. Compliance and imitation are the costly result. It can even be impossible to tell the two apart, since the False Self is capable of mimicking the True Self. Perhaps—a disturbing implication that Winnicott does not pursue—the self is only ever mimicry after all. The child grows up to be just like its mother, nurse, aunt, or brother, along the lines of the cramped imitative trajectory sketched by 'The Immortality Ode' ('The little actor cons another part').

The Winnicottian False Self is the ultimate defence against the unthinkable 'exploitation of the True Self, which would result in its annihilation' (*MPFE* 147). To avoid this catastrophe, the False Self hides the True Self 'by complying with environmental demands'. Meanwhile the True Self—the instinctual self—remains unknowable and unknown. Winnicott's True Self turns out to be a loose *congerie* of perceptions and feelings that 'does no more than collect together the details of the experience of aliveness'—this means the body's life-sustaining functions, 'including the heart's action and breathing' (*MPFE* 148). Just sense. But sense includes a potential passage to thought and a conceptual becoming.[34] Winnicottian subjectivity (true to its Romantic origins) involves a repetition of the Coleridgean Imagination, at the level of the body rather than the mind: 'I AM, I am alive, I am myself'[35]—a transformation of being far different from John Clare's diminished void, where there is nothing but the bare sense of existing ('I only know I am—that's all'). Communication between False and True Self depends for Winnicott on the original availability (or unavailability) of symbolic mediation. He is saying nothing so essentialist as that the True Self will out, nor so utopian as that the False Self must be outed. Rather, their relation depends on what he calls the facilitating maternal environment. In a letter to Bion, Winnicott takes him to task for neglecting to interpret a despairing remark by Bion's most Beckettian patient—'I ought to have telephoned my mother'—in terms of failed communication. Telephoning one's mother, according to Winnicott, represents 'a failure of the more subtle communication which is the only basis for communica-tion that does not violate the fact of the essential isolation of each individual'.[36] So much for phoning home.

In 'Fear of Breakdown', Winnicott defines 'breakdown' as 'the unthinkable state of affairs that underlies the defence organisation' (*PAE* 88). This breakdown involves a catastrophic failure to contain anxiety. Freud had defined trauma in

[34] Cf. Nancy, *The Restlessness of the Negative*, 46–54, for a philosopher's gloss on Hegel's 'sense': 'Sense is being as sense, being torn away from subsistence and away from fixed determination; and it is the appropriation of being by the subject, as subject' (ibid., 50).
[35] See D. W. Winnicott, *Playing and Reality* (1971; rpr. London and New York: Routledge, 1991), 56.
[36] 7 October 1955 (*The Spontaneous Gesture*, 91). Winnicott's letter, which alludes to Bion's con-cept of maternal 'reverie' as the capacity to sense (and make sense of) what is going on inside the infant, also expresses his impatience with the 'plugging of terms' by Kleinians (e.g., 'internal objects', 'projective identification', 'envy'); see ibid., 92.

Beyond the Pleasure Principle as the failure of anticipatory anxiety to defend against the fear of annihilation. Trauma is the event for which anxiety has not prepared us—at once the fear of something that has not yet happened, and the breakdown that has already happened prior to being known. The phenomenology of breakdown includes a return to an unintegrated state; depersonalization; loss of a sense of the real; and loss of object relations. Linking fear of breakdown to fear of death, Winnicott uses the phrase 'phenomenal death' to refer to a threat of annihilation prior to the possibility of its being experienced at all. This premature encounter gives rise to a sense of 'personal non-existence' that defends against feelings of guilt and persecution. Yet, Winnicott insists paradoxically, '*only out of non-existence can existence start*' (*PAE* 95). This 'unthinkable state of affairs' provides my point of entry into the first and earliest of the 'spots of time' that form the traumatic *punctum* of the 1798–9 *Prelude*. Pivotal to its evolving architecture, the spots of time imply the simultaneously spatial and temporal location (or isolocation) of a wound. They represent a fixation-point, a mark on landscape or memory that permanently anchors meaning for the subject, like the Lacanian *point de capiton* or quilting-point: 'There are in our existence spots of time, | Which with distinct preeminence retain | A Fructifying virtue...' (1799 *Prelude*, i. 288–90).[37] Originally the basis for an aesthetic theory of mind, the spots of time only took on their renovating function in the wake of post-Revolutionary disillusion, when they were moved to Book XI of *The Prelude*—counter-intuitively, since each of these well-known passages involves an untoward or unanticipated encounter with something so devastating that it has to be obscured or reasoned away: a gibbet where a murderer had been executed in times past, or an anxious Oedipal encounter at the crossroads marked, retrospectively, by the death of Wordsworth's father. The first and most enigmatic of these spots of time, the encounter with the gibbet, is specifically said to be located at 'the twilight of rememberable life' (1799 *Prelude*, i. 298), when memory (according to Freud) is most liable to revision.[38]

A lost 6-year-old stumbles on the hollow 'where in former times | A man, the murderer of his wife, was hung | In irons' (1799 *Prelude*, i. 308–10).[39] Nothing is left but the grim traces of this long-ago execution: 'mouldered was the gibbet mast, | The bones were gone ... Only a long green ridge of turf remained | Whose shape was like a grave' (1799 *Prelude*, i. 310–13). But, by 1805, Wordsworth's spare narrative is spectacularly overwritten with the story of a second murder:

> on the turf
> Hard by, soon after that fell deed was wrought,

---

[37] The word 'fructifying' is replaced by 'renovating' in the 1805 *Prelude*.

[38] For a contestatory 'Freudian' discussion of this spot of time, see David Ellis, *Wordsworth, Freud and the Spots of Time* (Cambridge: Cambridge University Press, 1985), 62–83; Ellis discusses the second spot of time under the heading of Oedipality (ibid., 17–34).

[39] The gibbet is a composite one, conflating two different hangings—that of a local murderer near Penrith in the 1760s; and the Hawkshead hanging of a wife-murderer a century before, on a gibbet close to where Wordsworth lodged with Ann Tyson; see *The Prelude*, 9 n.

> Some unknown hand had carved the murderer's name.
> The monumental writing was engraven
> In times long past, and still from year to year
> By superstition of the neighbourhood,
> The grass is cleared away; and to this hour
> The letters are all fresh and visible.
>
> (*Prelude*, xi. 290–301)

The revision erases both domestic violence and the unmarked 'ridge of turf . . . Whose shape was like a grave'. Yet this heavy-handed engraving is no ordinary form of erasure. The hyper-legibility of fresh and visible lettering overlays a trope of resemblance. What or who is buried here is not a name, but a 'shape'—a euphemism for death, or its uncanny afterlife.[40]

It would be a stretch to equate the unknown hand of superstition with the reviser's hand. But someone is seeing things. Revision disappears, reappearing as a kind of second sight. The lines that follow (virtually unchanged from the 1799 version) strip landscape to its bare elements—then run the list again, as if to enact the iterative force of traumatic memory. The turbulence of the child's anxiety is displaced onto a single, dream-like figure, forever crossing and recrossing an imaginary field of vision:

> I left the spot
> And, reascending the bare common, saw
> A naked pool that lay beneath the hills,
> The beacon on the summit, and more near,
> A girl who bore a pitcher on her head
> And seemed with difficult steps to force her way
> Against the blowing wind. It was, in truth,
> An ordinary sight, but I should need
> Colours and words that are unknown to man
> To paint the visionary dreariness
> Which, while I looked all round for my lost guide,
> Did at that time invest the naked pool,
> The beacon on the lonely eminence,
> The woman, and her garments vexed and tossed
> By the strong wind.
>
> (*Prelude*, xi. 301–15)

How extraordinary can an ordinary sight be? And what colour is 'visionary dreariness'? The real returns as something seen—ambiguously inside and outside—that

---

[40] For a discussion of revision in *The Prelude* that focuses on the episode of the drowned man (preceding the spots of time in the 1799 *Prelude*), see Susan J. Wolfson, *Formal Changes: The Shaping of Poetry in British Romanticism* (Stanford, Calif.: Stanford University Press, 1997), 100–32.

seems to invest the naked pool, the beacon, and the pitcher-bearing girl with hallucinatory intensity.[41]

The more recent meanings of 'dreary' include 'dull', 'dismal', and 'melancholy'; Milton, for instance, describes 'the dreary plain' of Hell as 'the seat of desolation' (*Paradise Lost*, i. 180). But this literary usage obscures its sensational pre-history: 'gory', 'cruel', 'dire', 'horrid' (*OED*)—fit words to describe a spot associated with archaic violence and death by hanging, or the scene of a moors murder. The guilty aftermath of the boat-stealing episode produces the same unsettling estrangement from the visible world:

> In my thoughts
> There was a darkness—call it solitude
> Or blank desertion—no familiar shapes
> Of hourly objects, images of trees,
> Of sea or sky, no colours of green fields . . .
>
> (*Prelude*, i. 421–5)

By a kind of visionary *après coup*, the insistent negativity of Wordsworth's language—*no* familiar shapes, *no* colours of green fields—redefines darkness as something blanked out, not just as the absence of colour. The list renders darkness cumulatively visible. Like 'colours and words that are unknown to man', Wordsworth's 'no colours of green fields' retain the traces of an erased figure. Seeing nothing is not the same as nothing to see; it implies something once seen but now occluded or disappeared. A short seminar piece by Winnicott, 'Hallucination and Dehallucination' (1957), explores what he calls 'the special use that children and adults make of blackness'. Blackness, he notes, can be welcome as well as traumatic—and black the best colour of all (as it was for Manet). But he has in mind a more active and destructive form of negation, a phenomenon that involves 'the blacking out of pictures after they have been painted'.

Winnicott refers to a patient who 'always blacks out his works of art' and to a prototypical isolate, a schizophrenic boy who blacks over every white sheet of paper: 'Sometimes he would lift the veil and paint or draw and allow me to see what there was to be dehallucinated, but for him it was traumatic if a drawing was snatched from him and displayed' (*PAE* 41). To illustrate the process that he terms dehallucination, Winnicott describes a strangely literary nightmare in which 'an old-fashioned little boy' of 6 runs forward in the dream-space like a ghost, as if asking for help. Recognizing this apparition as a hallucination, the dreamer screams and throws a cushion. The child is forcibly removed by his nanny and the dream-space becomes blurred, erasing both the original object of terror and the hallucination. The process, says Winnicott, involves first of all 'something seen,

---

[41] For Lacan, the Real (what cannot be integrated into the symbolic order) may return in the form of hallucination; see Jacques-Alain Miller (ed.), *The Psychoses: The Seminar of Jacques Lacan*, Book III, trans. Russell Grigg (London and New York: Routledge, 1993), 46.

then something dehallucinated, and then a long series of hallucinations so to speak filling the hole produced by the scotomization' (*PAE* 41). Compare the hole filled by the too-fresh, too-legible writing of the 1805 text, or the woman who forces her way against the wind with such hallucinatory agitation and turbulence. The spot of time is also a blind-spot or a 'scotomization' of superstition's lurid writing, diffused across the landscape as visionary dreariness.

Call it 'blank desertion' (*Prelude*, i. 423). 'Blank' is a word that recurs in *The Prelude*—notably, as the 'blank confusion' that makes London hard to see (*Prelude*, vii. 696).[42] Blankness signifies both whiteness and pallor (the colourlessness of unmarked paper, for instance), and something void of interest or expression, threatening vision and perhaps even causing eye problems; we know that Wordsworth's eyes gave him trouble when confronted by paper and that he feared blindness (hence his green eye-shade and team of female domestic scribes).[43] Blankness has privative force, like the 'blank misgivings' and 'Fallings from us, vanishings' of 'The Immortality Ode' (ll. 146–7)—surely an example of what Nancy means by the language of thought ('saying within language what language does not say'). As well as the blank of an eye, it can also refer to a blank domino, to the blank at the centre of a target, and even to the telling absence of rhyme at the turn of the blank-verse line. If one adds the blank space of an omitted letter, a missing word or name, or the space left for a signature, the resulting convergence of blankness, erasure, and writing argues compellingly for the over-determined meanings of blankness in *The Prelude*. Dehallucination belongs to the realm of not seeing, just as hallucination belongs to the visual register. Bion writes of the unreliable eye in need of an eye doctor, or two. But there is also the case of the not-seeing eye—an eye that does not so much refuse insight as it *refuses to see*.

Teasing out what he calls 'the intuition of the negative' in Winnicott (who had almost certainly not read Hegel), the French psychoanalyst André Green replaces the term 'dehallucination' with the phrase 'negative hallucination'.[44] By this he means not just the absence of representation, but the *'representation of the absence of representation'*.[45] The space occupied by hallucination is 'whitened' (his term), marked by the pressure of external reality against an unyielding internal psychic reality. Green re-reads Winnicott in terms of his interest in these 'states of non-representation, emptiness and blankness in which thought becomes anaemic

---

[42] Cf. the aftermath of the visions produced by the Cave of Yordas, a passage originally written to describe Wordsworth's anticlimactic crossing of the Alps when the seer is left with a 'a blank sense of greatness passed away' (*Prelude*, viii. 744).

[43] Wordsworth's attacks of eye-inflammation (trachoma) began in 1805 and recurred at intervals, making him hypersensitive to light and unable to read or write; see Gill, *William Wordsworth: A Life*, 287, 350, 358, 368.

[44] See André Green, *The Work of the Negative*, trans. Andrew Weller (1993; Free Association Books, 1999), 5. Green suggests that Winnicott became aware of 'the work of the negative' only retrospectively, and without actually reading Hegel. For Green's re-reading of Winnicott's paper 'Transitional Objects and Transitional Phenomena' (1951, rev. 1971), see also 'The Intuition of the Negative in Winnicott's Work', in Gregorio Kohon (ed.), *The Dead Mother: The Work of André Green* (London and New York: Routledge, 1999), 205–21, and Ch. 4 above.

[45] Green, *The Work of the Negative*, 276.

against the background of the negative hallucination of its own psychical productions'.[46] The mechanisms of what he calls 'blank thought' (*'les mécanismes du blanc de la pensée'*)—blank psychosis—include thinking deprived of images or words, or 'the non-perception of thoughts without language'. Green invokes the difference between 'My memory's failing me' and the phrase, 'My mind's gone blank':

> I think that we would be able to understand it if we could imagine thinking, not only without images—without representation—but also without words to perceive what one thinks. It is in this respect that language is both a representation and a perception...
> The negative hallucination of thought also manifests itself in the analytic situation as the inability to express oneself with words. This is not the silence of an absence of speech but that of the formation of words as tools for thinking, or of the relation between the morphology and semantics of words. Words can in this case just about be perceived on a sensory level, but what is lost is the relation of the words to their meaning in accordance with the reference to the unconscious.[47]

Wordsworth's marvellously evocative phrase 'Colours and words that are unknown to man' (*Prelude*, xi. 309) conveys with the greatest economy the silent convergence of language's exhaustion, negative hallucination, and the loss of words themselves as tools for thinking—a de-formation that unmoors the elements of landscape from their reference to the unconscious. Language and the unconscious turn out not to be talking to one another after all. It is the work done by this failure—the work of the negative—that communicates.

The same holds true at times for those other would-be imaginary twins, psychoanalysis and literary criticism. That is to say, they are not always talking, or at any rate they are sometimes not talking about the same thing, or in the same way. Each punctuates the too-harmonious functioning of the other's system by speaking their own language, or simply by not communicating. Psychoanalytic criticism, if it is to be at once psychoanalytic and literary, has to take account of this interruption instead of silencing it. Where Green (writing as a clinician) explores a psychotic break in his patient's capacity for verbal thought—*'j'ai un blanc'*—a literary critic might point to a breakdown in the relations between figural and literal, or (in more deconstructive mode) to the opening of a gap between the phenomenal world and the materiality of language.[48] Green's psychoanalytic account of 'the inability to express oneself with words' studiously resists the ineffability of non-verbal communication (compare Nancy's caution about the

---

[46] Ibid., 182. Cf. Green, quoting himself: 'This fading of the internal representations is what I relate to the inner representations of the negative, "a representation of the absence of representation"...which expresses itself in terms of negative hallucination, or in the field of affects, in terms of a void, emptiness or, to a lesser degree, futility, meaninglessness'; see *The Dead Mother*, 208.

[47] Green, *The Work of the Negative*, 198, 196–7; Green comments: 'I am thinking of those patients whose difficulties lie on the level of thinking, as Bion has described' (ibid., 196).

[48] Cf., for instance, Cynthia Chase's discussion of Hegel and Paul de Man, where the rise of aesthetics is seen as a response to 'the gap opened between meaning and language, between the phenomenal world and the materiality of language'; see 'Literary Theory as the Criticism of Aesthetics: De Man, Blanchot, and Romantic "Allegories of Cognition"', in Cathy Caruth and Deborah Esch (eds.), *Critical Encounters* (New Brunswick, NJ: Rutgers University Press, 1995), 54.

language of thought: 'it is above all not to enter the ineffable'). By contrast, both Winnicott's isolate and Wordsworth's points of singleness in their own way pay tribute to a silent reservoir of being. Even Blanchot, in 'The Essential Solitude of the Writer', risks succumbing to the lure of a pure void as 'the opaque and empty opening on what is when there is no more world, when there is no world yet'.[49]

Winnicott and Wordsworth convert this empty opening into a place-holder for the figure of breath or voice. Breathing life into the psychotic core, Winnicott startlingly defines aliveness as 'the moment-by-moment living of the backward child who is enjoying breathing'.[50] Breath, 'which never decides whether it comes primarily from within or without' becomes the first form of communication.[51] Wordsworth's equivalent is the phenomenality of lyric voice, or *The Prelude*'s 'breathings for incommunicable powers' (*Prelude*, ii. 188). Winnicott ends 'Communicating and Not Communicating' by imagining a mode of communication that is 'like the music of the spheres, absolutely personal' (*MPFE* 192). One could call this the personal idiom of the True Self, or the poetry of not communicating—what is sometimes referred to optimistically in a literary context as 'finding one's own voice', just as Winnicott insists (however irritatingly) on saying things in his own language, or Nancy's Hegel puts pressure on the language of thought. The same poetry can be heard in the boating-song of Wordsworth's Blind Highland Boy, the subject of a whimsical domestic tale composed in 1806. I want to close with this wishful performance of Winnicott's theme, if only because, in the insistent negativity of its idiolect, it bears on the poetics of not communicating.

A reprise of earlier and better known Wordsworthian isolates, this hard-to-reach child voyages (like Newton's statue) in strange seas of thought, alone, borne out to sea in a wash-tub on the tide of Wordsworth's home-grown conservative isolationism. His sly domestication of the writer at work floats serenely in a Blanchotian solitude where there is no more world, no world yet, but only the potential spaces of Romantic poetry. The rhythm of inhalation and exhalation in his Gaelic refrain (spelling by courtesy of Sir Walter Scott) utters the most untranslatable of lyric protests against being prematurely found or communicated with, influenced or intruded on:

> 'Lei-gha—Lei-gha'—then did he cry,
> 'Lei-gha—Lei-gha'—most eagerly;
> Thus did he cry, and thus did pray,
> And what he meant was, 'Keep away,
> And leave me to myself!'
>
> ('The Blind Highland Boy',
> ll. 161–4)[52]

[49] Maurice Blanchot, *The Gaze of Orpheus* (Barrytown, NY: Station Hill Press, 1981), 77.
[50] Winnicott, *Playing and Reality*, 69.
[51] Winnicott, *Through Paediatrics to Psycho-Analysis*, 154.
[52] In a letter of 20 January 1807, Wordsworth wrote to Sir Walter Scott with 'a singular sort of request, which is, that you could furnish me by application to some of your Gaelic friends, with a

'Beware! Beware! | His flashing eyes, his floating hair!' Perhaps Wordsworth and Winnicott have been reading each other all along.

The negative poetics that link Winnicott and Wordsworth can also be found in Blanchot. I have in mind not so much 'The Essential Solitude of the Writer' as the traumatic reticence of *The Writing of the Disaster* (*L'Écriture du désastre*, 1980). Blanchot has his own take on negativity and its arguable relation to an unconscious which (according to Pontalis) 'knows nothing of negation because it *is* the negative'—a negativity, however, that is sometimes operative ('speaking with language'), and sometimes inoperative ('the nonoperation of sheer inertia').[53] In this context, the unrepresentability of death in the unconscious is an idea that Blanchot attributes not only to Freud but to Winnicott's 1963 paper, 'Fear of Breakdown': 'Nothing can be done with death that has always taken place . . . the disaster would be beyond what we understand by death or abyss, or in any case by *my* death, since there is no more place for "me" ' (*WD* 119). At the heart of *The Writing of the Disaster* is a punctuating spot of time, a childhood memory or 'primal scene', to which Blanchot returns at intervals throughout his book. He introduces it by paraphrasing (without naming it) Winnicott's 'Fear of Breakdown'. In particular, he invokes Winnicott's memorable phrase for early, unremembered trauma, 'primitive agonies'.

Blanchot takes issue with Winnicott's developmental view of the child. This doubtful, anterior, and uncertain death, he writes,

cannot be explained, as Winnicott would have it, simply by the vicissitudes characteristic of earliest childhood, when the child, still deprived of a self, is subject to overwhelming states (primitive agonies) which he cannot know since he does not yet exist, which happen thus without taking place and later lead the adult, in a memory without memory and through his fissured self, to expect them (either with desire or with dread) from his life when it ends, from the collapse of his existence. Or rather, this understanding of Winnicott's is only an explanation, albeit impressive—a fictive application designed to individualize that which cannot be individualized or to furnish a representation for the unrepresentable . . . . The introduction of such a detour is perhaps therapeutically useful, to the extent that . . . it permits him who lives haunted by the imminent collapse to say: this will not happen, it has already happened; I know, I remember. (*WD* 66)

---

phrase in that language of eight syllables . . . . the Erse word sounded in my ears like Lega; but will you be so good as to send me a proper phrase to stand in the line, signifying—"beware", keep away, let me alone, or anything that might be translated by the words in the text.—'; see Ernest de Selincourt and Mary Moorman (eds.), *The Letters of William and Dorothy Wordsworth: The Middle Years*, Part I: *1806–11*, 2nd edn. (Oxford: Clarendon Press, 1969), 123–4 and n. By 1820, the 'Household Tub' (ll. 113) had become 'A Shell of ample size'.

[53] *The Writing of the Disaster*, trans. Ann Smock (1980; Lincoln, Nebr.: University of Nebraska Press, 1986), 118 (*WD*); Blanchot cites Pontalis on the negativity of the unconscious in relation to Freud's assertion that death is unrepresentable: 'a death that is always other, with which we do not communicate' (*WD* 118).

Winnicott's 'fictive application' makes it possible to remember the fear of one's own death. We live and speak, writes Blanchot, only because death has already taken place as an unsituatable and unremembered event which we entrust to 'the work of the concept (negativity)' or to the work of psychoanalysis (*WD* 67).

Blanchot (the most reticently non-autobiographical of writers) places the Winnicottian child—'The child who, before living, has sunk into dying' (*WD* 68)— at the heart of the writing of the disaster. Here is his own version of a spot of time as a death that has already happened, in all its extraordinary ordinariness. '*Suppose*', he writes,

> ... *suppose this: the child—is he seven years old, or eight perhaps?—standing by the window, drawing the curtain and, through the pane, looking. What he sees: the garden, the wintry trees, the wall of a house. Though he sees, no doubt in a child's way, his play space, he grows weary and slowly looks up towards the ordinary sky, with clouds, grey light—pallid daylight without depth.*
>
> *What happens then: the sky, the same sky, suddenly open[s], absolutely black and absolutely empty, revealing (as though the pane had broken) such an absence that all has since always and forevermore been lost therein—so lost that therein is affirmed and dissolved the vertiginous knowledge that nothing is what there is, and first of all nothing beyond.*
> (*WD* 72, emphasis in original)

Inexplicably overwhelmed with joy, the child bursts into a flood of tears. In this prelude, Blanchot reads the conditions of a premature death that gives him over to the silence of words. Like Wordsworth in his *Prelude*, Blanchot can only rehearse the mnemic elements that anchor his experience of emptiness and absence ('*the vertiginous knowledge that nothing is what there is*') to linear time, space, and affect: '*the tree, the wall, the winter garden, the play space and with it, lassitude.... Nothing has changed.—Except the overwhelming overturning of nothing*' (*WD* 115).

Throughout *The Writing of the Disaster*, Blanchot identifies writing with the overwhelming negativity that both vivifies and eludes it. He remains profoundly mistrustful of any reliance on 'word-things', sceptical about what can be 'communicated' or shared with someone else. He writes about what is non-transmissible, problematizing the idea of an inner self divorced from the literary:

> It is language that is 'cryptic': not only as a totality that is exceeded and untheorizable, but inasmuch as it contains pockets, cavernous places where words become things, where the inside is out and thus inaccessible to any cryptanalysis whatever—for deciphering is required to keep the secret secret. The code no longer suffices. The translation is infinite. And yet we have to find the key word that opens and does not open.   (*WD* 136)[54]

As Blanchot reminds us, aphoristically, '*To keep a secret—to refrain from saying some particular thing—presupposes that one could say it*' (*WD* 137). The secret, he

---

[54] Blanchot cites Derrida: '... something gets away safely, something which frees loss and refuses the gift of it. "*I* can only save *an inner self by placing it in 'me,'* separate from myself, *outside.*" (Derrida). This is a sentence with unlimited developments' (*WD* 136). Indeed.

concludes, is not autobiographical, but linguistic and impersonal—'*not linked to an "I" but to the curve of a space which cannot be called intersubjective*'. The space of the literary is the one place where communication can occur. *The Writing of the Disaster* defines the negative poetics that allows Wordsworth and Winnicott to keep reading each other's books.

PART III

TRANSFORMATIONS

7

Palinurus and the Tank: *Bion's War*

o nimium caelo et pelago confise sereno
nudus in ignota, Palinure, iacebis harena.

Virgil, *Aeneid*, v. 870–1

'For counting
Overmuch on a calm world, Palinurus,
You must lie naked on some unknown shore.'[1]

An unexpected feature linking psychoanalysis, military assault vehicles, and thinking is that all three elicit the idea of a container. To take tanks first, the lumbering prototype of the First World War was affectionately (or ironically) known as 'Mother' when it was first developed during 1915–16 (Figure 13).[2] The term 'tank' emerged as a catchy shorthand—competing with 'container', 'receptacle', 'reservoir', or 'cistern'—designed to conceal the existence of a secret weapon.[3]

---

[1] *The Aeneid*, trans. Robert Fitzgerald (New York: Vintage, 1990), v. 1139–41.

[2] For a contemporary, deadpan recollection of the genealogy of the tank, see Major-General Sir Ernest Swinton, *Eyewitness: Being Personal Reminiscences of Certain Phases of the Great War, Including the Genesis of the Tank* (London: Hodder & Stoughton, 1932), 146 and n., 147 n.: 'Later on the first actual Tank was known as "Mother", and the original Mark I tanks of the same type were called *Big Willies* in contradistinction to *Little Willie*. The *Centipede*, which became "Mother", was the prototype of all the Mark I Tanks, of *Big Willies*, which took the field in September, 1916. It may help to avoid confusion if it is explained that "Mother" was a Male Tank. It was dubbed "Mother" before there were two sexes in the Tank species' (ibid., 184). Swinton suggests that the first canvas-swathed prototypes were called 'Big Willie' and 'Little Willie' because they 'suggested a gigantic canvas covered sow with a sucking pig alongside her' (ibid., 168). For the cultural history, imagery, and language associated with the development of the First World War tank, see Trudi Tate, 'From Little Willie to Mother: The Tank and the First World War', *Women: A Cultural Review*, 8 (1997), 48–64, rpr. in Trudi Tate, *Modernism, History, and the First World War* (Manchester: Manchester University Press, 1998), 120–46. The names 'Mother' and 'Willie'—already a slang word for penis—inevitably gave rise to gender jokes and gender innuendos. For a comprehensive history of the First World War tank, including its representations by war correspondents and war artists, see also Patrick Wright, *Tank: The Progress of a Monstrous War Machine* (London: Faber & Faber, 2000), esp. 23–110; for a witty recapitulation of Wright's book from the perspective of modern aesthetics and technology, see also Peter Wollen, 'Tanks', *Paris Manhattan: Writings on Art* (New York: Verso, 2004), 35–50.

[3] Swinton recalls: 'I was instructed…to try to find some non-committal word to take the place of "landship" or "landcruiser", which tell-tale names, it was realized, gave away the whole secret…The structure of the machine in its early stages being boxlike, some term conveying the idea of a box or container seemed appropriate. We rejected in turn–"container"–"receptacle"–"reservoir"–"cistern." The monosyllable "tank" appealed to us as being likely to catch on and be remembered' (*Eyewitness*, 161).

BUT·THE·MAN· THAT·SHALL·TOUCH ·THEM·MUST·BE·FENCED ·WITH·IRON·

Figure 13 'But the Man that Shall Touch Them Must Be Fenced with Iron'; Tank Light, First World War Window; St Mary's, Swaffham Prior; National Monuments Record.

Tanks were sometimes transported under canvas disguised as water-carriers, and even masqueraded as snow ploughs destined for the Russian front.[4] The modern think-tank evokes a metaphorical reservoir of a different kind—a concentration of experts employed to generate knowledge and ideas, often from a shared political perspective. This semantic happenstance, whereby armoured caterpillar-tractors and groups of like-minded policy-wonks are collectively known as 'tanks', is especially provocative in conjunction with the work of Wilfred Bion. During the 1950s and 1960s, Bion transformed Melanie Klein's theories of infant phantasy— particularly her concept of the infant's projection of unwanted emotions and sensations into the mother's body (projective identification)—into an epistemological 'theory of thinking' of his own. According to Bion, the infant learns to think provided that a maternal receptacle or 'container' is available to modify its anxiety, thereby transforming toxic states of mind into manageable thoughts

---

[4] According to Swinton, tanks were 'later talked of as water-carriers, sometimes as snow ploughs' (*Eyewitness*, 168). He adds: 'It was possible only in the early stages to conceal from the hundreds of men engaged in the production of the Tanks the nature of what they were making. Reports were deliberately spread that the machines were water-carriers for our troops in Palestine, snow-ploughs for the Russian Army, etc., but . . . these fictions could not be kept up. Still further to mislead, the Tanks were numbered from 700 and not from 1, and the legend "WITH CARE TO PETROGRAD" was painted in Russian letters twelve inches high on both sides of each machine' (ibid., 203).

and feelings.[5] Bion's term, routinely used in contemporary Kleinian Object Relations psychoanalysis, applies especially to containment of the infant's unbearable dread of dying.

For Bion, thinking is at once crucial to survival, potentially catastrophic, and frequently impeded. Proto-mental states subtend feelings, meaning, and thought—thought conceived as spanning both contact with reality (hence essential to survival) and the capacity for creative dreaming or the creation of abstract concepts. The primitive building-block for thought is the Kleinian concept of projective identification, which Bion understands both as a primitive form of linking and also as a potentially destructive form of unlinking. Intolerance of frustration, envy, and psychosis, or a mother impervious to, or intolerant of, infantile anxiety, are all conducive to the negative form of thought that Bion termed '–K' (that is, the destruction of knowledge, or 'the link constituted by NOT understanding i.e., *mis*-understanding').[6] The conditions of war provide a fertile site for fears about annihilation, while inevitably intensifying both destructive and persecutory phantasies. In 1940, in an essay called 'The "War of Nerves"', Bion speculated about the effects of warfare on the civilian population during the Second World War. He suggests that 'the object of the combatant is to exploit unconscious phantasies, both in the enemy and in himself, in such a way that the enemy is discomfited and he himself benefited'.[7] No less than the combatant's, the patient's unconscious aim may be to disorient the analyst and sabotage thought. The analytic session becomes a potential battlefield—dangerous and frightening to both parties, and intensely lonely for the bombarded analyst.[8] Bion compares giving interpretations to the problem of using one's brains 'while you are being bombed and shot at'.[9] This, as it happens, was an experience that he himself had undergone as a young tank officer during the First World War.

Enlisting fresh from his British public school, where he was mainly distinguished as an athlete owing to his size and strength, Bion joined the newly formed Tank Corps out of curiosity about tanks because, he wrote, 'it was the only way to penetrate

---

[5] See, for instance, Wilfred R. Bion, 'A Theory of Thinking', *Second Thoughts: Selected Papers on Psycho-Analysis* (1967; rpr. London: Karnac Books, 1987), 116 (*ST*): 'Normal development follows if the relationship between infant and breast permits the infant to project a feeling, say, that it is dying into the mother and to reintroject it after its sojourn in the breast has made it tolerable to the infant psyche'.

[6] Wilfred R. Bion, *Learning from Experience* (1962; rpr. London: Karnac Books, 1984), 52 (*LE*).

[7] See Wilfred R. Bion, 'The "War of Nerves"', E. Miller and H. Crichton-Miller (eds.), *The Neurosis in War* (London: Macmillan, 1940), 180.

[8] See Francesca Bion, 'The Days of Our Years', *Melanie Klein and Object Relations*, 13 (1995), 18–19, on '*the dangerous nature of the analytic experience*': 'it is a stormy, emotional situation for both people. The analyst, like an officer in battle, is supposed to be sane enough to be scared while at the same time remaining articulate and capable of translating what he is aware of into a comprehensible communication.'

[9] 'A famous general once said, "You do not have to be very intelligent to be a general, but you must be able to use such brains as you have while you are being bombed and shot at". It does not sound very dramatic, but I think most psycho-analysts know what it feels like to be giving an interpretation in front of a patient'; see Wilfred R. Bion, *Brazilian Lectures* (London: Karnac Books, 1990), 5.

the secrecy surrounding them'.[10] He records that he was frightened by his first sighting of this 'queer mechanical shape, immobilized and immobilizing' and wanted to get away from it.[11] He survived the war, much against the odds of a tank officer's average life-expectancy—in part because his promotion to section commander took him out of tanks themselves.[12] At this early stage in their evolution, tanks were vulnerable, unreliable, primitive, 4–5 mph mechanical dinosaurs—sitting targets for enemy fire, frequently disabled, easily 'ditched' or bogged down in trenches or the heavy Flanders mud, and constantly in need of maintenance and spare parts. But as well as being recalcitrant material objects, tanks were a potent source of anthropomorphic phantasy. Modernist monsters or primitive cyborgs (one eye-witness saw them as 'a species of gigantic cubist steel slug'), they generated a flurry of jocose hybrid epithets in the journalism of the time: 'Old Ichthyosaurus', 'Giant Toad', 'Motor-Monster', 'Jabberwock with eyes of Flame', 'Hush-Hush', 'Touring Fort', 'Travelling Turret', 'Whale', 'Slug', and 'Boojum'.[13]

Politically and culturally, tanks were seen as a means not only to transform the war abroad but also to rally flagging economic and moral support for the war at home. For all their teething problems (slowness, unmanoeuvrability, unreliability), tanks appeared to hold the promise of mobility, mechanical power, and armoured protection in the midst of stasis and carnage—a strategic lever to overcome the crippling stalemate and overwhelming infantry losses that already characterized trench warfare by 1915.[14] First developed by the navy rather than the army, tanks were originally envisaged as 'landships' or landcruisers, running on primitive caterpillar tracks derived from agricultural machinery (the earliest prototype was called HMS *Centipede* in nautical fashion).[15] Much of the romance attached

[10] See Wilfred R. Bion, *The Long Week-End 1897–1919: Part of a Life* (1982; rpr. London: Karnac Books, 1991), 115 (*LWE*). For a brief account of Bion's war years, see Gérard Bléandonu, *Wilfred Bion: His Life and Works 1897–1979*, trans. Claire Pajaczkowska (London: Free Association Books, 1994), 24–34. Bion also refers to curiosity in the 1970s commentary on his earlier war diaries: 'I was extremely anxious to see these newly invented things, and joining seemed the only way of seeing them'; see Wilfred R. Bion, *War Memoirs 1917–1919*, ed. Francesca Bion (London: Karnac Books, 1997), 200 (*WM*). Bion's *War Memoirs* are illustrated with his own drawings and with photographs that illustrate both the technical aspects of tank warfare and their anthropomorphic menace as they loom over trenches, sink in the mud of a water-logged battlescape, or break through enemy barbed wire.

[11] Bion recalls: 'I was ordered to Bovington Camp at Wool where I saw my first tank . . . The queer mechanical shape, immobilized and immobilizing, was frightening in the same way as the primitive tiger trap near Qualior; I wanted to get away from it' (*LWE* 115); for the frightening, box-like tiger trap of his Indian early childhood (a contraption baited with a live goat), see ibid., 32.

[12] Towards the end of the war, a third of every section was wiped out by each battle; in one battle, Bion lost his entire section and all his tanks (see *LWE* 258). By the end, only Bion and two other officers were left of those who had served with the battalion from the start, and none of their men (see *LWE* 286).

[13] See Swinton, *Eyewitness*, 170, 245. Tate cites the *Daily Mail* correspondent, writing in 1916: 'Whales, Boojums, Dreadnoughts, slugs, snarks—never were creatures that so tempted the gift of nick-naming' (see *Modernism, History, and the First World War*, 124).

[14] See ibid., 120–46, and Wright, *Tank*, 81–100.

[15] See Swinton, *Eyewitness*, 139, for the work of the Admiralty 'Landships Committee', which had been working independently from the War Office in 1915 to develop a trench-crossing machine.

to these slow-moving machines derived from the idea of an armoured land-destroyer, advancing unstoppably ahead of infantry troops, crushing barbed-wire entanglements, crossing trenches, and rolling over enemy machine-gun outposts (not to mention bodies).[16] Although the military bureaucracy of the time has often been seen as unable to harness the potential of tanks, let alone envisage their future uses, substantial financial and technical resources were actually committed to their development early on in the war.[17] At the front, reactions by army professionals were mixed—a weapon peripheral to conventional warfare, or a new technology capable of winning a war in which military-industrial capacity had become crucial? The effective deployment of tanks required, among other things, careful co-ordination, timing, and communications; accurate and detailed assessment of terrain; and an essential element of tactical surprise. These conditions were often neglected, absent, bungled, or simply ignored. For the eight-man crews who drove them, tanks entailed maximum vulnerability and frustration, given their propensity to attract enemy gunfire, the difficulty of getting out if they were hit, or their tendency to simply break down and get hopelessly stuck. Often they failed even to reach the starting line. Mechanical problems with engines, gears, and tracks, combined with intractable elements such as mud, darkness, unsuitable terrain, and (most catastrophically) fire, turned the inside of a tank into a mobile hell—hot, noisy, blinding, fume-filled, and above all, liable to explode, with fatal consequences for the entire crew.[18] Officers drove or guided their tanks under conditions of semi-blindness, steering by compasses that were thrown off by the mass of metal that surrounded them. Radio communication was still at a rudimentary stage, leaving communications dependent on people waving flags or on homing pigeons. Section commanders who co-ordinated their tank sections on foot—as Bion did—were more likely to survive than were their vulnerable crews, often becoming helpless onlookers from a distance at the destruction of their tanks and the teams of men for whom they were responsible and to whom they had become attached.

As Bion informed his parents, 'The worst of it was that the splinters would usually kill or wound the crew and set the tank alight. The wounded often couldn't get out and simply were burned to death' (*WM* 35 n.). Wounded foot soldiers tended to regard tanks as armoured ambulances or shelters, begging agonizingly

[16] See Bion's idiotic (female) questioner on one of his leaves: ' "What was it like... when you drove your tank over people?"... But I had never driven over anyone; I had to admit that the experience had so far escaped me' (*LWE* 266).

[17] David J. Childs, in *A Peripheral Weapon? The Production and Employment of British Tanks in the First World War* (Westport, Conn.: Greenwood Press, 1999), argues against the generally accepted view that the army dragged its heels in the development and use of tanks; eyewitness accounts such as Swinton's are apt to claim lonely prophetic status for themselves as the sole 'inventors' or proponents of the tank.

[18] See Tate, *Modernism, History, and the First World War*, 140, for Arthur Jenkin's vivid account of conditions inside in *A Tank Driver's Experiences; or, Incidents in a Soldier's Life* (London: Elliot Stock, 1922), 179.

for lifts that had to be refused, or crawling into stranded tanks to die under their shelter.[19] For those who saw them looming from the other side, tanks instilled fear, resembling inhuman, death-dealing monsters coming unstoppably on, undeterred by barbed wire or trenches.[20] But for the tank-crews themselves, the overwhelming anxiety was that of being blown up (tanks were often packed with explosives to self-destruct and prevent them falling into enemy hands). In a recorded flashback at the end of his life, Bion graphically evoked the terrifying symbiosis of man and machine that resulted from a direct hit: 'the bodies were charred and blackened, and poured out of the door of the tank as if they were the entrails of some mysterious beast of a primitive kind which had simply perished then and there in the conflagration'.[21] Elsewhere, he writes of bodies flung from an exploded tank 'like the guts of some fantastic animal hanging out of a vast gaping wound' (*WM* 254). Bion's later accounts link this primitive anthropomorphism with the stupefied 'mindlessness' produced by being part of the army itself, and specifically by battle conditions; the tank comes to figure mindlessness rather than primitive life, let alone shelter.[22] Under heavy artillery fire, a solid steel tank shook continuously 'like a wobbling jelly' in 'an inferno of slammed doors' (*LWE* 130). This was an experience whose loneliness and vulnerability Bion had evoked in his *War Memoirs* with the same desolate, ear-slamming image: 'It seemed as if you were all alone in a huge passage with great doors slamming all around' (*WM* 30). The tank was an armoured refuge or carapace that could not protect its inmates—a place of imaginary security, or a container that failed to contain: 'No protection more solid than a figment of the imagination' (*LWE* 130).

In 'A Theory of Thinking', Bion writes of a breakdown of thought whereby 'the appropriate machinery' for thinking 'is felt to be, not an apparatus for thinking the thoughts, but an apparatus for ridding the psyche of accumulations of bad internal objects' (*ST* 112)—a primitive ejection mechanism. When an infant who feels that it is dying is unable to arouse the same fear in its mother, the consequence (according to Bion) is both an escalation in the force and frequency of the projective identifications with which it bombards its unresponsive maternal

---

[19] Bion explains: 'As we trundled along, we were hailed by numbers of wounded who called to be carried back. The position was a difficult one. Tanks were expressly forbidden to take back wounded if limbs were broken. In a previous action they had been ordered . . . to carry back all they could. The result was a tragedy. At the end of half an hour's ride . . . every wounded man that had been picked up with broken bones was found to be dead . . . The result was we were forced to refuse these people our help. It was an incredible business. They of course saw a tank as their great chance of safety' (*WM* 151).   [20] See Tate, *Modernism, History, and the First World War*, 138–9.

[21] Transcript of a tape recording on 8 August 1978 (the sixtieth anniversary of the Battle of Amiens); see W. R. Bion, *Cogitations*, ed. Francesca Bion (London: Karnac Books, 1994), 368 (*C*). Cf. the primitive anthropomorphism of his earlier autobiography: 'Out of the door hung three blackened bodies like disembowelled entrails' (*LWE* 251).

[22] 'I do not remember that any of us for a moment thought that a forty-ton tank could float; the mud must have seeped into the place where our minds were supposed to be. The army, of which we were part, was mindless' (*LWE* 126). Cf. the mindlessness induced by heavy bombardment: 'Could a shell fall short or over? It could—so I gave up thinking about it, thus taking shelter instinctively in mindlessness' (*LWE* 130).

object, and the denuding of the projection of meaning.[23] Bion's accounts of such primitive states of mind have something in common with his description of a war similarly characterized by escalating artillery bombardment on both sides, which came to seem increasingly meaningless and inhuman. In his later commentary on his wartime experiences, Bion describes the tank soldier's inadmissible depression and fear before battle and the prospect of death as 'a curious sense of being entirely alone in company with a crowd of mindless robots—machines devoid of humanity. The loneliness was intense' (*WM* 204). Bion's reconstructed journal of his wartime years, from 1917 until his demobilization in 1919 (a record written while he was at Oxford) is a belated communication to his parents, and particularly his mother.[24] This near-contemporary record offers a detailed, factual, and increasingly disillusioned account of his experience of tank warfare. His retrospective journal was subsequently overlaid by accounts that return, fugue-like, to unpack this traumatic period in his life, along with the regressed and proto-mental states it deals with, as if the writing had to be done over and over again. Bion continued to write and dream about the war at intervals for the next fifty years, reworking his memories at the very end of his life in his autobiographical trilogy, *A Memoir of the Future* (1975–9): 'These old ghosts, they never die' (*LWE* 264). Bion's accounts of the war convey his stamina, resourcefulness, and intelligence—as well as his conventional public-school piety—along with his growing identification with the helplessness and hopelessness of a hunted animal, and his weariness as the war dragged to a close: 'I had the sense of being a cornered rat which a giant was nonchalantly aiming to club to death' (*LWE* 262). Feeling himself 'merely an insignificant scrap of humanity that was being intolerably persecuted by unknown powers' (*WM* 94–5), he experienced the persecutory anxiety that he later associated with psychosis, and with the persistence of myths involving a hostile, omnipotent deity. Wartime trauma offered a template for the psychotic states he later described in his analytic patients.

Bion was decorated after the Battle of Cambrai in 1917, when tanks first played a prominent role and he himself was still a relatively enthusiastic and inexperienced young officer.[25] Later he received the Légion d'honneur after the Battle of

---

[23] 'If the mother cannot tolerate these projections the infant is reduced to continued projective identification carried out with increasing force and frequency. The increased force seems to denude the projection of its penumbra of meaning' (*ST* 115).

[24] In 'Aftermath', Parthenope Bion (Bion's daughter) notes 'that although the diaries were dedicated to his parents, it is his mother alone who is invoked every now and again as reader, as though Bion felt that she was a fundamental participant in an internal dialogue'. She speculates that Bion's inability to write to his mother during the war may have been 'an unconscious attempt to preserve her in his own mind as a container as undamaged as possible by hideous news' (*WM* 310).

[25] The gallantry of W. R. Bion is described in a footnote to the official history of his regiment, which conveys the early ethos of these mechanically 'mounted' cavalry; see Captain B. H. Liddell Hart, *The Tanks: The History of the Royal Tank Regiment and its Predecessors, 1914–45*, 2 vols. (London: Cassell, 1959), i. 143 n.: 'Some of the tankmen fought on when "dismounted". A striking example was that of Lieutenant W. R. Bion, who, when his tank was knocked out, established an advanced post in a German trench with his crew and some stray infantry and then climbed back on the roof of his tank with a Lewis gun, to get better aim at an opposing machine-gun. When the

Amiens, the decisive Allied advance of 8 August 1918—a devastating experience for Bion himself, however, who wrote: 'I never recovered from the survival of the Battle of Amiens' (*WM* 209). In his dreams, death, not survival, was the reality: 'Oh yes, I died—on August 8th 1918' (*LWE* 265), along with so many of his fellow-soldiers. This was the battle that elicited Bion's most memorable account of traumatic disorientation and never-to-be-completed mourning. He returns again and again to the death of the boy-soldier, his runner, Sweeting—seemingly haunted as much by his own panic and aversion as by the dying boy's maddeningly repeated 'Write to my mother, mother, mother... You will write to her, Mother, Mother...' (*WM* 255). Tank warfare and mothers converge like a refrain in Bion's repeated reliving and rewriting of this, the Mother of all battles: 'Never have I known a bombardment like this, never, never—Mother, Mother, Mother—never have I known a bombardment like this' (*WM* 256). I shall return to the traumatic episode of Sweeting. But, to start with, I want to focus on a different aspect of Bion's war experience. Modern trauma theory is often said to have its origins in early twentieth-century psychologists' attempts to understand the impact on soldiers of the technologies of modern war.[26] Pre-Freudian railway trauma gave way to the trauma of shellshock, just as hysterical reminiscence became the soldier's *malaise* rather than the *fin-de-siècle* woman's, later to be replaced by a deepened understanding of the relation between trauma, grief, and object loss. Freud's well-known reference to the piercing of the psychic organism's protective shield (using a metaphor drawn from cell biology) is among his lasting legacies to the discourse of psychical trauma. But this legacy includes, as well, the metaphor of falling along with the elusive death-drive, or the compulsion to repeat—the mutter—*Mutter* effect that recurs in Bion's telling and retelling of the Battle of Amiens and in his stuttering account of the death of the boy-soldier, Sweeting ('never never—Mother, Mother, Mother').[27]

The metaphor that Bion himself uses for trauma might more properly be called a literary allusion that takes on the status of a personal myth or psychoanalytic 'construction', or reconstruction. It becomes, in fact, one of Bion's touchstones for

Germans counter-attacked in strength he kept them at bay until his ammunition ran out and then continued the fight with the use of an abandoned German machine-gun, until a company of the Seaforths came up. Its commander was soon shot through the head, whereupon Bion temporarily took over the company. He was put in for the V.C., and received the D.S.O.'

[26] See, for instance, Ruth Leys, *Trauma: A Genealogy* (Chicago: University of Chicago Press, 2000), 83–119. John Rickman—Bion's analyst and Second World War colleague—describes a Second World War soldier's traumatic hysteria in terms of his mourning and depression in response to object-loss; see John Rickman, 'A Case of Hysteria—Theory and Practice in the Two Wars' (1941), *Selected Contributions to Psycho-Analysis* (1957; rpr. Karnac Books: London, 2003), 90–4: 'It was observed that he nursed his arm, it was all he could think about, he stroked it and tried to make it warm (it was blue and cold)... It was soon clear, when he was got to talk, that the "poor arm" represented in his thoughts a person who was dead, and one for whom he would have given his right hand—his best companion in the dreary first winter of the war' (ibid., 91).

[27] For a grim anecdote about a dying 16-year-old German soldier crying out 'Mutti—Mutti' and being consoled by 'a British Tommy sitting wounded by a knocked-out tank... saying... "It's all right chum, Mother's here with you"', see Tate, *Modernism, History, and the First World War*, 137.

psychoanalytic construction more generally, in the archaeological sense in which Freud had used the term.[28] This metaphor also suggests the possibility of re-reading Bion's most original contribution to the affective terminology of primitive experience, his phrase 'nameless dread'. This is a form of anxiety that has its origin and prototype in the failure of the maternal container to contain—to process or return in manageable form—the baby's psychic experience of being attacked by painful internal sensations, and especially its fear of dying: 'It therefore reintrojects, not a fear of dying made tolerable, but a nameless dread' (*ST* 116). Strictly speaking, such dread precedes both thought and any traumatic encounter with the external world. But, in the light of Bion's war memoirs, it might be seen as a retroactive back-formation that paradoxically gives meaning to his traumatic experience of tank warfare. Whatever its origins, the figure of a failed maternal container ('Mother') is a constant in Bion's writing, both on the battlefield and in what he later called his 'Theory of Thinking'. Because the conditions of tank warfare involved such powerful conscious and unconscious phantasies of combined omnipotence and helplessness (and such devastating internal and external conditions), it is tempting to link Bion's war writings with an episode from Virgil's *Aeneid* which he invokes on a number of occasions in his later writing. The story of the pilot, Palinurus, who falls asleep in Book V of the *Aeneid* while guiding the lead ship of Aeneas' fleet, acquires particular resonance when re-read in the context of Bion's war writings. It also invokes the phenomenology of falling, a recurrent trope in Second World War writing about trauma that coincides with Bion's confessed fear of falling under his own tank: 'The tank commander's private fear now possessed me—the fear that I would fall wounded, unobserved by the crew, and so be driven over by the tank' (*LWE* 130).[29]

UNUM PRO MULTIS

In the *Aeneid*, Palinurus—the pilot of the leading ship in Aeneas' fleet—is the victim arbitrarily offered up to Neptune by Venus in exchange for a safe voyage for Aeneas and the rest of his companions: ' "*unus erit tantum, amissum quem gurgite quaeres;* | *unum pro multis dabitur caput...*" ' (*Aeneid*, v. 814–15; ' "One shall be

[28] See Sigmund Freud, 'Construction in Analysis' (1937), *SE* xxii. 257–69: '[The analyst's] work of construction, or, if it is preferred, reconstruction, resembles to a great extent an archaeologist's excavation of some dwelling place that has been destroyed and buried or of some ancient edifice... It must be borne in mind that the excavator is dealing with destroyed objects of which large and important portions have quite certainly been lost, by mechanical violence, by fire and by plundering' (*SE* xxii. 259). Cf. Bion, 'On Arrogance', writing of a psychic spectacle, 'to borrow Freud's analogy, similar to that of the archaeologist who discovers in his field-work the evidence, not so much of a primitive civilization, as of a primitive catastrophe' (*ST* 88).
[29] See, for instance, Eleanor Kaufman, 'Falling from the Sky: Trauma in Perec's *W* and Caruth's *Unclaimed Experience*', *Diacritics: Trauma and Psychoanalysis*, 28/4 (1998), 44–53; Kaufman draws attention to the link between falling from the air and post-Holocaust accounts of trauma.

lost, | But only one to look for, lost at sea: | One life given for many" ").[30] As the crew lie sleeping on their benches, Somnus, the God of sleep, approaches Palinurus (a responsible helmsman who is specified as 'guiltless') disguised as his shipmate Phorbas, and brings him bad dreams. The god tempts Palinurus to sleep, since the sea is calm, but Palinurus refuses to give up the tiller. He speaks scornfully from all his accumulated experience as a pilot, refusing to trust to the treachery of the sea:

> *'mene salis placidi vultum fluctosque quietos*
> *ignoreare iubes? Mene huic confidere monstro?'*
>
> (*Aeneid*, v. 848–9)
>
> 'Forget my good sense for this peaceful face
> The sea puts on, the calm swell? Put my trust
> In that capricious monster?'[31]

Palinurus refuses to lose his hold on the tiller, keeping his eyes on the stars by which he pilots the lead ship. His fate is to be cast into the sea and washed up on a strange shore, left unburied and lamenting his lack of a tomb. In Cyril Connolly's appropriation of the story, 'His is the core of melancholy and guilt that works destruction on us from within.'[32]

Bion's own interpretation is more complex and more intimately bound up with his psychoanalytic system. Apropos of the turmoil of the analytic consulting room that may belie its superficial calm, his late paper, 'On a Quotation from Freud' (1976), invokes Palinurus' response to Somnus—that he is too experienced to trust 'the calm and beautiful surface of the Mediterranean'.[33] As if to punish him for his confidence, the persistent god shakes his Lethe-dipped bough over Palinurus' temples, dissolving his swimming eyes in sleep as the fleet sails serenely on. Hardly has Palinurus fallen asleep when Somnus flings him headlong into the sea, breaking off with him the helm and part of the stern, while Palinurus

---

[30] *The Aeneid*, trans. Fitzgerald, v. 1064–6.   [31] Ibid., v. 1110–12.

[32] See Cyril Connolly, *Palinurus' The Unquiet Grave: A Word Cycle* (1945; rpr. London: Pimlico, 1992), p. xiii. For Connolly, not only must the ghost of Palinurus be appeased by a cenotaph, but his death may not have been as accidental as Aeneas imagines (perhaps Palinurus was tired of the war). Connolly devotes his final chapter to a psychoanalytic interpretation which emphasizes Palinurus as the myth of 'a certain will-to-failure or repugnance to success, a desire to give up at the last moment, an urge towards loneliness, isolation, and obscurity. Palinurus, in spite of his great ability and his conspicuous public position, deserted his post in the moment of victory and opted for the unknown shore' (ibid., 137). This interpretation might have struck a chord in Bion in the wake of his departure for Los Angeles in 1968.

[33] See Francesca Bion (ed.), Wilfred R. Bion, *Clinical Seminars and Other Works* (1987; rpr. London: Karnac Books, 1994), 308: 'Palinurus is described, at the end of the fifth book of the *Aeneid*, as saying that Somnus must think he is very inexperienced if he can be led off course while steering his fleet on the calm and beautiful surface of the Mediterranean. This is something we should not forget; we should not be misled by the superficial and beautiful calm which pervades our various consulting rooms and institutions.' Here, as well as in 'Emotional Turbulence' (1976), Bion invokes Leonardo's drawings of hair and water as images of mental turbulence (see ibid., 308, 303).

calls on his unhearing comrades:

> *vix primos inopina quies laxaverat artus,*
> *et super incumbens cum puppis parte revulsa*
> *cumque gubernaclo liquidas proiecit in undas*
> *praecipitem ac socios nequiquam saepe vocantem . . .*
>
> (*Aeneid*, v. 857–60)

> His unexpected drowse barely begun,
> Somnus leaned over him and flung him down
> In the clear water, breaking off with him
> A segment of the stern and steering oar.
> Headfirst he went down, calling in vain on friends.[34]

In this moment of gratuitous violence, when a man specified as guiltless is hurled overboard for refusing to hand over the tiller, Virgil's narrative too seems momentarily rudderless. How wrong can an experienced pilot be?

The breaking-off of the stern along with the steering oar makes this a peculiarly violent 'fall'. Is the helmsman a victim of bad luck or of his own misplaced pride? Was he indeed guiltless, or was he (as Virgil makes Aeneas lament) too trustful of the calm of sea and sky? And what kind of hostile deity drowns the pilot so that the fleet may reach port? Bion's scattered but prominent references to the episode shed some light on how he himself may have read it towards the end of his life. In the 8 August 1978 recording made on the sixtieth anniversary of the Battle of Amiens, he refers telegraphically to the difficulty of using a term like 'omnipotence' when it must always be described in terms of what he calls its 'reciprocal' (elsewhere, its 'co-ordinate')—that is, 'helplessness'. Palinurus, Bion recalls, 'was put to sleep by the god disguised as [Phorbus], and hurled into the depths of the ocean'; he might have felt as betrayed as Jesus did 'when he found that God did not protect him'. An inhuman and incommensurate power is registered in such episodes, 'and yet people talk about "omnipotence" as if they knew what it meant and as if it had a simple connotation' (*C* 370–1). In an earlier essay, 'The Grid' (1971), Bion describes what he calls 'C constructs'—dream-thoughts, dreams, and myths possessing a vivid pictorial quality ('a verbal picture gallery') and facilitating conceptual thought in psychoanalytic work. His examples include Freud's Oedipus myth, along with catastrophic events such as the mass burials at the royal cemetery of Ur in 3500 BC, the plundering of the grave five hundred years later, and the Biblical stories of the Tree of Knowledge and the Tower of Babel. He also cites the episode of Palinurus as his own particular contribution to a collection of psychoanalytic constructs that combine elements of religion, ritual, magic, and drugs with an overwhelmingly hostile deity.[35]

---

[34] *The Aeneid*, trans. Fitzgerald, v. 1122–6.
[35] See Wilfred R. Bion, *Two Papers: The Grid and Caesura* (1977; rpr. London: Karnac Books, 1989), 11, 29.

These stories evoke primitive or violent components in Bion's psychoanalytic table of elements: destructive forms of ignorance allied to curiosity; murderous greed or envy; and hostility on the part of an all-powerful and persecutory god. Such stories are needed, Bion proposes, because—unlike 'theory'—they reveal 'that certain elements are constantly conjoined; that fact may escape attention but for a model of this kind.'[36] His summary of the death of the pilot Palinurus is used to illustrate the reciprocal or 'conjoined' meanings of omnipotence and helplessness. Bion's retelling of the story emphasizes Palinurus' contemptuous response to Somnus, along with Aeneas' lament for the apparent fecklessness of his helmsman: ' "*o nimium caelo et pelago confise sereno* | *nudus in ignota, Palinure, iacebis harena*" ' (*Aeneid*, v. 870–1 ' "For counting | Overmuch on a calm world, Palinurus, | You must lie naked on some unknown shore" ').[37] Stunned by the fate of his pilot, Aeneas takes over the helm, steering his ships away from the Sirens. But whose is the omnipotence, and whose is the helplessness, in this (re)construction? Palinurus, who is too trustful of the calm weather, falls asleep like a baby, and must lie naked on an unknown strand. His professional pride is humbled by its 'co-ordinate'. In 'A Theory of Thinking', Bion writes that Klein's phrase 'excessive projective identification' should be understood not only to refer to the frequency of its employment, 'but to excess of belief in omnipotence' (*ST* 114). For Bion, unconscious omnipotent phantasy arises as a defensive response to the baby's actual helplessness. In benign circumstances, such omnipotence is managed relatively realistically via the combined operation of projective identification and the subtle adjustment of mother to child (just as Winnicott believes that the role of the mother is to protect the infant against the too-early impingement of the environment). But, in battle conditions, omnipotent phantasy may bring with it the kind of dissociation that Bion elsewhere describes as 'spontaneous, automatic, but potentially costly as it involved not knowing of the imminence of death' (*LWE* 132).[38]

This costly means of achieving security by losing contact with reality approximates to Palinurus' over-confident condition of unknowing. He has no inkling of his own danger and imminent fall—no sense of his vulnerability, whether to sleep or to death. Bion claims that psychoanalysis is particularly deficient when it comes to models that involve the relation between omnipotence and helplessness, both features of primitive thinking, and perhaps (he speculates) inseparable from thought itself. Along with other myths such as the Tree of Knowledge, the Tower of Babel, and the Oedipus myth, the story of Palinurus sketches the specialized, paradoxical, and problematic concept of omnipotence that had become central to

---

[36] Wilfred R. Bion, *Two Papers: The Grid and Caesura* (1977; rpr. London: Karnac Books, 1989), 30.   [37] *The Aeneid*, trans. Fitzgerald, v. 1139–41.
[38] Bion describes a similar moment of omnipotence (or lunacy) when he walks along the top of a trench to rejoin his men: 'from the point of view of sheer unadulterated lunacy what followed was the maddest and most dangerous thing I ever did. I must have been very nearly mad to do it. But I never *thought* more clearly in my life' (*WM* 106).

Bion's thinking. But the episode also emphasizes what is gratuitous and arbitrary in Palinurus' fate: an innocent man, doing his job, flung headlong into the sea; part of the stern and the steering oar torn off violently as he goes overboard; his comrades not hearing his cries. In his São Paulo lectures of 1973, Bion singles out elements such as the story's ostensible focus on religion: 'The story of Palinurus is a *serious* simplification, through the poetical capacity of a great man to draw attention to religion.' He narrates Somnus' attempted seduction, Palinurus' haughty reply, and the violent sequel: 'This is a moral story, a *serious* moral story. If we ask ourselves what words we should have to use to tell that story today, we should have to talk about things like memory, desire, drugs (the waters of Lethe), violence and great hostility.'[39] With this opaque interpretation, Bion turns to the clinical situation—not so much to illuminate the story's confusing morality (or lack of it), as to underline the potential role of aesthetics, narrative, and language in psychoanalytic practice:

Aeneas sees his helmsman has gone, his ship is veering wildly and the fleet has nothing to navigate by. He says: 'Poor Palinurus! How sad that you should be taken in by something so commonplace as the smooth appearance of the sea.' Nobody gains anything. Aeneas cannot believe he has a faithful, experienced helmsman; Palinurus cannot feel that his leader knows anything about his fidelity or his ability. That is a moral story; plus or minus. Therefore, when your patient makes you feel that he is being omnipotent, it would be useful if you had evidence which might show what kind of god he is talking about and what kind of morals he is experiencing. In the consulting room, the analyst has to be a kind of poet, or artist, or scientist, or theologian to be able to give an interpretation or a construction . . . The analyst must be able to construct a story. Not only that, he must construct a language which he can talk and which the patient can understand.[40]

When it comes to the unquiet seas of interpretation, the analyst has to be a poet as well as a pilot. He needs Virgil's *Aeneid* as his guide, especially if he is to avoid the fate of Palinurus—the occupational hazard of falling asleep at the helm, or in the analytic consulting room, for all his professional pride and experience. But worse than falling asleep would be having too much confidence in his own expertise. Not being able to let go of the helm has its own dangers.[41]

Michael Putnam's account of Virgilian language in the *Aeneid* emphasizes the violence and destructiveness implied by Virgil's use of the adjective '*adfixus*' to describe Palinurus' fast hold on the tiller. The term is associated variously with attachment, rootedness, stinging, piercing, fiery combustion, and, in Book V, with Palinurus himself, '*adfixus et haerens*' (*Aeneid*, v. 852). Putnam writes: 'The bees leave poison and make a wound, as they put their life into the sting, and by clutching

[39] Bion, *Brazilian Lectures*, 16.   [40] Ibid., 17.
[41] The Palinurus episode has also been glossed elsewhere 'as a metaphor to explain the danger faced by the analyst when he is not ready to give up memory, desire, and understanding during analytic listening'; 'the metaphor is used to explain the danger of remaining stubbornly harnessed to memory and desire as Palinurus did with the helm'; see Rafael E. López-Corvo, *The Dictionary of the Work of W. R. Bion* (London: Karnac Books, 2003), 206.

tightly to his rudder Palinurus maims his ship as he falls.'[42] He notes that Palinurus, like fire on a Trojan defence-tower, clings with mutilating adhesiveness to the very thing he is trying to preserve. This fatal inability to let go will recur in Bion's account of tank warfare, where abandoning a tank might feel like risking court-martial, but is the only way to save the lives of the crew and the driver. The element of fixation turns out to be a specific feature of trauma as Bion rewrites it—not only in relation to the temporal recurrence of traumatic memories, and not only in his various returns to the story of Palinurus, but thematized in a more literal way as sticking fatally to one's tank (just as Palinurus clings to his helm). The Palinurus episode surfaces in Bion's writing as if the charged language of fixation enacts the fixation of war trauma itself, shaping the very forms of memory: 'Every course I had initiated seemed to be an irretrievable blunder. It was not a repetition, it was not a reminiscence'—not death-drive, not hysteria. Rather, Bion recalls, what he experienced was a sense of overwhelming persecution: 'again I had the sense of being a cornered rat' (*LWE* 262).

Bion's 8 August 1978 recording, marking the sixtieth anniversary of the Battle of Amiens, opens by quoting from the last phantasmal battle scene in Tennyson's *Idylls of the King*: 'The faces of old ghosts look in upon the battle' (*C* 368).[43] Commemorating the dead soldiers he had known—a litany of the names memorialized in his memoirs (Asser, Cartwright, O'Toole)—Bion recalls the charred and blackened bodies pouring out of the doors of Cartwright's tank, then turns to feelings prompted by a recent visit to the Keats–Shelley museum in Rome. The associations with poetry, death, and literary rivalry usher in reflections on what we would now call (perhaps too knowingly) the anxiety of influence. Bion contrasts the varieties of poetic rivalry between Shelley and Keats, on one hand, and Byron and Keats on the other, in terms of the difference between generosity and envy. But he also invokes kinds of influence beyond articulate speech, alluding obscurely to 'stimuli that come from without, the unknown that is so terrifying and stimulates such powerful feelings that they cannot be described in ordinary terms' (*C* 369). In making this commemorative tribute to his dead companions, Bion clearly has in mind, among other things, Shelley's lament for the dead Keats in *Adonais*. As Bion's editor reminds us, Shelley's preface to *Adonais* begins with a Greek quotation from Moschus' 'Epitaph for Bion'—'A poison came, Bion, to thy lips . . . He was immune to song' (*C* 369).[44] In this literary association between the ghosts of

---

[42] Michael C. Putnam, *Virgil's Aeneid: Interpretation and Influence* (Chapel Hill, NC: University of North Carolina Press, 1995), 35: 'At the end of the fifth book we find Palinurus "affixed and clinging" (*adfixus et haerens*, 852) to the helm of Aeneas' ship, soon to tear part of the poop and rudder with him as Sleep plunges him into the water.'

[43] See Tennyson, *Idylls of the King*, 'The Passing of Arthur', ll. 103–5: 'And some beheld the faces of old ghosts | Look in upon the battle; and in the mist | Was many a noble deed, many a base . . . '. Bion might well have had his own First World War associations with the misty limbo of Arthur's deathbed struggle: 'Sweat, writhings, anguish, labouring of the lungs | In that close mist, and cryings for the light, | Moans of the dying, and voices of the dead' (ibid. ll. 115–17).

[44] 'Φαρμακον ηλθη, Βιον, ποτι σον στομα . . . εκφϑγεν ωδαν'; Moschus, epitaph for Bion, 'Preface', *Adonais* (1821). Bion refers to Moschus, *Theocritus, Bion, and Moschus* (1911); see *C* 392.

dead soldiers and the Dead Poets' Society, Bion (or so it is implied) identified himself with a celebrated lament for a dead pastoral poet of the same name. His younger self had died on the Amiens–Roye road, and now, like Tennyson's Arthur, he anticipates his own passing at the end of his life. The movement of thought in this memorial recording suggests that Bion was willing to allow his ideas to emerge associatively. Elsewhere, he links these ideas with the inarticulateness and unformedness that characterize the transition between paranoid–schizoid and depressive positions (the Positions, as he calls them in *Cogitations*, to indicate that they always function in tandem). For Bion, one might note, this oscillatory mode not only has creative potential but can be thought of as underlying creativity itself. No wonder poetry was in, or on, his mind.

The loose, free-associative train of ideas in Bion's recorded talk provides the context for his segue to the term 'omnipotence', which he insists has no meaning without its reciprocal, 'helplessness'. The point Bion seems to be making is that meaning exists in essentially dynamic relation to its others (object relations psychoanalyst that he is, he instances Buber's '*I and thou*', subject in relation to object), rather than as isolated entities. But language, like narrative, becomes strained by the attempt to evoke forces beyond the reach of human imagination, rationality, and words. In this context, Bion's reference to Palinurus, 'put to sleep by the god disguised as Somnus, and hurled into the depths of the ocean' (*C* 370), functions as a submerged metaphor for the struggle to apprehend immense unknown forces as well as the letting go of memory and desire. The fate of Palinurus becomes a figure for death itself—not only considered as the prototype for a disorganized state of mind but also for a devastating sense of abandonment on a par with that of Jesus—'Why hast thou forsaken me?' (*C* 371). The implied reproach in Sweeting's repeated 'Mother, Mother, Mother'—why did you send me to war?—is the question that many young soldiers must have been tempted to ask their mothers (patriotic or not) during the First World War. *The Long Week-End* describe the lengths to which Bion's own parents went to get him enlisted as an officer, and his mother's pained non-comprehension during his brief, unhappy, uncommunicative leaves from the front. Bion's thinking aloud in this recording also refers, punningly, to a '*crise de foi*' or '*crise deux fois*'—a (double) crisis of faith (*C* 370). The death of Palinurus provokes a crisis of faith (revealing a hostile god), much as the events of the First World War had disillusioned the conventionally 'pi' (pious) Bion, who had enlisted as a curious 18-year-old, games-playing, ex-public-school boy. But one could also read the episode as having to do with the movement beyond rationality, by way of bafflement, that Bion associates with the evolution of new thoughts. In this sense, thinking is a disaster, although it may lead to something unexpected.

Bion's recorded talk follows a circuitous, associative path from old ghosts, the anxiety of influence, and epitaphs, via the Palinurus episode and the adjacency of

Wilfred Owen also read the pastorals of Theocritus, Bion, and Moschus alongside Barbusse's *Under Fire* during the First World War; see Paul Fussell, *The Great War and Modern Memory* (London: Oxford University Press, 1975), 232.

love and murderousness, to the apocalyptic possibility of the extinction of the entire human race. This doubling between fixation on the past and anxiety about the future—between being stuck in historical repetition and imagining its catastrophic end—suggests that for Bion (at least in his later life) literary commemoration and the apprehension of death were liable to converge. Much has been written about the role of memorialization in the Great War, along with the part played by the Great War in literary modernism and its persistence in modern memory.[45] Bion reveals the modern(ist) analyst reaching for constructions that can explain his patient's otherwise incomprehensible experiences, drawing indirectly on his own experience as he does so. But he also invokes a revised account of the anxiety of influence, and of creativity itself. Just as there can be no literature without envy of literary precursors, and no thought without risk of catastrophe, so there can be no poetry without disorganized states of mind—and perhaps no memory without an element of traumatic fixation as well. In all its violence and indirection, the Palinurus episode becomes a point of reference for an apparently rudderless ship. As a conscientious tank officer, Bion had marked out the route of his tanks in advance, taking elaborate compass bearings that in battle could either turn out to have been crucial or prove utterly useless. He often experienced disorientation, not knowing where he and his tanks were going, or whether he had led them in entirely the wrong direction. Like falling unobserved in battle, or the intense loneliness of coming under enemy bombardment, being thrown off course provides a powerful metaphor for the analytic situation. Palinurus, the helmsman who falls asleep, conveys the loneliness of the long-distance pilot who has nothing to rely on but his own mind when it comes to the perilous encounter with psychical reality. Bion wrote that one of the elements of psychoanalysis was the analyst's intense deprivation, stemming from the need for detachment and the accompanying fear of desertion.[46] The scrutinizer of the primitive mind feels cut off from its own vitality, while the primitive part of the mind risks feeling abandoned. One could argue that this peril-fraught view of thinking informs Bion's entire *œuvre*, at once an irreducible element in his theory of thinking and a recurrent aspect of its difficulty.

NAMELESS DREAD

Bion's terse account in *Learning from Experience* of what he calls 'nameless dread' ('the infant who started with a fear he was dying ends up by containing a nameless dread') identifies its chief characteristic, in a telling neologism, as 'without-ness' or

[45] See, for instance, Fussell, *The Great War and Modern Memory*, esp. 310–35.
[46] See Wilfred R. Bion, *Elements of Psychoanalysis* (1963; rpr. London: Karnac Books, 1989), 16: 'Detachment can only be achieved at the cost of painful feelings of loneliness and abandonment experienced (1) by the primitive animal mental inheritance from which detachment is effected and (2) by the aspects of the personality that succeed in detaching themselves from the object of scrutiny. . . .'.

'an internal object without an exterior'. In the relation that Bion calls '–K', it is not just a matter of depletion but of what is returned empty to the infant: 'the breast is felt enviously to remove the good or valuable element in the fear of dying and force the worthless residue back into the infant' (*LE* 96, 97). This viscerally charged language of negativity, emptying out, and 'envious denudation' recalls Bion's descriptions of the gutted interiors and gaping intestines of exploded tanks. In 1958 he wrote that it was his own interior 'gut' that remembered his wartime fear: 'I was and am still scared. What about? I don't know—just scared. No, not even "just" scared. Scared' (*WM* 209–10). In this formulation, the model of a negative alimentary process is precisely calibrated: the process of stripping does its work at the level of a syntactically unmodified fear ('No, not even "just" scared. Scared'). What makes Bion scared, in this case, is remembering a smell: 'That "sweet smell of the dead" I remember. It was pervasive' (*WM* 210). 'Sweet' brings in its train the association with Sweeting, the boy-soldier wounded during the Battle of Amiens, when part of his torso was stripped away to leave his lung exposed, while Bion struggled to cover the wound with a pitifully inadequate field-bandage. Bion's war writings record other traumatic experiences, other close encounters with death, other recurrent nightmares.[47] But the death of Sweeting returns to him over and over again, as if to flag the convergence of a moment of traumatic guilt (his own) with guilt at his contrasting failure to communicate with his own mother during the war.

'Write to my Mother' is Sweeting's refrain as well as his dying request. It drives Bion frantic as the two take shelter during the disorienting, fog-shrouded early morning bombardment that ushers in the Battle of Amiens. ' "Mother, Mother, write to my mother, sir, won't you? You'll remember her address, sir, won't you? 22 Kimberley Avenue, Halifax. Write to my mother—22 Kimberley Road, Halifax. Mother, Mother, Mother, Mother." "Oh, for Christ's sake shut up", shouted Bion, revolted and terrified' (*WM* 255). And so on, over and over: ' "Write to my mother, sir, you will write to my mother, won't you?" ' until his voice grows faint. Here Bion (' "Yes, for Christ's sake shut up" ') reacts like the mother of a screaming child who is unable to bear the infant's projection of the anxiety that he is dying. This excerpt comes from Bion's later and more candid attempt to narrate his war memoirs in the third person. In the contrastingly stiff-upper-lipped diary he wrote for his mother and father immediately after the war while at Oxford, he simply records, like any good officer, 'He gave me his mother's address, and I promised to write' (*WM* 127). But as well as Sweeting's hideous chest wound ('He kept trying to cough, but of course the wind only came out of his side' (*WM* 127)), both accounts narrate a prior experience: Bion's panicked visual disorientation as

---

[47] 'At Oxford, when I was writing the diary, I used to have a recurrent dream of clinging to the slimy bank of a torrent that rushed by some twenty feet below. As I was slipping, I tried to dig my finger-nails into the mud. But as I became tired I moved to ease myself—and this meant a further slither. This vast raging torrent waiting for me below was the Steenbeck. I have described the trickle of dirty water that was the geographical fact' (*WM* 207–8).

the two cower in their shell-hole. By a trick of perspective, the tall grasses on the other side of the sunken road in which the pair take shelter look like the poplar trees lining the Amiens–Roye road: 'What are those trees there? . . . there in the distance it seemed, through the lifting fog, that there was this row of poplars, a long straight line of poplars. What could it possibly mean? This long straight line of trees?' (*WM* 254). It could mean only one thing: Bion 'must have got his compass bearings wrong. He was sure then that some terrible blunder had occurred', as he guided his tanks into position through the fog. It meant that 'he had launched the battalion tanks not towards the enemy, but across the British Front' (*WM* 255). This was the tank pilot's worst nightmare. Bion's temporary loss of his bearings resembles his later accounts of the disorientation that may arise in the face of radically opposed possibilities for psychoanalytic interpretation. This—or that? To make a mistake is not just to be on the wrong road, but dangerously out of touch with reality. With the pilot lost or his ship helplessly adrift, the entire fleet is at risk.

The Battle of Amiens had been preceded by Bion's thorough reconnaissance of the ground his tanks would have to cross next day, in the company of a distinguished, risk-taking spy—a kind of Scarlet Pimpernel, visibly amused by the painstaking compass bearings which Bion took to cover up his nervousness as they crawled about in broad daylight beyond their own lines. The dense fog next morning proved that Bion was right to have taken these precautions. But the question of his fallibility haunts his narrative. Survival often turns out to depend on chance or blind thinking, rather than on foresight or intelligence. One such episode of the same riddling nature—although less desolating and less traumatic than the death of Sweeting—involved Bion's decision to abandon a tank to its inevitable fate. Potentially punishable by court-martial, this inspired impulse towards survival overtook Bion without any pause for reflection. It saved not only the lives of his crew, but his own life, although it cost him the tank itself. The episode makes Bion a kind of anti-Palinurus—a pilot who has the sense to abandon his ship at a critical moment, rather than remain adfixed to it under the omnipotent illusion that he has any control over his fate. In the aftermath of the Battle of Amiens, Bion had watched his tanks purring forward over the grass in broad daylight, unsupported by infantry or covering fire, to certain, slow-motion destruction: 'The whole four had flowered. Hard bright flames, as if cut out of tinfoil, flickered and died, extinguished by the bright sun. One tank, crewless, went on to claw at the back of one in front as if preparatory to love-making; then stopped as if exhausted' (*LWE* 254). The reason for the flowering was that each tank carried a charge of high explosives, as Bion notes facetiously, army staff 'foreseeing the danger that a tank commander would surrender his tank to the enemy—"You know what these tank commanders are"' (*LWE* 257).

This, in fact, is just what Bion decides to do. He has a raging fever, and a sizeable dose of alcohol by way of antidote. Realizing that his tank is under observation from enemy balloons and that it is only a matter of time before it receives a direct hit, he orders his crew out and makes them walk behind. He takes over driving the tank himself, 'meaning to drive a zig-zag course with the escape hatch over [him] open'. But without a crew, there is no way to change course to left or right; he can only drive straight ahead: 'I had no sense of fear. I opened the throttle so that the tank was at full speed. Before I knew what I was doing I had left the driver's seat and joined the crew behind' (*LWE* 262). Immediately afterwards, he is overwhelmed with panic: 'Suppose they were *not* firing at us? Suppose they did not hit us? A fully equipped tank in complete working order would have been handed over to the enemy, abandoned on my orders by its crew' (*LWE* 262). Running frantically to catch up with his driverless tank, Bion trips and falls, just as the tank is blown up by a shell: 'The tank stopped, flames spurting everywhere. In a moment it was a total wreck.' Bemused, Bion is unable to grasp what has happened—'I only knew that I had failed in my desperate resolve to get back to the tank. Had I succeeded I could not possibly have survived.' Survival entails abandoning ship while retaining a precarious hold on reality. Yet, once more, he has the sense of having blundered involuntarily and incompetently: 'it was not a repetition, it was not a reminiscence, but again I had the sense of being a cornered rat... Even as a rat I was incompetent' (*LWE* 262). This experience of survival as sheer mistake—a sense of persecution that is neither repetition nor reminiscence— runs through Bion's entire record of the experience of combat.

Like Freud's account of the repetition compulsion, Bion's account of 'nameless dread' resembles a pure culture of death. The infant who is filled with nameless dread (because 'the breast is felt enviously to remove the good or valuable element in the fear of dying') experiences a total evacuation of all personality, losing even the will to live:

Indeed it is as if virtually the whole personality was evacuated by the infant. The process of denudation... is therefore more serious, because more extensive, than is implied in the simple example of the projection of a fear of dying. The seriousness is best conveyed by saying that the will to live, that is necessary before there can be a fear of dying, is a part of the goodness that the envious breast has removed. (*LE* 97)

This powerful projection, Bion suggests, denudes the psyche to such an extent that 'There is therefore hardly any infant to re-introject, or into whom the denuded fear of dying can be forced.' Melanie Klein's definition of the death-drive as the ego's destructive attack on its own mental processes (reconceptualized by Bion as 'attacks on linking') becomes for Bion himself 'an envious assertion of moral superiority without any morals... an envious stripping or denudation of all good'. In this process of stripping or denudation, what is left is an overwhelming negativity, 'hardly more than an empty superiority–inferiority that in turn degenerates to nullity' (*LE* 97). Bion links such an experience of degenerate nullity with finding fault, hatred of new developments in the personality, rejection of any search for truth or contact with reality, and above all with the arousal of meaningless guilt. He writes: 'The power to arouse guilt is essential and appropriate to the operation of projective identification in a relation between infant and breast. This guilt is peculiar in that its association with primitive projective identification implies that the guilt is meaningless' (*LE* 98). 'Meaningless guilt'—as opposed to appropriate or meaningful guilt—could be understood as the most primitive, paranoid–schizoid precursor of depressive guilt; primitive anxiety about survival has not, or has not yet, given rise to the guilt feelings of the depressive position, with its connotations of concern for an attacked or damaged object. Instead, guilt pre-exists both the sense of an object and the possibility of repairing it.

Confronted by the fatally wounded Sweeting, Bion—revolted, terrified, and vomiting—wishes he would shut up and die. Unable to contain either Sweeting's fear of annihilation or his own, he throws up instead. In the aftermath, once Sweeting has been moved to a casualty station, he was 'filled with passionate hatred of himself for his hatred of the wounded man' (*WM* 290). This is meaningless guilt with a vengeance, corresponding to what Bion means by nullity, without-ness, or denudation. Such internal states are aptly embodied by the dying Sweeting as he tries to cough with no lung, or by the spectacle of an exploded tank with its guts hanging out of a gaping wound. In *Learning from Experience*, Bion sums up the operation of '–K' as the process that strips, denudes, and devalues persons, experiences, and ideas. 'In –K neither group nor idea can survive partly because of the destruction incident to the stripping and partly because of the product of the stripping process', envy and its concomitant, meaningless guilt (*LE* 99). This process is the antitype of a satisfying relation to a good breast. Bion's war writings raise the question of whether, at least in unconscious phantasy, the Mother tank was a figure for the bad breast that the infant is aware of inside it—'a breast that is "not there" and by not being there gives it painful feelings'; or else, in Bion's own, much-decorated case of heroism, provides no actual reservoir of courage, but only a carapace of steel. This bad object that is felt to be evacuated, or else an unsatisfied 'need-of-a-breast' form of the bad breast (which produces a collapse of the emotion and the thing-in-itself into one undifferentiated state), corresponds to what Bion would call a beta-element, or undigested sensation. Elsewhere in *Learning from Experience*, Bion tries to define an evacuated no-breast that is made worse by being a concrete, bizarre representation—'an evacuated object and therefore indistinguishable from a beta-element'—and to link alimentation with thinking (*LE* 59).

These dense and difficult pages in *Learning from Experience* grope towards the means by which the mind and thinking may arrive at models or abstract conceptions of themselves. A model, as Bion defines it in contrast to an abstraction, is 'a construction in which concrete images are combined with each other; the link between concrete images often gives the effect of a narrative implying that some elements in the narrative are the causes of others' (*LE* 64). The Palinurus episode can be read as just such a construction, in which powerful beta-elements (Bion's term for primitive proto-mental experiences) are linked together so as to form a narrative that only seems to imply causation. In this case, however, we have both a 'model' and an 'abstraction'. Elements in the narrative simultaneously become indices of Bion's individual past and express the abstract relationship between omnipotence and helplessness—'a moral story, a *serious* moral story'. Bion goes on to emphasize the difference between phantasies of omniscience, as opposed to the capacity to tolerate the actual frustrations involved in learning ('K') that he calls 'learning from experience', where model-making and abstraction (both integral aspects of 'K') imply ' "knowing" in the sense of "getting to know" something' (*LE* 65). Bion's daughter, Parthenope, in her 'Aftermath' to the war writings, raises the question of just how (and how far) her father was shaped as an analyst by his wartime experiences.[48] A partial answer may lie in the ongoing struggle to which his war writings testify— the struggle to 'get to know' his wartime experiences in all their persecutory and traumatic aftermath. But his later writings also suggest that they provided him with powerful and original models for psychoanalytic understanding.[49]

As Bion himself writes, 'The use of a model has a value in restoring a sense of the concrete to an investigation which may have lost contact with its background through abstraction and the theoretical deductive systems associated with it.' Models for thinking with, he suggests, 'are constructed with elements from the individual's past, whereas the abstraction is, as it were, impregnated with preconceptions of the individual's future' (*LE* 64). Both draw on previous emotional experience and try to apply it to fresh emotional experience. Model-making—an attempt to think about thinking—is comparatively primitive as a form of thinking in its use of the concrete elements or visual images drawn from past experience. But Bion's war memories provide just such primitive models or rudimentary containers for thought. As he notes in *Learning from Experience*, the idea of 'containing' and the implied model of the container that goes with it are unavoidable once one uses the terms 'external' or 'internal' objects:

The model is one I employ with reluctance as I think it is more appropriate to immature than mature scientific thinking. Yet the nature of this work and the lack of a language adequate for a scientific approach to it compels the employment of models sometimes known and more often suspected to be inappropriate, but unavoidable because there is none better.   (*LE* 102)

Like Bion's war writings, his later theories may serve as models or containers for the anxiety of annihilation aroused by traumatic experience and memory. Tanks for the memories.

***

[48] Parthenope Bion Talamo, 'Aftermath' (*WM* 309–12), suggests that Bion's war writings 'present the reader with raw, basic, almost primitive experiences that had been dealt with at the time of their occurrence by a mind that was recognized as being ill-equipped to do so', underlining Bion's later concern with the coexistence of regressed or proto-mental states alongside more sophisticated ones.

[49] See Paulo Cesar Sandler, 'Bion's War Memoirs: A Psychoanalytical Commentary: Living Experiences and Learning from Them: Some Early Roots of Bion's Contribution to Psychoanalysis', Robert M. Lipgar and Malcolm Pines (eds.), *Building on Bion: Roots* (London: Jessica Kingsley, 2003), 59–84. Sandler compares the writings that comprise *War Memoirs* to *Cogitations* 'in the sense that both contain preparatory notes—a laboratory?—for books that were written later' (ibid., 59).

The self-reflexive turn in Bion's psychoanalytic thinking about 'learning from experience' did not at once emerge as the hallmark of his writing. His First World War experiences, combined with his subsequent analytic training and professional experience at the Tavistock Clinic, led him towards a pre-war analysis with John Rickman during the late 1930s.[50] Although the analysis was interrupted by the war, it resulted in Bion's collaboration with Rickman on the then-innovative theory and practice of group psychotherapy and the therapeutic community.[51] The aim was to encourage the Northfield patients to take charge of their immediate environment, thereby countering their sense of helplessness, demoralization, and persecution (the same sense that Bion records so vividly as an aspect of his combat experience in the First World War).[52] Through the leaderless group, soldiers who had broken down or lost their nerve moved into greater dependence on, and communication with, one another, rather than remaining isolated, atomized, and infantilized. The Northfield experiment was brought to a halt by the military authorities, for whom the unit's apparent indiscipline and untidiness did not represent army-style order, and whom Bion and his colleagues had failed to bring along with them in undertaking their short-lived experiment. As Bion writes with characteristic sardonic humour, 'it was assumed either that we were trying to get troops into battle, or alternatively that we were concerned to help a lot of scrimshankers to go on scrimshanking'.[53] But it gave rise to the form of group-analytical psychotherapy that was practised extensively after the war at the

---

[50] Bion's first 'analyst', whom he refers to as 'Dr FiP' ('feel-it-in-the-past'), has been identified as J. A. Hadfield, whose psycho-dynamically oriented work dating from this period included *Psychology and Morals* (1923), *Psychology and Modern Problems* (1935), and *Psychology and Mental Health* (1950); Bion would have encountered him first at University College, London, where he trained as a doctor, and afterwards when he joined the staff of the Tavistock Clinic in 1932, where he received his analytic training and where 'Hadfieldeans' were a powerful group during the 1930s. Bion's subsequent analysis with John Rickman lasted from 1937 until 1939, when it was interrupted by the outbreak of the Second World War; Rickman, who had been in brief analyses with Freud and Ferenczi, and prominent from the early years onwards in the British Psycho-Analytical Society, was by then himself in analysis with Melanie Klein from 1934 until 1941 (see Bléandonu, *Wilfred Bion*, 42–7).

[51] For an account of Rickman's work, see Pearl King, 'Introduction: The Rediscovery of John Rickman and his Work', Pearl King (ed.), *No Ordinary Psychoanalyst: The Exceptional Contributions of John Rickman* (London: Karnac Books, 2003), 1–68. For Bion's and Rickman's joint *Lancet* paper, 'Intra-group Tensions in Therapy: Their Study as the Task of the Group' (1943), see ibid., 220–31, and Bion, *Experiences in Groups*, 11–26.

[52] For a brief account of Rickman's and Bion's short collaboration and abrupt transfer, see King (ed.), *No Ordinary Psychoanalyst*, 40–3; for a full account of the Northfield experiment, see Tom Harrison, *Bion, Rickman, Foulkes and the Northfield Experiment: Advancing on a Different Front* (London: Jessica Kingsley, 2000), esp. 184–91; and see also Ben Shephard, *A War of Nerves* (London: Jonathan Cape, 2000), 257–71.

[53] Bion continues: 'The idea that treatment was contemplated was regarded as an elaborate, but easily penetrable deception. We learned that leaders who neither fight nor run away are not easily understood'; see *Experiences in Groups and Other Papers* (1961; rpr. London and New York: Routledge, 1989), 65. For accounts by those who had first-hand knowledge of the Northfield experiment and the work that Bion later did with groups at the Tavistock Clinic, see Patrick B. de Maré, 'Major Bion', in Malcolm Pines (ed.), *Bion and Group Psychotherapy* (London and New York: Routledge, 1985), 108–113; Eric Trist, 'Working with Bion in the 1940s: The Group Decade', ibid., 1–46; and Harold Bridger, 'Northfield Revisited', ibid., 87–107.

Tavistock by Bion and others, as well as to Bion's widely influential work on groups, collected as *Experiences in Groups* (1961).[54] Bion's post-Second World War writing about groups emphasized the group's reluctance to face anxiety and fear of change, its preference for internal or external scapegoats or redeemers, and the mechanisms of psychotic splitting and defensive pairing that work against the group's ostensible aims, producing a regression to primitive forms of thinking. Group analysis was predicated on the fundamental reluctance of groups to learn from experience, along with their conscious and unconscious hostility to the therapeutic rationale of the group itself.[55]

Bion's therapeutic method at Northfield hospital consisted in gathering together his patients in small groups and drawing attention to what was happening at each moment in the group, especially in relation to their feelings about him. Rather than steering the discussion or offering interpretations or solutions, he waited until complex feelings in himself made him aware of complex feelings in the group towards him. Instead of serving as 'leader', Bion encouraged the group and its individual members to find their own solutions to the problems confronting them, in the face of their palpable resentment at his refusal to do it for them. His hope was that the group, by studying its real-life internal tensions, could also confront what actually needed to be done in an equally realistic fashion. The idea underlying the Northfield experiment was to produce a greater capacity for trust and friendliness within military units, so that hostility could be externalized and directed at the enemy—the neurotic enemy within as well as without—while allowing individual soldiers to re-enter civilian as well as military worlds. But, at the time, the experiment was not judged a success by the military authorities. Bion's and Rickman's methods of working proved too slow, too productive of anxiety, too disorganized, and too cerebral for the other army psychiatrists involved, and they were briskly transferred to different hospitals before their work could take hold. Bion himself, however, laconically identified a specific problem for the analyst who was treating combatant soldiers—'his feeling of guilt that he is trying to bring them to a state of mind in which they will have to face dangers, not excluding loss of life, that he himself is not called upon to face'.[56] These were dangers of which he had first-hand knowledge. But his personal relation to guilt about dangers (faced or not faced), 'not excluding loss of life', is oddly distanced by Bion's impersonal formulation. One wonders why.

[54] Recent work that continues to build on Bion's lasting contribution in *Experiences in Groups* and his work at the Tavistock Clinic includes, for instance, R. D. Hinshelwood and Marco Chiesa (eds.), *Organizations, Anxieties and Defences: Towards a Psychoanalytic Social Psychology* (London: Whurr, 2002); Robert M. Lipgar and Malcolm Pines (eds.), *Building on Bion: Branches* (London: Jessica Kingsley, 2003); and Claire Huffington, David Armstrong, William Halton, Linda Doyle, and Jane Pooley (eds.), *Working Below the Surface: The Emotional Life of Contemporary Organizations* (London: Karnac Books, 2004).

[55] See Bion, 'Group Dynamics' (1952), *Experiences in Groups*, 141–91.

[56] See W. R. Bion, 'The Leaderless Group Project', *Bulletin of the Menninger Clinic*, 10 (1946), 77–81; quoted in Harrison, *Bion, Rickman, Foulkes, and the Northfield Experiment*, 171.

During the Second World War, tank officers came to constitute a distinct group, whom Tom Main (Bion's Northfield colleague and fellow pioneer in the treatment of war neuroses) described as traumatized by the fiery deaths of their successive crews, increasingly unwilling to risk intimacy, and depressed by the lack of opportunity for mourning the men with whom they had lived on such intimate terms.[57] These tank officers were seen as a remote and stand-offish group, and were given (by Tom Main) the unorthodox and seemingly inhumane treatment of three days' solitary confinement in a darkened room, on a bread-and-water diet, with instructions to 'bloody well cry mate!'—a draconian measure whose result was not only to sanction the grief that the army had failed to sanction but also to elicit all their pent-up anger and bitterness in place of a numbing sense of loss.[58] Superficially at least, the saurian, aloof, and ungrieving Bion described by his second, post-First World War volume of autobiographical memoirs, *All My Sins Remembered* (1985), fits the same diagnostic category. Personal tragedy in the course of the Second World War (the loss of his wife in childbirth, leaving him with a baby daughter to care for) seems to have reactivated an earlier numbness and inability to yield to ordinary feelings. Bion records his inhibition in a painful domestic vignette. Watching his infant crying piteously as she tries to crawl towards him across the garden, he remains immobile, refusing to get up and fetch her. This was a version of letting the members of the group solve their own problems; except that, in the case of his small daughter, he felt in the vice-like grip of his own incapacity for spontaneous response—followed by a keen sense of loss: 'But I, I had lost my daughter.'[59] The baby's nurse, unable to bear her cries, picks her up and comforts her. The aftermath of Bion's own war experience was his return to analysis, not with Rickman—by now his colleague once more—but with Melanie Klein, eventually inaugurating a new and creative period of psycho-analytic work as well as unlocking his capacity for renewed personal happiness and family life.

Sometime during the Second World War, after Rickman left London, Bion was to have had an analytic consultation with Donald Winnicott, since his own

---

[57] See Harrison, *Bion, Rickman, Foulkes, and the Northfield Experiment*, 176–7 (unpublished interview by Harrison with T. F. Main, 1984) for Tom Main's graphic account of the typical trau-matized Second World War tank commander's experience is reminiscent of Bion's experience in the First World War: 'There was a particular lot of people I paid attention to. This was the depression that hit some tank commanders who refused to fight...They were good human material: sergeants, young lieutenants. And they had lived with their crews in intense group loyalty, they depended on each other for their lives. The tank would get hit and when a tank gets hit the metal that's just been struck by a shell blows in at once, white hot, and the ammunition inside starts to burn...A great flash of flame envelops the tank. And the tank commander has time to get out. But he hears the people, cries, screaming, he gazes at them, covered in flame, burning, probably die at once. But these were people he'd lived with intensely, slept with nights, enormous crew loyalty.' The tank commander would be given successive tanks and crews and expected to go into battle again, each time becoming more cautious about getting to know his men.   [58] Ibid., 177.

[59] See Francesca Bion (ed.), Wilfred R. Bion, *All My Sins Remembered: Another Part of a Life and the Other Side of Genius* (1985; rpr. London: Karnac Books, 1991), 70.

analyst, Rickman, had been called up.[60] Had he done so (Bion himself left soon after), one can imagine a fascinating correspondence and difference of views—if not then, later, although Winnicott's home-front war work (his involvement with child evacuees), took him in a different direction.[61] Winnicott's highly speculative 1960s paper 'Fear of Breakdown' represents another contribution to the experience of overwhelming primitive anxiety that Bion calls 'nameless dread'. Winnicott identifies a particular fear, the fear of breakdown, which he defines as the fear of a breakdown that has already taken place—an unthinkable collapse of defences and a return to an earlier unintegrated state. Under the heading of 'primitive agonies' (Winnicott writes that 'anxiety is not a strong enough word here'), he lists 'falling for ever', 'failure of [psycho-somatic] indwelling', 'loss of sense of the real', and loss of the capacity to relate to objects.[62] Falling for ever (the infant's primitive fear) is reminiscent of the experience of the headlong fall and abandonment encapsulated by the Palinurus episode, or even by Bion's fear of falling unobserved under his own tank. Winnicott locates this primitive trauma, not in Virgilian epic or war but in infancy, prior to the possibility of being experienced at all. More specifically, the fear of a breakdown that has already happened is the fear of death, akin to the nameless dread of the Bionic infant: 'Death, looked at in this way as something that happened to the patient but which the patient was not mature enough to experience has the meaning of annihilation'.[63] Winnicott's paper focuses on the phenomenology of emptiness against which, paradoxically, the only defence is a search for non-existence—a means of getting rid of everything personal via projection. His speculation resonates with Bion's 'nameless dread', the state of absolute nullity or 'without-ness' which similarly results in the total evacuation of all personality and even destroys the will to live (*LE* 97). In Winnicott's emphasis on 'holding' and the importance of the maternal environment, one can find an analogy of sorts for Bion's maternal container. His attempt to define the

---

[60] Pearl King, personal communication; based on the Archives of the British Psycho-Analytical Society. When Rickman left London during the war, the Training Committee suggested that Bion should consult Winnicott, who was not fighting; in the end, however, this was not pursued since Bion was also called away to the war.

[61] See F. Robert Rodman, *Winnicott: Life and Work* (Cambridge, Mass.: Perseus Publishing, 2003), 89–105. For clues to the subsequent prickly relations between Bion and Winnicott, see Winnicott's letter to Bion (7 October 1955) commenting on a reading of his paper 'Differentiation of the Psychotic from the Non-Psychotic Personalities' (1957), and later to John Wisdom (26 October 1964); see F. Robert Rodman (ed.), *The Spontaneous Gesture: Selected Letters of D. W. Winnicott* (1987; rpr. London: Karnac Books, 1999), 89–93, 144–6. Winnicott's letter to Wisdom complains that although he likes 'the way he goes ahead in his own grooves', Bion pays insufficient attention to the work of others, including Winnicott's work: 'It is important to me that Bion states (obscurely of course) what I have been trying to say for 2½ decades but against the terrific opposition of Melanie [Klein]' (ibid., 145); cf. also Winnicott's letter to Donald Meltzer for the supposed similarity between his own and Bion's views (ibid., 159).

[62] See D. W. Winnicott, *Psycho-Analytic Explorations*, ed. Clare Winnicott, Ray Shepherd, and Madeleine Davis (Cambridge, Mass.: Harvard University Press, 1989), 87–95. Probably written in 1963 (see ibid., 87 n.), the paper was posthumously published in *The International Review of Psycho-Analysis*, 1 (1974), 103–7.   [63] Winnicott, *Psycho-Analytic Explorations*, 93.

worst of all primitive terrors, the primitive agony of falling, suggests that Bion was not alone in placing the Palinurus episode on the site previously occupied by Freud's account of the retrospective effects of trauma.[64] The Palinurus episode could be redefined, with Winnicott's help, as the narrative of a fall that has already taken place, but could only be experienced as a sense of overwhelming helplessness in the face of unknown hostility and omnipotent persecution. The tank that fails to contain, or contains only the evacuation of nameless dread, is the 'Mother' to whom the dying runner, Sweeting, addresses his last, unwritten letter.

[64] For an account of Winnicott's 'Fear of Breakdown' in conjunction with trauma, see Max Hernandez, 'Winnicott's "Fear of Breakdown": On and Beyond Trauma', *Diacritics: Trauma and Psychoanalysis*, 28/4 (1998), 134–41.

8

Prometheus on the Couch:
The Language of Terror

οὔκουν, Προμηθεῦ, τοῦτο γιγνώσκεις, ὅτι
ὀργῆς νοσούσης εἰσὶν ἰατροὶ λόγοι;

Aeschylus, *Prometheus Bound*, 379–80[1]

[Don't you know, Prometheus: | a sick mind may be cured by words.][2]

It is not thought that the disaster causes to disappear, but rather questions and problems—affirmation and negation, silence and speech, sign and insignia—from thought.

Maurice Blanchot, *The Writing of the Disaster*[3]

Terror today can hardly be thought about separately from the threat of terrorist acts and the war on terror. But terror has long been recognized as a war of words as well as a form of psychological warfare. In an essay published in the year of his death, Wilfred Bion wrote: 'In war the enemy's object is so to terrify you that you cannot think clearly, while your object is to continue to think clearly no matter how adverse or frightening the situation.'[4] For Bion, 'thinking' means retaining vital contact with an unwelcome reality—not just the bombardment that he had experienced during the First World War but states of nameless psychic dread, along with the proto-mental processes of the primordial mind. Although war remained a life-long preoccupation in Bion's autobiographical writing, psychosis was the central focus for his psychoanalytic work both during and after his analysis with

---

[1] Aeschylus, *Prometheus Bound*, ed. Mark Griffiths (Cambridge: Cambridge University Press, 1983), 54.

[2] Aeschylus, *Prometheus Bound*, trans. James Scully and C. J. Herington (London: Oxford University Press, 1975), 47.

[3] *The Writing of the Disaster*, trans. Ann Smock (1980; Lincoln, Nebr.: University of Nebraska Press, 1995), 52 (*WD*).

[4] Wilfred R. Bion, 'Making the Best of a Bad Job' (1979), *Clinical Seminars and Other Works* (1987; rpr. London: Karnac Books, 1994), 322. See also Bion's wartime essay, 'The "War of Nerves": Civilian Reaction, Morale and Prophylaxis', in E. Miller and H. Crichton-Miller (eds.), *The Neuroses in War* (London: Macmillan, 1940), 180–200.

Melanie Klein.[5] He became an expert on the sense of overwhelming persecution by an incomprehensible and omnipotent agency that is especially conducive to terror. For Bion, it was the psychotic's dread of internal reality that led to the destruction of his capacity for thought, including—especially—verbal thought. Thought involves what he calls linking, that is, the connection between ideas, or between words and things, thoughts, and feelings (ultimately, the link between baby and breast, or the sexual link between the parents). The psychotic subjects the link to furious attack, rendering it cruel or sterile. The link of language is not just destroyed; it becomes destructive.

Bion's personal collection of organizing myths, or psychoanalytic 'constructions', foregrounds a variety of persecutory narratives. As well as the episode of Palinurus from Book V of the *Aeneid*, the list includes the tomb-burials of Ur around 3500 BC. In a late essay, 'The Grid' (1977), he reads the archaeological evidence pieced together from this site of mass immolation as evidence for the persistence and prevalence of human acts of destruction and self-destruction. The same place served as both cemetery and rubbish dump. Bion describes how the dead monarch had been laid to rest in a funeral rite that included the live burial of his heavily drugged, splendidly clothed courtiers after a ceremonial death-march to the funeral pit:

The site chosen for this cemetery was the city's refuse heap. We may assume that the magic performed that day was held to have sanctified the ground chosen and thus to have overlaid not only the real rubbish deposited on that site but also the view, if it existed, that the human remains were rubbish and that the appropriate place for the disposal of rubbish was the rubbish heap. Sanctification made the ground desirable for those who sought a resting place of magic property for their own dead rubbish. Thus the sanctified place, together with the sanctity which made it desirable, came in the course of time to lose its virtue as it became vulgarized, too full for further burials, and finally reverted to its former use.[6]

Five hundred years later, plunderers returned to the site. Undeterred by the ghosts of the dead, they robbed the graves of their funeral treasures. Bion ponders this ambiguous record of rubbish and religious narcosis: 'The Royal mourners demonstrated the power of Religion, Ritual, Magic, Drugs. The plunderers demonstrated the power of gain... how powerful must be the force, emotional, cultural, religious, which can impose on a group of people a course of action certain to lead to their death' (*Grid* 9–10). But only a cocktail as potent as curiosity and cupidity could have made the grave-robbers brave murderous forces still associated with the ceremonial death-pit five centuries later. Greedy as they were (Bion speculates),

[5] For Bion's experience as a tank commander in the First World War, as well as for his work as an army psychiatrist during in the Second World War, see Ch. 7. Bion's war experiences in the First World War are described in his memoirs, *The Long Week-End 1897–1918* (1982) and *War Memoirs 1917–19* (1997), as well as in *A Memoir of the Future* (1975–9). Bion's analysis with Melanie Klein began in 1945 and lasted until 1953; see Gérard Bléandonu, *Wilfred Bion: His Life and Works 1897–1979*, trans. Claire Pajaczkowska (London: Free Association Books, 1994), 93–101.

[6] *Two Papers: The Grid and The Caesura* (1977; rpr. London: Karnac Books, 1989), 8 (*Grid*). Bion's source is Sir Leonard Woolley, *Excavations at Ur: A Record of Twelve Years' Work* (London: E. Benn, 1954).

these taboo-breakers might even be considered proto-scientific pioneers, undeterred by the secrets of death.

Bion's way with his psychoanalytic constructions is to read them aslant, against the grain of their received meaning. This tendency illustrates the swerve that makes him a strong reader of Klein rather than her follower, even as he continues to work with the basic tools of Kleinian concepts such as splitting and projective identification. The tomb-burials at Ur provide an unsettlingly prophetic instance. One thinks not only of the looting and destruction that followed the US invasion of Iraq, but of the vast rubbish site which the World Trade Centre became in the wake of 9/11, at once tomb and underground mall, plundered in the aftermath by thieves undaunted by the still-smouldering wreckage. The aptly named Fresh Kills garbage dump to which the debris of the Twin Towers was afterwards transferred, piece by piece, has been called the scene of 'the biggest and grimmest forensic investigation in New York's history'. Apropos of the painstaking sifting of the debris for human fragments and clues to the identity of the unknown and uncounted dead, one New York City chief of police is quoted as saying: 'This is a special place . . . this is a very humbling and holy place.'[7] The need to believe that burial sites are sacred overrides the perception that this is a rubbish dump and that its contents will return to rubbish again: dust to dust and ashes to ashes. Understandably, memorialization of those whose eviscerated remains were ferried to Fresh Kills by the truckloads has tended to focus on images of lives tragically interrupted, rather than on processing the grim forensic evidence. It is absence—a gaping hole—that draws both mourners and tourists to the site, and poses a problem for architectural schemes to memorialize the disaster. No one likes to live, work, or rent 'In the shadow of No towers', let alone next to a death-pit.[8]

Bion was writing during the Cold War, at a time when 'Ground Zero' meant something other to the collective imagination than what it has since come to mean. His main professional life as a psychoanalyst coincided with the post-Hiroshima era, when the prospect of mass civilian deaths in the event of nuclear catastrophe might disturb the most robust psychoanalyst. The language of atomic fission also gave rise to what became briefly ensconced in literary theory as the Nuclear Sublime—a reminder that responses to a uniquely twentieth-century form of terror derived from pre-existing aesthetic languages and hyperboles, ironized, however, by contemporary resistance to the aestheticizing impulses within the discourse of the Sublime itself. As early as 1947, Bataille had written: 'between the mind's habitual standards and the atomic effect there remains a disproportion that makes one's head spin, leaving the imagination before the void'.[9] Bataille's head-spinning

---

[7] *Guardian*, 16 January 2002.

[8] The title of Art Spiegelman's graphic response to 9/11, *In the Shadow of No Towers* (New York: Pantheon Books, 2004). Spiegelman's front cover has a stylized black-on-black silhouette of the Twin Towers; the back and inside cover feature silhouettes of falling comic-book figures.

[9] See Georges Bataille, 'Concerning the Accounts Given by the Residents of Hiroshima' (1947), trans. Alan Keenan, in Cathy Caruth (ed.), *Trauma: Explorations in Memory* (Baltimore: Johns Hopkins University Press, 1995), 223.

metaphor—along with his salutary emphasis on the instant of the disaster—
remains devastatingly apt. One thinks of the dizzying, slow-motion collapse of the
Twin Towers, folding into themselves like packs of cards under the impact of collision and fire.[10] The tiny, flailing Xs tumbling through the air from their flaming
tops recapitulate—in a different register—the figure of a falling body that is a
recurrent trope in contemporary trauma theory.[11] The collapse of high buildings
has been associated from antiquity with the traumatic origins of rhetoric and the
intertwined arts of memory, as well as with the collapse of civilization. But Bataille's
essay on Hiroshima implicates 'civilization' itself in bringing about the catastrophe.

The same figure of a falling body undergirds Winnicott's psychoanalytic
emphasis on the infant's need for a 'holding' or facilitating environment. Falling
from a great height—more than just a metaphor when it comes to the clinging,
uncoordinated neonate—remains a heart-stopping fear for even the most well-
grounded adult. But vertigo also belongs to the phenomenology of terror that can
be traced back, for instance, to Burke's *Philosophical Enquiry into . . . the Sublime
and Beautiful* (1757), where Burke had alluded to the image of a precipitous fall
that may accompany bodily relaxation on 'falling' asleep.[12] Winnicott's metaphorical
'holding' and 'dropping' are propped on everyday maternal handling and the
infant's Moro reflex. One might see the omnipotent phantasy associated with the
Sublime as lined with the same instinctual dread. Extreme helplessness forms
the underside of the terror of immense, impersonal persecution that continued to
fascinate Bion as a result of his First World War experience; together, he uses
helplessness and omnipotence to define a single complementary field of meaning.
Apropos of Bion's theory of thinking, André Green draws attention to what he
calls 'blank psychosis' or 'states of blankness' resulting in 'a "blank hole in the mind" ',
acting as an inner void and attracting related mental contents into the black hole.
The psychotic's awareness 'of an image of himself that will terrorize him' and his
terror in the face of mental death (writes Green) result in 'black holes of the mind,
attracting and destroying the thoughts'.[13] Elsewhere, in *The Work of the Negative*,

[10] For a thought-provoking collection which brings together past and present psychoanalytic
reflections on terror, terrorism, and war in the wake of 9/11, see Coline Covington, Paul Williams,
Jean Arundale, and Jean Knox (eds.), *Terrorism and War: Unconscious Dynamics of Political Violence*
(London: Karnac Books, 2002); and for the languages of terror and hyperbole that connect the events
of 9/11 to the discourse of terrorism more generally, see also Alex Houen, *Terrorism and Modern
Literature, from Joseph Conrad to Ciaran Carson* (Oxford: Oxford University Press, 2000), 1–17.

[11] See, for instance, Cathy Caruth, 'The Falling Body and the Impact of Reference', *Unclaimed
Experience: Trauma, Narrative, and Theory* (Baltimore, Md.: Johns Hopkins University Press, 1996),
73–90. Eyewitnesses of the collapse of the Twin Towers also comment on the air being filled with
pieces of office paper; see Justin Beal, 'Thoughts and Photographs, World Trade Centre: 11th
September 2001', in Coline Covington *et al.* (eds.), *Terrorism and War*, 23–9.

[12] David Womersley (ed.), Edmund Burke, *A Philosophical Enquiry into the Origin of our Ideas of
the Sublime and Beautiful* (Harmondsworth: Penguin Books, 1998), 176 (*PE*): 'I have often experienced,
and so have a thousand others; that on the first inclining towards sleep, we have been suddenly
awakened with a most violent start; and that this start was generally preceded by a sort of dream of our
falling down a precipice . . .'.

[13] André Green, 'The Primordial Mind and the Work of the Negative', in Parthenope Bion
Talamo, Franco Borgogno, and Silvio A. Merciai (eds.), *W. R. Bion: Between Past and Future* (London:
Karnac Books, 2000), 113–14, 123.

Green describes this domain of negativity associated with the death-drive (with a touch of the negative Sublime on his own account) in terms of 'catastrophic or unthinkable anxieties, fears of annihilation or breakdown, feelings of futility, of devitalisation or of psychic death, sensations of a gap, of bottomless holes, of an abyss'.[14] In this deathward plunge, the endangered body comes sharply into focus along with the physical sensation of a gap or bottomless abyss.

Bion's psychotics live with the sense of imminent evisceration, as if the internal world were a perpetual ground zero. Terms like 'anxiety' or 'fear' hardly begin to evoke the visceral sensations that accompany such unbearable states of mind: the knot in the throat, the pain in the gut, the dissolution of ligaments or sphincters. Fears of imminent annihilation, catastrophic breakdown, or unchecked fall are relocated in the body, as if terror surprises us into the concreteness that marks primitive thinking. These proto-mental and primitive states may be experienced as painful or negative breaches of the bodily envelope, just as traumatic events, by analogy, can be thought of as breaching the psychic envelope that forms Freud's model for trauma in *Beyond the Pleasure Principle* (1920). Burke argues in his psychological model of the Sublime that terror mimics pain. This may not be only because the worst of all imaginable terrors is the threat of bodily annihilation but because fear of death forces signification violently into the bodily realm. Writing in the shadow of nuclear anxiety, Bion (I shall argue) articulated a modern psychoanalytic discourse of terror, predicated on psychotic body-language as well as on Klein's premiss that the fear of annihilation is the first and worst fear that afflicts the infant.[15] But his work also offers a point of critical purchase on the language of 'shock and awe' which appropriates Burke's language of power for political ends in order to terrify. The war on terror is also a war of words.

'NOTHING IS REALLY A HERNIA'

> How will thy soul, cloven to its depth with terror,
> Gape like a Hell within!
>
> P. B. Shelley, *Prometheus Unbound* (1819),
> i. 55–6[16]

Thus Prometheus, the forethinker, defiantly addressing the all-powerful and tormenting Jupiter. Shelley's language evokes the universe of terror and terrorization

[14] André Green, *The Work of the Negative*, trans. Andrew Weller (London: Free Association Books, 1999), 84.

[15] For a suggestive meditation on fear in the context of both Klein's and Winnicott's thinking, see Adam Phillips, 'Fears', *Terrors and Experts* (London: Faber, 1995), 46–63: 'Psychoanalysis... is a story of what there is to fear; like the symptoms it can sometimes explain, it is grounded in terror' (ibid., 49).

[16] Quotations from Shelley's *Prometheus Unbound* (1819) are from Kelvin Everest and Geoffrey Matthews (eds.), *The Poems of Shelley*, Volume 2: *1817–1819* (London: Longman, 2000).

that Prometheus opposes through the very speech that perpetuates it. While recognized as having far-reaching implications for psychoanalysis, Bion has been comparatively neglected by literary critics, for whom his system often appears impenetrable and his preoccupations idiosyncratic. But his writing (besides its resonances with the high Romanticism of Shelley's verse drama) has elements in common with the linguistic and thought experiments of mid-twentieth-century avant-garde practice. The highly original, path-breaking essays of the 1950s and 1960s, included in *Second Thoughts* (1967), reveal a modernist fascination with dislocating, alienating, and defamiliarizing the world of physical objects, especially the world of ordinary sense perceptions, as a means to understand the language and thought of psychosis. Bion's oblique angle on consciousness—the province he carved out for himself, just as Freud had previously made his province the unconscious—foregrounds modern technologies of communication and perception. The psychotic patient experiences his senses and insights as if dispersed into the mechanical objects by which he is terrorized. Bion's exploration of this bizarre world focuses on the transformation of sight and insight into alienated and alienating forms of persecution, including hallucination.

An early essay, 'Notes on the Theory of Schizophrenia' (1953), provides an illustration of Bion's compressed and idiosyncratic working style, with its propositional exactitude and even its jokes.[17] 'Interpretation', he writes, 'should be in language that is simple, exact, and mature.' The language of his case-material is not only exact but exacting, stretching the reader's mind and even credulity. Here is a representative mini-dialogue:

Patient. I picked a tiny piece of skin from my face and feel quite empty.
Analyst. The tiny piece of skin is your penis, which you have torn out, and all your insides have come with it.
Patient. I do not understand . . . penis . . . only syllables.
Analyst. You have split my word 'penis' into syllables and it now has no meaning.
Patient. I don't know what it means, but I want to say, 'If I can't spell I cannot think'.
Analyst. The syllables have now been split into letters; you cannot spell—that is to say, you cannot put the letters together again to make words. So now you cannot think.[18]

---

[17] See Edna O'Shaughnessy, 'W. R. Bion's Theory of Thinking and New Techniques in Child Analysis' (1981), in Elizabeth Bott Spillius (ed.), *Melanie Klein Today: Developments in Theory and Practice*, 2 vols. (London and New York: Routledge, 1988), ii. 177: 'It is not easy to convey the rare originality of Bion's thought. He expressed himself in austere propositions with a high yield of exact meaning. They repay the reader's repeated return, as, for diversion, do his occasional and lastingly funny jokes.' See also Edna O'Shaughnessy, 'Psychosis: Not Thinking in a Bizarre World', in Robin Anderson (ed.), *Clinical Lectures on Klein and Bion* (London and New York: Routledge, 1992), 89–101.

[18] Wilfred R. Bion, *Second Thoughts: Selected Papers on Psycho-Analysis* (1967; rpr. London: Karnac Books, 1987), 28 (*ST*). An earlier version of 'Notes on the Theory of Schizophrenia' (based on a still earlier paper of 1953) appeared as 'Language and the Schizophrenic' in Melanie Klein, Paula Heimann, and R. E. Money-Kyrle (eds.), *New Directions in Psychoanalysis* (1955; rpr. London: Karnac Books, 1985), 220–39.

Lesson One: spelling and psychosis. The reader might be forgiven for thinking this mode of ordinary-language interpretation ('simple, exact, and mature') guaranteed to drive the patient mad if he was not already so. Bion himself notes dryly 'the patient's belief that the analyst strives, by understanding the patient, to drive him insane' (*ST* 107). So it seems. In the next session, the patient complains that his 'socks are a mass of holes'. The analyst responds by connecting the state of his clothes with the tiny injury done to his body the previous day. The patient complains that his socks constrict his feet. The analyst offers the startling interpretation that—having in phantasy torn out *both* their penises—there is nothing left interesting to eat, 'only a hole, a sock. But even this sock is made of a mass of holes', felt to be joined together 'to constrict, or swallow and injure' the patient's foot. All that is left, apparently, is a hole 'so persecutory that he had to split it up. As a result of the splitting the hole became a mass of holes which all came together in a persecutory way to constrict his foot' (*ST* 28).

Like the patient's socks ('a mass of holes'), Bion's mode of analysis could be defined as a series of holes joined together by the loopy string of interpretation. The idea of being swallowed up by the black hole of an empty sock illustrates, if nothing else, the deadpan humour with which Bion communicates his clinical material, without overt reference to its dark comedy or evident surrealism. Freud, however, had been there before him, as Bion's essay reminds us with a brief but pointed segue to his discussion of schizophrenic 'organ-speech' in *The Unconscious* (1915). Freud refers to a black-head-picking, psychotic patient who (like the Wolf Man) imagined that there were deep holes in his face, seeing every hole in the light of a potential castration. Freud goes on to mention another patient reported by Tausk, who can claim to be the first patient to get his socks into analysis: 'In putting on his stockings . . . he was disturbed by the idea that he must pull apart the stitches in the knitting, i.e. the holes, and to him every hole was a symbol of the female genital aperture' (*SE* xiv. 200). In Freud's signifying system, black holes (whether in skin or socks) imply not so much the terror of engulfing absence as castration anxiety. But this is not the end of it for Bion's patient. Some days later, he says sorrowfully, a tear welling up, 'Tears come from my ears now'. The analyst hears this poignant remark as yet another instance of his patient's inability to connect words in a meaningful way. Tears come from his ears, sweat oozes from his pores, urine seeps from the hole left by his torn-out penis; even his tongue has been torn out. The trickle turns into a flood, causing catastrophic linguistic meltdown—the 'completely chaotic series of words and noises' now emitted by the terrified and terrorized patient. Bion interprets this chaos of disorganized sounds as meaning that the tongue is now felt to be as bad as the ear—'it just poured out a flow of destroyed language'.

Communication itself is under attack, and the verbal link between analyst and patient is in danger of being destroyed: 'In short, it appeared that . . . we could not, or he felt we could not, communicate.' The patient's assault on language gives rise to empty word-play on tears ('*teers*' or '*tares*'?), play that is expressly designed, so Bion asserts, to prevent objects or words from coming together in any way except arbitrarily and without affect. The psychotic with his torn-out tongue is the first anti-language poet. The dread of verbal thought causes the patient to attack communication itself. Glimpsing the possibility of integration brought about by the analytic process, the patient resorts to violence, pushing the capacity for language on which analysis depends back into the analyst. As he gets better, he has greater reason to dread the pain ushered in by the depressive position (associated in Kleinian aesthetics with access to both language and symbolization). The pain that accompanies increased insight comes from having to recognize his own insanity. Bion suggests that by rendering language meaningless, the patient avoids confronting his own destructiveness. Terror impedes thought—but thought arouses terror. Any change of state (for instance, from the paranoid–schizoid position to the pain and guilt of the depressive position) is therefore experienced as potentially catastrophic. Bodily apertures—ears, mouths, genitals, even pores—map the topography of an intimate disaster. For Klein, these apertures are associated in unconscious phantasy with the taking-in and evacuation of objects, part-objects, or primitive affects. Bion continues to deploy the Kleinian language of evacuation, but he re-imagines the organs of the body as organs of distorted perception. Combining Klein's unconscious body-based phantasy with Freud's perception-based consciousness, he foregrounds sight and hearing, eyes and ears. In so far as the psychotic thinks, in fact, it is with his intestines (the digestive tract that eliminates and evacuates). In so far as he perceives, it is with the prosthetic apparatus of modern technology. Rather than seeing through a glass darkly, he hallucinates negatively.[19]

In what is probably his best-known essay, 'Differentiation of the Psychotic from the Non-psychotic Personalities', Bion transforms Klein's ideas about projective identification into a theory of primitive mental functioning. According to Bion, the psychotic's fear of what his own perceptions and insight may bring causes him to split them into minute 'particles' (this was the era of elementary particle physics as well as nuclear physics), then lodge them in the angry, so-called 'bizarre objects' by which he feels persecuted and controlled. 'Bizarre'—a term that crops up routinely in contemporary clinical discussions of schizophrenic language and ideation—derives ultimately from the medieval Italian figure of the angry man, the disturbing figure of the *bizarro*.[20] Bion's account of the schizophrenic's persecutory object-world makes things rather than persons angry, swollen up with the split-off parts of the psychotic personality that engulf them. Bion writes that the predisposing causes for this primitive form of projective identification include the following: preponderance of destructive impulses, hatred of reality, dread of imminent annihilation, and a premature formation of object relations. It is not

---

[19] See Bion's essay 'On Hallucination' (1958), *ST* 65–85; and see also 'The Work of the Negative and Hallucinatory Activity', in Green, *The Work of the Negative*, 161–214.

[20] See Sander Gilman, 'Seeing the Schizophrenic: On the "Bizarre" in Psychiatry and Art', *Disease and Representation* (Ithaca, NY: Cornell University Press, 1988), 231–43.

that the psychotic has no relation to the world, but rather that he relates to the world destructively, and as if to a world of destruction.

In Bion's account, this deadly combination results in a kind of bodily bio-terrorism, or 'eviscerating attacks' on all forms of awareness—sense-impressions, attention, memory, judgement, thought itself—'that lead to them being minutely fragmented and then expelled from the personality to penetrate, or encyst, the objects' (*ST* 47). The schizophrenic feels himself surrounded and threatened by encysted bizarre objects that listen to or watch him in a persecutory way. His world is made up of strange mechanical devices associated with sight and sound, surveillance and persecution, their hybrid functions travestying those of the sense-organs to which they refer:

The nature of this complete particle will depend partly on the character of the real object, say a gramophone, and partly on the character of the particle of personality that engulfs it. If the piece of the personality is concerned with sight, the gramophone when played is felt to be watching the patient; if with hearing, then the gramophone when played is felt to be listening to the patient. The object, angered at being engulfed, swells up, so to speak, and suffuses and controls the piece of personality that engulfs it: to that extent the particle of personality has become a thing. (*ST* 48)

The object-world inhabited by the psychotic, Bion suggests, is made up of these minutely split 'particles' of his personality—atomized forms of subjectivity that animate, control, and persecute him. Thing not person, the bizarre object is endowed with all the attributes of a primitive self. The cruel and archaic super-ego within (a primitive, spit-off internal object) is misheard as His Master's Voice.

Whether or not Bion intended the allusion to HMV, the psychotic's bizarre object is both a mechanism of terror and surveillance and the means of his forcible interpellation into a persecutory world. In Bion's theory of thinking, the unconscious interaction of introjection and projection has the potential to forge creative and linguistic links (links that might also be associated with the animating tropes of poetry). But the psychotic part of the personality uses the primitive mechanism of projective identification to fragment and fracture rather than think or connect. Nothing (absence) becomes a hostile and persecutory no-thing, or a negative hole in the mind.[21] Part of the patient's own perceptual apparatus has been ejected and lodged in the bizarre object. Instead of being a means to encounter reality, consciousness becomes the instrument of reality's destruction. For Bion, as for Freud, primitive thought attaches at the outset to pictographs or ideograms, prior even to language. Without words, objects remain incapable of being thought about; without the capacity to relate objects to each other, symbolic meanings and creative re-combinations are foreclosed. Splitting serves the psychotic as a substitute for repression or dreaming; he has no access to the work of the unconscious or its symbolizing capacities. Such a patient, Bion writes, 'moves,

[21] For a discussion of the no-thing in Bion's work, see Michael Eigen, *Psychic Deadness* (Northvale, NJ: Jason Aronson, 1996), 45–67.

not in a world of dreams, but in a world of objects which are ordinarily the furniture of dreams' (*ST* 51).

Like Shelley's tormented Prometheus, the undreaming psychotic beholds his world 'with sleepless eyes' and 'eyeless in hate' (*Prometheus Unbound*, i. 4, 9). Because he cannot dream, he can never wake from his terrible nightmare. The mutilation of sense-impressions and language leaves him prey to a generalized universe of destruction. In a figure drawn from contemporary astronomy, Bion suggests that 'The sense of imprisonment is intensified by the menacing presence of the expelled fragments within whose planetary movements he is contained' (*ST* 51). Primitive ideas ('expelled fragments') behave like material objects orbiting unpredictably in an exploded galactic system. Material objects, by contrast, are felt to behave as if they were mental functions. The return of the ejected thought is therefore experienced not as an access of insight but as an assault—the revenge of the object world on the sleepless psychotic. The endlessly repeated footage of passenger jets aimed at the World Trade Center literalized this persecutory phantasy of the return of an expelled idea in the form of a deadly missile.

Both the strangeness and the reticence of Bion's clinical vignettes might be seen as a trace of Bion's former patient, Samuel Beckett.[22] Earlier in his career, Bion had treated Beckett in the mid-1930s for a range of psychological and physical problems when he was at work on his first novel, *Murphy* (1938). Unemployed and unemployable, Murphy (like Beckett himself) finds a job in a mental hospital. In this 'society of psychotics', he feels at home among the patients. He accidentally blows himself up in the rocking-chair to which he retreats in his off-duty hours in order to cultivate the state of perfect blankness that is epitomized by the schizophrenic inmate Mr Endon, whose hallucinations and 'bizarrerie' is accompanied by 'a psychosis so limpid and imperturbable that Murphy felt drawn to it as Narcissus to his fountain'.[23] Listening to Murphy, his girlfriend, Celia, felt 'spattered with words that went dead as soon as they sounded; each word obliterated, before it had time to make sense.... It was like difficult music heard for the first time.'[24] Though less lyrical, the effect of Bion's psychoanalytic vignettes—their rhythm of pause and non sequitur, their covertly observed stage business, their bleak, unforgiving humour—comes close to Beckett's difficult music heard for the first time, just as Bion's patients aspire to the opacity of Beckettian characters. Take, for instance, the patient in 'Differentiation of the Psychotic from the Non-psychotic Personalities', who comes in, lies down, turns from side to side as if to

---

[22] It has been suggested that Beckett is 'The Imaginary Twin' of Bion's 1950 essay (see *ST* 3–22); but for Bion's own guarded remarks on the identity of 'The Imaginary Twin', see *ST* 120. For the argument that their mutual awareness permeates their work see, for instance, Didier Anzieu, 'Beckett and Bion', *International Review of Psycho-Analysis*, 16 (1989), 163–9; and see also David Mayers, 'Bion and Beckett Together', *British Journal of Psychotherapy*, 17/2 (2000), 192–202.

[23] Samuel Beckett, *Murphy* (1938; rpr. London: John Calder, 1963), 128. As Beckett has him say numinously ('words demanding so strongly to be spoken that he spoke them') in the final eye-to-eye scene between himself and the unseeing Mr Endon, 'Mr Murphy is a speck in Mr Endon's unseen' (ibid., 171).   [24] Ibid., 31–2.

make himself comfortable, and then utters the following despondent prophecy: ' "I don't suppose I shall do anything today. I ought to have rung up my mother." He paused and then said: "No; I thought it would be like this." A more prolonged pause followed; then "Nothing but filthy things and smells", he said. "I think I've lost my sight" ' (*ST* 53).

Before addressing this obscurely loaded communication, however, Bion turns his attention to the patient's bodily manœuvres on the couch.[25] Five years before, his patient had undergone an operation for a hernia. Invited by Bion to attach some meaning to his movements, 'his reply had been, "Nothing" ' ('a thinly veiled invitation to me to mind my own business as well as a denial of something very bad'). But nevertheless, Bion stealthily observes his body-language—a form of bodily theatre whose obscure but precise choreography he describes as follows:

I continued, over the weeks and years, to watch his movements. A handkerchief was disposed near his right pocket; he arched his back—surely a sexual gesture here? A lighter fell out of his pocket. Should he pick it up? Yes. No, perhaps not. Well, yes. It was retrieved from the floor and placed by the handkerchief. Immediately a shower of coins spilled over the couch on to the floor. The patient lay still and waited. Perhaps, his gesture seemed to suggest, he had been unwise to bring back the lighter. It had seemed to lead to the shower of coins. He waited, cautiously, furtively. And finally he made the remark I have reported. It reminded me of his descriptions . . . of the tortuous manoeuvres through which he had to go before he went to the lavatory, or went down to breakfast, or telephoned to his mother.   (*ST* 53)

Reflecting on this furtive but copious overspill of cautious gestures and small mishaps, Bion speculates that what he is witnessing is 'a series of miniature dramatic presentations, preparations for a baby's bath or feed, or a change of nappies, or a sexual seduction' (*ST* 54). Perhaps this 'conglomeration of bits out of such scenes' is a form of 'ideo-motor activity, that is to say a means of expressing an idea without naming it', thus rendering it obscure. This would confirm Bion's previous interpretation about the patient's deliberate obscuration of meaning.

Bion points out that the patient feels much the same about his movements as he does about a dream he has told his analyst:

[H]e had no ideas about the dream and he had no ideas about the movements. 'Yes', he had agreed, 'that's so.' 'And yet', I replied, 'you once had an idea about it; you thought it was the hernia'. 'That's nothing', he replied, and had then paused, almost slyly I thought, to see if I had grasped the point. So, 'Nothing is really a hernia', I said. 'No idea', he replied, 'only a hernia'.   (*ST* 54)

This is what Green means by the feeling of persecution being felt 'inside' as a non-idea, then rendered 'nothing', unavailable to thought (an example of negativity

²⁵ Winnicott's letter to Bion of 7 October1955 interprets this moment in Bion's paper ('I would know that he was talking about communication and his own incapacity for making communication') as a transference communication about the mother's and the analyst's failure to be fully oriented to the baby's needs as communicated by his movements; see F. Robert Rodman (ed.), *The Spontaneous Gesture: Selected Letters of D. W. Winnicott* (1987; rpr. London: Karnac Books, 1999), 91.

at work).[26] The exchange conveys the tenacity of Bion's pursuit of the analytic conversation—his grasp of the point being made by the patient, however slyly. Bion calls such moments of sly obstruction 'mutilated attempts at communication'. But (this is his point) they also represent attempts to mutilate and destroy communication itself. Bion puts meaning back into the absent 'nothing' (the painful no-thing) that is 'only a hernia'. As another of his patients puts it, 'Thoughts are a nuisance . . . I don't want them.'[27] To use Green's definition again, they tend to be delivered as messages 'directly evacuated from the unconscious and projected to the object outside'.[28] Taking his cue from the patient's fear that he has lost his sight, Oedipus-like, Bion tells him that the 'filthy things and smells' are what, in phantasy, the patient has made the analyst do (i.e., defecate his own dirty thoughts and sight). This filth now surrounds him as a hallucinatory form of visual air pollution.[29] The patient's statement, 'I can't see' refers to his evacuation of the capacity for insight itself; earlier, he had complained that the analysis itself is 'torture'. No wonder he now complains: 'My head is splitting; maybe my dark glasses' (*ST* 56). Insight under such psychic conditions is dazzlingly painful.

Dark glasses provide Bion with an ideograph richly susceptible to interpretation: made of glass like a baby's bottle, two like the breasts, dark because frowning and angry, dark because of what the patient wants to use them for (spying on his parents), and so on. But this is the non-psychotic, meaning-making part of the patient's personality. What interests Bion is the psychotic part of the personality. In the ensuing exchange, the analyst addresses psychotic mental functioning, since this is the part that needs repair:

Analyst. Your sight has come back into you but splits your head; you feel it is very bad sight because of what you have done to it.
Patient. (moving in pain as if protecting his back passage). Nothing.
Analyst. It seemed to be your back passage.
Patient. Moral strictures.   (*ST* 58)

Bion abstains from interpreting this last enigmatic phrase ('Moral strictures') on the grounds that it would keep him talking much longer than the patient. Insight becomes a primitive and punitive form of conscience—not only because the patient has tried to get rid of it but because of the destructive use to which he puts it (spying on his analyst's imagined week-end activities). During the impending week-end break, Bion tells him, the patient will need the same long-range mental

[26] See Green, 'The Primordial Mind', in *W. R. Bion: Between Past and Future*, 123.

[27] See Wilfred R. Bion, *Learning from Experience* (1962; rpr. London: Karnac Books, 1984), 34–5, where Mr Murphy meets Mr Endon again, in the afterlife of Bion's musings on a patient's obscure utterance: ' "Thoughts are a nuisance" said one of my patients, "I don't want them." Is a "thought" the same as an absence of a thing? If there is no "thing", is "no thing" a thought and is it by virtue of the fact that there is "no thing" that one recognizes that "it" must be thought?'

[28] Green, 'The Primordial Mind', in *W. R. Bion: Between Past and Future*, 117.

[29] Compare the hallucinatory 'blue haze' that seems to fill the room in 'Attacks on Linking' (1959), where Bion defines 'the use of the word "blue" as a compact description of vituperative sexual conversation' (*ST* 96).

capacity to stay in touch with his analyst that he employs when he telephones his mother:

Patient. Brilliant interpretation. (With a sudden convulsion) O God!

Analyst. You feel you can see and understand now, but what you see is so brilliant that it causes intense pain.

Patient. (clenching his fists and showing much tension and anxiety). I hate you.

Analyst. When you see, what you see—the week-end break and the things you use darkness to spy on—fills you with hate of me and admiration.   (*ST* 59)

Sight (insight) returns as the god of punitive moral strictures or what Bion glosses elsewhere as 'the function of a severe and ego-destructive superego' (*ST* 107). No wonder the patient is convulsed by his painful hernia. At such moments, he comes close to glimpsing the alienated image by which he is terrorized—not so much the persecuting analyst (despite the tendency of Kleinian interpretation to arouse persecutory anxiety) but a cruel and archaic agency within himself which has led to the painful herniation of his psychic reality.

Bion notes with admiration 'the tour de force by which primitive modes of thought are used by the patient for the statement of themes of great complexity' (*ST* 62). The close reader of Bion's writing (and especially his stage directions) may be moved to admire the same *tour de force* in his own statement of complex themes. Clarifying the painful process by which expelled ideas re-enter the patient, making him feel 'intruded upon, assaulted, and tortured' (*ST* 62–3), Bion makes it retrospectively possible to understand the patient's earlier convulsive movements on the couch and his agonized response to the analyst's 'brilliant interpretation' ('O God') as forms of hallucinatory thinking. The senses themselves, like Bion's penetrating interpretations, are felt to be painfully compressed in the process of being taken back into the patient, giving rise to 'the extremely painful, tactile, auditory, and visual hallucinations in the grip of which he seems to labour' (*ST* 63). Noting a gradual lessening in intensity of the inner drama rehearsed for his benefit, Bion suggests that the mutilation of verbal and pre-verbal thought may be reversed by the same primitive means. An intestine can digest thoughts as well as expel them. In the same way, 'agglomeration'—a favourite word in Bion's psychoanalytic lexicon—can result not only in a meaningless jumble of sensations and ideas but may also give rise to the complex layers of meaning represented by an everyday but suggestive ideograph like 'dark glasses'.[30] Indeed, Bion's reflections on the interplay between psychotic and non-psychotic functioning could be read as an embryonic theory of poetry, bringing to mind Shelley's account in *Prometheus Unbound* of another patient chained to the couch of a primitive and punitive super-ego.

---

[30] The temporal and temporary nature of agglomeration—as opposed to articulation—is an antecedent of the bizarre object and indistinguishable from incoherent speech; see Rafael E. Lopez-Corvo, *The Dictionary of the Work of W. R. Bion* (London: Karnac Books, 2003), 24.

In Shelley's utopian psycho-drama, an authoritarian régime can be successfully neutralized only by its linguistic recall into the self from which it originated, inaugurating the downfall of tyranny and the dawn of a psychic revolution, and breaking the recurrent cycle of tyrannical régimes and their overthrow. Shelley's preface famously announces that his imagery is 'drawn from the operations of the human mind, or from those external actions by which they are expressed'.[31] Bound to a precipice in his icy Caucasian ravine, Prometheus undergoes the return of expelled ideas (ideas that pierce, eat, tear, mock, and wrench) with all the torturing effects experienced by Bion's hernia-afflicted patient, writhing and hallucinating on the couch:

> The crawling glaciers pierce me with the spears
> Of their moon-freezing crystals; the bright chains
> Eat with their burning cold into my bones.
> Heaven's wingèd hound, polluting from thy lips
> His beak in poison not its own, tears up
> My heart; and shapeless sights come wandering by,
> The ghastly people of the realm of dream,
> Mocking me: and the Earthquake-fiends are charged
> To wrench the rivets from my quivering wounds . . .

> > (*Prometheus Unbound*, i. 31–9)[32]

Notice how only the body and its organs are concretely realized in Shelley's lines, while everything else becomes shapeless, mocking, and ghastly. This is not only to suggest that Shelley's coruscating poetry of Promethean torture anticipates Bion's psychic vocabulary, although it surely does—nor, for that matter, that Bion intends to recapitulate Shelley's revolutionary psychic politics, his self-described 'passion for reforming the world' (a crucial difference, to be sure).[33] But, with hindsight, Bion's clinical drama on the couch can be read as a kind of back-formation that leads by way of Shelley's *Prometheus Unbound* to a reclamation of the eighteenth-century aesthetic discourse of the Sublime.

In the painful prelude to unsaying his high language, Prometheus is assaulted by the return of his disowned hatred in the form of a piercingly concrete universe. 'Nothing is really a hernia' and 'Moral strictures' represent mutilated ideas that express similarly complex thoughts relating to internal persecution, without actually naming them. The quiveringly sensible body functions as both repository and figure for undigested mental pain, when the victim's curse returns to torment him on his glacial couch, as Prometheus laments in his refrain: 'Ah me, alas, pain, pain

---

[31] Everest and Matthews (eds.), *The Poems of Shelley*, ii. 473.

[32] Shelley's language recapitulates the language of Prometheus' torture in Aeschylus' *Prometheus Bound*; see ibid., 479 n.; although Shelley is deliberately departing from his Aeschylean model.

[33] Ibid., 475; but (according to Shelley) 'it is a mistake to suppose that I dedicate my poetical compositions solely to the direct enforcement of reform' (ibid., 475). For the contemporary resonances of the politics of *Prometheus Unbound*, see, for instance, Stuart Curran, 'The Political Prometheus', *Studies in Romanticism*, 25 (1986), 429–55.

ever, forever!…Ah me, alas, pain, pain ever, forever!' (*Prometheus Unbound*, i. 23, 30). Surrounded by the Furies, Prometheus acknowledges, 'Pain is my element, as hate is thine' (*Prometheus Unbound*, i. 477). That the gaping hell within (the hell that Prometheus wishes, in turn, on Jupiter) is located in the intestines for Bion's patient confirms what Shelley had imaged as the eyelessness of hatred—the eyes-wide-shut condition of not being able either to sleep or to wake from the Promethean nightmare of torment and perpetual punishment. Just as what pains the mind is located inside the body, hateful thoughts are hallucinatorily externalized by Shelleyan metaphor. Shelley's utopian claim that language and love offer the means to unsay the bound condition of humanity under the yoke of injustice and hatred anticipates the grand narrative of twentieth-century psychoanalysis, if only in its emphasis on the power of saying and unsaying. Drawing political oppression into the domain of the psychic, Shelley's *Prometheus Unbound* privileges verbal thought as a means to confront and undo the shapeless forms of internal persecution that collaborate with institutional oppression to bind the suffering subject to his rocky couch. When the Phantasm recalls Prometheus' curse to Jupiter (the shadowy oppressor created and sustained through Prometheus' own mental action), he repeats the Promethean taunt against Omnipotence: 'let the hour | Come, when thou must appear to be | That which thou art internally' (*Prometheus Unbound*, i. 297–9). The Shelleyean drama of untransformed internal states (hatred, persecution, and Omnipotence) is fiercely ironic as well as liberatory, constantly threatened with exposure for what it is not, as well as for the mental tyranny it is. Traces of Shelley's irony surface in Bion's twentieth-century re-imagining of schizophrenic language and thought, which is itself ironized, however, by the return of hatred in the twenty-first century, on a scale and in a form that makes Shelley's utopian intra-psychic world-change no longer imaginable.

A PROBLEM IN PHONATION

No passion so effectually robs the mind of all its powers of acting and reasoning as fear.

Edmund Burke, *PE* 101

The language of the Sublime has long-standing associations, not only with terror but with figurations of domination and power.[34] Burke's account of terror, for instance, is linked not only to obscurity but to secrecy, power, and superstition.

---

[34] See, for instance, Peter de Bolla, *The Discourse of the Sublime: Readings in History, Aesthetics, and the Subject* (Oxford: Basil Blackwell, 1989), 61–72; de Bolla (who is concerned to distinguish a theory of the subject from the discursive 'emission' of power) argues persuasively for 'the power of sublimity as a discursive *techne*' in Burke: 'the discursive counter "power" behaves exactly as a trope, since it figures, or rhetorically orders, the discourse of analysis… [power] does not produce sublimity in itself, by itself, but in connection to its accompaniment, terror' (ibid., 69).

Despotic governments keep their rulers out of the public eye and their workings hidden. Heathen temples are dark; druids hide under spreading oak-trees, and so on. This foray into the relation between political power, paranoia, and eighteenth-century ethnography ushers in Burke's most striking literary example of the relation between linguistic obscurity, terror, and the Sublime. The shapeless figure of Death, 'the portrait of the king of terrors', epitomizes the despotic eloquence of Miltonic description, 'dark, uncertain, confused, terrible, and sublime to the last degree', and almost too familiar to rehearse:

> The other shape,
> If shape it might be called that shape had none
> Distinguishable, in member, joint, or limb,
> Or substance might be called that shadow seemed,
> For each seemed either; black it stood as night,
> Fierce as ten furies, terrible as hell,
> And shook a dreadful dart; what seemed his head
> The likeness of a kingly crown had on.
>
> (*Paradise Lost*, ii. 666–73 (*PE* 103)) [35]

Bin Laden himself, surely? It was a stroke of genius on the part of al-Qaeda to disseminate the information that ten terrible look-alikes were roving the mountains of Afghanistan to confuse Bin Laden's American captors (a strategy of confusing self-multiplication adopted more recently by Saddam Hussein in the build-up to the invasion of Iraq).[36] The proliferation of gaunt and shapeless figures yokes obscurity with terror in a way that only a student of mass communication, or Milton, could have dreamed up.[37]

The verbal legacy of Death's shapelessness ('that shape had none') is its negativity; compare the 'shapeless sights' that mock Prometheus. Milton's lasting contribution to the aesthetics of the Sublime was the linguistic war he waged against the visible image: 'If shape it might be called', 'Or substance might be called that shadow seemed', 'what seemed his head'. Likeness (resemblance) is called into question along with visibility. Death becomes at once a problem of representation and of versification. The joints and limbs in play are concretions of the formal jointing and limbing—simultaneously, the un-jointing and dis-limbing—of Milton's blank verse. Freud, like Burke, associates the thought of death with the problem of representation, believing (unlike Klein, however) that it had no representative in the unconscious.[38] In 'Our Attitude towards Death' (Freud's title for

---

[35] Quotations from *Paradise Lost* are taken from John Carey and Alastair Fowler, *The Poems of Milton* (London: Longmans, 1968).

[36] 'Bin Laden Uses 10 Lookalikes to Foil Hunt' (Reuters, 17 November 2001).

[37] As Bion writes in 'The Grid', 'The visual image, as television and the movies have shown, has great power of lateral communication' (*Grid* 23).

[38] See Melanie Klein in 'The Theory of Anxiety and Guilt' (*E&G* 29–30). Klein's account of the fear of annihilation complements this discussion of Burke: 'If we try to visualize in concrete form the primary anxiety, the fear of annihilation, we must remember the helplessness of the infant in face of internal and external dangers. I suggest that the primary danger-situation arising from the activity of the death instinct within is felt by him as an overwhelming attack, as persecution' (*E&G* 31).

Part II of his sobering wartime *Thoughts for the Times on War and Death* (1915)), Freud notes that 'in the unconscious every one of us is convinced of his own immortality'. But, in times of war, 'Death will no longer be denied; we are forced to believe in it. People really die; and no longer one by one, but many, often tens of thousands, in a single day' (*SE* xiv. 289, 291). The denied reality of death intrudes, painfully and concretely. Those bombs fall on people like ourselves, tens of thousands in a single day.

The reality of death, unwaveringly registered by Freud, is reversed by Burke so that it appears as the opposite problem—the difficulty of comprehending the related ideas of eternity, and infinity. These ideas Burke pronounces to be 'among the most affecting we have, and yet perhaps there is nothing of which we really understand so little as of infinity and eternity' (*PE* 105). Thinking about the *absence* of finality and finitude (time and space without end) represents a chronic failure of understanding. As if to figure his simultaneously obscure and obscurantist meaning, Burke cites Milton's description of the ruined but still glorious archangel, Satan, who 'In shape and gesture proudly eminent | Stood like a tower', although bright, diminished like the rising sun seen through the mist; or eclipsed by the moon, and portending the fall of kings:

> . . . as when the sun new risen
> Looks through the horizontal misty air
> Shorn of his beams, or from behind the moon
> In dim eclipse disastrous twilight sheds
> On half the nations, and with fear of change
> Perplexes monarchs.
>
> (*Paradise Lost* i. 594–9 (*PE* 105))

These are images of glory dimmed, to be sure—but also of anticipatory confusion and dread. We too have seen sights that 'disastrous twilight sheds | On half the nations' and 'with fear of change' perplexes presidents. Art Spiegelman's *In the Shadow of No Towers* (2004) takes up the theme of human diminishment, confusion, and anxiety in the wake of urban capitalist disaster, attempting its own computer-generated vision of the incandescent after-image of the Twin Towers. Spiegelman shows us how a vision of catastrophic change can become a powerful tool for mobilizing the so-called war on terror, with its bellicose and patriotic rhetoric, precisely because it is obscure. Burke comments similarly on Milton's spectacle of monarchs ruined and kingdoms overturned: 'The mind is hurried out of itself, by a croud [*sic*] of great and confused images; which affect because they are crouded and confused . . . The images raised by poetry are always of this obscure kind' (*PE* 106). This is why, for Burke, sublime poetry works better than painting when it comes to communicating affect; it stops us in mid-thought—or rather, it acts like Blanchot's disaster, turning thought 'into the body of its absence' (*WD* 52).

Apropos of Shakespeare's *Coriolanus*, Hazlitt argues fiercely, from his own passion for reform, that the language of poetry and the language of power—the language of sublimity and despotic rule—have totalitarian potential during periods of national and international conflict.[39] Burke, we might recall, insists that big thoughts are necessarily obscure: 'A clear idea is . . . another name for a little idea' (*PE* 106). He quotes the apocalyptic poetry of the Book of Job (another mega-sufferer subjected to Almighty persecution): 'In thoughts from the visions of the night, when deep sleep falleth upon men, fear came upon me and trembling, which made all my bones to shake . . . and I heard a voice—Shall mortal man be more just than God?' (*PE* 106; Job 4: 13–17). In Burke's aesthetic argument, His Master's Voice eschews visual representation. Obscurity necessarily envelops the terrors of the Sublime, whether satanic or divine, malevolent or righteous. The reason to privilege poetry over painting, Burke argues, is poetry's non-pictorial status, or rather, its figurality—'Its apparitions, its chimeras, its harpies, its allegorical figures' (*SE* 107). Paradoxically, Burke's own language enacts the collapse of figuration into figure. In the effort to imagine abstract ideas, metaphors that convey affects and ideas are allegorized and personified. Klein identifies personification as the trope of the primitive or childish imagination (just as projective identification is the mechanism of primitive thought). Hence, the tendency for what Burke calls the 'sensible image' (*PE* 110) to impinge on obscurity, even in the case of the Deity. In a primitive counterpart of the same process, we have already seen how nothing (absence) becomes a sensible, pain-producing no-thing ('Nothing is a hernia') for Bion's psychotic patient.

Bion's Job-like sufferers, with their hallucinations, convulsive movements, and allegorical personifications, inhabit a world of shadowy persecution ('Moral strictures'). In his writing, we see how the aesthetics of the Sublime continue to underpin psychology.[40] Whereas Milton's poetry provides Burke with illustrations of sublime negativity, Bion's psychotics embody the catastrophic failure of figuration, the breakdown of verbal thought. The psychotic who is terrorized by the obscurity of his own ideas is simultaneously tortured by the concreteness of his thinking and his fear of bodily annihilation. Burke's *Enquiry* imagines death as a primal fear, like the fear of God himself, '*primos in orbe deos fecit timor*' (*PE* 112; 'fear made the first gods on earth')—as a Sublime catastrophe. In the face of superior power, the ideas of pain and death are overwhelming: 'strength, violence, pain and terror, are ideas that rush in upon the mind together' (*PE* 108). Unable to contain this traumatic onrush of ideas, the mind goes blank. The operation of the Sublime is therefore privative; its terrible imagery is that of '*Vacuity, Darkness, Solitude* and *Silence*' (*PE* 113). Hence its negativity. We are left with the no-thing and its companion, the no-idea. Burke writes that the passion aroused by the Sublime in nature is astonishment and that astonishment suspends the motions

---

[39] See William Hazlitt, 'Coriolanus', *Selected Writings* (Harmondsworth: Penguin, 1982), 284–8.
[40] See Thomas Weiskel, *The Romantic Sublime: Studies in the Structure and Psychology of Transcendence* (Baltimore, Md.: Johns Hopkins University Press, 1976), 83–106, on the relation between the Sublime and the psychology of terror. For Weiskell, whose psychoanalytic interpretation continues to be an important account of the Sublime, Burke's sublime moment is epitomized by its Oedipal identifications (ibid., 88–92).

of the soul with horror. But the word he uses, 'stupefaction' (Lat. *stupeo*), tips astonishment in the direction of the loss of the capacity for thought or mindlessness (with its associations of stupidity). What is terrible gives rise to fear, and fear is an emotion that resembles pain in its paralysing effect on mental functioning: 'No passion so effectually robs the mind of all its powers of acting and reasoning as fear. For fear being an apprehension of pain or death, it operates in a manner that resembles actual pain' (*SE* 101). In Burke's mimetic theory, terror can only be perceived as a trope of resemblance or as a bodily spectacle. The body becomes a primitive signifying system, forcing terror into the realm of mimesis as well as literality: 'I say a man in great pain has his teeth set, his eye-brows are violently contracted, his forehead is wrinkled, his eyes are dragged inwards, and rolled with great vehemence, his hair stands on end, the voice is forced out in short shrieks and groans, and the whole fabric totters' (*PE* 161). Pain becomes the (failed) figure—the embodiment or personification—of terror, or the apprehension of pain or death that has not yet occurred. Since they act similarly on the nerves, pain and terror are impossible to differentiate. Even a dog (writes Burke) writhes in anticipation of its punishment. Death is apprehended on the model of pre-traumatic anxiety, that is, as anticipatory fear, or the anxiety we have not had time to master. Building on the later Freud, Klein came to understand the death-drive as exactly that—the fear of annihilation and death in the unconscious.

In 'Attacks on Linking' (1959), Bion defines the destruction of mental processes as a clinical manifestation of the death-drive. The nothing that is a hernia is an undigested idea (a content-less, disorganized state) evacuated in the form of painful fragments or minute particles. Bion's figure for obscurity in 'Attacks on Linking' is the 'probability cloud'—a phrase derived from elementary particle physics, where something may be split up and ejected 'in particles so minute that they are the invisible components of a continuum' (*ST* 99). The patient experiences his own capacity for judgement as an alienated form of judgement, shapeless and persecutory, 'enigmatic and intimidating', qualities derived from a primitive breast (*ST* 100). The characteristics of this 'agglomeration of persecutory objects', Bion asserts, 'have the quality of a primitive, and even murderous, superego' (*ST* 101). He redefines Freud's archaeological analogy for psychoanalysis itself, not as the evidence of a primitive civilization to be uncovered and reconstructed but instead—like the burial-pit at Ur—as evidence of a primitive disaster that leaves its traces in the dispersed fragments littering the site (*ST* 101).[41] But Bion's theory of thinking is also a theory of affect. As a result of this primitive disaster, feeling has been split off. What is hated and destroyed is the link of emotion that gives meaning to things, both present and absent, ancient and modern. This is also what gives verbal form to thoughts and feelings. Bion's psychotic discourse of terror includes the linguistic manifestation of

---

[41] Bion is referring to 'On Arrogance' (1957): 'the spectacle presented is one, to borrow Freud's analogy, similar to that of the archaeologist who discovers in his field-work the evidences, not so much of a primitive civilization, as of a primitive catastrophe' (*ST* 88).

evacuated affect. 'Attacks on Linking' is Bion's clearest statement of the precise form of cruelty involved—'an overprominence in the psychotic part of the personality of links which appear to be logical, almost mathematical, but never emotionally reasonable. Consequently the links surviving are perverse, cruel, and sterile' (*ST* 109). The history of totalitarian thought is full of such attacks on the linking function of emotion.

This description of negative and dis-linking mental processes has a disconcerting parallel in the style and manner that Bion assumes in his own clinical writing—its logical and almost mathematical distinctions, its dryness, dark humour, and distance; even its moments of sheer emotional unreasonableness and verbal torsion. Bion's terse, irascible style is nothing if not difficult. One might argue that the analyst has to allow his thinking to approach that of the psychotic in the interests of communication. But another, and more interesting, way to read Bion's well-known impenetrability would be to envisage his patients as engaged in a shadow-play (perhaps even a dramatization) of aspects of the analyst's own mental functioning. Bion's 'Commentary' on the papers included in *Second Thoughts* shows him capable of extended self-commentary and self-reflexivity (as well as self-criticism) in relation to his own psychoanalytic writing.[42] The patient's phrase 'probability clouds', for instance, doubles as an allusion to the unlocalized, but continuous, field of minutely shifting meaning which is the object of Bion's own scientific observation in the clinical setting. The language of elementary particle physics—a modern science of the unobservable—offers new forms of knowing that can only be inferred, and new ways of thinking about the psychoanalytic universe that are strikingly counter-intuitive.[43] The theories of psychoanalysis, like theoretical physics, are frequently observable only in the sense they make of otherwise unintelligible results (a modern form of scientific inquiry). But whereas the patient's language is obscure, that of the analyst, by contrast, draws on the language of physics in order to describe minute and constantly shifting psychic phenomena with ever greater clarity, specificity, and precision. Klein's terminological emphasis on paranoid–schizoid splitting is refined as 'minute eviscerating

---

[42] Bion emphasizes the fictitiousness of his papers at the outset: 'If the distortions are judged effective, the narrative must be regarded as fiction. If the narrative were a work of art it might be reasonable to regard it as more nearly representative of truth than any literal transcription; but this psychoanalyst is not an artist. Expectations that the record represents what actually took place must be dismissed as vain' (*ST* 120). Bion similarly ponders the problem of communicating with his readers—'the communication between the psycho-analyst reading and the psycho-analyst writing' (*ST* 122)—as well as criticizing his own papers 'because their defect is not peculiar ... but typical' (*ST* 125).

[43] For Bion's interest in the transformative work of mathematicians and quantum theorists such as Henri Poincaré and Max Planck, see *Grid* 17. A sampling of Bion's reading in mathematics, contemporary philosophy of science, and quantum theory can be found in the bibliography to W. R. Bion, *Cogitations*, ed. Francesca Bion (London: Karnac Books, 1994). He would have found in Heisenberg not only the thesis that observation alters the thing observed but concepts such as probability waves and cloud chambers; see Werner Heisenberg, *Physics and Philosophy* (London: George Allen & Unwin, 1959), 42, 47. Cf. also the Cambridge philosopher Braithwaite, who includes 'unconscious mental processes' along with atoms among theoretical concepts; see Richard Braithwaite, *Scientific Explanation* (Cambridge: Cambridge University Press, 1955), p. ix.

splitting', her crude 'bits' become Bion's 'minute fragments' or 'stream of particles', like the continuous product of a collision between atoms, electricity, and gas in elementary particle physics.

One form of minute splitting to which Bion draws particular attention, as we have already seen, is linguistic (the split-up syllables and letters that prevent his patient thinking because he can no longer spell). Near the start of 'Attacks on Linking', Bion provides another example of linguistic splitting—a patient who responds to an interpretation with a prolonged fit of stammering. His stammer, Bion remarks, 'had the effect of spreading out his remark over a period of as much as a minute and a half. The actual sounds emitted bore resemblance to the gasping for breath; gaspings were interspersed with gurgling sounds as if he were immersed in water' (*ST* 94). Bion interprets the stammer, in line with his theory of thinking, as an assault on the verbal link between analyst and patient. But his fluent articulation of the patient's contrastingly breathless impediment suggests an obscure pleasure. At this point, an obvious question presents itself. What are the stakes of speech, viewed as a container for thoughts and feelings, for the analyst himself? Bion writes elsewhere of the stammerer that 'he was trying to "contain" his emotions within a form of words, as one might speak of a general attempting to "contain" enemy forces within a given zone'.[44] A battle is in progress. 'The Grid', the same late essay in which Bion invokes the tomb-burials of Ur, also stages an anguished performance of mutilated vocalization—compared, elaborately and at length, to a one-man band. Bion recounts a hilarious and (to modern ears) disablist episode involving a patient whose speech impediment cuts in at the precise moment when he tries to articulate the nature of his disability.

Bion's language of terror culminates in a piece of high tragicomedy which evokes a moment of clinical reminiscence. The patient in question is a research scientist, well acquainted with psychoanalysis. At first, he appears to be lying silently on the couch, until his analyst becomes gradually aware that he is not so much silent as stammering helplessly—unable, in fact, to say anything at all. Here is Bion's account:

I listened intently . . . He would breathe deeply, pause, let out his breath and start again. Each time he would draw in his breath suddenly and sharply and then suddenly let it out again as if experiencing considerable relief. I could make nothing of it. After a few moments he became silent again.

After a further pause I realized I had been listening in the expectation that he would speak and not listening to what I could hear. At first my impression was that he was

---

[44] See Wilfred R. Bion, *Attention and Interpretation* (1970; rpr. London: Karnac Books, 1984), 94. Bion develops the military metaphor to explain his patient's 'boring' modes of expression: 'the verbal formulation could not "contain" his emotions, which broke through and dispersed it as enemy forces might break through the forces that strove to contain them . . . His verbal formulation could be described as like to the military forces that are worn by the attrition to which they are subjected by the contained forces' (ibid., 94).

straining to pass a motion. Again he relapsed into a silence. This time it was broken by sounds as if he were swallowing, perhaps nearly retching. I drew his attention to the facts and said that they could, if I ignored all impressions other than sound, be evidence of activity at both ends of his alimentary canal. He agreed verbally but as if the 'stammer' continued; as nearly as I can represent it he breathed out sharply 'Hah, hah, just . . . hah . . . a problem . . . hah . . . hah . . . in ph . . . huh . . . her . . . nation'. I said he seemed to be making both a sarcastic comment on what was taking place—his 'stammer' and my interpretation. He then said, after a preliminary check in his voice but not in his lips, 'I think you are quite right.' (*Grid* 13)

Here Burke's voice of terror, 'forced out in short shrieks and groans', is swallowed down by the incapacitated stammerer. Bion disconcertingly confesses that the most striking feature of this implicitly sarcastic comment on the analytic dialogue (Hamlet's 'words, words, words') is the discovery of his own sense of exasperation in the face of the patient's speech impediment. Exasperation is followed, however, by astonishment at its sheer severity. What is going on?

Bion is prompted to reflect that any quest for a general psychoanalytic theory might lead him to overlook the observable facts. Instead of being 'deafened by the uproar of what the patient is *not* saying or doing' (*Grid* 14), he listens to the uproar of the noise that he *is* making—a noise that Bion proceeds to rehearse, conveying a practised raconteur's enjoyment at the retelling: 'There he lay, spluttering and farting and sucking away with his lips, and never a word of English. Had he been in command of the knowledge one would expect of a man of his age, I should say it was a perfect symphony concert of rude noises. It was, had I realized it earlier, a virtuoso performance' (*Grid* 17–18). A virtuoso performance, one might add, ventriloquistically appropriated by Bion himself—a speaker as much in command of rude knowledge as he is of English. Prompted by the spectacle of his stammering patient, Bion launches into a memory, presumably from his Indian childhood, involving a one-man band whose performance he was not allowed to watch as if it were indecent. But this time, he offers an uncensored version of the spectacle in the form of a comic turn of his own that leads, as it must, to the naming of body parts:

With an arrangement of pulleys, strings, a drum and a sort of harmonium he could be kicking up his heels, waving his arms, throwing his head back violently and suddenly, and thereby putting up a tolerable imitation of a musical performance, sounding his drum with his forehead, ringing a bell with his occiput and so forth. For some reason I could not understand, I was not allowed to watch this performance but used to be hauled off as if from some indecent spectacle. I was reminded of this . . . as I dragged myself into contact with the patient. After a time I said it sounded as if his mouth, his anus, his throat, were all engaged in a struggle for attention, for who should be supreme. 'Fff . . .', he replied, 'F.f.f . . . Ffonation', he finally exploded. 'It sounds', he said with increasing freedom, 'as if they were trying to settle who was top. But . . .' and again he became inarticulate.   (*Grid* 18)

The one-man band jubilantly enacts the forbidden pleasures of a body engaged in a clamorous instinctual argument with itself. At a loss for an interpretation (but not for words), Bion hazards a guess that these organs—mouth, anus, and throat—have a personality of their own, all trying to make use of the patient's 'phonation' to express themselves, staging a sort of open-mike poetry slam. 'Like trying to get hold of the microphone, and keep all others out', suggests the suddenly unimpeded stammerer.

Fluently, the patient begins to speak about his situation as a scientist. In his laboratory, he might have to work with a partner whose intelligence he doubted on 'an explosive project that might be extremely dangerous. Once before, a man had caused an explosion in the laboratory which seemed to fragment every glass vessel in the room. They might both have been killed. As it was, his companion had lost an eye. He did not want to lose his' (*Grid* 19). Bion interprets this story both in the light of Oedipal anxiety and as a transferential attack on his own analytic skills. The scenario of the stammer forms part of a dramatic represen-tation of an Oedipal trio (father, mother, child); the analyst is only as good as a bottle, compared to the breast; and so on. But as Bion continues to reflect on the plight of the patient with a prejudice (as he puts it) in favour of the truth, while cursed with the inability to speak, we begin to see the stammerer as a figure for the analyst himself. He, too, attempts to 'contain' emotion in verbal form in the face of the forces that struggle to break through. Not only that, but in order to hear 'sounds which would formerly have passed unnoticed' (*Grid* 23), he has to silence the competing voices of his own theoretical pre-conceptions, along with what he calls 'the clamour of psychoanalytical gang warfare' that surrounds him (a reference, presumably, to competing factions within the psychoanalytic world). Listening to the speeches of Hitler in German, he says, has allowed him to hear inarticulate elements that lie outside the spectrum of 'thought' as vocal elements that can set off dangerous explosions and chain-reactions.

Bion's polyphonic scene of phonation draws attention to a primitive musical score struggling for expression at the level of the body, via mouth, lips, tongue, throat, even anus. He refers to the feelings of 'men in battle conditions, prisoners of war or civilians in similar stress' as evidence of dormant forces acting on the analogy of 'the capillary blood system which in ordinary conditions is dormant but in extraordinary conditions may dilate as in surgical shock' (*Grid* 23, 24). The shock registered at the level of the lips is revealed as a 'silent metaphor' that has become 'dead' conversational metaphor. Having observed that the muscles of the patient's mouth 'fibrillate' uncontrollably like heart muscle, for instance, Bion refers to the animating of dead metaphor when 'brought to life by juxta-position with another metaphor whose inappropriateness, non-homogeneity, sends a galvanic-like flutter through it' (*Grid* 26). Shades of *Frankenstein*. The man with the stammer is in the grip of his bodily functions because he is galvanized by dead metaphor—or rather, by 'inappropriate' (i.e., improper) metaphor. To his patient, phonation meant defecation or urination; the mouth was not a means to speech but 'an object to be sensuously gratified by the tongue' (*Grid* 26). The reduction of the patient to the level of an indecently galvanic spectacle or uncontrollable muscular automatism draws attention to an explosive and traumatic potential within language itself. War in the mind becomes war in the mouth: the shockingly unpronounceable f-word that the patient is unable to spit out.[45]

If the rude Fff-word stops the mouth of the stammerer, all the more reason for the analyst to articulate his own thoughts and words in terms 'simple, exact, and mature', the appropriate speech of analytic interpretation. Failed phonation enacts what 'Attacks on Linking' identifies as hatred of emotion, hatred of reality, hatred of life itself. Bion sees this state of mind at work both in attacks on normal projective identification (the most primitive form of thinking, linking, and communication) and—at the opposite end of the spectrum—in potential attacks on 'the most sophisticated forms of verbal communication and the arts' (*ST* 108). 'Verbal communication and the arts' are also potential bearers of the negative aesthetics of psychotic mental functioning: the obscure poetry of psychosis, the explosive performance art of the stammerer, the bizarre object of Surrealism. Language and art (the language of art, including poetry) contain more destructive and narcissistic elements than allowed for by orthodox Kleinian aesthetics, with its emphasis on reparation, mourning, and artistic creation, and its ethical insistence on the relation between symbolization and the depressive position.[46] Emotion, writes Bion, is ultimately hated because 'it gives reality to objects which are not self and therefore inimical to primary narcissism' (*ST* 108). Primary narcissism is destructive in its hostility to recognizing the reality of others (not-selves). Bion's writings about psychosis gesture towards the pressure-point for liberal-humanist beliefs in the ethics of imagination. Any attempt to imagine the other—via literature, for instance—is ultimately forced to confront the recalcitrance and negativity of psychic processes.[47] Subjectivity, you might say, is not ours to give.

In 'The Grid', Bion writes of the need to protect and maintain the fragile link of language connecting analyst and patient. Among the more incapacitating terrors for the analyst might be that of losing his own tongue—being reduced to the helpless condition of the stammerer on the couch, mouth fibrillating like a muscle, speechlessly gurgling and gasping for breath; unable to contain the attack of his

---

[45] Cf. Bion, *Attention and Interpretation*, 94: 'His attempt to use his tongue for verbal expression failed to "contain" his wish to use his tongue for masturbatory movement in his mouth' (presumably the indecent spectacle the child is not allowed to watch).

[46] The classic statement is Hannah Segal, 'A Psychoanalytic Approach to Aesthetics', *The Work of Hannah Segal* (London: Free Association Books, 1986), 185–205.

[47] Cf. Blanchot: 'if so-called subjectivity is the other *in place* of me, it is not more subjective than objective; the other is without interiority' (*WD* 28).

own and the patient's emotional forces. The capacity for verbal thought keeps in mind questions and problems (Blanchot's 'affirmation and negation, silence and speech, sign and insignia') in the face of emotional assault, psychic breakdown, inner or outer catastrophe. The capacity to think and speak may even seem a guarantee of survival in the wake of unimaginable disaster. The tomb-burials of Ur, Hiroshima, the wreckage of the Twin Towers, recent scenes of devastation in Iraqi cities reassert the painful reality that Freud faced in his wartime essay of 1915, when his sons were fighting at the front: 'Death will no longer be denied; we are forced to believe in it'. As Freud remarks with understated irony, there is one sole condition on which we can reconcile ourselves to dying, 'namely, that behind all the vicissitudes of life we should still preserve a life intact' (*SE* xiv. 291). What Beckett in *Texts for Nothing* (1954) calls 'the old ceasing voice', a voice that never quite ceases 'when all would be silent and empty and dark... when all will be ended', is his bleak way of imagining death going on without us, beyond feelings, questions, or speech.[48]

In a similar vein, Blanchot's *The Writing of the Disaster* (1980) invokes 'The interruption of the incessant'. The defining characteristic of fragmentary writing is 'interruption having somehow the same meaning as that which does not cease' (*WD* 21). Blanchot re-imagines Beckett's ceasing, unceasing voice as writing itself. His pregnant phrase resituates the language of terror in a different, but no less relevant, frame. As Blanchot reminds us, the non-arbitrariness of writing 'makes of the most "reasonable" language a contaminated process, rich in what it cannot say, inappropriate for what it does say, and stating in secret (well or ill kept) the indefinable impropriety' (*WD* 136). What is the 'appropriate place' for the burial of human remains? What is an 'inappropriate' use of metaphor, when all metaphor (living or dead) is in some sense inappropriate? Language—rude language—sticks in the throat of a truthful patient, overwhelmed by the force of his emotions, producing a comically desperate explosion of 'Ffphonation'. Blanchot invokes Mallarmé's subversive aphorism, '*There is no explosion except a book*' (*WD* 7). But, as he aptly puts it, in a formulation that might have been arrived at by Bion, 'Consciousness can be catastrophic without ceasing to be consciousness' (*WD* 49). This is not to say that a catastrophe involving consciousness, or the explosiveness of books and words, can be measured on the same scale as the incandescent implosion of the Twin Towers. Nor is the incessant self-interruption of the stammerer, let alone the catastrophe of psychosis, to be equated with Blanchot's writing of the disaster (the end of writing and the chiastic writing of ends)—a meta-language for the experience of death that we can never have. What links them, however, is Blanchot's expressed wish 'for a psychoanalyst to whom a sign would come from the disaster' (*WD* 9). Although he eschews psychoanalytic vocabulary for himself as 'only the convenient language of an established culture', Blanchot explicitly states that for those who practise psychoanalysis in the battle

---

[48] Samuel Beckett, *Texts for Nothing* (1954; rpr. London: Calder and Boyars, 1974), 63–4.

zone, 'analysis is a risk, an extreme danger, a daily test' (*WD* 67). This is the risk conveyed by Bion's writings on terror and psychosis. Literary criticism (a less dangerous calling, to be sure) is left with its own test: how to read the signs from the disaster; how to remember the collapse of high buildings, while refusing the rhetoric of the war on terror.

9

Catastrophe in the Poppy Field: *Bion's Aesthetics*

Suppose a painter sees a path through a field sown with poppies and paints it: at one end of the chain of events is the field of poppies, at the other a canvas with pigment disposed on its surface. We can recognize that the latter represents the former, so I shall suppose that despite the difference between a field of poppies and a piece of canvas, despite the transformation that the artist has effected in what he saw to make it take the form of a picture, *something* has remained unaltered and on this *something* recognition depends. The elements that go to make up the unaltered aspect of the transformation I shall call invariants.

Wilfred R. Bion, *Transformations*[1]

Bion's poppy field is also a minefield. For all its invariants—the unaltered elements that allow it to be recognized as a poppy field—catastrophe haunts the scene of representation. Just when we think we recognize a familiar field of meaning (poppies, paint, canvas, Impressionism), the point of view or 'vertex' suddenly shifts, leaving us struggling to adjust to an unfamiliar perspective. In *Transformations* (1965)—generally regarded as his most problematic book—Bion broaches the aesthetics of psychoanalysis. His subject is the psychoanalyst's representation of clinical material.[2] Sometimes he approaches it by way of analogies that are easy to grasp, but at other times he uses the most abstract terms available to him, drawing on his reading in twentieth-century philosophy of science, mathematics,

---

[1] W. R. Bion, *Transformations* (1965; rpr. Karnac Books, 1984), 1 (*T*).

[2] For a helpful and accessible discussion of *Transformations*, see Gérard Bléandonu, *Wilfred Bion: His Life and Works 1897–1979*, trans. Claire Pajaczkowska (London: Free Association Books, 1994), 195–214; see also the more idiosyncratic discussion by Donald Meltzer, *The Kleinian Development, Part III: The Clinical Significance of the Work of Bion* (1978; rpr. London: Karnac Books, 1998), 341–63, and, for a brief overview of *Transformations*, James S. Grotstein, 'Bion the Navigator of the Deep and Formless Infinite', in Robert M. Lipgar and Malcolm Pines (eds.), *Building on Bion: Branches* (London: Jessica Kingsley), 17–22. For an interesting discussion of the emotional valance of catastrophic change in relation to emotional growth and insight, see also Lia Pistiner de Cortiñas, 'Transcending the Caesura: The Road Towards Insight', ibid., 225–52.

and geometry.[3] His discussion of painting swiftly mutates towards what later came to be known as catastrophe theory (in the wake of René Thom), with its emphasis on abrupt, unpredictable changes from one apparently stable state to another.[4] Atomic explosions disrupt the familiar Impressionist landscape, just as projective geometry takes over from traditional painterly perspective—sometimes with added projectile force.[5]

As a week-end painter himself, Bion had observed landscape with a meteorologist's eye, transforming his own visual perception of cornfields and cloudscapes in paint and on canvas.[6] But, as well as the Suffolk cornfields, the familiar Impressionist analogy with which *Transformations* opens may suggest (with hindsight) the poppies and carnage of Bion's First World War experiences. Add to this an item from Bion's list of theoretical preconceptions in *Transformations*— 'the theory of violence in primitive functions' (*T* 51)—and the potential for violence is ever-present in the calmest of summer landscapes. From Bion's perspective, nothing is ever quite what it looks, not even a poppy field, even though in Monet's 'Les Coquelicots' ('The Poppy Field', 1873) he evokes an easily recognizable Impressionist painting with its distinctive vision, light, and atmosphere. As he puts it, 'the invariants of an impressionist painting are not the invariants of a painting by a member of, say, a realist school of painting' (*T* 5).[7] We know what

---

[3] The bibliography of *Cogitations*, ed. Francesca Bion (London: Karnac Books, 1994) (*C*), provides a guide to Bion's reading in mathematics, algebra, and philosophy of science; the list includes R. B. Braithwaite, *Scientific Explanation* (1955); Euclid's *Elements*; Werner Heisenberg, *Physics and Philosophy* (1958); Charles Peirce, *Collected Papers of Charles Sanders Peirce*, Vol. VII: *Science and Philosophy* (1958); Henri Poincaré, *Science and Method* (1914); Karl Popper, *The Logic of Scientific Discovery* (1959); Willard van Orman Quine, *Mathematical Logic* (1955); G. Semple and G. T. Kneebone, *Algebraic Projective Geometry* (1952); and A. N. Whitehead and Bertrand Russell, *Principia Mathematica* (1925 and 1927).

[4] By the 1970s, although his work had circulated during the mid-1960s, René Thom was the main exponent of catastrophe theory or 'morphogenesis', which provides mathematical models for applications that have been extended from physics and biology to brain-modelling, prison riots, and semiotics; see René Thom, *Structural Stability and Morphogenesis: An Outline of a General Theory of Models*, trans. D. H. Fowler (1972; London: W. A. Benjamin, 1975), and *Mathematical Models of Morphogenesis*, trans. W. M. Brookes and D. Rand (1974; Chichester: Ellis Horwood, 1983). For an overview with an insistence on the mathematical basis of Thom's theory, see also Tim Poston and Ian Stewart, *Catastrophe Theory and its Applications* (London: Pitman, 1978). It has been suggested that Bion's concept (which precedes the publication of Thom's work and the popularization of catastrophe theory) is closer to the idea of 'catastrophic reaction' in Gestalt theory; see Bléandonu, *Wilfred Bion*, 283, 35 n.

[5] In *Cogitations*, Bion refers to catastrophe in the apocalyptic context of his vision that psychoanalysis might disappear, perhaps 'because it arouses or will arouse fear of the unknown to the point where the protective mechanisms of the noösphere compel it to destroy the invading ideas for fear they will cause a catastrophe in which the noösphere disintegrates into the no-amorph. This catastrophic change could be brought about by advances in astronomy, physics, religion, or indeed any domain for which there may as yet be no name' (*C* 320); cf. 'The Resistance of the Thinker to the Unthought Thought', W. R. Bion, *Attention and Interpretation* (1970; rpr. London: Karnac Books, 1984), 118 (*A&I*).

[6] See Francesca Bion (ed.), Wilfred R. Bion, *All My Sins Remembered: Another Part of a Life and The Other Side of Genius* (1985; rpr. London: Karnac Books, 1991), for reproductions of Bion's paintings, including 'Cornfield, from The Little Cottage'.

[7] Bion borrows his terminology from projective geometry; see, for instance, J. G. Semple and G. T. Kneebone, *Algebraic Projective Geometry* (Oxford: Clarendon Press, 1952), 1–8, which provides a source for a number of terms in Bion's lexicon (transformations, invariants, realization, co-ordinates,

we are looking at if we know anything about painting. But for Bion, *interpretation* is the representational and aesthetic practice (as well as the action) specific to psychoanalysis, and here it may not be so easy. This is the domain of 'technique', considered not only as a set of clinical protocols but also as the representation of psychoanalytic work and the theories on which it depends.

At once a theory of object relations and an epistemology (a way of both seeing and knowing), psychoanalytic interpretation implies what Bion calls a transformation, or change of vertex. He conceives of interpretation as arising from the subjective emotions of the observer (painter/analyst) in response to the behaviour of the object observed (landscape/patient), which is itself necessarily altered by observation. 'Red-to-red' (taking red as an 'invariant') is less important than communicating the emotional experience of redness, along with the psychoanalyst's ability to evoke emotion in the reader. For Bion, it is not a matter of redness becoming (more) so by virtue of its relation to its surroundings, as it might be for the phenomenological Maurice Merleau-Ponty.[8] Without evoking the relationality of red, let alone non-representational conceptions of painting, Bion turns to the abstract notation of contemporary algebraic mathematics, philosophy, and physics to convey subjective feelings and psychic processes. In aesthetics, Bion is a neo-Kantian for whom reality, or the thing-in-itself (O), can only be known through its sensory perception and representation.[9] He suggests that both observer and landscape may be subject to unexpected turbulence, and sometimes even to catastrophic change. *Transformations* vividly evokes the dangers of unpredictable psychotic upheaval, as well as the risk that the observer will become caught up in the surrounding turbulence. Bion's 'invariants' are the equivalent of reference points and conventions built into, or implied by, a particular

and even O). It would be interesting to know if Bion progressed from the easier exercises at the end of ch. II to the concluding exercise of ch. XVI: '. . . Show also that the section of Ω by a quadratic Ω through such a double-four of planes represents a tetrahedral complex in S_2' (ibid., 397). The concept of 'plastic invariants' also had currency in mid-century art criticism (see Bléandonu, *Wilfred Bion*, 196). For Bléandonu's critique of Bion's reduction of painting to a representation of the external world, see ibid., 196–7.

[8] See Merleau-Ponty's turn to the visual arts and aesthetics in his late writings: 'Claudel has a phrase saying that a certain blue of the sea is so blue that only blood could be more red. The colour is yet a variant in another dimension of variation, that of its relations with the surroundings: this red is what it is only by connecting up from its place with other reds about it, with which it forms a constellation . . . It is a concretion of visibility, not an atom'; Claude Lefort (ed.), Maurice Merleau-Ponty, *The Visible and the Invisible*, trans. Alphonso Lingis (1964; Evanston, Ill.: Northwestern University Press, 1968), 132; cf. also the discussion of red in Merleau-Ponty's notebooks as a form of seeing 'accessible only through the seeing' (ibid., 247).

[9] For a clarificatory discussion of Bion's epistemology, and particularly his relation to the Kantian 'thing-in-itself', see Victor L. Schermer, 'Building on "O": Bion and Epistemology', in Robert L. Lipgar and Malcolm Pines (eds.), *Building on Bion: Roots* (London: Jessica Kingsley, 2003), 226–53. For Bion's use of the sign 'O', in the sense of ultimate reality, the (unknowable) thing in itself, and its relation to mystical experience as well as Kant, see Rafael E. López-Corvo, *The Dictionary of the Work of W. R. Bion* (London: Karnac Books, 2003), 197–201. It seems unlikely that Bion read Husserl, but here, too, he would have found (as did Merleau-Ponty) the view that there can be no knowledge of things-in-themselves except as accessible to perception and consciousness.

representational style, technique, or point of view. According to his extended aesthetic analogy, analytic interpretation transforms clinical experience, 'Just as impressionism can be regarded as a method of transforming landscape into a painting' (*T* 5). No two painted poppy fields are alike, any more than any two painter's styles resemble each other, even if they belong to the same school; and the same holds true for psychoanalysis. A Kleinian 'transformation' will differ from a Freudian one. Even within the same school, interpretations will not necessarily be identical. Yet two psychoanalysts would probably recognize the same psychic situation, much as two painters would recognize a poppy field.

Side by side with this extended Impressionist analogy, however, Bion develops another model, based on projective geometry. Euclidean geometry, the most abstract of representational forms, deals with points, lines, and circles that represent the spatial world from the point of view of a centre of embodied perception. The optical effects of parallel lines that meet, or circles that appear as ellipses, are the domain of traditional perspective. But multi-dimensional geometry poses a conceptual challenge to the bodily understanding of space. Vertices (which change from one system to another) are not the same as relationships (which remain constant even when transposed to a different plane). Bion applies the analogy to the vertices and invariants of psychoanalytic interpretation, where familiar situations appear startlingly different when viewed from another vertex, although the points of reference remain constant. What interests Bion is the idea that the same situation can be transformed and understood in a hitherto unknown way when it shifts to a different vertex. How it is understood has implications for the psychoanalytic knowledge it provides. Bion's melding of the subjective and affective vision of Impressionism with mathematical logic and the mind-bending abstractions of projective geometry says something about his own notoriously demanding style. His writing uses a deceptively ordinary vocabulary while drawing on the repertoire of mathematical and algebraic philosophy. It aims to be a sensitive barometer of the psychoanalyst's emotions, conveyed by means of ordinary language and close observation. Yet it also lays claim to forms of symbolic notation capable of being applied to other psychic situations and clinical contexts.[10] Bion's observations

---

[10] See also Bion's interest, apropos of the need for a study of scientific method, in finding abstract terms for defining and describing feelings and mental states. He contrasts the 'statement-forming assignatory functions' of mathematical logic, in which 'the mathematical logician is attempting by abstraction to gain in precision a method of communication that is more exact than that of ordinary speech', with 'a method of communication and thought that is quite different from that of ordinary speech' (*C* 158)—a fine but significant distinction; cf. Poincaré, *Scientific Method*, 156, for a critique of '*logistic* mathematics', or '*pasigraphy*, that is to say, the art of writing a treatise on mathematics without using a single word of the ordinary language'. Bion also refers to the mathematical logician, J. H. Woodger, *Technique of Theory Construction* (Chicago: University of Chicago Press, 1939), 10; Woodger's short book (Vol. 2/5 of the *International Encyclopedia of Unified Science*) provides an example of (unsaturated) meta-logical construction derived from foundational texts such as Bertrand Russell, *Principles of Mathematics* (1903; 2nd edn., London: George Allen & Unwin, 1937). Bion's allegiance is closer to Poincaré's Kantian (*synthetic a priori* intuitionist) position rather than to the logicistic approach of Bertrand Russell.

and intuitions are frequently conveyed in terms of bodily perception and the language of subjective emotion. But they are converted into mathematical and theoretical models that are no longer corporeal or subjective.[11] This is the mark of the construction of scientific theory for Bion.

By introducing catastrophe theory into the representational realm of the Impressionist poppy field, or the management of a psychotic crisis, Bion risks generating a peculiar form of anxiety (and even frustration) in his readers. He unmoors us from the perceptual and affective world by means of concepts that are both obscure and intellectually challenging. This effect of a world turned sideways—rendered strange and unrecognizable—resembles the mental vertigo produced by the *n*-dimensional realm of projective geometry. *Transformations* begins with its familiar aesthetic analogy (Monet's painting), but rapidly segues to a clinical crisis (a psychotic breakdown) in order to view what has happened from a new perspective. Bionic interpretation is redefined as a modernist mode that breaks with familiar representational contours, whether in art or life, where the empirical viewer remains securely located. It transforms the reassuring certainties of bodily, affective, or spatial perception, much as abstraction had transformed the rules of representation in the realm of art, or the twentieth-century revolution in quantum physics had transformed the idea of observation itself. Through their encounter with the violence of catastrophic change and new ideas, both clinical experience and theory undergo a transformation. In this new mode of psychoanalytic thinking, uncertainty becomes central. What, precisely, are we seeing? Bion's aesthetics remain anchored in the problematics of vision. Hence, they are inseparable from his interest in hallucination. The thematics of sight involve both Oedipal wounding and Miltonic blinding. Seeing means seeing things—but also *not* seeing them; insight may be projected as out-sight; the seen can be deformed as well as transformed. The analyst has to be able to hallucinate blindly along with the psychotic patient, in order to understand both what the psychotic sees and what he annihilates.

SEEING THINGS

Bion's aesthetics are heavily invested in the idea that symbolic or narrative violence is implied by any aesthetic transformation. The peculiar mode of psychoanalytic

---

[11] Bion cites Poincaré: 'our methods of mensuration, which have played and still play a considerable part in the concept of space, are clearly related to man's awareness of his own body' (*C* 85); cf. Henri Poincaré, *Science and Method*, trans. Francis Maitland (London: Thomas Nelson and Sons, (1914)), 100: 'It is in reference to our own body that we locate exterior objects, and the only special relations of these objects that we can picture to ourselves are their relations with our own body. It is our body that serves us, so to speak, as a system of axes and co-ordinates.' For the pervasive influence of Poincaré on twentieth-century aesthetics, cf. the sculptor Bruno Adriani for Poincaré's idea of the construction of physical space in relation to the body; see Suzanne Langer, *Feeling and Form* (London: Routledge & Kegan Paul, 1953), 90–1.

narrative that he employs to illustrate his meaning is 'catastrophic', in the sense that there is no 'during', but only a before and after—a sudden, unpredictable, and absolute change of state. This change may be experienced less as an oscillation (as in Bion's concept of the PS←—→D, the oscillation between paranoid–schizoid and depressive positions within the patient and the analytic session) than as an explosion. However retrospectively predictable, it occurs unforeseeably, and its effects are violent. The introductory chapter of *Transformations* narrates the situation of 'a man' (later referred to as Patient A), a borderline psychotic who unexpectedly has a breakdown. What can be learned from this embedded narrative?

We might expect that Bion's telling of the story ('man having a psychotic breakdown') would bear the marks of his previous discussion of Impressionism. But his clinical illustration appears to have no connection whatever with aesthetics. As often happens in Bion's writing, the pace changes as soon as the clinical vignette is introduced. At first there is nothing much to report ('Analysis seems to proceed slowly'). But suddenly the rhythm picks up. The air is heavy with anxiety and intimations of alarm:

> Then a change: friends or relations who have been denying that there is anything the matter cannot ignore his illness. He has been strange: he spends hours seated morosely in a chair; he appears to be hearing voices and seeing things . . . In analysis he is hostile and confused. There is a sudden deterioration. The alarm of relatives is evident in letters and other communications . . . There appears to be reason for the analyst to be alarmed.   (*T* 7)

We sense that this is a clinical set-piece. Confronted by a situation of generalized but unspecific anxiety, the reader is as confused as the analyst. But rather than turning the spotlight on the patient (who is now, in lay terms, 'mad' or 'mental', no longer 'normal'), Bion describes the effects on himself and on the patient's relatives. All of them are now in the grip of an urgent and uninspected need to 'do something'. Something has to be done. But what and by whom?

The sudden change of state in the patient (from stable to unstable) is registered by a sequence of escalating statements that describe what feels (if only to the analyst) like an unmanageable disaster:

> It is catastrophic in the restricted sense of an event producing a subversion of the order or system of things; it is catastrophic in the sense that it is accompanied by feelings of disaster in the participants; it is catastrophic in the sense that it is sudden and violent in an almost physical way. This last will depend on the degree to which analytical procedure has produced a *controlled* breakdown.   (*T* 8)

Instead of thinking, acting takes over. The story of Patient A (the story of a psychotic breakdown) does more than overturn order or generate anxiety; it releases a sudden violence that is almost physical in its conversion of ideas into actions. What had previously been described as '*theoretical* violence' becomes violently enacted. This is one definition of a psychotic breakdown and the turbulence it causes. Where violence was previously latent and theoretical, now it is manifest—but almost impossible to think about: 'Emotion is obvious and is aroused in the analyst' (*T* 9). The invariants of Bion's psychoanalytic system (in this case, Klein's theories of projective identification and internal objects) had previously informed an interpretive frame for the patient's hypochondriac pains in the knee, legs, abdomen, or ears. Metaphorically speaking, his internal objects had been giving him trouble.

Now, however, the patient's problems present themselves in the form of 'anxious relatives, impending law-suits, mental hospitals, certification, and other contingencies apparently appropriate to the change in circumstances'. The psychoanalyst is in danger of substituting doing for thinking, losing his grip on psychic reality. The same invariants are present, but their meaning is transformed by their reappearance on a different plane. Reality impinges in ways that appear intractable, inevitable, and even natural. Internal objects previously experienced as internal are experienced as external, just as the impulse to act is lodged in others ('Do something!') in place of the patient's own hypochondriacal symptoms. 'The change is violent change and the new phase is one in which violent feelings are violently expressed' (*T* 9). The analyst risks being caught up in the cumulative violence, since he is the one expected to 'do something' in light of the patient's alarming change. Bion's model is that of 'an explosion and its expanding pressure-waves' (*T* 9). Like an explosion, the patient's breakdown sets up chain-reactions. What has been psychic now takes a social form, or at least becomes a matter for the group. As we can see from this example, the 'model' (that of an explosion) is also a transformation. But is it necessarily violent? There is all the difference between a representation (whether a painting, a narrative, or a psychoanalytic interpretation) and a catastrophe. Transformation is the controlled change of state proper to analytic interpretation (which tends towards thought), as opposed to the uncontrolled change involved in a psychotic breakdown (which tends towards unthinking action).

In lay terms, Bion asks: is the patient normal or mad? Psychosis has gone public, acquiring social reality. But the business of the psychoanalyst—as Bion reminds us—is what is going on in his patient and himself, rather than the social dimensions of catastrophe. In other words, 'In general terms the analyst's point of view differs from those we have considered because it is psycho-analytic.' His function is to observe, reflect on, and describe his experience of both pre- and post-catastrophic states in order to understand their psychic meaning. If the reader finds this strange (Bion suggests), 'he will realize that any apparent strangeness lies in the method of approach and not in the experience described' (*T* 11). The apparent 'madness' has method in it; or rather, the madness lies in Bion's method, which refuses to regard the world of telegrams and anger as self-evident, natural, or normal. Bion's psychoanalytic theory includes in the category of 'action' the body-based phantasy 'that the mind, acting as if it were a muscle and a muscle acting as a muscle, can disburden the psyche of accretions of stimuli' (*T* 36).[12] His representation (his interpretation) will therefore differ from a non-psychoanalytic one, although it involves the same set of circumstances. Bion's stance is predicated on Heisenberg's proposition that 'in atomic physics, a situation has arisen in which the scientist cannot rely on the ordinarily accepted view that the researcher has access to facts, because the facts to be observed are distorted by the very act of observation' (*T* 45).[13] Things are not only not what they seem; they are changed by being seen.

Psychoanalysis, for Bion, deals with psychotic breakdown or psychotic thought in a way analogous to quantum physics. Observation is never neutral but is distorted in the act of observation, and inevitably distorts what it observes. Even if the realm of psychoanalytic discourse and description is finite, the phenomena described contain a theoretically infinite realm of possibilities—just as Heisenberg's philosophy of quantum mechanics abolished the walls of his laboratory: 'If a patient says that he knows that his "char" is in league with the postman because his friend left white of egg in the bathroom the relatedness implied by his statement may differ from forms of relatedness to which I am accustomed because his statement represents phenomena related to each other in an infinite universe' (*T* 46).[14] Only a theory (a preconception) can produce coherence, given this infinitude of possible relations. But even a theory will not be able to describe the total reality.[15] Perhaps this is why the analyst turns to aesthetics in order to grasp

---

[12] Bion is referring to Freud's 'Formulations on the Two Principles of Mental Functioning' (1911), where Freud distinguishes between alteration of the environment by muscular action and a stage when the capacity for thought has come into being: 'Thinking was endowed with characteristics which made it possible for the mental apparatus to tolerate an increased tension of stimulus while the process of discharge was postponed' (*SE* xii. 221).

[13] See Bion's 9 August 1959 reflections on the opening pages of Heisenberg's *Physics and Philosophy: The Revolution in Modern Science* (London: George Allen & Unwin, 1958), 32–3 ('every tool carries with it the spirit by which it has been created'; 'the spirit of modern physics . . . will connect itself in different ways with the older traditions'). Bion re-reads and reverses Heisenberg's propositions in terms of the hypertrophying of man's tool-making capacity (much 'as the defensive armour of stegosaurus hypertrophied and led to its extinction'), as well as the impact on modern science of powerful older traditions (instead of vice versa); still more boldly, he reformulates the contradiction between particle theory and wave theory in terms of primitive phantasies, equating elementary particles with the paranoid–schizoid and wave theory with the depressive positions (*C* 60–1).

[14] See Bion: 'Heisenberg's exposition of the philosophy of quantum mechanics shows that the dependence of the physicist's observed facts on a relationship with facts that are not and can never be known has abolished the limiting walls of his laboratory, and therefore the laboratory itself, so that the physicist has difficulties with his laboratory analogous to the analyst's difficulty with his consulting room and analytical situation' (undated; *C* 263). As Heisenberg puts it, experiments involving atomic events 'have to do with things and facts' but atoms and elementary particles 'form a world of potentialities or possibilities rather than one of things and facts'; see Heisenberg, *Physics and Philosophy*, 169. Cf. also Bion's 4 October 1959 comment on Heisenberg and Nils Bohr, and the Copenhagen School: 'no single fact is unrelated to and uninfluenced by the totality of facts, and that totality must remain unknown' (*C* 85).

[15] In the same entry, Bion cites Semple and Kneebone's *Algebraic Projective Geometry* (1949)—a totality of facts will not 'support the view that there is a realization . . . which corresponds to the mathematical calculi and the scientific deductive systems they represent'—and quotes Heisenberg on the limited applicability represented by a mathematical scheme or a coherent set of concepts (see *C* 86). Cf. Heisenberg on 'the often discussed lesson that has been learned from modern physics: that

the internal reality of the psychotic patient: 'His thought processes were extremely disturbed, many of his utterances being incomprehensible even after prolonged analysis. When I thought I grasped his meaning it was often by virtue of an aesthetic rather than a scientific experience' (*T* 52). The analytic function intervenes in a model of transformation that holds equally good for painting, music, mathematics, sculpture, or even a relationship between two people.

The principle at work is that 'observation' (like primitive phantasy) is embedded in the meaning-making and theory-producing process. A fact is a fact, not because it is naturally or inevitably so but because it has acquired meaning from a pre-existing theory. This theory may itself correspond to, or be unable to transcend, unconscious phantasy. In support of his argument, Bion appeals to what is possibly the most traditional of representational and mimetic tropes, that of reflection—a lake holding a reflected image. This is not only an optical model, but a model taking into account atmospheric effects that disturb both surface and reflection: 'A lake in calm bright weather reflects trees upon the bank on the shore opposite the observer. The image presented by the trees is transformed in the reflection: a whole series of transformations is effected by atmospheric changes' (*T* 7). So far, so (non)transparent. Bion has in mind not only the observer's ability to deduce the nature of the trees on the basis of their representation (like the Kantian thing-in-itself, the reality that can only be known through perceived phenomena)—a task made more difficult if he has to deduce the species of tree or even the microscopic features of leaf-structure. But how much more difficult if changes intervene, from light to dark, or from calm to turbulence; then 'the demands on him could be impossibly exacting' just as 'atmospheric conditions could be impossibly distorting' (*T* 47). The complexities of the emotional link, whether Love or Hate or Knowledge (L, H, and K—the Bionic relational triad), produce effects analogous to shifts in atmospheric conditions.

The lake with its changing reflections becomes an image of observation changed, disturbed, and rendered opaque to such an extent that it is reversed, a refraction of a reflection that alters the original landscape: 'the atmospheric change disturbs the reflection, but (it would be necessary to say), the disturbed reflection affects (or "causes") the atmospheric change' (*T* 71). As things change, seeing things changes them. This may not be a tenable theory about lakes, but it offers a plausible aesthetic analogy for transformation. The difference, Bion argues, is analogous to what distinguishes a portrait from a caricature or a cartoon, in which a pictorial representation is affected by essential components in the transformation (whether L, H, or K). Form and feeling inhere in any transformation of the original 'invariants' (in this case, the identifying characteristics of the sitter). Bion is anxious enough about his portrait-painterly analogy to acknowledge its limits; it would be repugnant, he says, to think 'that the analyst works on

every word or concept, clear as it may seem to be, has only a limited range of applicability' (*Physics and Philosophy*, 111). Bion concludes that mathematics may be 'an important element in the mental processes of the individual which makes it possible for him to be a psycho-analyst' (*C* 87).

his patient's emotions as a painter might work on his canvas' (*T* 37). The psycho-analyst does not set out to manipulate the patient's state of mind. Instead, he turns 'to the domain of the Aesthetic' in the absence of what might be called hard scientific evidence. He only has at his disposal his position in the optical model, looking across the lake (observing both reflection and trees), alert to changes in surface or light that alter appearances. In making this appeal to aesthetics in a scientific context, Bion could rely on an established scientific and mathematical privileging of the aesthetic (as well as the unconscious) when it came to the realm of hypothesis and explanation.

Given the long-running controversy surrounding psychoanalysis—how can an empirically unverifiable method be called a science?—it is hardly surprising that Bion turned to the twentieth-century conceptual revolution that had transformed theoretical physics and the philosophy of science along with it.[16] *Cogitations* provides ample evidence of his reflections on contemporary scientific thought and method. Specifically, he draws on the vocabulary of particles, elements, combinations (physics), or vertices, invariants, and matrices (mathematics and geometry)— a vocabulary crucial to twentieth-century quantum-physics theory, mathematical philosophy, and to the revision of classical geometry by projective geometry.[17] Bion attempts a similarly rigorous rearticulation of psychoanalytic theory in terms of the problem of observing phenomena that are constantly subject to uncertainty and change. The precursor for Bion's turn to aesthetics in a scientific context is the thinking of the early twentieth-century mathematician Henri Poincaré. Bion derived from Poincaré not only the idea of an inductive method alert to minute differences in the initial state of a given system, and their unpredictable consequences for subsequent states, but the concept of the 'selected fact' around which a hypothesis coheres. Poincaré also foregrounded the aesthetics and the unconscious psychological processes of mathematical discovery; the study of mathematics included emotion and elegance, or 'the feeling of mathematical beauty', along with sudden flashes of illumination. What Poincaré called 'the delicate sieve' of 'aesthetic sensibility' was an essential corrective for mathematical thought.[18]

Poincaré also provides an autobiographically based account of the unconscious work that led to mathematical discovery. *Scientific Method* describes a period of unformed ideas, fruitless work, mental restlessness and blockage, followed by the coalescence of ideas in a stable combination around a 'selected fact', or else by a

[16] Bion argues that Freud's work elicited criticism for being 'unscientific because it does not conform to the standards associated with classical physics and chemistry', while it constitutes 'an attack on the pretensions of the human being to possess a capacity for objective observation and judgement by showing how often the manifestations of human beliefs and attitudes are remarkable for their efficacy as a disguise for unconscious impulses' (*C* 84–5).

[17] For a brief account of the profound changes brought about in the early decades of the twentieth century by the revolution in quantum mechanics, see Phillip Stehle, *Order, Chaos, Order: The Transition from Classical to Quantum Physics* (New York: Oxford University Press, 1994).

[18] See Poincaré, *Science and Method*, 60. Like other philosopher-mathematicians who influenced Bion, Poincaré took a Kantian position, refusing the purely logical manipulation of symbols for a more intuitive and aesthetic approach.

sudden and dazzling illumination—resonating with ideas inscribed in Kleinian accounts of the role of the depressive position as it affects the capacity for symbol formation and creativity.[19] If Bion needed a description of what he was attempting with his own work, he would have found it in a passage quoted in *Learning from Experience* (1962), apropos of 'the process of creation of a new mathematical formulation':

If a new result is to have any value, it must unite elements long since known, but till then scattered and seemingly foreign to each other, and suddenly introduce order where the appearance of disorder reigned. Then it enables us to see at a glance each of these elements in the place it occupies in the whole. Not only is the new fact valuable on its own account, but it alone gives a value to the old facts it unites. Our mind is as frail as our senses are; it would lose itself in the complexity of the world if that complexity were not harmonious; like the short-sighted, it would only see the details, and would be obliged to forget each of these details before examining the next, because it would be incapable of taking in the whole. The only facts worthy of our attention are those which introduce order into this complexity and so make it accessible to us.[20]

Order is introduced into complexity by the 'fact' that makes sense of otherwise meaningless details (details that confuse the short-sighted).

Elsewhere, with Poincaré explicitly in mind, Bion refers to 'the coming together, by a sudden precipitating intuition, of a mass of apparently unrelated incoherent phenomena which are thereby given coherence and meaning not previously possessed'.[21] The new pattern of material produced by the patient falls into place like the reconfigured elements in a kaleidoscope. Poincaré was referring, among other things, to his realization that his first treatise had defined Fuchsian functions by applying the 'transformations' of non-Euclidean geometry. For Bion, too, non-Euclidean geometry occupies a key position in his transformation of psychoanalysis. Prominent aspects of his terminology—including the term 'transformation' itself, derived in its most specific usage from the transformation onto multiple planes of n-dimensional projective geometry—are derived from this context. The revolution in quantum physics depended on forms of inquiry and

[19] See ibid., 52–5 for Poincaré's account of the vicissitudes of creative mathematical work, and Bion: 'the mental state described by Poincaré is quite compatible or even identical with that described by Melanie Klein in her discussion of the paranoid–schizoid and depressive positions' (*C* 85). Bion sees the 'uncoordinated and incoherent elements' of modern physics as analogous to the mental domain from which Poincaré tried to escape by means of the 'selected fact'.

[20] Wilfred R. Bion, *Learning from Experience* (1962; rpr. London: Karnac Books, 1984), 72; cf. Poincaré, *Science and Method*, 30. Poincaré goes on to stress the importance to mathematicians of the elegance of their methods and results: 'Elegance may result from the feeling of surprise caused by the unlooked-for occurrence together of objects not habitually associated' (ibid., 31). Cf. also Suzanne Langer, who sees the part played by symbolism in science exemplified by Poincaré in the context of new philosophical, scientific, and psychological epistemologies where the 'given fact' (a theoretical hybrid of concept and percept) has taken over; see Suzanne Langer, *Philosophy in a New Key* (Cambridge, Mass.: Harvard University Press, 1942), 274.

[21] Wilfred R. Bion, *Second Thoughts: Selected Papers on Psycho-Analysis* (1967; rpr. London: Karnac Books, 1987), 127 (*ST*).

discovery expressed in mathematical equations. Bion's awareness of these competing strands in the philosophy of science inflects his attempt to develop psychoanalytic concepts analogous to mathematical or algebraic formulae. His transformation of Klein's theory of projective identification and internal objects into a theory of knowledge involves just such a tension between registering affect, on one hand, and achieving abstraction, on the other. This is the tension that underlies his approach to the aesthetics of psychoanalysis.

Transformations develops Bion's concern with model-making in the direction of general propositions capable of explaining a broad range of psychic phenomena.[22] At stake for Bion is a science that is both empirical and non-positivistic, observed and abstract, yet capable of functioning as a recognizable form of representation for both psychic states of mind and psychoanalytic theory. His aim is to provide an account of the psychical field—much as a theoretical physicist might describe the behaviour of elementary particles—on the basis of mathematical formulae or theoretically inflected 'facts', as the kaleidoscope shifts or the field explodes, creating previously unperceived patterns and meanings. What has become of his familiar aesthetic touch-stone, Monet's 'Poppy Field'? No wonder Bion acknowledges that, when he sees things, he may be as 'mental' as his patient.

THE PAIN IN THE PATIENT'S KNEE

In what sense can a personality be said to have a form? Bion asks this surprising question apropos of the word 'transformation'. As well as form, there is deformation, in Poincaré's sense of 'deformation'—not only of our view of the world (as in a distorting mirror) but of self-perception (the body as an instrument of measurement).[23] The patient may indeed be a shapeless lump; but a different distortion is involved if he interprets the analyst's greeting as a hostile attack. For every transformation there exists its negative form. Take Bion's example, the meaning attributed to the opening psychoanalytic ritual—the formality of shaking hands performed by analyst and patient at the start of a session. In order to understand the multiplicity of meanings present in this initial handshake, we have to understand 'what [the patient] says or does as if it were an artist's painting. In the session the facts of his behaviour are like the facts of a painting and from them [the analyst] must find the nature of his representation' (*T* 15). Patient A returns

[22] See, for instance, the chapter 'Models for Scientific Theories', in Richard Braithwaite, *Scientific Explanation* (Cambridge: Cambridge University Press, 1953), 88–114, a book to which Bion often refers in *Cogitations*.

[23] Cf. Poincaré, *Scientific Method*, 98, on deformation involving the body: 'If we look at the world in one of those mirrors of complicated form which deform objects in an odd way, the mutual relations of the different parts of the world are not altered . . . we readily perceive the deformation, but it is because the real world exists beside its deformed image . . . But if we imagine our body itself deformed, and in the same way as if it were seen in the mirror, these measuring instruments will fail us in their turn, and the deformation will no longer be ascertained.'

at this point, bringing with him a dream (dreamed just before a week-end break) that a tiger and a bear are fighting. He wakes with his own shout of fear in his ears, and the dream reminds him of a story of a famous big-game shoot. A fierce tiger is driven off its kill by a bear, but the bear has its nose bitten off: 'It made him shudder to think of it. (Here he screwed up his face and shuddered)' (*T* 16). The material that follows is sexually and Oedipally inflected. But at first Bion chooses not to emphasize this. Instead, he asks, 'in more conversational terms, what was the patient talking *about*? One answer is that he was talking about the week-end break. Let us examine this' (*T* 17). Another answer would be that he was talking about the primal scene. Bion asks why the patient should see the week-end break as an object of fear: 'What, when he contemplates the week-end break, does he see?' (*T* 18). Notice the emphasis on sight.

A transference interpretation would argue that Patient A has transferred a fragment of infantile sexuality to the analyst with relatively little deformation, preserving the truth of an earlier childhood situation. Like the transformation of projective geometry, it contains as little change as possible; the analyst can gauge the original state of affairs with some accuracy (what Patient A is seeing in relation to his dream of the tiger and the bear). But, in a brilliantly observed sequel, Bion offers a very different scene of greeting, this time between himself and another, less accessible patient, Patient B. Here is Bion's brief but startling, apparently verbatim record of the session's opening exchange, which immediately challenges both his and the reader's understanding with its incoherence:

The patient came in, but, though he had been attending for years, seemed uncertain what to do. 'Good morning, good morning, good morning. It must mean afternoon really. I don't expect anything can be expected today: this morning, I mean. This afternoon. It must be a joke of some kind. This girl left about her knickers. Well, what do you say to that? It's probably quite wrong, of course, but, well, I mean, what do *you* think?' He walked to the couch and lay down, bumping his shoulders down hard on the couch. 'I'm slightly anxious . . . I think. The pain has come back in my knee. You'll probably say it was the girl. After all. This picture is probably not very good as I told him but I should not have said anything about it. Mrs X . . . thought I ought to go to Durham to see about, but then' and so on.   (*T* 19–20)

'I cannot do justice to the episode', Bion observes of this obscure, rapid-fire, and altogether Beckettian communication, noting its swift 'changes of tone expressing depression, fear, anxiety, confidentiality, and others'. He takes a moment to observe that he remembers 'only the general impression and the general impression . . . was itself intended to give a general impression' (*T* 20)—that is, to obfuscate—before deciding that his first record of the experience is misleading.

The thick description of Bion's second attempt relies on the tools of precision and nuance in the face of deliberate deformation—and on a prior theory. Instead of losing his mind to the impression of generality deliberately created by the patient, the analyst tries to decipher (interpret) what he is actually 'talking *about*'. Bion notes that his sustained meta-reading of the patient's initial (non)communication involves 'a high proportion of speculation' and that these 'speculations depend on [his] theoretical pre-conceptions' (*T* 21). Preconceptions give meaning to what would otherwise be baffling in the patient's obscure communication. This approach to interpreting the patient's opening remarks constitute his psychoanalytic 'transformation'. Bion's account derives its meaning both from the theory of the Oedipus complex and from the particular way it functions in the transference situation between patient and analyst:

> After his pause of uncertainty he whispered his good mornings as if he were pre-occupied with an object he had lost but expected to find close at hand. He corrected himself in a tone that might imply a mental aberration that had led him to think it a 'good morning'. The speaker of the words 'good morning', I gathered, was not really the patient, but someone whose manner he caricatured. Then came the comment that nothing could be expected. That was clear enough, but who was making the comment, or of whom nothing could be expected, was obscure. It might have been myself; I did not think it was he. Then he spoke of the joke. The way this term was used implied that the joke had no tincture of humour about it . . . When he spoke of 'this' girl it was evident that I was supposed to know her; in fact I did not nor did I know whether she had left her knickers lying about or given notice on account of some episode connected with her knickers. 'What do you say to that?' meant that in either case I would know as well as he did what her behaviour signified, though, as his next sentence showed, the significance (unmentioned) attached to her behaviour by both of us was probably mistaken, girls being what they are.   (*T* 20)

Bion's commentary conveys, in great detail (yet with a considerable degree of abstraction) the minutiae of the patient's behaviour and speech. The effect is not joking, exactly—but nor does it have (unlike the patient's own communication) 'no tincture of humour about it'.

The analyst's interpreting presence directs us to the patient's subtle, indirect, and persistent attempts at communicative obfuscation, including his attempt to confuse the analyst's mind. The patient, so Bion tells us—in a way that immediately implies we too shall be able to 'gather' or infer it from his account—does indeed have something in mind; although precisely what it is he is unable to render with any 'verbal exactitude'. But, at this point, I want to break off to pursue another tack. Who is the girl about whose essential nature—'girls being what they are'—the patient and (by implication) the analyst are imagined as being in such collusive, knowing, and altogether mistaken masculine agreement? The passage from *Transformations* brings to mind Bion's recollection, in a quite different context, of a painful personal episode involving a different girl. In his bleak, posthumously published autobiography of the inter-war years, *All My Sins Remembered* (1985), Bion describes a painful episode which also has obvious Oedipal resonances. On a solitary walking holiday, he unexpectedly encountered his ex-fiancée ('an extremely beautiful young woman'), apparently week-ending in the company of another man. The meeting, Bion records, aroused a storm of feeling in him, and he abruptly cut his own week-end short. Outwardly, he behaved with civilized composure towards the couple, as they did towards him. But a very different scenario—a veritable 'scene of violence at the crossroads'—was played out in his imagination. Imperceptibly, Bion's narrative of the episode assumes the form of a police inquiry. What really happened as a result of this painful week-end encounter? And what bearing might the episode conceivably have on the obscure communication of Patient B about the pain in his knee?

Walking along the river after his meeting with the maddeningly happy and conventional couple (seemingly oblivious to his jealousy), Bion imagines, vividly and murderously, the following crime of passion involving a knee injury:

> I was haunted by that walk along the reedy path of the river. If I had had my service revolver with me I would have shot him. Then I would have shot her through the knee in such a way that the joint could not be repaired and she would have had a permanently rigid leg to explain to her future lovers. I would not give myself up because that would not be enough of a mystery to occupy the newspapers. But when in the course of ordinary routine inquiries they closed in on me I would make my report.[24]

'*A sordid little murder*', comments Bion's imaginary interlocutor (a version of his older self), unimpressed. This is certainly true as far as the fate of his rival is concerned. But into this lurid phantasy involving two men and a girl, Bion also projects a crippling pain (or deforming rigidity) which he locates elsewhere, in his beautiful ex-fiancée's knee. Operating in a peculiarly omnipotent and concrete fashion, his phantasy deserves to be described as 'hallucinatory', in the sense that a painful perception is ejected as a hostile and retaliatory assault on an object imagined as persecutory or frustrating.[25] Bion reproaches himself retrospectively for his failure to negotiate the Oedipal scene as regards both sexual and generational difference—that is, for not having known, when he became engaged to the 'girl', the crucial difference 'between a boy and a girl, a wife and a girl, a husband and a boy, a wife and a mother, or a husband and a father'.[26] His imaginary interlocutor (still unimpressed) dismisses the dismal litany of Bion's exploits in love and war as an '*extremely uninteresting and commonplace story*'.[27] But the other Bion (the autobiographical Bion who recounts the episode and his misery afterwards) replies, still smarting: 'It was very painful to me'.

So perhaps the question is not who was this girl over whom two men are presumed to be struggling, but, rather, to whom does the pain in the knee belong? It appears to circulate, like the part-object it is, among all the parties in this violently transferential and counter-transferential Oedipal triangle. Elsewhere in *Transformations*, Bion writes of the psychotic personality's probing as 'incessantly

---

[24] Bion, *All My Sins Remembered*, 29–30.

[25] Cf. Bion's earlier paper, 'On Hallucination' (1958), in connection with a seriously disturbed schizophrenic: 'The patient had been hostile and afraid that he would murder me. I was able to show him that he was splitting off painful feelings, mostly envy and revenge, of which he hoped to rid himself by forcing them into me' (*ST* 68).   [26] Bion, *All My Sins Remembered*, 30.

[27] Ibid., 32. Bion gives a graphic account of his time as a tank commander in the First World War in his posthumously published autobiography, *The Long Week-End 1897–1919* (1982) and *War Memoirs 1917–19* (1997); see also Ch. 7 above.

active, designed to tap sources of counter-transference. The patient's associations are directed to obtaining evidence of meaning and emotion (here broadly divided into two all-embracing categories of love and hate)' (*T* 81–2). The focus is on Love and Hate (L and H), rather than the knowledge (K) that is properly at stake in psychoanalytic inquiry. The link (whether of Love or Hate) constitutes reassuring a antidote to the problem, rather than an approach to its solution. Both the patient's and the analyst's assumed familiarity with the typical behaviour of girls ('girls being what they are') probes an old wound, a hallucinatory counter-transferential pain in the knee. Both men are supposedly at a loss about a girl, viewed here as an internal object—'an object [the patient] had lost but expected to find close at hand' (*T* 20), presumably in the analyst's possession: 'but, well, I mean, what do *you* think?' (*T* 19). It is not so much the girl but the capacity to think that the patient has lost, and now expects to find in his analyst ('what do *you* think?').

This brief clinical vignette in *Transformations* suggests how lying down on the couch can turn into a scene of obfuscation which simultaneously creates a deceptive sense of complicity between men, while probing their Oedipal rivalry. The patient seems to be trying to get a rise out of the analyst, or else covertly testing the enemy's defences. Bion's narrative implies that 'internal, mental pain' has something to do with the loss of an object, along the lines of Freud's speculative analogy with physical pain. The chief characteristic of psychical pain is that it is apt to be located in—or fantastically inflicted upon—someone other than one self. Bion's extended commentary on Patient B's opening remarks conveys the mix of envy, destructiveness, and violence in the micro-movements of the analytic encounter:

When he lay on the couch he did so as if trying to express surreptitiously his wish to damage my property. I thought his next comment compatible with this surmise in that it might mean that, being confused with me and yet detached from both of us, he hazarded a guess that I was anxious at his violence, that I supposed him to be anxious and not aggressive, that he thought the feelings he experienced were what I would call anxiety. His reference to the pain in his knee was typical of certain very rare statements in that it meant 'The pain in my knee, which I now experience, is what you as analyst think is really the girl inside me.' Such a statement meant that despite evidence to the contrary he had knowledge of my analytic theories and that he was now having an experience which I would explain by that particular theory. It might mean that he wished me to know what experience he was having and that the correct interpretation could be arrived at through the theory of internal objects.   (*T* 20–1)

We are now in a better position to understand Bion's interpretation of the patient's peculiar manner of lying down on the couch. Bion suggests that the patient caricatures and attacks—with deliberately hostile and aggressive intent— the very psychoanalytic theory by which the analyst tries to understand the patient's pain.

Klein's 'theory of internal objects' is often regarded as among the most complex and crucial, but also the most mysterious, of her theoretical innovations.[28] At one extreme, the internal object can be imagined as a troublesome physical object literally located inside the body. At the other, it implies the introjected objects whose assimilation into the ego constitutes our very identities. In his wish to damage the analyst's intellectual property, Bion's patient attacks not only his couch but his theory. In this context, the question 'to whom does this property belong?' is already moot. The patient is so confused in his own mind with the caricature of a stereotypically avuncular analyst ('Good morning, good morning, good morning') that he attacks his own mental functioning when he attacks the analyst. Bion comments: 'His "after all" is typical; it is meaningless, but can act as a stimulus to speculation' (*T* 21). This may be equivalent to saying that the patient's convoluted opening communication comes down ('After all') to his need to reduce Bion's theory to meaninglessness. The patient's efforts seem devoted to ensuring that his communication will be regarded not just as obscure but as 'bad'—leading it to be forcefully evacuated to a great distance by the analyst (this is how Bion explains the puzzling allusion to a picture and a journey to Durham).[29] The patient's personality is in fragments and the bits are meant to get under the skin of the analyst, in order to confuse him and prevent him from thinking—or else to make him think of his own difficulties instead of the patient's (and perhaps even conjure up some earlier scene of violence at the crossroads).

Bion's meta-commentary mentions his dependence on both 'classical analytical [i.e., Freudian] theory' and 'Kleinian theories of splitting and projective identification', as if he were combining classical physics with the revolution in quantum-physics theory along the lines of Copenhagen School physics.[30] His own position is predicated on the classical theory of Oedipal anxiety combined with Kleinian paranoid–schizoid functioning. Bion adds that he expected to find that the confusion between analyst and patient in the patient's mind 'would be illuminated by applying the theory of projective identification' (*T* 21). But even this primitive level of relating represents a form of thought. However rudimentary, a primitive communication is taking place via the mechanism of projective identification. Bion goes on to ask a characteristically difficult question that involves two utterly opposed answers about the obscurity of the patient's communication: 'Is its obscurity due to the difficulty of the matter of the problem for which he seeks help

[28] See R. D. Hinshelwood, *A Dictionary of Kleinian Thought* (London: Free Association Books, 1991), 68–83; and see also Meir Perlow, *Understanding Mental Objects* (London and New York: Routledge, 1995).

[29] 'Subsequent remarks meant that what had been taking place in the session was a pictorial representation, an externalization of a visual image, not likely to be regarded by me as good and therefore evacuated by me with such force that this fragment of his personality would be projected as far away from me as Durham is from London' (*T* 21).

[30] Cf. Heisenberg, *Physics and Philosophy*, 46, on the model provided by the paradox of the reliance of contemporary physics on both classical concepts and the uncertainty principle.

or is it due to his need to conceal? The analyst's task is to distinguish one from the other' (*T* 22). This is not a question of radical un-decidability. Far from it. Rather, Bion advances a model which might be called radical *decidability* in the context of unpredictability.[31] Two distinct and opposed meanings masquerade as a single confusion in the analytic encounter (the same confused and confusing pain, as distinct from an accurately differentiated pain).

Psychoanalysis is not, for Bion, a relativistic science; it may be an epistemology that involves uncertainty, but there is a crucial difference between K and –K (knowledge and its deliberate destruction). Similarly, there is all the difference in the world between the pain in the patient's knee and a cruel joke; between a surreptitious attack on the analyst and the actual insolubility of the patient's problem—not to mention the difference between the patient's pain, any pain hypothetically felt by the analyst, and the phantasized nature of the injury done to his ex-fiancée, from whom (Bion recalls) he had withdrawn to a great distance after their chance encounter. In *All My Sins Remembered*, Bion's imaginary interlocutor remarks: '*that must have been a terrible loss to her*'.[32] *Transformations* observes that 'The sense of being at a loss, which will be apparent to the reader, is not quite so profound in the consulting room as the written account makes it appear, because the clinical experience affords a mass of detail that cannot be communicated in print' (*T* 22). The mass of detail provides a foundation for interpretation. None the less, the analyst's 'sense of being at a loss'—ultimately a loss or failure of understanding—parallels what the patient seems to have lost, 'but expected to find close at hand' (*T* 21) when he arrives at his analytic session. What has been destroyed is at once an emotional tie (an affective link) and a relation to knowledge (a cognitive link). In this context, the patient's 'After all' can be heard as a moment of insistent stasis in his stalled, repetitive, and baffling monologue.

The barriers erected against communication reveal the extent to which the psychoanalytic scene involves a considerable degree of covert or open hostility, and even hallucinations of murderous violence. But, Bion seems to say, better a hostile link than none at all. At least there is a pain somewhere in the room, or in the patient, even if it masquerades as a girl or a part-object, or travesties the Kleinian theory of internal objects—and even if it takes the form of an uncanny doubling with the analyst's private history of pain and envy. On one level, the Oedipal pain in the patient's knee is the part-object that stands for an entire body of internalized theoretical knowledge belonging to the analyst and susceptible of being imagined as lodged in, or forcibly ejected into, another physical body. The patient 'knows' the analyst's theoretical stance, envies it, and seeks to destroy it, because the insights it brings cause him pain. There is 'understanding' psychoanalysis, and

---

[31] Cf. Poincaré, *Science and Method*, 68: 'it may happen that small differences in the initial conditions produce very great ones in the final phenomena. A very small error in the former will produce an enormous error in the latter. Prediction becomes impossible, and we have the fortuitous phenomenon.' Poincaré's example is the unpredictability of meteorological disaster produced by unstable atmospheric conditions.   [32] Bion, *All My Sins Remembered*, 29.

then there is the 'psychoanalysis' of understanding, including the potential destruction and deformation of knowledge. Reversible perspective (a term used to describe a peculiarly intractable and destructive form of psychoanalytic *impasse*) might be used to conceptualize this oscillation between the possibilities of clinical insight and its loss, the difficult terrain involving the chiasmic alternative of suffering as opposed to avoidance.[33] As Bion defines it, 'Reversible perspective is evidence of pain; the patient reverses perspective so as to make a dynamic situation static.'[34] The patient's reversal renders a dynamic situation static, so that the psychoanalytic process stalls. But in that stalling, pain speaks.

Bion observes in *Transformations* that the pressure on the analyst to give interpretations can serve to disguise an anxiety about meaninglessness. Intolerance of meaninglessness leads the patient to 'pour out a flood of words so that he can evoke a response indicating that meaning exists either in his own behaviour or in that of the analyst' (*T* 81). This recalls the flood of false *bonhommerie* in the patient's parodic opening greeting ('Good morning, good morning, good morning'). The effect, according to Bion, is to stifle curiosity about the possibility of no-meaning as well as meaning. Without the possibility of a no-thing (absence), the temptation is to substitute a thing—something or anything (a pain in the knee). For instance, 'The actual murder is to be sought instead of the thought represented by the word "murder"' (*T* 82). The dangerousness of acting out, or the concretization of phantasy, would have replaced thinking, just as Oedipus misunderstood Tiresias' words to him by taking them literally. Such processes, Bion reminds us, induce states of stupor, hallucination, or megalomania. They also lead to the abolition of boundaries. No distinction exists for the analysand between himself and the analyst (no 'dividing membrane').

The penetration of this protective barrier or membrane had provided Freud with his founding analogy between physical pain and mental trauma. According to the Freud of *Inhibitions, Instincts, and Anxiety* (1926), even 'If the pain proceeds not from a part of the skin but from an internal organ, the situation is still the same' (*SE* xx. 170–1). Internal objects as well as organs can cause pain that resembles physical pain. For the psychotic patient, concrete thinking denies the difference between the patient's pain and his knee, or between his pain and the analyst's pain, not to mention their internal objects—the theory, or the girl over whom they struggle in unconscious phantasy. The consequence is not just to elide differences between persons but to destroy meaning itself, along with the boundary between inside and outside, while simultaneously evacuating a disowned pain into someone else. Pain circulates without being owned or understood, just as

[33] See Bléandonu, *Wilfred Bion*, 180–2: 'Bion shows how reversible perspective facilitates the avoidance of the mental pain that is essential to all growth . . . Here the conflict is between the analyst's point of view and the patient's . . . The inverted perspective enables the patient to avoid the discomfort of acknowledging the existence of the parental couple, and of being in overt conflict with his analyst.' The classic instance of reversible perspective would be Oedipus' misunderstanding of Tiresias' words.
[34] Wilfred R. Bion, *Elements of Psycho-Analysis* (1963; rpr. London: Karnac Books, 1984), 60.

psychoanalytic knowledge and understanding are obscured by the patient's hostile, obfuscating communication. The analyst's interpretation—his transformation— puts the pain back where it belongs.

THE INVISIBLE VISUAL

The problematic status of the visual in Bion's psychoanalytic aesthetics— his emphasis on the pictorial, whether as landscape, reflection, or portrait—has hallucination as its corollary. In 'Reality Sensuous and Psychic', Bion writes that the analyst needs a capacity for what he calls 'the state of hallucinosis', not so much an exaggeration of a pathological condition but rather 'a state always present, but overlaid by other phenomena, which screen it' (*A&I* 36).[35] Its ubiquity makes it possible for the analyst to participate in the patient's (and his own) hallucinations in order to arrive at a state where they can be transformed into interpretations by something Bion views as a scientific state of mind—'an act of faith' (*A&I* 32).[36] Hallucination is intrinsically far-fetched. It might lead a patient to see the analyst's words as flying over his head, or to detect them in the patterns of a cushion so that 'he was able, in a state of hallucinosis, to see that the patterns were really my words travelling, through his eyes, to him' (*A&I* 37).[37] Only through the analyst's own capacity for hallucinosis can the meaning of the patient's hallucination be grasped, as a prelude to understanding its meaning(lessness): 'In the domain of hallucinosis the mental event is transformed into a sense impression and sense impressions in this domain do not have meaning; they provide pleasure or pain' (*A&I* 37). Hallucination implies a reversal of sense perception. Instead of meaning being taken from the outside to the inside, it is expelled from inside to outside.

'On Hallucination' (1958) describes a situation in which a patient experiences the obstruction of his feelings of love towards a prospective mate. His hatred and envy render him impotent in the face of phantasized parents or rivals. His posture is that of a muscular scowl directed at the entire world:

The unburdening of the psyche by hallucination, that is by the use of the sensory apparatus in reverse, is reinforced by muscular action which may best be understood as being an extremely complex analogue of a scowl; the musculature does not simply change the expression to one of murderous hate but gives effect to an actual murderous assault . . . The assault is but the outward expression of an explosive projective identification by virtue of which his murderous hatred, together with bits of his personality, is scattered far and wide into the real objects, members of society included, by which he is surrounded.   (*ST* 83)

---

[35] For a discussion of 'Transformations in hallucinosis', see López-Corvo, *The Dictionary of the Work of W. R. Bion*, 292–6.

[36] Bion sees the relationship of 'acts of faith' to thought as analogous to the relationship of a priori knowledge to knowledge (*A&I* 35).

[37] Cf. the patient who responds to Bion's words as if to 'visible objects which were passing over his head to become impacted on the opposite wall' (*ST* 75).

Scowling at the world, Bion had reached in phantasy for his service revolver. Committing a murderous assault goes a stage further than scowling, to the police inquiry or the realm of psychosis. In the domain of hallucination, however, 'the violence of the explosion leaves him denuded also of his feelings of love' (*ST* 84). Hence Bion's misery after the encounter and the hallucinatory sequel recorded in *All My Sins Remembered*.

Exploring the subject of hallucination in *Cogitations* during 1959, Bion suggests that unwelcome interpretations and even dreams may also be evacuated by being 'seen' or got rid of in the form of visual hallucinations.[38] This evacuation includes an invisible form of visual hallucination by means of minute fragmentation of the analyst's words, as if by teeth or typewriter: 'the words are taken in aurally, broken up into letters of the alphabet, and thus not only fragmented but transformed from sound into visual objects and ejected through the eyes to become further mutilated' (*C* 79). The paradoxical result would be not so much visual or pictorial images as 'invisible visual hallucinations that are the outcome of transformation into pictorial images, extremely minute fragmentation, and ejection by the eyes to a great distance' (*C* 79)—perhaps as far away as Durham ('I ought to go to Durham...'). In 'Attacks on Linking' (1959), Bion describes how, in response to an interpretation to the effect that the patient 'felt he had been and still was witnessing an intercourse between two people, [the patient] reacted as if he had received a violent blow... my impression is that he felt it as delivered from within' (*ST* 95). Logically, the blow comes from outside (in the form of the analyst's words), but the patient experiences it as 'a stabbing attack from inside'. Here a verbal 'attack', registered as internal, becomes a hallucinatory assault that paradoxically abolishes the visual element of the hallucination altogether: 'He sat up and stared intently into space. I said that he seemed to be seeing something. He replied that he could not see what he saw. I was able from previous experience to interpret that he felt he was "seeing" an invisible object' (*ST* 95–6). It is not that the patient cannot see; rather, he annihilates what he sees (the analyst's words) by splitting them into minute fragments. The hallucination has become 'invisibly visual', since it has been fragmented to such an extent that it can no longer be seen. André Green refers to this phenomenon as negative hallucination that does not stop 'at the gates of language'; indeed, he suggests, language may be 'the preferential target of negative hallucination'.[39]

'On Hallucination' describes the unseen drama involved in the action of psychoanalysis (interpretation) as a bizarre form of mirroring. Bion describes how

[38] Speculating about the prevalence of visual images in dreams, Bion suggests that they may be a form of visual evacuation like that of the hallucinated patient 'taking in the interpretation and evacuating it as far as possible away from himself by "seeing" it, i.e., visually evacuating it as a hallucination' (2 August 1959; *C* 49).

[39] See André Green, *The Work of the Negative*, trans. Andrew Weller (London: Free Association Books, 1999), 207: 'There is no reason to believe that negative hallucination ... stops at the gates of language because the latter consists of verbal matter. On the contrary, there is every reason to suppose that language, owing to its relational vocation, may be the preferential target of negative hallucination.'

the patient exerts an automatized control over the analyst, as revealed by 'the charade-like episode, when he was coupled with [Bion himself], so that both appeared as lifeless automatons' (*ST* 82). This episode refers to yet another greeting-scene at the start of the analytic session, where the two protagonists are brought into relation by 'the bizarre automaton-like synthesis of physical movement in which patient and analyst are geared together like clockwork toys' (*ST* 68). As the sequence of movements unfolds, in a pantomime of the analyst's behaviour, it becomes evident to Bion that the patient is hallucinating. The purpose of the hallucination is to keep an eye on the analyst even though he cannot be seen, and ultimately to denude him of life so that the two of them are locked in a reciprocal yet lifeless relationship. Bion stages this strange performance by keeping his own eyes firmly fixed on the patient:

While I close the door he goes to the foot of the couch, facing the head pillows and my chair, and stands, shoulders stooping, knees sagging, head inclined to the chair, motionless until I have passed him and am about to sit down. So closely do his movements seem to be geared with mine that the inception of my movements to sit appears to release a spring in him. As I lower myself into my seat he turns left about, slowly, evenly, as if something would be spilled, or perhaps fractured, were he to be betrayed into a precipitate movement. As I sit the turning movement stops as if we were both parts of the same clockwork toy. The patient, now with his back to me, is arrested at a moment when his gaze is directed to the floor near that corner of the room which would be to his right and facing him if he lay on the couch . . . He reclines slowly, keeping his eye on the same corner of the floor, craning his head forward now and then as he falls back on the couch as if anxious not to become unsighted.   (*ST* 66)

As Bion explains this mechanical choreography, 'When the patient glanced at me he was taking a part of me into him. It was taken into his eyes' (*ST* 67). Whose eyes are watching whom?

The patient's eyes are felt to suck something out of the analyst 'so that it was deposited in the right-hand corner of the room where he could keep it under observation while he was lying on the couch' (*ST* 67). But the analyst may equally be felt to extract something from the patient whom he keeps under observation. Bion's prose records a reciprocal (verbal) tremor of satisfaction when the patient's shudder signals that the expulsion is complete, and the hallucination comes into being. Here the bizarre object is the analyst himself, experienced as a hostile watcher located in the right-hand corner of the room, where he can be kept under observation. Bion's interpretation depends on his hypothesis that the patient 'felt his sense organs to expel as well as to receive' (*ST* 67). But in this play of insight and hallucination, hallucinosis is mutually constitutive. In Bion's terms, the hallucinating patient is not just seeing things; he is ejecting Bion's analytic observation through his eyes. The content of the hallucination is the activity of a hostile observer whom the patient attempts to control by depositing him in the far corner of the room. Otherwise puzzling exchanges are similarly interpreted. The patient not only believes that he is seeing the analyst in front of him; he also believes that his sight is destroyed as a result of the analyst having seen the same man. When he says 'It's all gone dark. I can't see' (*ST* 70), Bion interprets his statement as evidence that he has experienced the analyst's perception as the sucking in of the part of his personality vested in the gaze of the analyst; a bit of himself had been swallowed up and blinded by the analyst's eyes. These recursive transactions produce convulsive movements, as if the patient feels that something is being violently obtruded into him. When his convulsive movements stop, the patient announces: 'I have painted a picture' (*ST* 71).

The patient is a painter, but sightless. The picture he has painted includes the analyst and himself, depicted as a pair of lifeless automata. For Merleau-Ponty, the reciprocity of seeing turns the self inside out: 'As soon as we see other seers, we no longer have before us only the look without a pupil, the plate-glass of the things with that feeble reflection, that phantom of ourselves they evoke by designating a place among themselves whence we see them: henceforth through other eyes we are for ourselves fully visible . . . For the first time I appear to myself completely turned inside out under my own eyes.'[40] Bion comments that when the patient paints his picture, he pushes life and sexuality out of himself and his analyst. 'Quite right', the patient assents (*ST* 72). Who or what is the source of these violent reversals and intrusions—the patient, Bion, or the system of relations in which they are linked as observer and observed? Psychotic and analytic actions mirror one another in perfect sync. The two kinds of seeing are locked together in a hallucinatory vision system which parodies that of vision itself; as Merleau-Ponty puts it, 'One has to understand that it is the visibility itself that involves a non-visibility'.[41] The inextricability of sense-perception, primitive thought processes, and observation, combined with the theory of projective identification, provides a psychoanalytic basis for understanding the relation between hallucination (the patient's) and hallucinosis (the analyst's). Yet the peculiar form of transformation provided by hallucinosis—while it rivals and even destroys psychoanalytic understanding—may be a necessary prelude to psychoanalytic insight.

In *Transformations*, interpretation often seems to skew the patient's already skewed thought still further. Yet the effect on the patient confirms that (however blindly) Bion has somehow hit the bull's eye of psychic reality. He describes his position in terms of the viewer of an invisible artwork executed in an unfamiliar medium, scale, or colour-code:

[T]he analyst is in a position analogous to that of a listener to the description of a work of art that has been implemented in materials and on a scale that is not known to him. It is as if he heard the description of a painting, was searching on a canvas for the details represented to him, whereas the object had been executed in a material with which he is unfamiliar. Such a patient can talk of a 'penis black with rage' or an 'eye green with envy' as being visible in a painting. These objects may not be visible to the analyst: he may think the patient is hallucinating them.   (*T* 114–15)

---

[40] Merleau-Ponty, *The Visible and the Invisible*, 143.   [41] Ibid., 247.

Such objects are 'sense-able', along the lines of Freud's suggestion that analytic intuition can function like a psychic sense organ. In *Memoirs of the Blind*, Derrida writes that the blind are always of interest to the draftsman because he is an interested party, 'which is to say, he is engaged and works *among them*. He belongs to their society, taking up in turns the figures of the seeing blind man, the visionary blind man, the healer'. The painter 'takes away sight in order finally to show or allow seeing'.[42] The blind are the means, as well as the object, of his own (in)sight. Derrida's assemblage of the graphic archive of blindness and seeing invokes what he calls the '*hypothesis of intuition*' as well as the '*hypothesis of sight*'. There is always an element of conjecture in the process of imagining both the artist at work and the work of the artist. The artist and the spectator, the artist and his mirror, are bound together in a play of impossible or self-blinding reflexivity. It is this relation that Bion's patient mimics when he says 'It's all gone dark. I can't see' (*ST* 70).[43]

Derrida's specular hypothesis offers a way to read *Transformations* as a scene of analysis where interpretation and hallucinosis are mutually constitutive in the realm of the visible-invisible. But Bion is not so much a theorist of perception as a model-maker in search of analogies. His awareness of the role of analogy in psychoanalytic theory is taken up in a late paper, 'The Grid'. Here he not only emphasizes the relationship between the two images but connects analogy on an ascending scale of emotional intensity that leads (via transference, delusion, and illusion) to hallucination.[44] *Transformations* offers another clinical example to show the mirroring of free-floating attention and speculative analogy. The two work together like hallucinosis and interpretation, taking as their starting-point a perception couched in terms of the analogy between a cloudscape and the clouds that appear in elementary particle physics:

Two people are present: myself and a patient. I am detached and so is he, though for both of us the experience is important. As he lies on the couch and I sit I imagine that a cloud begins to form rather in the way that clouds can sometimes be seen to form above a hot-point on a summer's day. It seems to be above him. A similar cloud may be visible to him, but he will see it arising from me. These are probability clouds.

Soon other clouds form: some of these are new clouds, some formed from old ones, probability clouds that have changed into possibility clouds.   (*T* 117)

As more clouds form (new or old), probability clouds mutate into possibility clouds, producing clouds of both scientific knowledge and uncertainty.[45] Bion

---

[42] Jacques Derrida, *Memoirs of the Blind: The Self-Portrait and Other Ruins*, trans. Pascale-Anne Brault and Michael Naas (1991; Chicago: University of Chicago Press, 1993), 20. For Derrida's discussion of Merleau-Ponty and the visible-invisible, see ibid., 52–3.   [43] Ibid., 60–2.

[44] See Wilfred R. Bion, *Two Papers: The Grid and The Caesura* (1977; rpr. London: Karnac Books, 1989), 27 (*Grid*).

[45] Bion would have found in Charles Sanders Peirce (whose pragmatism provides a scientific source for Bion's modified Kantian idealism) a relevant statement of the theory of probability: 'A probability . . . is nothing but the degree to which a hypothesis accords with one's preconceived notions, and its value depends entirely upon how those notions have been formed'; see Arthur W. Burks (ed.), *The Collected Papers of Charles Sanders Peirce*, Vol. VII: *Science and Philosophy* (Cambridge, Mass.: Harvard University Press, 1958), 177; and cf. Bion's note on 'Probability' (*C* 212–15).

develops an analogy drawn from observing the weather which also alludes to the physicist's cloud-chamber, where events are located now in one place, now another, but never with complete certainty; for the philosopher of physics, probability describes, not a certain event, but an ensemble of possible events.[46] Bion writes of this increase of tension, clouds, and doubt, as a kind of wandering analogue: 'To every cloud there corresponds its hot point, but the cloud, like its analogue in nature, may have wandered far from it' (*T* 117). The wandering of analogy makes thought possible, as the analyst's mind drifts associatively ('I associate pressure with both tension and clouds').

At moments such as these, the Bion of *Transformations* is revealed to be in search of a system of representation that is not pre-saturated with meaning. The analyst represents a 'no-thing' (which occupies, or once occupied, a space that should be, or is now vacated) by means of a sign. The clinical situation can also be re-presented (transformed) in terms of the patient's aggressive occupation of the couch, which involves a pre-emptive usurpation or 'saturation' of meaning: 'The patient occupies the couch because he is determined that no one else should. His aim is to "saturate" the session so that I cannot work and no one can take *his* place' (*T* 118). The only words he will use are ones which once had meaning but whose meaning has now been erased ('the terms mark the place where the meaning used to be'). The absent meaning will not allow anything else to takes its place. The visual elements have to be replaced—for the analyst, in this case, by abstract algebraic signs, elements, or geometrical schema involving points and lines to denote lost meaning. Bion shifts from analogy to a more precise, yet general, formulation, and from precise formulation back to analogy again: 'all these changes are examples of transformation' (*T* 119). The model that corresponds to dream thoughts and myths (category C in Bion's grid) involves a cloud—which might be replaced by a point, or by another category (breast, penis, or no-thing), in a system of transformation involving different vertices.[47] A cloud may be generated by emotions such as greed, hostility, envy; the hot-point may be the genital of the analyst or of the analysand. The weather may be a function of observation, or of tension in the room (felt as pressure) between patient and analyst. The rules for manipulating signs are also the rules governing the reciprocal relationship of personalities.

[46] Cf. Heisenberg, *Physics and Philosophy*, 47–8: 'We can, for instance, predict the probability for finding the electron at a later time at a given point in the cloud chamber. It should be emphasized, however, that the probability function does not in itself represent a course of events in the course of time. It represents a tendency for events and our knowledge of events.' Popper, lecturing on indeterminacy and unpredictability, also uses the cloud image: 'My clouds are intended to represent physical systems which, like gases, are highly irregular, disorderly, and more or less unpredictable . . . some natural phenomena, such as the weather, or the coming and going of clouds, are hard to predict'; see Karl Popper, *Of Clouds and Clocks* (St Louis, Mich.: Washington University, 1965), 2.

[47] For Bion's 'Grid', as the representation of an instrument of observation but also as instrument of knowledge (both mirror and invention), see Bion, *Elements of Psycho-Analysis*, 81: 'The grid as a representation of an instrument used by the analyst in scrutinizing the patient is equally a representation of the material produced by the patient as an instrument for scrutinizing the analyst. But if the analyst scrutinizes the material . . . to see in what category the representation lies to which the realization approximates the grid is an instrument and not merely a representation.' See also Bion, *Grid*, 3–33, and López-Corvo, *The Dictionary of the Work of W. R. Bion*, 115–31.

Bion's insistent turn and return to the visual analogy at the start of *Transformations* suggests both his restlessness under the domination of the visual, and a persistent testing of analogy, as if his own susceptibility to what Freud calls 'the seduction of an analogy' risks super-saturation of the visual metaphor—much as beta-elements (thoughts or perceptions rendered as things) come to occupy the place of alpha-elements (the materials of meaning-making, dreaming, and symbolization): 'The combination of terms such as "hot-point" with other terms such as "cloud" and "probability" denied the model any variety of applicability but restricted its usefulness to one context. Terms such as "probability" and "cloud" are not homogeneous. Can they be replaced by signs that are? Yes: if they are replaced by points' (*T* 121).[48] Geometry's '*intra-psychic* origin is experience of "the space" where a feeling, emotion, or other mental experience "was" ' (*T* 121); points (the most minimal of signs) were once spaces occupied by a feeling that has become 'no-feeling' (the space where a feeling used to be), just as lines indicate tendencies, uses, or 'pre-conceptions'. Bion's risky aesthetic wager in *Transformations* is matched by the challenge he sets himself to achieve precise mathematical formulations that can achieve propositional status for psychoanalytic theory: 'It is said that a discipline cannot properly be regarded as scientific until it has been mathematized' (*T* 170). The mathematics of hallucinosis means that 1 breast + 0 breast = 1 breast (as opposed to 1 breast + 0 breast = 0 breast); nothing becomes a (no-)thing.

Bion compares hallucinosis to Shelley's description of a state of mind in which ideas 'assume the force of sensations through the confusion of thought with the objects of thought, and the excess of passion animating the creations of imagination' (*T* 133). Hallucinosis animates the imagination by an excess of passion, demonstrating its independence of anything but its own creations and its striving for God-like self-sufficiency. Bion invokes the figure of '*Hyperbole*' to suggest the part played by exaggeration, not only in the creation of an autonomous universe (the realm of hallucinosis) but in scientific inquiry itself. Like Poincaré's 'selected fact', the phenomenon of hyperbole can be used to achieve coherence where incoherence would otherwise reign. But the term 'hyperbole' is intended 'to convey an impression of exaggeration, of rivalry' as well as 'throwing out and out-distancing' (*T* 141). Bion links the figure of 'hyperbole' to his theory of projective identification. When the patient says 'I have always believed you are a very good analyst', he may be claiming to be the limit of the analyst's goodness ('I am "it" '), or to be its embodiment, or to have incorporated and possessed analytic goodness (*T* 161). But in all such 'transformations in hallucinosis', we see 'projection conjoined

---

[48] Cf. Braithwaite, *Scientific Explanation*, 90–2, on model-making, defining the difference between the theory and the model in terms of their different epistemological structures (i.e., a model is an interpretation of a scientific theory that depends on logically prior premises, whereas the meaning of a theory is determined by logically posterior consequences for the calculus of the premises): 'To use . . . the metaphor of a zip-fastener, the calculus is attached to the theory at the bottom, and the zip-fastener moves upwards; the calculus is attached to the model at the top, and the zip-fastener moves downwards' (ibid., 90).

with rivalry, ambition, vigour which can amount to violence' (*T* 162)—literally the 'throwing beyond' (*hyperbole*) or projection to a distance of an object, as if projected by explosive force.

Milton's God enters the argument of *Transformations* in the guise of the unknowable nature of Godhead, which has appeared earlier as the alone-dwelling and self-knowing 'Eternal Light' of Dante's *Paradiso* (*T* 138); the same Godhead is 'Darkness and Formlessness' for the mystic, Meister Eckhard.[49] Bion alludes to the moving 'exordium' at the start of Book III of *Paradise Lost*, as Milton enters the divine presence. The blind poet's invocation to light is autobiographical as well as theological and philosophical. It also places him in the line of blind poet-prophets (Thamyris and Maeonides, Tiresias and Phineus) for whom the world is no longer a visible source of knowledge. Milton's invocation to light—'which at the voice of God invested "The rising world of waters dark and deep, | Won from the void and formless infinite"' (*T* 162; *Paradise Lost*, iii. 11–12)—forms part of Bion's discussion of 'Ultimate Reality or Truth and the phenomena which are all that human beings can know of the thing-in-itself' (*T* 162). Since the thing-in-itself can only be known in its realizations, it can never be fully known except through becoming one with it, a state that Bion calls 'at-one-ment'. His distinction is between knowledge and being, or knowing 'about' and becoming. O resembles Milton's blind illumination—a revelation or intuition of the truth that exists even before the sun, and (at God's command) clothed the formlessness of the deep.

The transformation of O into something communicable by musician, artist, or poet is accompanied by violence. Bion's example is Oedipal, 'the scene of violence at the crossroads at Thebes' (*T* 97); but it might equally be the catastrophe of psychotic breakdown with which *Transformations* begins.[50] This glimpse of the ineffable, the unknown or unknowable, constitutes the form of illumination proper to the analyst, as opposed to the mystic (who may gain access to Godhead). To be identified with O would constitute a form of hyperbolic megalomania. But, at the other extreme, to be entirely inaccessible to intuition would constitute a form of resistance to the shift from transformations involving K (knowledge) to transformations involving O. This compressed train of thought at the end of *Transformations* returns the reader to Bion's starting-point, the opening of a psychoanalytic session: 'The beginning of a session has the configuration already formulated in the concept of the Godhead' (*T* 171). Everything is there to be won by the analyst, as if from Milton's 'void and formless infinite', or Pascal's terror at infinite space, his *horror vacui*: '*Le silence de ces espaces infines m'effraie*' (*T* 171). The risk is that the analyst will be unable to tolerate fear of the unknowable, as the pedestrian conscious lumbers after the nimble unconscious.[51] The analyst can

---

[49] See *T* 138: 'God in the Godhead is . . . so elemental that we can say nothing about it.'

[50] Cf. 'a transformation in which an intense catastrophic emotional explosion O has occurred (elements of personality, link, and second personality having been instantaneously expelled to vast distances from their point of origin and from each other)' (*A&I* 14).

[51] '. . . as if . . . an extremely active, flexible and speedy unconscious were being pursued by a slow, rigid, lumbering conscious' (Bion, *Grid*, 25).

only win interpretations from the formlessness of the patient's unconscious by way of the patient's (equally hard-won) statements.

Bion's culminating example of resistance to the unknowable (i.e., of a preference for transformations in K rather than O) is that of preferring a reproduction over the original of 'Les Coquelicots', the painting which had provided his aesthetic reference-point:

> The photograph representing Monet's Les Coquelicots (or any other artistic representation) is preferred to exposure to the painting itself: exposure to the painting is restricted to perceiving that it is 'about' a field of poppies. No matter what the domain may be, the resistance by 'knowing about' against 'becoming' is sure to be in evidence and is by no means restricted to psychoanalysis. (*T* 163)

Preference for the photograph as opposed to the painting (a preference that Bion equates with opting for 'about-ness' as opposed to at-one-ment) amounts to refusing the experience of the thing-in-itself, or a Keatsian 'becoming' that is tolerant of uncertainties, mysteries, and doubts.[52] In the last resort, however, *Transformations* abandons the realm of visual or aesthetic analogy altogether, gesturing instead towards 'the sense of the undiscovered or the unevolved' (*T* 171): what is unknowable and provisional in the unconscious.[53]

Apropos of the book that became *Learning from Experience*, Bion wrote: 'the book will have failed for the reader if it does not become an object of study, and the reading of it an emotional experience itself' (*C* 261).[54] As an object of study, *Transformations* is his most demanding book. By Bion's own admission, his focus on the aesthetics of psychoanalysis sheds little direct light on psychoanalytic practice: 'The bearing on psycho-analysis and interpretation of what I have said may seem obscure'. It is not surprising that he should invoke *Paradise Lost*—a poem by a blind man who asks for inner illumination as he gauges the magnitude of his task. Bion risks hyperbole if he identifies too closely with either divine omniscience or Miltonic vision. But blindness is the necessary condition for his seeing. *Paradise Lost* poignantly emphasizes the poet's exile from sight to 'cloud in stead, and ever-during dark'. Loss of sight expunges and razes natural appearances, turning nature's book of knowledge into 'a universal blank' (*Paradise Lost*, iii. 45–8).

---

[52] Cf. *A&I* 125, where Bion quotes Keats on Shakespeare ('capable of being in uncertainties, mysteries, doubts'), apropos of the peculiar language of psychoanalysis which is 'both prelude to action and itself a kind of action'.

[53] Cf. Peirce, *Collected Papers*, vii. 512–17, where Peirce (who relates pragmatism to evolution) speculates on the evolution or failure to evolve of the human mind in its adaptation to the changing laws of nature; and cf. also Peirce's proposition (which could have been written by Bion in gnomic mode): 'It is evolution (Φυσις) that has provided us with the emotion. That situation is what we have to study' (ibid., vii. 191).

[54] For reading Bion, including *Transformations*, see Thomas H. Ogden, 'An Introduction of the Reading of Bion', *International Journal of Psychoanalysis*, 85 (2004), 285–300; Ogden emphasizes the mix of obscurity and clarity in Bion's earlier writing, in contrast with the capacity for the negative demanded by his later work.

Milton's invocation razes knowledge gained through the eye, the prime organ of perception. But his plea for inward seeing—'the mind through all her powers | Irradiate, there plant eyes'—amounts to what Bion might term a 'Transformation in vision', a transformation that allows the unsighted to 'tell | Of things invisible' (*Paradise Lost*, iii. 52–5). The invisible is what interests him in *Transformations*.

Bion admired Freud for his remark to Lou Andreas Salomé that in writing he 'had to blind [himself] artificially in order to focus all the light on one dark spot.'[55] For Bion, this artificial blinding involved not only the erasure of memory and desire but a heightened perception located at the limits of seeing.[56] In *Cogitations*, he writes: 'Psycho-analysis tells you nothing; it is an instrument, like the blind man's stick that extends the power to gather information' (*C* 361). *Transformations* simultaneously privileges and problematizes the visual, as we have seen. Like the blind man's stick, 'seeing things' yields only a provisional form of information. Hallucinosis marks the point where perception disappears, reappearing as a new form of psychoanalytic knowledge. Not being able to see plants eyes in the mind. Bion's aesthetics—the invisible-visual, or the visible-invisible—have an uncanny resemblance to the experience of reading, where we have to not-see what we are seeing, or see it only in the mind's eye, in order to understand it. It is this that makes reading an emotional experience and links it to psychoanalytic insight.

[55] See Bion, *Grid*, 38.   [56] See ibid., 17, and cf. *A&I* 43.

ENVOI

10

The Unexpected: *Bionic Woman*

Any culture, civilization, or temporarily exposed characteristic of persons
or peoples is subject to penetration and displacement by the unexpected.
They say animals are aware of the imminence of an earthquake. Humans are
sensitive to the imminence of emotional upheaval.

Wilfred R. Bion, *A Memoir of the Future*, 1975–91[1]

A Memoir of the Future, Bion's experimental autobiography of the 1970s, is not an
obvious point of departure for thinking about the relation between women and
psychoanalysis. I want to propose it, by way of *envoi*, if only because Bion's writing
is not often read for what it has to say about women, although it has much to say
about change. Anxiety about the future tends to focus on the idea of catastrophic
change—a revolution in politics or climatic conditions, an apocalypse, an earthquake, or a terrorist attack; even a new thought can upset an existing equilibrium.
We may be scared or hopeful; things and bodies (or personalities) may fall apart
or cohere; borders or régimes may change; we may be afraid of breakdown in its
multiple forms: 'Break up, down, in, out, or through?' (*MFIII* 539), Bion asks
rhetorically in *A Memoir of the Future*. Or we may be resentful about being
invaded by the germ of an anticipatory idea.[2] In the terms of Wilfred Bion's early
work on groups, futuristic thinking can also resemble the 'basic assumption' associated with the pairing group, as opposed to the work group—a feeling of hope, or
the expectation of a Messianistic birth located somewhere in the future, destined
to save the group from its hatred and destructiveness, but which must at all costs
be aborted in order not to upset the status quo.[3] A new leader or a new future can

---

[1] Wilfred R. Bion, *A Memoir of the Future* (1975, 1977, 1979; rpr. London: Karnac Books, 1991),
538 (*MFI, MFII, MFIII*). Useful accounts of *A Memoir of the Future* are to be found in León
Grinberg, Darió Sor, and Elizabeth Tabak de Bianchedi, *New Introduction to the Work of Bion*, 3rd edn.
(Northvale, NJ: Jason Aronson, 1993), 135–40, and Gérard Bléandonu, *Wilfred Bion: His Life and
Works 1897–1979*, trans. Claire Pajaczkowska (London: Free Association Books, 1994), 249–64. For
an imaginative literary and psychoanalytic reading, see also Meg Harris Williams, 'The Tiger and
"O" ', *Free Associations*, 1 (1985), 33–56.

[2] Cf. Wilfred R. Bion, *Learning from Experience* (1962; rpr. London: Karnac Books, 1988), 98, for
the super-ego's 'hatred of any new development in the personality as if the new development were a
rival to be destroyed'.

[3] See Wilfred R. Bion, *Experiences in Groups and Other Papers* (1961; rpr. London and New York:
Routledge, 1989), 150–2.

easily become the focus for such abortive hopes and expectancy. 'Beware the charismatic individual! Beware the stigmata of messianic future!' (*MFII* 251), warns the psychoanalytic *alter ego* of Bion's paradoxically entitled *A Memoir of the Future*.

For the later Bion, the psychoanalytic encounter itself was a site of turbulence, ' "a mental space" for further ideas which may yet be developed'.[4] He spent the final years of his long and distinguished professional life furthering these ideas in the form of a futuristic trilogy in which he is answerable to no one but himself. *A Memoir of the Future* is a blackly humorous, seriously self-parodic, mono-dialogical inquiry into his past, present, and future selves, whether aborted or oblivious, forward-looking or traumatized by the past. It is also a sustained reflection on the theory and practice of contemporary psychoanalysis in the wake of Freud and Klein. At once an apology and a critique, it disturbs, provokes, and (above all) refuses to prophesy. Bion reminds us that desires for the future are bound up with remembering the past, and he implies that the real difficulty is to recognize the past in the formless, fluid, tumultuous chaos of the here-and-now for which foetal life is both metaphor and precursor. His introduction speaks of 'modes of thinking to which no known realization has so far been found to approximate' (*MFI* ix). Terms like 'memory', 'desire', and 'understanding' refuse the troublesome discovery of the unthought thought or the unobserved phenomenon.[5] Given his Kantian stance—'the thing-in-itself' (*MFI* 4) is radically unknowable except in its secondary manifestations—Bion eschews the pre-emptive knowledge that shuts off thought; his version of psychoanalysis is anticipatory, perplexed, and often perplexing (negative capability is the Keatsian phrase invoked by Bion himself). At times he writes like a ludic cross between a latter-day Wittgenstein or Beckett and a 1960s new-maths teacher—analytically, laconically, abstractly, unstoppably. At other times, far from seeming post-modern (let alone post-historical), he can sound as retrograde as one of the primitive dinosaurs that roam his fiction alongside the tanks of his traumatic war memories.[6]

Born at the turn of a previous century, Bion was subsequently formed (or deformed, as he strongly implies) by his military experience during the First

---

[4] 'Making the Best of a Bad Job', in Wilfred R. Bion, *Clinical Seminars and Other Works*, ed. Francesca Bion (1987; rpr. London: Karnac Books, 1994), 325. Bions paper begins with the proposition: 'When two personalities meet, an emotional storm is created' (ibid., 321)—a description of the meeting between analyst and patient, but also of the conditions that prevail in *A Memoir*, whether imagined as an encounter between different personalities or between differing parts of the personality.

[5] See 'Opacity of Memory and Desire', in Wilfred R. Bion, *Attention and Interpretation* (1970; rpr. London: Karnac Books, 1984), 41–54, where Bion links the eschewing of memory and desire to Freud's artificial 'blinding' of himself (ibid., 43). See also Melvin R. Lansky, 'Philosophical Issues in Bion's Thought', in James S. Grotstein (ed.), *Do I Dare Disturb the Universe? A Memorial to Wilfred R. Bion* (London: Karnac Books, 1983), 428–39, esp. 433–4.

[6] For Bion's war experience as a tank commander, see Ch. 7, and Wilfred R. Bion, *The Long Week-End 1897–1919: Part of a Life* ed. Francesca Bion (1982; rpr. London: Karnac Books, 1991), as well as the contemporary war diaries and later reminiscences in Wilfred R. Bion, *War Memoirs 1917–19*, ed. Francesca Bion (London: Karnac Books, 1997). For the dinosaurs of *A Memoir* (named Albert Stegosaurus and Adolf Tyrannosaurus), locked in sado-masochistic battle, see *MFI* 83–4.

World War, with its legacy of saurian, armour-plated emotional defence. Most of Bion's writings belong to the last three decades of his life, the 1950s, 1960s, and 1970s. This was the nuclear age; the Cold War froze what fission was simultaneously heating up, and the Big Bang lay in an anxious, hypothetical future rather than in the cosmic past. Bion can facetiously wish his readers a 'Relativistic Fission . . .' (*MFIII* 578) by way of droll pessimistic *envoi* to his work in a post-Einsteinian age. *A Memoir of the Future* is infused with a sense of imminent danger and potential explosiveness—silent, internal menace and the risk of final oblivion. The author's own death looms, unknowably; he evidently feels free enough to say what he thinks, if only (he writes) 'To prevent someone who KNOWS from filling the empty space' (*MFIII* 578). But Bion's unconventional autobiography happens to be one of the few places where he writes about women, imagining them (whether futuristically or anachronistically) as co-habitants of his personal, soma-psych(ot)ic world. Elsewhere, his epistemic rewriting of Kleinian concepts finds a place for women as mothers whose capacity to receive and detoxify the infant's primitive projective identifications, dread, or distress provides a model for the analyst's containing receptivity.[7] For the post-Kleinian Bion, the myth of Oedipus concerns investigatory curiosity—the quest for knowledge—rather than sexual difference; the other main character in the Oedipal drama becomes Tiresias (the false hypothesis erected against anxiety about a new theory).[8]

Having experienced the mixed benefits and tribulations of analysis with Melanie Klein in the 1950s, and despite some initial resistance to her ideas, Bion thoroughly assimilated and transformed Kleinian concepts during the aftermath. But (as Winnicott had also done in his way), he also strove towards new meanings and distinctive contributions of his own.[9] Although Bion analysed women such as the child analyst Frances Tustin, he rarely, if ever, addresses the subject of women directly in his psychoanalytic writings.[10] In his straightforwardly autobiographical memoirs of the First World War and the period leading up to the Second World War, girls and women (whether sister, mother, fiancée, or wife) play roles that are often annoying, guilt-inducing, tantalizing, or enigmatic. Both sex and women were a problem, according to Bion himself. He is understandably reticent

---

[7] See, for instance, 'A Theory of Thinking' (1962), Wilfred R. Bion, *Second Thoughts*, 115–16.

[8] See Wilfred R. Bion, *The Elements of Psychoanalysis* (1963; rpr. London: Karnac, 1984), 48–9.

[9] For Bion's account of his analysis with Klein, see Wilfred R. Bion, *All My Sins Remembered: Another Part of a Life*, ed. Francesca Bion (1985; rpr. London: Karnac Books, 1991), 66–8; cf. PA in *A Memoir*: 'I found it difficult to understand Klein's theory and practice though—perhaps because—I was being analysed by Melanie Klein herself. But after great difficulty I began to feel there was truth in the interpretations she gave and that they brought illumination to many experiences, mine and others, which had previously been incomprehensible, discrete and unrelated. Metaphorically, light began to dawn . . .' (*MFIII* 559). But, he goes on, although 'Melanie Klein's interpretations began to have a vaguely but truly illuminating quality' (*MFIII* 560), when he employed the same interpretations with his patients, 'none of the good results that [he] anticipated occurred' (*MFIII* 559).

[10] See Frances Tustin, *Autism and Childhood Psychosis* (London: Karnac Books, 1995), p. vii. For Bion's better known work with Beckett during the 1930s, see Bléandonu, *Wilfred Bion*, 44–6, and Didier Anzieu, 'Beckett and Bion', *International Journal of Psycho-Analysis*, 16 (1989), 163–9.

about the wartime marriage he embarked on in his forties, which was tragically cut short by the death of his wife in childbirth, leaving him with a small daughter to take care of.[11] Yet *A Memoir of the Future* shows that he took a lively psychoanalytic interest in women and in their different points of view, and did not regard them simply as metonymic place-holders for the breast or as 'containers' for foetal sensations and infant projections. Bion's women, in fact, have voices of their own, both shrewd and shrewish, and they play a prominent and sometimes discomfiting part in the unfolding psycho-drama of his life. They function as characters in their own right while serving as critical interlocutors for a loose *congerie* of Bionic *alter egos* (variously called 'Bion', 'Myself', and 'PA', or 'Psycho-Analyst').

The Bion of *A Memoir* tends to associate women with disturbance, persistently imagining them in terms that are provocative, disruptive, or associated with dangerous invasion by both retrograde and 'anticipatory' thoughts. Take the character named Alice who opens 'The Dream' (Book I of *A Memoir of the Future*): ' "O dear, oh dear," said Alice, rubbing her eyes and pushing away the shower of leaves that had awoken her. "I had such a queer dream . . ." ' (*MFI* 7). In Bion's 'Pro-Logue', Alice is the generic name for the author's bedfellow; she shares his restless night of psychosomatic or soma-psychic farts and belches: 'Alice didn't think much of it obviously. But what was *she* up to then? Must remember to ask her' (*MFI* 4). What Alice was up to will provide the highly selective, and far from impartial focus for my reading of Bion's gender perspective in *A Memoir*. One thread among many, Alice's adventures are intertwined with those of his various multiple personae. Not surprisingly, Bion belongs to a pre-feminist rather than to a proto-feminist era. But that is not to say he is unenlightened or incurious about the women of the past, present, and future, even if he views them through the lens of his own history, which is necessarily coloured by his period, gender, and class. *A Memoir* explores the transformations and shifts in his thinking about women, but it also explores the thinking of his women characters, who are at once the objects of masculine phantasy and subjects with their own phantasies.

Bionic woman has plenty to say for herself, and at times takes over the conversation altogether. Indeed, *A Memoir* is aggressively even-handed when it comes to the war between the sexes. But while Bion does not denigrate what passes for 'female intuition' or 'common sense', he does not privilege it either—nor does he exempt it from analysis. His women pose provocative questions (provoking to both men and to women), but they do so in a context that is argumentative, dialogical, and speculative. Bion's approach to gender also holds some interest for the indirect light it sheds on the culture of post-Kleinian psychoanalysis during the 1970s. Even if Bion's women risk seeming dated to present-day, post-millennial feminists, their role in *A Memoir* also has a tendency to unsettle the status quo in ways that are unexpected—although not always progressive, as we shall see.

[11] See Bion, *All My Sins Remembered*, 60–1, 69–70, for an anguished and self-castigating account of these events and their aftermath; included in the same volume, Bion's letters to his second wife and to his children testify to his later happiness.

ALICE IN ANACHRONOMOUS LAND

Bion calls his *Memoir* 'a fictitious account of psychoanalysis including an artificially constructed dream'. He goes on to claim 'definitary status . . . for the constructions of wakefulness, scientific alertness and scientific theory' (*MFI* 4). In what he also refers to as 'science fiction', he explores the multiple selves that make up a 'personality' (or a group) and the unending struggle between psyche and soma, as well as a seemingly irresolvable war between, and within, the sexes. His women characters express their deflating or practical viewpoints, and punctuate the discussion with their criticisms and complaints about men, while observing (accurately) that the conversation between men often excludes them entirely: 'ALICE: You have been monopolizing articulate speech' (*MFI* 142). Alice, of course, is a well-known dreamer in her own right. She belongs to a Wonderland of logical nonsense, distorted bodily perspectives, and inverted reflections (or what Bion calls 'reversible perspective': two independently experienced views or phenomena whose meanings are incompatible).[12] We might expect both Alice and Dodgsonian mathematics to have intrigued the mathematically minded Bion, given his interest in projective geometry—not to mention his creation of the Grid as a form of notation that resembles a game of snakes and ladders (or a periodic table), where ascents and descents chart sudden and unpredictable changes from one state to another. But Bion's Alice is also a throw-back to a more recent Age of Anxiety, reminiscent as it is of the rise of fascism during the 1930s recorded in Auden's and Isherwood's *The Dog Beneath the Skin* (1936), where sexual and political dissidence meld with psychoanalysis in an atmosphere of impending totalitarian takeover, and a class-bound, conventional, and repressive England has been mysteriously 'pacified' or 'liberated' (depending how you look at it).[13] The polyphonic narrative—shifting without warning from autobiographical reminiscence to dialogical argument to abstruse reflection—reveals Bion's fascination with turbulence, transformation, and reversal, along with the sheer difficulty of thinking at all.

This difficulty, which it is tempting to attribute to Bion himself, includes thinking about women. Alice is a 'fabulous monster' (*MFI* 5), with her conventional marriage to Roland (a romantic hero drawn from a former era), and not-so-conventional relationship with her uppity maid, Rosemary. The world of 'drab fidelity' and equally 'drab infidelity' is unmasked as a class-inflected nightmare,

---

[12] See Bion, *Elements of Psychoanalysis*, 50, 54–9; see also Bléandonu, *Wilfred Bion*, 165–72.

[13] Cf. *A Memoir*: 'Alice may be in Wonderland, but Wonderland is not Victorian England' (*MFII* 293). Although Bion makes a number of references to the pre-First World War period of his boyhood, the world of Books I and II of *A Memoir* approximate to that of the inter-war years, particularly in its critique of ruling-class assumptions and general atmosphere of menace. The scene of 'The Dream' involves Mundens, a reference to *The Long Week-End*, where Mundens is the name of the farm to which the two boys must drive a recalcitrant cow and where the cowman has committed suicide; see Bion, *The Long Week-End*, 56–61. Alice (*MFI* 72) is reminiscent of the younger sister who refuses to go to church (ibid., 62).

played out against a background of gentlemanly farming and sexual carrying-on above and below stairs. Upper-middle-class marriage is propped upon an underclass of urban prostitution and lurid violence. The mutually seductive, sado-masochistic relation of mistress and maid, feared yet desired, parodies the master–slave dialectic to the tune of 'a well-drilled representation of sexual life' (*MFI* 17). But where do these dreadful clichés come from?—the 'insolent expressions' and 'hardening eyes' that litter the stage directions of a perverse and dated soap opera. The pornographic banality of the fiction that opens Book I of *A Memoir* disconcertingly replicates a misogynistic fantasy about what women do when they are alone: sexually humiliate one another. Women not only despise men, they hate each other. Bion calls this 'fact and nightmare . . . indistinguishable from hallucination', or 'married love' viewed from 'the vantage point of the maid and whore' (*MFI* 22, 24). The content of Rosemary's dream (so Bion tells us in his 'Key' to *A Memoir*) is 'the reciprocal of Alice's experience of conscious waking reality' (*MFIII* 656). When the tables are turned, the maid is on top, pleasuring her mistress by degrading her.

Domination and submission structure same-sex relations as much as they structure the relation of one class to another. Stripped of their social roles, the women shed their clothes and their inhibitions, while Roland and his friend Robin (bonding weakly with each other) become boys-on-the-run in the face of the vaguely defined threat of invasion. Routine acts of violence (rape, guns) titillate and menace. Sado-masochistic sexuality is allotted to women, schoolboy paranoia to men, as if viewed through the gendered lenses of a dated thriller. In this mutilated dream-world, all encounters—sexual and otherwise—are reduced to the same brutal fiction of dominance or submission, fight or flight. The prevailing emotions are envy, boredom, and dread. A masque of allegorical speakers stages the phantasmagoria of 'thought without a thinker . . . the content that explodes its possessive container' (*MFI* 38). The Bion of *Learning from Experience* had likened this nameless dread to a process that strips and denudes thought of all that is good.[14] 'The Dream' is just such an obscene strip-show. The women get down—'We knew that fucking was a nuisance . . . The clitoris for me every time' (*MFI* 45), says Rosemary, in ex-prostitute mode—while the men seem hardly able to get it up, preoccupied as they are with war, philosophy, and the homo-erotics of male friendship and mutual admiration. The women openly prefer each other, mocking or deriding the men while simultaneously seducing and manipulating them.

Bion's cast of characters inhabits a fragmented, paranoid–schizoid world, or a world of empty abstraction. When Alice asks whether 'we are just a part of [Roland's] dream', the answer comes back from a character called, simply, 'Voice': 'You'll see; we shall fade away. Our place will be taken by a mass of meaningless

---

[14] See Bion, *Learning from Experience*, 97: 'The process of denudation continues till [the absence of a container/contained relations] represent hardly more than an empty superiority/inferiority that in turn degenerates to nullity'.

abstractions. Listen . . .' (*MFI* 68). Even the robust Roland—a vehicle for the knee-jerk emotional responses of his outdated class and type—fades away into a similarly disembodied thinker. Perhaps it was all a dream: 'ALICE: What a night! Roland, what an earth were you up to? . . . I could hardly get a wink of sleep. ROLAND: What were *you* up to?' (*MFI* 82). Rosemary (defiantly grandiose) answers this question about her own activities by claiming to be the eternal 'She': 'My profession is the oldest profession in the world . . . Thais, Eve, Lillith . . . *there* is a lineage which you cannot begin to match . . . If I were to unveil my beauty you would—shrivel up and die' (*MFI* 78–9). Strip the mistress and you find the compliance of the doormat; strip the maid, and she blossoms into a scornful *femme fatale*. Women like Rosemary are sure that they are fascinating, 'and that is more than you [Bion] can claim to be' (*MFI* 100). Not for her the gentlemanly Roland, let alone the shadowy 'Bion'. Her chosen mate is the chocolate-bar-wielding, gun-toting, genially brutal, allegorical, and macho Man.

Downtrodden Alice may fleetingly express an interest in psychoanalysis, but Rosemary remains preoccupied with her looks and with sensational developments in the plot, frivolously egging her Man on to gratuitous violence ('Are you going to shoot him? Oh, *do* shoot him—please, *please!*' (*MFI* 109). With hindsight, we can begin to understand the banal sexual phantasy vested in the Roland/Alice and Rosemary/Man parallel plots as 'scraps of a conversation destroyed and fragmented by a jealous, hostile, curious and destructive, excluded, but none the less present, well . . . personality, shall we call it?' (*MFI* 120–1; Bion's ellipses). This is an old-fashioned Oedipal plot—call it a 'personality' driven by triangulated rivalry, combined with a gendered phantasy that combines masculine envy and feminine betrayal. The opening scenario may have been 'only Roland', 'Only pornography, "only" sex' (*MFI* 131)—or rather (according to the speaker whom Bion calls Myself), 'The sentence, "That was only Roland", would have to be replaced by many terms such as "jealousy", "triumph", "envy", "rivalry", "revenge", "love", "sex"' (*MFI* 132). This is much the same *congerie*, of murderous but excluded emotions that Bion attributes to himself in *All My Sins Remembered*, when he recalls meeting his ex-fiancée in the company of another man ('If I had had my service revolver with me I would have shot him. Then I would have shot her through the knee . . .').[15] According to Alice, the scenario at the start of the book represented 'Alice in Anachronomous Land': 'MAN: . . . you come from Pornography don't you? ALICE: Not really—Wonderland' (*MFI* 136). In the land of porno-anachronomism, what Alice and Rosemary are up to turns out to be a function of an ancient sexual grudge, with its anachronistic and primitive storm of affects: humiliation, murderous rage, rivalry, and exclusion.

---

[15] Bion, *All My Sins Remembered*, 29–33; in retelling this triangulated episode of rivalry, murderous feelings, and guilty retribution, Bion lapses into the mode of a police report and confession to an imaginary interlocutor (see Ch. 9 above).

Roland's 'dream' explores the infancy of the spectrum of 'love at one extreme, rivalry and hate at the other'—a spectrum found even in 'The psycho-analyst, the artist, and the entertainer' (*MFI* 121). Bion's theory of creativity involves what he calls the 'excluded middle' as well as 'the excluded personality' (*MFI* 121). His theory of the oscillating relations of PS← →D (the unresolved, ever-shifting movement between Klein's paranoid–schizoid and depressive positions) is analogous to the shift between ugly and beautiful that characterizes Bion's women. Rosemary (the whore who turns into Helen of Troy) asks, 'Has anyone seen an artist paint a picture "about" or "of" something ugly which was nevertheless beautiful? Has anyone seen a skivvy or whore turn into a beautiful woman? Or pander turn into a man?' (*MFI* 128). Throughout *A Memoir*, Bion's exploration of aesthetic transformation associates beauty with the potential for abstract thought that is achieved, for instance, when mathematics is freed from the world of sense perception by concepts like imaginary numbers or Cartesian co-ordinates.[16] Beauty also resides in 'the formless infinite' (*MFI* 156) of chaos or wave theory— the writhing coils of hair and swirling masses of water drawn by Leonardo da Vinci that Bion uses as a metaphor for emotional turbulence.[17] But in a sudden shift of mood, we see the obtrusive apparition of an old beggar woman, with the 'built-in ugliness' of the beautiful girl (*MFI* 145).[18] What is going on?

Obscurely associated with this filthy, sombre, and squalid reminder of carnal aims and mortality is the figure of a woman dying in childbirth: 'BION: Childbirth? ROSEMARY: It seems simple, doesn't it' (*MFI* 151). Rosemary heartlessly manicures her nails ('sharpening her claws'). But Myself, as she points out acutely, is ' "sharpening [his] moral claws"—that is not a pretty sight either' (*MFI* 153). Has she put her finger on Myself's moral masochism? Things turn nasty. Primitive Man beats in a woman's skull and sucks out her brain like a cannibal. 'This is an anachronism', says Man, giving 'Bion' a lecture on the evolution of thought. A vision shows 'The skull-crushing object and sucking object . . . overwhelmed by depression at the failing supply of nutriment from the dead [container] and the failure to restore it to life' (*MFI* 161). A thought arises and is transformed into Leonardo da Vinci's aesthetic forms as they are revealed in chaos. This, says Man,

---

[16] See *MFI* 130, where 'Man' refers to the transformation of mathematics which is 'effected by imaginary numbers, irrational numbers, Cartesian co-ordinates freeing geometry from Euclid by opening up the domain of algebraic de-ductive systems' and compares it to a similar freeing of psychoanalysis 'from the domain of sensuality-based mind'. Cf. also Bion's account of the 'selected fact' (*Learning from Experience*, 72), and *MFII* 243 ('Poincaré talks of the Beauty of a mathematical construction').

[17] Cf. *MFI* 156 ('the form that lay concealed within the formless infinite'), as well as Bion's essay, 'Emotional Turbulence' (1976): 'Leonardo's drawings of hair and water give a good idea of what turbulence looks like. Mental turbulence, whether one's own or that of the community in which one lives, is much more difficult to depict: its existence and significance cannot be understood if the turbulence is not observed' (Bion, *Clinical Seminars*, 303).

[18] Cf. *MFII* 268: 'a beautiful girl instinctively wraps an ugly soul in her looks'. Is this old beggar woman obscurely related to the 'vicious old bitch', Imagination (*MFII* 349), who used to torture Alice in her childhood?

is 'the taste of your brother's brains and blood and guts'—in other words, the laws of 'mental cannibalism' (*MFI* 162, 164). Thinking about women oscillates between the built-in ugliness of the beautiful girl and a dead or stripped empty container, a cannibalistic or failed supply of nutriment and the possibility of aesthetic transformation.

To whom does all this gratuitous violence, swirling emotion, and visceral savagery belong? Surely not only to primitive, gun-toting Man. And why are they directed specifically against women?—as they are when Man imagines 'a man going out with a girl at a holiday resort' in terms of taking her off into the bushes where he 'savaged the woman's breasts and genitalia with his teeth, devouring the flesh of both regions in a manner that would be comprehensible if he were a wild carnivore' (*MFI* 166), a psychotic scenario worthy of Hitchcock. Bion seems not only to be saying that everyday acts involve primitive emotional experiences but that where thought (alpha-function) is not, there psychosis returns with a vengeance—the ugliness of untransformed beta-elements, or dream-thoughts gone awry, as unprocessed and undigested raw sensations take over. Mental activity contains the taste of blood; the emotions connected with erectile tissue are those of a carnivore; primal Man is little better than the beast of Rosemary's lurid phantasies about her mother's life as a prostitute. As Alice observes, no wonder women are less 'keen on the survival of the "good old days" of the British Empire' than men are (*MFI* 173). Bion's female characters are instinctive anti-imperialists, pointing out how much importance men attach to 'conflict, rivalry, victory' (*MFI* 174). Rosemary and Alice have reasons of their own for welcoming their country's downfall, since 'their nation or culture undergoes a change which makes it possible for each individual to pursue a life which they would not otherwise have been free to do' (*MFI* 174; 'Bion' is speaking here). Catastrophic change, even in the guise of war, may emancipate women.

The argument of Book I spins on and off course, man-to-man, between men and women, or woman-to-woman, until the women get fed up and threaten to leave: 'ROSEMARY: It sounds very highbrow till you listen to it' (*MFI* 199). As Myself explains, accurately but with a touch of masculine condescension, 'This isn't psychoanalysis: it is talking *about* psychoanalysis' (*MFI* 199)—a very different activity from experiencing it, which he does not think 'you two ladies' would enjoy (*MFI* 200). But, in the end, as in a romantic comedy, the two couples are reconciled and walk off together for a cup of coffee. Man remains eternally seduced by Rosemary; Roland and Alice are still together after their years of conventional marriage. Alice observes, 'we are back to square one' (*MFI* 215). But, not quite unchanged. Bion reminds us that, according to Heisenberg's law, 'the thing itself is altered by being observed' (*MFI* 216). At the end of Book I, we begin to see how 'the thing itself' (the group or the personality) may be altered by scientific observation, and even by its potential for self-observation, the mode of thinking that is analogous to it in the mental domain.

'IDÉES MÈRES'

In Book II of *A Memoir of the Future* ('The Past Presented') we meet Roland and Alice again, both in daylight and in dreamtime, this time as members of a kitchen-table, country week-end discussion group. How do we know what we know, and how do we talk about it? (Bion in his epistemological mode). When Alice comments ironically, 'I am most impressed—as I think I am meant to be—by the brilliance of these logical constructions and the brilliance of masculine thought' (*MFII* 234); Roland responds by complimenting her condescendingly on her illogicality and her innate female wisdom. As the conversation shifts to the pos-sibility of a new birth, a new conception or species in the psychoanalytic 'zoo', one of the characters remarks satirically: 'A feminine psycho-analyst perhaps' (*MFII* 235). This monstrous birth, 'a monster not apparent but real' (*MFII* 236), recalls the 'fabulous monster' or 'serpent Alice' (*MFI* 5) whom we met at the start of Book I—the wisdom of the serpent combined with the cunning of the dove: 'ROLAND: You women are all the same. She's a cruel snake' (*MFII* 273). Alice objects: 'You often talk as if, because I am a woman, I can't ever have had an intel-ligence from which to be separated' (*MFII* 249). According to PA, the part of Roland's primordial mind from which he remains unseparated 'is still dominated by the belief that as a woman has not got a penis she cannot have a capacity of masculine thinking' (*MFII* 249).

Could this monstrous birth, or new thought, be a wise feminine psychoana-lyst with a capacity for 'masculine thinking'? Apropos of his fearsome zoo of psychoanalytical concepts—'fearsome and dangerous creatures', 'as fearsome and as non-existent as the cockatrice and the bandersnatch' (*MFII* 239, 250)—PA tells us that, 'like all really simple things they are slippery and hard to grasp' (*MFII* 250). Perhaps there is an analogous difficulty in thinking about women, since they too, for Bion at least, are at once simple and hard to grasp—at once slippery and serpentine. 'The brilliance of masculine thought' (*MFII* 234) anticipates a moment when Alice invokes Milton's tropes of darkness and illumination, singing 'of Chaos and Eternal night' (*MFII* 254) in Book III of *Paradise Lost*. At one point, PA refers to his own use of Freud's 'penetrating shaft of darkness' to illuminate 'obscure areas of the mind' (*MFII* 271).[19] The obscu-rity that comes to light at this point, however, is his own traumatic memory of sheltering in a shell-hole beside the dying runner whose chest had been blown away, destroying his lung and exposing his heart: 'Mother, Mother—you'll write to my Mother, sir, won't you?' (*MFII* 256), the young soldier repeats over and over again (' "Yes, blast you", I said'). The episode, told and retold elsewhere in

---

[19] Cf. Bion, *Attention and Interpretation*, 43, and Wilfred R. Bion, *Two Papers: The Grid and Caesura* (London: Karnac Books, 1989), 38; the reference is from Freud's letter to Lou Andreas Salomé ('I know that in writing I have to blind myself artificially in order to focus all the light on one dark spot').

Bion's writings about his wartime experience, represents the return of chaos in its most traumatic form.[20]

Feelings of remorse and shame, as PA vividly testifies, 'hang across the gaping wound of my mind like a ridiculous field dressing' (*MFII* 256). Yet again, PA locates his own death at the scene of this catastrophic 'advance' of 8 August 1918: 'I would not go near the Amiens–Roye road for fear I should meet my ghost—I died there' (*MFII* 257). As these traumatic memories and mythologies suggest, 'The Past Presented' is the backward-looking, purgatorial book of *A Memoir of the Future*. What Alice calls 'the woman's view' (*MFII* 261) intrudes sporadically, but Roland's loyal friend, Robin, asserts: 'No woman, even one as sensitive as Alice, will understand that life cannot be the same for a man who has been in fighting' (*MFII* 262). Roland's nightmare of 'DU' (his foreign 'Ought o'Nomic' *alter ego*) is inhabited by such '*idées mères*'—the breeding place of untransformed beta-elements, the unacceptable and traumatizing ideas that make him toss and turn restlessly in his sleep as his 'mind bursts with all this stuff' (*MFII* 274, 247). Bion's 'Key' to *A Memoir* defines '*idées mères*' (a phrase derived from Joyce) as fissile, radio-active ideas that 'provoke breeder-reactions' (*MFII* 622).[21] Ought o'Nomic 'DU' refers to Roland's heroism as being 'in reality blown up by your super-intelligent mechanical evacuation' (*MFII* 278)—'your bloody heroism and conceptual rubbish' (*MFII* 279). Do mother-ideas breed such reactions, such mental explosions and super-intelligent mechanical evacuations of unbearable reality?

When the hero Roland pronounces it 'a man's world' (*MFII* 293), Alice promptly rejects it for her own reality: 'A man's world is and always has been a figment of the imagination. Love and all that—compare that with childbirth and maternal death . . . a woman's world is a far more somber one than that discerned by the man' (*MFII* 293). Romantic idealization—'He . . . kept on dreaming and fell in love' (*MFII* 290–1)—is the other side of Bion's soldierly heroism ('bloody heroism'). Rosemary, 'That bloody bitch!' (*MFII* 314), according to Roland, turns out to represent for PA a reflection of 'the England I lived in and how it then looked to you. Not a flattering portrait, but true as far as appearances go' (*MFII* 320). Spoiling for a fight, Rosemary offers her hideous vision of male sexploitation of women (battered, prostituted, and mutilated, the victims of combined sexual and class hatred). Violence against women points to the incompatibility between masculine and feminine definitions of 'Love' and 'Honour' (*MFII* 323).

In this world of class and sexual domination, the only way out for the oppressed is to turn into the oppressor. The once-prosperous Alice—related to 'the Trojan

[20] See Bion, *The Long Week-End*, 248–9, where Bion offers a less condensed and more compassionate version of the episode involving his younger self and the wounded runner: 'And then I think he died. Or perhaps it was only me' (ibid., 249). The episode is pre-told in *War Memoirs*, 124–70, and reappears in his 1958 attempt to relive the Battle of Amiens (ibid., 254–6, 289–90); see. Ch. 7 above.

[21] See Bion's 'Key' to *A Memoir*: 'In analysis, certain ideas . . . are soon seen to provoke breeder reactions . . . It is against this vent that either of the two people can strive to defend himself by a closure', by refusing to sleep or 'by sleep or by being deaf, dumb and blind to the surrounding universe' (*MFIII* 622).

women before Troy fell'—is now a weeping skivvy, subject to Rosemary's whims
and tyranny. Rosemary tells Alice: 'I can see now what a terrible pair you and
Roland were as master and mistress. Were all your governing class friends as bad as
this?' (*MFII* 336). Clytemnestra ('a murderous woman') stalks the dreams of men
like Robin, avenging ancient female wrongs with a sharp axe-blow behind the
knees; Roland, true to form, suggests the comparison with Rosemary: 'You've got
Rosemary on the brain—sharp but not very sensitive' (*MFII* 338). PA defines the
active principle of 'seduction and intimidation' as 'the stimulation of one part of a
personality against another' (*MFII* 346). Seductive Rosemary and vengeful
Clytemnestra are two sides of the same coin; she and Man form a well-matched
pair. The ill-assorted discussion group adds up to a divided personality. It
includes, among others, 'two members of a defeated army, one member of a force
successfully mobilized to destroy a nation, [and] a woman from a subjected class'
(*MFII* 347), all set against each other by greed, war, murder, want, starvation, and
social inequality.

According to PA, the experience of such a group might promote 'growth of
health and strength of the individuals' if their meetings turn out to have 'developmental generative force' (*MFII* 347). But when Sherlock Holmes's Watson joins
the cast and asks Alice to 'answer for "womanhood"'—'Do you think you are a
real woman?' (*MFII* 348)—her response, in an apparent non sequitur, is to
denounce her ex-hero and ex-husband, Roland, to his face as a 'fictitious and
flattering version of the blackguard you were' (*MFII* 348). Perhaps Alice and
Rosemary are as much a function of Roland's bloody-mindedness as he is a function of the bloodiness of women. But, later, we learn that the flaunting Rosemary
is also 'a desire of Alice's; what P.A. would call a "sexual desire"' (*MFII* 411). In the
end it is the hapless Roland, for whom 'Sex is an unpredictable force' (*MFII* 350),
who gets shot when a murderous impulse allies itself with the death-instinct—an
impulse associated, according to PA, with an abortive birth or a Frankenstein's
Monster that kills its creator: 'The death instinct killed Eros' (*MFII* 352).
This 'ugly monster' or new birth is a thought or thinker giving rise to murder at
its inception, like a massacre of the innocents—that is, if the fragile barrier that
ought to be interposed between thought and action is destroyed. In this case, the
new idea turns out to be a monstrous plot hatched between Roland and Robin
against Man, caused by jealousy over his possession of Rosemary, who now
represents 'the spoils of war', just as Alice herself is now part of the spoils of
Rosemary's war (*MFII* 358). While murderous Man contemplates marriage,
and Rosemary cynically plots her reproductive strategy—'No pregnancies'
(*MFII* 367)—Robin and Roland argue over her, until suddenly: 'ROLAND
(*white with rage*) I'll teach the whole damn lot of you! (*A shot is heard, soft and
muffled. Roland falls dead*)' (*MFII* 370). Before Roland can kill Man, gun-toting
Man has turned the tables, shooting Roland with his Luger.

The murder initiates the final phase of Book II. Rosemary is troubled by the
apparition of the squalid old woman whom we saw before: '*A shattered ghost of a*

beggar woman slowly becomes apparent' (*MFII* 374). At once the 'herald of
impending disaster and a sign of that disaster . . . a symptom of a "mind
diseased"' (*MFII* 375), the hallucinatory figure haunts her in the guise of Lady
Macbeth. She is her own bad dream. She wakes from her nightmare screaming:
'Mad—and no one to talk to. Mad! And alone' (*MFII* 379). Is this a breakdown or
a breakthrough? Such an ambiguous breakdown might well have the effect of 'an
explosion of vast, tremendous and majestic proportions', or else represent a 'dark
night of the soul' (*MFII* 381).[22] PA refers to 'terrifying experiences' that include
'the awe-ful experience' of ' "going mad", some indescribable disaster, "break
down" '; or else people who 'express themselves by bringing about a disaster'
(*MFII* 382). This is a psychotic crisis. The unknown is rendered explicable only as
a violent 'explosion', perhaps a preconception or conception, or the birth of a
baby, or even the apocalyptic idea that a woman might 'have a thought worthy of
consideration' (*MFII* 382). PA speculates pointedly that 'People of different sex
find it easier to resolve their anatomical and physiological differences than their
differences in outlook' (*MFII* 389). But if (as PA does) you believe that 'there is a
mind' as well as a body, then 'the mental differences present goals and problems
which are far more difficult' (*MFII* 389). Women constitute a generative or
destructive force to be reckoned with—a force as great as that of quasars. As
Rosemary puts it: 'You should see what goes on in the psychoanalytic dovecote
when feminine intuition intrudes' (*MFII* 390). Bion had seen plenty of that.

As the tigerish Alice howls in the darkness for her dead mate, Roland, (recalling
the tigress grieving for her dead mate in the Indian childhood of Bion's *The
Long Week-End*),[23] the old marriage of Roland to Alice gives way to the unholy
wedding of neo-fascist Man and seductive Rosemary. In attendance is a cast of All
Souls that includes PA's ghostly wartime companions and even the 'Ghost of PA'
himself. Soliloquizing on the 'excluded middle'—the possibility excluded by
the choice of one extreme over another—PA had 'thought there could be some
alternative to an extreme course' (*MFII* 395), a middle way. Man objects that here,
on the contrary, 'Nothing is excluded' and '*everything*' is allowed: 'This isn't a
marriage—it's a riot' (*MFII* 405). Time Past's wild party, the domain of Regret
rather than psychoanalysis, includes all possible states of mind along with
untransformed auditory interference—snatches of song, jazz, poetry, waltzes; a
frenetic dance of death. Is some catastrophic change occurring, unobserved, like
the growth of a foetus? Or has a 'foetal idea' been killed off? (*MFII* 417).
The Bandmaster calls 'All change at Purgatory!' and PA announces the birth of

---

[22] For the relationship between violence and catastrophic change, see Wilfred R. Bion,
Transformations (London: Karnac Books, 1984), 8–10: 'The change is a violent change and the new
phase is one in which violent feelings are violently expressed' (ibid., 9); see Ch. 9 above for Bion's use
of the analogy of expanding pressure waves in the wake of an explosion for the effects of violent
emotions in the wake of psychotic breakdown.
[23] For the tiger mourning her mate, see Bion, *The Long Week-End*, 17; and, for a reading of this
episode, see Williams, 'The Tiger and "O" ', 38–41. The ghosts of Bion's wartime companions replicate
the trope of a purgatorial no man's land often associated with the writing of the First World War.

the 'post-Big Bang Era' (*MFII* 418–19). 'The Past Presented', however, ends not
with a bang but with a whimper. Or rather, it ends with Alice whimpering at the
traumatic memories of PA's First World War experiences and his dead comrades, a
terrible dream from which she wakes crying, depressed, and calling for Rosemary.

'XANTHIPPE DARLING'

In 'Making the Best of a Bad Job' (1979), Bion quotes Plato on Socrates' 'art of
midwifery'. According to Socrates, 'the only difference is that my patients are
men, not women, and my concern is not with the body but with the soul that is in
travail of birth'.[24] In the third and last Book of *A Memoir of the Future* ('The Dawn
of Oblivion'), Rosemary wonders if at last 'a mind will be generated' (*MFIII* 474)
from the riotous getting-together of Post-Natal Souls. Pervaded by foetal images
and metaphors of gestation and pregnancy, this final part of Bion's memoir opens
by announcing itself, satirically, as 'a psycho-embryonic attempt to write an
embryo-scientific account of a journey from birth to death overwhelmed by
pre-mature knowledge, experience, glory and self-intoxicating self-satisfaction'
(*MFIII* 429).

A number of preoccupations found elsewhere in Bion's late essays (Leonardo's
whirling hair and water, the Caesura of birth, foetal pre-experience) surface in this
recapitulated developmental journey from amniotic fluid to adulthood experience
and beyond. The same cast of characters emerges from the womb to resume their
debate, but during the course of what increasingly resembles a Socratic dialogue,
Alice and Rosemary change places, with Alice assuming the role of commonsensical
wife and mother, while Rosemary becomes the comical cockney maid, prone to
invoking her 'Mum', her Mum's sense of propriety, and her Mum's 'gentlemen'.
The women (as usual) are perceived by the men as intrusive butters-in on their
conversation: 'These women butted—I mean—"said" something' (*MFIII* 457).
PA notes that 'Alice, hostile, "thinks" I am an obtuse male' (*MFII* 459), while the
uneducated Rosemary is in awe of his learning. On her side, Alice speaks from the
authority of her own experience of pregnancy and childbirth: 'At last—something
I *do* understand; I have the advantage of knowing pregnancy' (*MFIII* 460). But, if
Rosemary is to be believed, men think that women do not necessarily 'know' what
they're talking about anyway: 'ROBIN: . . . Of course, they can't have known
what they were talking about. ROSEMARY: "Of course." Like women they
would not know' (*MFIII* 463). Bion does not commit himself to either side of the
argument. Instead, he focuses on the anger that occupies the excluded middle of
these competing viewpoints.

At one point, Roland calls Alice 'Xanthippe darling' after Socrates' supposedly
shrewish wife. Alice wonders: 'Do men agree with the dismissal of Xanthippe?

---

[24] Bion, *Clinical Seminars*, 330 (the quotation is from Plato's *Theaetetus*).

Do you consider the presence of myself and Rosemary an excrescence? Is our sexual equipment the only worthwhile contribution to the discussion?' (*MFIII* 480). Alice is allowed to express her perception of psychoanalysts in openly unflattering terms (a greedy, maladjusted, bigoted, bad-tempered, complacent, and ignorant lot on the whole). She and Rosemary interrupt PA—by now an increasingly long-winded, plaintive, and at times defensive character—with their scathing complaints: 'ALICE: My clitoris is passed by unnoticed by your mouth, "blinded," "glutted" by your penitential penis. What you don't know is knowledge; once you know it . . . you are too full of knowledge to be curious. ROSEMARY: . . . his eyes are so stuffed with Beauty that he cannot see me. Not even Homer had the wit to see that Helen of Troy was not just an ecto-dermal proliferation' (*MFIII* 467). Even the 'capacity for articulate speech' becomes 'more an opaque screen than a link' (*MFIII* 467) between these sexual opponents. From the incompatible perspectives of male fear and female hostility, each sees the other through a glass darkly, a dilemma that could only be resolved by Picasso's device of painting on a piece of glass, 'so that it can be seen from both sides of the screen—both sides of the resistance' (*MFIII* 465).

Into this linguistic impasse of recriminatory, mutual non-comprehension, Bion tosses a casual hand grenade: Roland's exasperated exclamation, 'You bloody women' (*MFIII* 463). Unremarkable in themselves, these words cause almost as much of an explosion as the birth of a new idea. Roland amplifies: 'I was scared of bloody women. Even the first man I saw spread-eagled in the shell hole we shared was not bloody—only faintly green parchment stretched over bones' (*MFIII* 464). War trauma and sex trauma, rather than Rank's birth trauma—a notion later contested by Alice, when she demands, 'Whose experience is traumatic?' (*MFIII* 563)—surface side by side in the shellhole occupied by thin-skinned ectodermal man. In an essay written during the same period, 'On a Quotation from Freud' (1976), Bion announces: 'I want to say something which sounds just like saying something for the sake of saying it; and perhaps it is. "Bloody cunt." "Bloody vagina." '[25] The first phrase, he speculates, is part of a 'universal language'—neither sexual, nor (like the second phrase) anatomical or obstetrical. What interests him is a primitive or archaic language that is connected not only with the sacred ('Bloody', Bion points out, is an abbreviation of 'By Our Lady') but with turmoil. This turmoil underlies the calm of consulting rooms or institutions, or the Socratic dialogue—where language may reach its limits and produce expressions of anger—or, for that matter, the seemingly civilized psychoanalytic discussion that is one mode of *A Memoir of the Future*.

When Roland tells Robin, 'Don't be a bloody cunt' (*MFIII* 483), Alice primly objects, 'surely it is not necessary to talk like that . . . I have to think of Rosemary'. Rosemary piously observes, 'My mum was very particular how she brought me up' (*MFIII* 483). Alice's squeamishness about 'such . . . language' contrasts with her

[25] 'On a Quotation from Freud' (1976), ibid., 307.

own ability to 'talk that stuff as well as you can' when she has to: 'Why don't you two fucking bastards shut up . . .?' (*MFIII* 484). PA explains carefully that 'This language, which clearly we all know though we have forgotten it. . . . makes an unrecognized—and unrecognized archaic and still vital—contribution to our intercourse' (*MFIII* 485). What PA refers to as 'the sacred "bloody" and the non-sexual "cunt" ' (*MFIII* 486) is acknowledged by Roland as archaic language whose purpose is to 'hide or disguise or preserve some powerful germ of vital develop-ment' (*MFIII* 487). PA draws an analogy between the 'storms that rage' beneath 'the calm and mirror-like surface' of Rosemary's character and the nature of language itself—'a distorted, distorting and turbulent reflective surface' (*MFIII* 490). Reality is neither civilized nor reasonable, but it speaks a universal language: 'The bloody cunt which is *not* anything to do with anatomical sex, not masculine, not feminine, not haematology, not religion but could be said to be sacred has . . . nevertheless an almost universal—western at least—comprehensibility' (*MFIII* 492). Even Alice speaks such 'cuntish language' as if she had been 'born to it, lived it, loved it as [her] very own favourite language' (*MFIII* 493).[26] So much for class privilege.

For PA, this 'cuntish' language is the language of the angry, inarticulate baby, a 'gem of obscene "water"—amniotic fluid, social freedom' (*MFIII* 494), that is brought to the surface by mental turbulence, tapping reserves of vitality to enliven an apparently somnolent or well-behaved psychoanalytic discussion group. PA himself is still preoccupied with his experiences as a tank commander in the First World War and its traumatic aftermath. Alice, however, for whom childbirth is 'No metaphor' (*MFIII* 507) but something she has experienced at first hand, asks: 'And the women? Or don't they matter? What should I tell my daughters—and their daughters—about childbirth?' (*MFIII* 508). What is woman's place in a new post-Bomb technological world order, if giving birth can still prove fatal? When Robin—a proto-Thatcherite already headed for the Falklands—says, 'We could do with a woman with some guts today', Alice responds sceptically: 'do you suppose that any woman would be allowed to clear up the mess . . . ?' (*MFIII* 511). The old Freudian question, 'What does woman want?' sounds different in this context: political power? Wages for housework? Material change? These were some of the feminist questions of the 1970s. The more PA sounds like a man trapped by the occupational demands and risks of his profession, the more Alice sounds like an under-appreciated, disempowered, un-waged housewife: 'If a house has to be kept liveable it is women who have to do so. How much respect do you think is paid to the minutiae to which we devote ourselves?' (*MFIII* 530–1). And, finally, with impatience, 'Oh, Freud! You people seem to believe that no one ever thought before Freud. Any *woman* knows . . .' (*MFIII* 532).

---

[26] Commenting, Bléandonu associates 'sexual insults such as "bloody cunt" ' with Rosemary's 'sadomasochistic sexuality' (Bléandonu, *Wilfred Bion*, 262), as well as with the amniotic fluid and meconium of early life; as we see, Alice is as quite at home in this medium as her maid.

What 'any *woman* knows' turns out to be what babies are trying to say—whereas psychoanalysts have to resort to jargon 'to express a minute particle of common sense which any woman would know' (*MFIII* 534). Not any woman, replies PA. But, wait a moment: what have domestic minutiae to do with minute particles of common sense? Bion's epilogue will proclaim his rebellion against common sense, as commonly understood, while his entire psychoanalytic *œuvre* explores the psychic action of minute splitting (perhaps domestic labour and psychoanalytic jargon are alike in splitting women's knowledge). Increasingly, Alice becomes the repository for a 'feminine' or 'maternal' intuition against which PA tries to maintain his own sceptical, agnostic view of the unknowable. The philosophic scold, Xanthippe, proclaims her respect for truth—'ALICE: Even women have been known to wish to bear children in whom a love of truth can germinate' (*MFIII* 561)—while she continues to insist on the medical fact that giving birth may be dangerous to mothers as well as infants. But, in the face of her way of knowing, PA defines his own role, which is to share not only the danger but 'the "smell" of that danger' (*MFIII* 517), while acknowledging both the 'bad smell' of obscene language and the 'evil smell' (*MFIII* 511) that accompanies creativity, which also has its origins in turmoil and danger. This is not quite common sense as we know it.

'Bion' speaks of the individual 'who behaves as if his wisdom and intelligence would be contaminated if he allowed himself to recognize that his body thought. Conversely, this individual believes that his physique would suffer if he allowed his body to know what his mind thought' (*MFIII* 566). We are back with the role of the psyche-soma? 'Suppose', asks Alice, 'while I am pregnant, I have some disturbing news. Would this affect the foetus?' (*MFIII* 575). PA suggests that news may be welcome or unwelcome, depending on whether the pregnancy is wanted or unwanted, the father loved or unloved. But the model of the pregnancy is like that of talk—its pains and frustrations have to be faced, rather than 'fall[ing] back on murder or war as a substitute for discussion' (*MFIII* 576). It is left to Alice to name an overwhelmingly feared outcome of failed discussions during the 1960s and 1970s: 'Nuclear war, for example'. By way of conclusion, PA gives himself the last word by responding uncompromisingly: 'There are no labels attached to most options; there is no substitute for the growth of wisdom. Wisdom or oblivion—take your choice. From that warfare there is no release' (*MFIII* 576). We might recall the unthinkable future or 'excluded middle' that confronted Bion himself at this stage in his life: wisdom *and* oblivion—not war, but his own inevitable mortality and death.

At the end of *A Memoir*, Bion takes leave of his group of characters in an epilogue spoken directly to the reader in his own voice. His book, he tells us, represents a rebellion against 'common-sense, reason, memories, desires and—greatest bug-bear of all—understanding and being understood' (*MFIII* 578). Kantian that he is, *sensus communalis* means a capacity for seeking the universal in the individual's experience. But, despite his uncompromising stance, 'sanity, like "cheerfulness," will creep in' (as they also do, for instance, in Alice's caricature of housewifely sanity, or Rosemary's cockney comic turn). In the last resort, *A Memoir of the Future* gives birth to a new-age foetus rather than a new-age feminist. We look in vain for 'a feminine psycho-analyst', although Bion had known many, among them his own analyst, Melanie Klein. 'All change'—or no change? Bionic woman reveals the extent to which futuristic thinking inevitably risks replicating uninterrogated, indeed conventional, representations of gender (the dualities of mistress and maid, Helen and whore). But she also plays her part in penetrating and displacing the 'masculine brilliance' and self-satisfaction of Bion's psychoanalytic culture at its blind-spot, the very focus of illumination: 'Too dark to see, or too blinded— . . . The difficulty is not only with the galactic centre. It is as difficult to see the centre of one's own personality' (*MFII* 254). *A Memoir* brings the inquiry home to Bion himself. And there his inquiry rests.

In *The Elements of Psychoanalysis* (1963), Bion had written: 'Self consciousness or curiosity in the personality about the personality is an essential feature of the story.'[27] His own curiosity in, and about, the personality is an essential feature of *A Memoir*, constitutive of its psychoanalytic self-inquiry. At the end of his last paper, 'Making the Best of a Bad Job' (1979), Bion calls for psychoanalysts to 'study the living mind': 'Will psycho-analysts study the living mind? Or is the authority of Freud to be used as a deterrent, a barrier to studying people?' Whose mind, after all, was he better placed to study than his own? 'Making the Best of a Bad Job' utters Bion's own warning against psychoanalytic orthodoxy of all kinds: 'The revolutionary becomes respectable—a barrier against revolution. The invasion of the animal by a germ or "anticipation" of a means of accurate thinking, is resented by the feelings already in possession. That war has not ceased yet.'[28] In the Bionic struggle against orthodoxy, *A Memoir* suggests, women fight unpredictably yet tenaciously on both sides of the barrier. Their role is at once reactionary and anticipatory; they function equally as respectable deterrents and as sources of emotional turbulence; they represent deathly forces, while also being repositories of essential (and potentially essentialist) knowledge about the risks of giving birth in the twentieth century; they voice opposition and generate change in their own way. In the last resort, Bionic woman can also be read, not just as the precursor of emotional upheaval but as a figure for 'the unexpected' itself—for that ultimately unknowable form of emotional turbulence about which no personality can fail to be curious: the end of one's life. It goes without saying that the association of women and death is the oldest myth of all.

The war between the sexes, at least for the Bion of *A Memoir*, is a displaced version of the struggle between life and death within the personality, whose essential feature is its curiosity about itself. Bion offers his own blueprint for the ways in which the not-seeing part of the psyche—its ideological blind-spot—is

[27] Bion, *Elements of Psychoanalysis*, 46.   [28] Bion, *Clinical Seminars*, 331.

bound to be implicated in all thinking, and particularly in thinking about the future, with its attendant anxieties about change, death, and the unknown. For a feminist reader, Bion's articulation of anticipatory thought reveals itself, like psychoanalysis, as powerfully and inescapably gendered, and at times downright retrograde in its underlying ideology. Its backward-looking 'post-modernity' is not modern and scarcely feminist. Yet Bionic woman—'the unexpected'—does more than define the limits of what was thinkable for Bion during the 1970s, a period when second-wave feminism took root and curiosity about feminine sexuality again became the focus of psychoanalysis, much as it had been fifty years before, during the 1920s and 1930s, when the newly emergent women psychoanalysts of the period began to interrogate Freud's account of femininity and Freud himself returned to the question. The unexpected offers an opportunity to scrutinize our own unacknowledged phantasies, along with the psychic conservatism that Bion identified as an impediment to change and (perhaps unintentionally) as latent in psychoanalysis itself. But it also allows an enlarged concept of the psyche—what Bion calls 'the personality'—to emerge from his harnessing of futuristic science-fiction and post-modern autobiography, making space for dream and phantasy, mental action and argument, to participate in that perennially absorbing project, the study of the living mind.

Bibliography

Abel, Elizabeth, *Virginia Woolf and the Fictions of Psychoanalysis* (Chicago: University of Chicago Press, 1989).

Abraham, Karl, 'A Short Study of the Development of the Libido' (1924), in *Selected Papers of Karl Abraham*, trans. Douglas Bryan and Alex Strachey (1927; rpr. London: Karnac Books, 1988), 418–501.

—— 'A Particular Form of Neurotic Resistance against the Psycho-analytic Method' (1919), in *Selected Papers of Karl Abraham*, 303–11.

Abram, Jan, *The Language of Winnicott: A Dictionary of Winnicott's Use of Words* (London: Karnac Books, 1996).

Adelman, Janet, *Suffocating Mothers: Fantasies of Maternal Origin in Shakespeare's Plays* (London and New York: Routledge, 1992).

Aeschylus, *Prometheus Bound*, trans. James Scully and C. J. Herington (London: Oxford University Press, 1975).

—— *Prometheus Bound*, ed. Mark Griffiths (Cambridge: Cambridge University Press, 1983).

Alexander, Franz (ed.), *Psychoanalytic Pioneers* (New York: Basic Books, 1966).

Anderson, Robin (ed.), *Clinical Lectures on Klein and Bion* (London and New York: Routledge, 1992).

Anzieu, Didier, *The Skin Ego*, trans. Chris Turner (1985; New Haven: Yale University Press, 1989).

—— 'Beckett and Bion', *International Journal of Psycho-Analysis*, 16 (1989), 193–9.

—— (ed.), *Psychic Envelopes*, trans. Daphne Briggs (London: Karnac Books, 1990).

Apollinaire, Guillaume, *Alcools: Poèmes 1898–1913* (Paris: Editions de la Nouvelle Revue Française, 1920).

Appignanesi, Lisa, and John Forrester, *Freud's Women* (London: Weidenfeld & Nicolson, 1992).

Arendt, Hannah, *The Human Condition* (1958; rpr. Chicago: University of Chicago Press, 1998).

—— *The Life of the Mind* (New York: Harcourt Brace Jovanovich, 1978).

Armstrong, Philip, *Shakespeare in Psychoanalysis* (London and New York: Routledge, 2001).

Bal, Mieke, *Quoting Caravaggio: Contemporary Art, Preposterous History* (Chicago and London: University of Chicago Press, 1999).

Balint, Michael, *Thrills and Regressions* (New York: International Universities Press, 1959).

Balmond, Cecil, 'Skinning the Imagination', in Anish Kapoor, *Marsyas* (London: Tate Publishing, 2002), 66–9.

Barthes, Roland, *La Chambre claire: note sur la photographie* (Paris: Gallimard Seuil, 1980).

—— *Camera Lucida: Reflections on Photography*, trans. Richard Howard (1980; rpr. London: Vintage, 1993).

Bataille, Georges, 'Concerning the Accounts Given by the Residents of Hiroshima', trans. Alan Keenan, in Cathy Caruth (ed.), *Trauma: Explorations in Memory* (Baltimore, Md.: Johns Hopkins University Press, 1995), 221–35.

Bateson, Gregory, 'A Theory of Play and Phantasy', *Psychiatric Research Reports*, 2 (1955), 39–51.

Beckett, Samuel, *Murphy* (1938; rpr. London: John Calder, 1963).

—— *Texts for Nothing* (1954; rpr. London: Calder and Boyars, 1974).

Berenson, Bernard, *Aesthetics and History* (London: Constable, 1950).

Bethell, S. L., *Shakespeare and the Popular Tradition* (London: P. S. King and Staples, 1944).

Bick, Esther, 'The Experience of the Skin in Early Object Relations' (1968), in Andrew Briggs (ed.), *Surviving Space: Papers on Infant Observation* (London: Karnac Books, 2002), 55–9.

—— 'Further Considerations on the Function of the Skin in Early Object Relations' (1986), in Andrew Briggs (ed.), *Surviving Space: Papers on Infant Observation*, 60–71.

Bion, Francesca, 'The Days of our Years', *Melanie Klein and Object Relations*, 13 (1995), 1–23.

Bion, W. R., 'The "War of Nerves": Civilian Reaction, Morale and Prophylaxis', in E. Miller and H. Crichton-Miller (eds.), *The Neurosis in War* (London: Macmillan, 1940), 180–200.

—— 'The Leaderless Group Project', *Bulletin of the Menninger Clinic*, 10 (1946), 77–81.

—— *Experiences in Groups and Other Papers* (1961; rpr. London and New York: Routledge, 1989).

—— *Learning from Experience* (1962; rpr. London: Karnac Books, 1988).

—— *Elements of Psycho-Analysis* (1963; rpr. London: Karnac Books, 1984).

—— *Transformations* (1965; rpr. Karnac Books, 1984).

—— *Second Thoughts: Selected Papers on Psycho-Analysis* (1967; rpr. London: Karnac Books, 1987).

—— *Attention and Interpretation* (1970; rpr. London: Karnac Books, 1984).

—— *A Memoir of the Future* (1975, 1977, 1979; rpr. London: Karnac Books, 1991).

—— *Two Papers: The Grid and Caesura* (1977; rpr. London: Karnac Books, 1989).

—— *The Long Week-End 1897–1919: Part of a Life* (1982; rpr. London: Karnac Books, 1991).

—— *All My Sins Remembered: Another Part of a Life and the Other Side of Genius*, ed. Francesca Bion (1985; rpr. London: Karnac Books, 1991).

—— *Brazilian Lectures* (London: Karnac Books, 1990).

—— *Clinical Seminars and Other Works*, ed. Francesca Bion (London: Karnac Books, 1994).

—— *Cogitations*, ed. Francesca Bion (London: Karnac Books, 1994).

—— *War Memoirs 1917–1919*, ed. Francesca Bion (London: Karnac Books, 1997).

Blanchot, Maurice, *The Gaze of Orpheus* (Barrytown, NY: Station Hill Press, 1981).

—— *The Space of Literature*, trans. Ann Smock (1955; rpr. Lincoln, Nebr.: University of Nebraska Press, 1982).

—— *The Writing of the Disaster*, trans. Ann Smock (1980; rpr. Lincoln, Nebr.: University of Nebraska Press, 1986).

Bléandonu, Gérard, *Wilfred Bion: His Life and Works 1897–1979*, trans. Claire Pajaczkowska (London: Free Association Books, 1994).

Bowie, Malcolm, *Lacan* (Cambridge, Mass.: Harvard University Press, 1991).

Braithwaite, Richard, *Scientific Explanation* (Cambridge: Cambridge University Press, 1955).

Bridger, Harold, 'Northfield Revisited', in Malcolm Pines (ed.), *Bion and Group Psychotherapy* (London and New York: Routledge, 1985), 87–107.

Briggs, Andrew (ed.), *Surviving Space: Papers on Infant Observation* (London: Karnac Books, 2002).

Britton, Ronald, *Belief and Imagination: Explorations in Psychoanalysis* (London and New York: Routledge, 1998).

Brome, Vincent, *Ernest Jones: Freud's Alter Ego* (London: Caliban Books, 1982).

Brooks Peter, and Alex Woloch (eds.), *Whose Freud? The Place of Psychoanalysis in Contemporary Culture* (New Haven: Yale University Press, 2000).

Budd, Susan, 'The Shark behind the Sofa: Recent Developments in the Theory of Dreams', in Daniel Pick and Lyndal Roper (eds.), *Dreams and History: The Interpretation of Dreams from Ancient Greece to Modern Psychoanalysis* (London and New York: Routledge, 2004), 253–69.

Burke, Edmund, *A Philosophical Enquiry into the Origin of our Ideas of the Sublime and Beautiful*, ed. David Womersley (Harmondsworth: Penguin Books, 1998).

Burne, Glenn S., *Julian Green* (New York: Twayne Publishers, 1972).

Butler, Judith, *The Psychic Life of Power* (Stanford, Calif.: Stanford University Press, 1997).

—— 'Moral Sadism and Doubting One's Own Love: Kleinian Reflections on Melancholia', in John Phillips and Lyndsey Stonebridge (eds.), *Reading Melanie Klein* (London and New York: Routledge, 1998), 178–89.

Caper, Robert, *A Mind of One's Own* (London and New York: Routledge, 1999).

Caruth, Cathy (ed.), *Trauma: Explorations in Memory* (Baltimore, Md.: Johns Hopkins University Press, 1995).

—— *Unclaimed Experience: Trauma, Narrative, and Theory* (Baltimore, Md.: Johns Hopkins University Press, 1996).

Caudwell, Christopher, *Illusion and Reality: A Study of the Sources of Poetry* (London: Macmillan, 1937).

Chase, Cynthia, 'Literary Theory as the Criticism of Aesthetics: De Man, Blanchot, and Romantic "Allegories of Cognition" ', in Cathy Caruth and Deborah Esch (eds.), *Critical Encounters* (New Brunswick, NJ: Rutgers University Press, 1995), 42–91.

Childs, David J., *A Peripheral Weapon? The Production and Employment of British Tanks in the First World War* (Westport, Conn.: Greenwood Press, 1999).

Colette, *L'Enfant et les sortilèges, oeuvres*, 5 vols. (Paris: Gallimard, 1991), iii. 151–6.

Conacher, D. J., *Aeschylus' Oresteia: A Literary Commentary* (Toronto: University of Toronto Press, 1987).

Conrad, Joseph, *The Arrow of Gold: A Story Between Two Notes* (1919; rpr. Philadelphia, Penn.: University of Pennsylvania Press, 2004).

Connolly, Cyril, *Palinurus' The Unquiet Grave: A Word Cycle* (1945; rpr. London: Pimlico, 1992).

Connor, Steven, *The Book of Skin* (London: Reaktion Books, 2004).

Cortiñas, Lia Pistiner de, 'Transcending the Caesura: The Road Towards Insight', in Robert M. Lipgar and Malcolm Pines (eds.), *Building on Bion: Branches* (London: Jessica Kingsley, 2003), 225–52.

Covington, Coline, Paul Williams, Jean Arundale, and Jean Knox (eds.), *Terrorism and War: Unconscious Dynamics of Political Violence* (London: Karnac Books, 2002).

Curran, Stuart, 'The Political Prometheus', *Studies in Romanticism*, 25 (1986), 429–55.

De Bolla, Peter, *The Discourse of the Sublime: Readings in History, Aesthetics, and the Subject* (Oxford: Basil Blackwell, 1989).

Deleuze, Gilles, *The Fold: Leibnitz and the Baroque*, trans. Tom Conley (1988; Minneapolis: University of Minneapolis Press, 1993).

—— *The Logic of Sense*, trans. Mark Lester and Charles Stivale (1969; London: Athlone Press, 1990).

de Maré, Patrick B., 'Major Bion', in Malcolm Pines (ed.), *Bion and Group Psychotherapy* (London and New York: Routledge, 1985), 108–13.

Derrida, Jacques, *Memoirs of the Blind: The Self-Portrait and Other Ruins*, trans. Pascale-Anne Brault and Michael Naas (1991; Chicago: University of Chicago Press, 1993).

—— *On Cosmopolitanism and Forgiveness*, trans. Mark Doolley and Michael Hughes (London and New York: Routledge, 2001).

—— *Without Alibi*, trans. Peggy Kamuf (Stanford, Calif.: Stanford University Press, 2002).

Dinnage, Rosemary, 'A Bit of Light', in Simon A. Grolnick and Leonard Barkin (eds.), *Between Reality and Fantasy: Transitional Objects and Phenomena* (New York and London: Aronson, 1978), 365–78.

Doane, Mary Ann, 'Film and the Masquerade: Theorizing the Female Spectator' (1982), in Katie Conboy, Nadia Medina, and Sarah Standbury (eds.), *Writing on the Body: Female Embodiment and Feminist Theory* (New York: Columbia University Press, 1997), 176–94.

Donald, James, Anne Friedberg, and Laura Marcus (eds.), *Close Up 1927–1933: Cinema and Modernism* (Princeton, NJ: Princeton University Press, 1998).

Dragstedt, Naomi Rader, 'Creative Illusions: The Theoretical and Clinical Work of Marion Milner', *Journal of Melanie Klein and Object Relations*, 16/3 (1998), 429–536.

Ehrenzweig, Anton, *The Psycho-Analysis of Aesthetic Hearing and Perception* (London: Routledge, 1953).

—— *The Hidden Order of Art* (London: Weidenfeld & Nicolson, 1967).

Eigen, Michael, *Psychic Deadness* (Northvale, NJ: Jason Aronson, 1996).

Ellis, David, *Wordsworth, Freud and the Spots of Time* (Cambridge: Cambridge University Press, 1985).

Etchegoyen, R. Horacio, *The Fundamentals of Psychoanalytic Technique*, trans. Patricia Pitchon (London: Karnac Books, 1991).

Evans, Dylan, *Dictionary of Lacanian Psychoanalysis* (London and New York: Routledge, 1996).

Fehl, Philipp, *Decorum and Wit: The Poetry of Venetian Painting* (Vienna: IRSA, 1992).

Felman, Shoshana (ed.), *Literature and Psychoanalysis: The Question of Reading, Otherwise* (Baltimore, Md.: Johns Hopkins University Press, 1982).

Fenischel, Otto, 'On Acting', *Psychoanalytic Quarterly*, 15 (1946), 141–60.

Fineman, Joel, *The Subjectivity Effect in Western Literary Tradition* (Cambridge, Mass.: MIT Press, 1991).

Frazer, J. G., *The Golden Bough: A Study in Magic and Religion*, Part III: *The Dying God* (London: Macmillan, 1911).

Freud, Anna, *The Psycho-analytical Treatment of Children*, trans. N. Proctor-Gregg (1927; London: Imago, 1946).

Freud, Sigmund, *The Standard Edition of the Complete Psychological Works of Sigmund Freud*, ed. James Strachey, 24 vols. (London: Hogarth Press, 1953–73).

Fussell, Paul, *The Great War and Modern Memory* (London: Oxford University Press, 1975).

Garber, Marjorie, *Shakespeare's Ghost Writers* (New York: Methuen, 1987).

Geissmann, Claudine, and Pierre Geissmann, *A History of Child Psychoanalysis* (1992; London and New York: Routledge, 1998).

Gill, Stephen, *William Wordsworth: A Life* (Oxford: Clarendon Press, 1989).

Gilman, Sander, *Disease and Representation* (Ithaca, NY: Cornell University Press, 1988).

Goldhill, Simon, *Language, Sexuality, Narrative: The Oresteia* (Cambridge: Cambridge University Press, 1984).

—— *Reading Greek Tragedy* (Cambridge: Cambridge University Press, 1986).

—— *Aeschylus: The Oresteia* (Cambridge: Cambridge University Press, 1992).

Green, André, *On Private Madness* (Madison, Conn.: International Universities Press, 1986).

—— *The Work of the Negative*, trans. Andrew Weller (1993; London: Free Association Books, 1999).

—— 'The Intuition of the Negative in *Playing and Reality*', in *The Dead Mother: The Work of André Green*, ed. Gregorio Kohon (London and New York: Routledge, 1999), 205–21.

—— 'The Primordial Mind and the Work of the Negative', in Parthenope Bion Talamo, Franco Borgogno, and Silvio A. Merciai (eds.), *W. R. Bion: Between Past and Future* (London: Karnac Books, 2000), 108–28.

—— *Life Narcissism, Death Narcissism*, trans. Andrew Weller (London: Free Association Books, 2001).

Green, Julian, *If I Were You* (New York: Harper, 1949).

—— *Si j'étais vous . . .* (Paris: Librarie Plon, 1970).

—— *The Apprentice Writer* (New York: Marion Boyars, 1993).

Grinberg, León, Darió Sor, and Elizabeth Tabak de Bianchedi, *New Introduction to the Work of Bion*, 3rd edn. (Northvale, NJ: Jason Aronson, 1993).

Grosskurth, Phyllis, *Melanie Klein: Her World and her Work* (Cambridge, Mass.: Harvard University Press, 1987).

Grotstein, James S. (ed.), *Do I Dare Disturb the Universe? A Memorial to W. R. Bion* (1981; rpr. London: Karnac Books, 1983).

—— 'Bion the Navigator of the Deep and Formless Infinite', in Robert M. Lipgar and Malcolm Pines (eds.), *Building on Bion: Branches* (London: Jessica Kingsley, 2003), 17–22.

Harris Williams, Meg, 'The Tiger and "O" ', *Free Associations*, 1 (1985), 33–56.

Harrison, Tom, *Bion, Rickman, Foulkes and the Northfield Experiment: Advancing on a Different Front* (London: Jessica Kingsley, 2000).

Harrison, Tony, *The Trackers of Oxyrhynchus* (London: Faber & Faber, 1990).

Hart, Captain B. H. Liddell, *The Tanks: The History of the Royal Tank Regiment and its Predecessors, 1914–45* , Vol. 1 (London: Cassell, 1959).

Hazlitt, William, *Selected Writings* (Harmondsworth: Penguin, 1982).

Heath, Stephen, 'Joan Riviere and the Masquerade', in Victor Burgin, James Donald, and Cora Kaplan (eds.), *Formations of Fantasy* (London: Methuen, 1986), 45–61.

Hegel, G. W. F., *Hegel's Science of Logic*, trans. A. V. Miller (New York: Humanities Press, 1989).

Heisenberg, Werner, *Physics and Philosophy: The Revolution in Modern Science* (London: George Allen & Unwin, 1958).

Hernandez, Max, 'Winnicott's "Fear of Breakdown": On and Beyond Trauma', *Diacritics: Trauma and Psychoanalysis*, 28 (1998), 134–41.

Hinshelwood, R. D., *A Dictionary of Kleinian Thought* (London: Free Associations Books, 1991).

—— and Marco Chiesa (eds.), *Organizations, Anxieties and Defences: Towards a Psychoanalytic Social Psychology* (London: Whurr, 2002).

Holland, Norman N., *Psychoanalysis and Shakespeare* (New York: McGraw-Hill, 1964).

Hopkins, Brooke, 'Wordsworth, Winnicott, and the Claims of the "Real"', *Studies in Romanticism*, 37 (summer 1998), 183–216.

Houen, Alex, *Terrorism and Modern Literature, from Joseph Conrad to Ciaran Carson* (Oxford: Oxford University Press, 2000).

Huffington, Claire, *et al.* (eds.), *Working Below the Surface: The Emotional Life of Contemporary Organizations* (London: Karnac Books, 2004).

Hughes, Athol (ed.), *The Inner World and Joan Riviere: Collected Papers 1920–1958* (London: Karnac Books, 1991).

—— 'Letters from Sigmund Freud to Joan Riviere (1921–1939)', *International Review of Psycho-Analysis*, 19 (1992), 265–84.

—— 'Personal Experiences—Professional Interests: Joan Riviere and Femininity', *International Journal of Psycho-Analysis*, 78 (1997), 899–911.

—— 'Joan Riviere and the Masquerade', *Psychoanalysis and History*, 6 (2004), 161–75.

Isaacs, Susan, *Intellectual Growth in Young Children* (London: Routledge & Kegan Paul, 1930).

—— 'The Nature and Function of Phantasy' (1943), in Riccardo Steiner (ed.), *Unconscious Phantasy* (London: Karnac Books, 2003), 145–98.

—— *Childhood and After: Some Essays and Clinical Studies* (London: Routledge & Kegan Paul, 1948).

Jacobus, Mary, 'Portrait of the Artist as a Young Dog', *First Things: The Maternal Imaginary in Literature, Art, and Psychoanalysis* (London and New York: Routledge, 1995), 173–204.

—— *Psychoanalysis and the Scene of Reading* (Oxford: Oxford University Press, 1999).

—— 'The Unexpected: Bionic Woman at the Millennium', *Women: A Cultural Review*, 11 (2000), 77–94.

Jenkin, Arthur, *A Tank Driver's Experiences; or, Incidents in a Soldier's Life* (London: Elliot Stock, 1922).

Johnson, Barbara, 'Using People: Kant with Winnicott', in Marjorie Garber, Beatrice Hanssen, and Rebecca L. Walkowitz (eds.), *The Turn to Ethics* (New York and London: Routledge, 2000).

Johnston, Kenneth, *The Hidden Wordsworth: Poet, Lover, Rebel, Spy* (New York: W. W. Norton, 1998).

Jones, Ernest, 'The Early Development of Female Sexuality', *International Journal of Psycho-Analysis*, 8 (1927), 459–72.

—— *Papers on Psycho-Analysis* (1948; rpr. London: Karnac Books, 1977).

—— *Essays in Applied Psycho-Analysis*, 2 vols. (London: Hogarth Press, 1951).

Joseph, Betty, *Psychic Equilibrium and Psychic Change: Selected Papers of Betty Joseph* (London and New York: Routledge, 1989).

Kahr, Brett, *D. W. Winnicott: A Biographical Portrait* (London: Karnac Books, 1996).

Kapoor, Anish, *Marsyas* (London: Tate Publishing, 2002).

Kaufman, Eleanor, 'Falling from the Sky: Trauma in Perec's *W* and Caruth's *Unclaimed Experience*', *Diacritics: Trauma and Psychoanalysis*, 28 (1998), 44–53.

Keats, John, *The Letters of John Keats*, ed. Hyder E. Rollins, 2 vols. (Cambridge: Cambridge University Press, 1958).

Kenner, Hugh, *A Homemade World: The American Modernist Writers* (New York: Knopf, 1975).

Kerrigan, John, *Revenge Tragedy: Aeschylus to Armageddon* (Oxford: Clarendon Press, 1996).

King, Pearl (ed.), *No Ordinary Psychoanalyst: The Exceptional Contributions of John Rickman* (London: Karnac Books, 2003).

—— and Riccardo Steiner (eds.), *The Freud–Klein Controversies 1941–45* (London and New York: Routledge, 1991).

Klein, Melanie, *The Psycho-Analysis of Children* (1932; rpr. London: Hogarth Press, 1975).

—— *Love, Guilt, and Reparation and Other Works 1921–1945* (London: Hogarth Press, 1975).

—— *Envy and Gratitude and Other Works 1946–63* (London: Hogarth Press, 1975).

—— and Joan Riviere, *Love, Hate and Reparation* (1937; rpr. New York: Norton, 1964).

—— Paula Heimann, Susan Isaacs, and Joan Riviere, *Developments in Psychoanalysis* (1952; rpr. London: Karnac Books, 1989).

—— Paula Heimann and R. E. Money-Kyrle (eds.), *New Directions in Psychoanalysis* (1955; rpr. London: Karnac Books, 1985).

—— *Narrative of a Child Analysis* (1961; rpr. London: Hogarth Press, 1975).

Kohon, Gregorio (ed.), *The Dead Mother: The Work of André Green* (London and New York: Routledge, 1999).

Kris, Anton O., 'Freud's Treatment of a Narcissistic Patient', *International Journal of Psycho-Analysis*, 75 (1994), 649–64.

Kris, Ernst, *Psychoanalytic Explorations in Art* (London: George Allen & Unwin, 1953).

Kristeva, Julia, *Powers of Horror: An Essay on Abjection*, trans. Leon S. Roudiez (New York: Columbia University Press, 1982).

—— *Melanie Klein*, trans. Ross Guberman (New York: Columbia University Press, 2001).

—— *Hannah Arendt*, trans. Ross Guberman (New York: Columbia University Press, 2001).

Lacan, Jacques, 'Desire and the Interpretation of Desire in *Hamlet*' (1959), trans. James Hulbert, in Shoshana Felman (ed.), *Literature and Psychoanalysis: The Question of Reading: Otherwise* (Baltimore, Md.: Johns Hopkins University Press, 1982), 11–52.

—— French transcripts of *Desire and its Interpretation*, Seminar VI (1958–9), http://www.ecole-lacanienne.net/seminaireVI.php3

—— *The Seminar of Jacques Lacan: Desire and its Interpretation 1958–1959*, Book VI, trans. Cormac Gallagher from unedited French ms. (n.d.).

—— '*Hamlet*, par Lacan', *Ornicar?*, 24 (1981), 1–31; 25 (1982), 13–36; and 26–7 (1983), 7–44.

—— *The Ethics of Psychoanalysis 1959–1960: The Seminar of Jacques Lacan*, Book VII, ed. Jacques-Alain Miller, trans. Dennis Porter (London and New York: Routledge, 1992).

—— *The Psychoses: The Seminar of Jacques Lacan,* Book III, ed. Jacques-Alain Miller, trans. Russell Grigg (London and New York: Routledge, 1993).

—— *Écrits: A Selection*, trans. Bruce Fink (New York: Norton, 2002).

Langer, Suzanne, *Philosophy in a New Key: A Study in the Symbolism of Reason, Rite, and Art* (Cambridge, Mass.: Harvard University Press, 1942).

—— *Feeling and Form* (London: Routledge & Kegan Paul, 1953).

Laplanche, Jean, and J.-B. Pontalis, 'Fantasy and the Origins of Sexuality', in Riccardo Steiner (ed.), *Unconscious Phantasy* (London: Karnac Books, 2003), 107–44.

Lawrence, D. H., *The Complete Poems of D. H. Lawrence*, ed. Vivian de Sola Pinto and Warren Roberts, 2 vols. (London: Heinemann, 1972).

Lecourt, Édith, 'The Musical Envelope', in Didier Anzieu, *Psychic Envelopes*, trans. Daphne Briggs (London: Karnac Books, 1990), 211–35.

Lewin, Bertram, 'Sleep, the Mouth, and the Dream Screen', *Psychoanalytic Quarterly*, 15 (1946), 419–34.

—— 'Reconsideration of the Dream Screen', *Psychoanalytic Quarterly*, 22 (1953), 174–99.

Leys, Ruth, *Trauma: A Genealogy* (Chicago: University of Chicago Press, 2000).

Likierman, Meira, *Melanie Klein: Her Work in Context* (London: Continuum, 2001).

Lipgar, Robert M., and Malcolm Pines (eds.), *Building on Bion: Roots* (London: Jessica Kingsley, 2003).

—— *Building on Bion: Branches* (London: Jessica Kingsley, 2003).

Little, Margaret, *Psychotic Anxieties and Containment: A Personal Record of an Analysis with Winnicott* (London: Jason Aronson, 1990).

López-Corvo, Rafael E., *The Dictionary of the Work of W. R. Bion* (London: Karnac Books, 2003).

Lupton, Julia Reinhard, and Kenneth Reinhard, *After Oedipus: Shakespeare in Psychoanalysis* (Ithaca, NY: Cornell University Press, 1993).

McFarlane, James Walter (ed.), *The Oxford Ibsen*, 7 vols. (Oxford: Oxford University Press, 1966).

McMillin, Scott, 'Lacan's Ghost: The Player in *Hamlet*' (unpublished paper).

Mao, Douglas, *Solid Objects: Modernism and the Test of Production* (Princeton, NJ: Princeton University Press, 1998).

Marcus, Laura (ed.), *Sigmund Freud's The Interpretation of Dreams: New Interdisciplinary Essays* (Manchester: Manchester University Press, 1999).

Mauss, Marcel, *A General Theory of Magic*, trans. Robert Brain (1950; London: Routledge & Kegan Paul, 1972).

Mayers, David, 'Bion and Beckett Together', *British Journal of Psychotherapy*, 17 (2000), 192–202.

Meltzer, Donald, *The Kleinian Development, Part III: The Clinical Significance of the Work of Bion* (1978; rpr. London: Karnac Books, 1998).

—— *Dream-Life* (Perthshire: Clunies Press, 1983).

Merleau-Ponty, Maurice, *The Visible and the Invisible*, ed. Claude Lefort, trans. Alphonso Lingis (1964; Evanston, Ill.: Northwestern University Press, 1968).

Miller, Arthur, *Jane's Blanket*, illustrated Al Parker (New York: Crowell-Collier Press, 1963).

Milner, Marion [Joanna Field], *An Experiment in Leisure* (London: Chatto & Windus, 1937).

—— *The Human Problem in Schools* (London: Methuen, 1938).

—— *On Not Being Able to Paint* (London: Heinemann, 1950).

—— *The Hands of the Living God: An Account of a Psycho-Analytic Treatment* (London: Hogarth Press, 1969).

—— *The Suppressed Madness of Sane Men* (London and New York: Routledge, 1987).

Milton, John, *The Poems of Milton*, ed. John Carey and Alastair Fowler (London: Longmans, 1968).

Murray, Gilbert, *The Oresteia Translated into English Rhyming Verse* (London: George Allen & Unwin, 1928); rpr. in *The Complete Plays of Aeschylus*, trans. Gilbert Murray (London: George Allen & Unwin, 1952).

Nancy, Jean-Luc, *The Restlessness of the Negative*, trans. Jason Smith and Steven Miller (1997; Minneapolis: University of Minnesota Press, 2002).

Netzer, Carol, 'Annals of Psychoanalysis: Ella Freeman Sharpe', *Psychoanalytic Review*, 69 (1982), 207–19.

Nussbaum, Martha, *Upheavals of Thought: The Intelligence of the Emotions* (Cambridge: Cambridge University Press, 2001).

Ogden, Thomas H., 'An Introduction to the Reading of Bion', *International Journal of Psycho-Analysis*, 85 (2004), 285–300.

O'Keefe, Daniel Lawrence, *Stolen Lightning: The Social Theory of Magic* (Oxford: Martin Robertson, 1982).

O'Shaughnessy, Edna, 'Psychosis: Not Thinking in a Bizarre World', in Robin Anderson (ed.), *Clinical Lectures on Klein and Bion* (London and New York: Routledge, 1992), 89–101.

Ovid, *The Metamorphoses of Ovid*, trans. Mary M. Innes (Harmondsworth: Penguin, 1955).

Padel, John, 'The Psychoanalytic Theories of Melanie Klein and Donald Winnicott and their Interaction in the British Society of Psychoanalysis', *Psychoanalytic Review*, 78 (1991), 325–45.

Palmer, John, *Political Characters of Shakespeare* (London: Macmillan, 1945).

Paskauskas, R. Andrew (ed.), *The Complete Correspondence of Sigmund Freud and Ernest Jones 1908–1939* (Cambridge, Mass.: Harvard University Press, 1993).

Payne, Sylvia, 'Obituary of Ella Freeman Sharpe', *International Journal of Psycho-Analysis*, 28 (1947), 54–6.

Peirce, Charles Sanders, *The Collected Papers of Charles Sanders Peirce*, Vol. VII: *Science and Philosophy*, ed. Arthur W. Burks (Cambridge, Mass.: Harvard University Press, 1958).

Perlow, Meir, *Understanding Mental Objects* (London and New York: Routledge, 1995).

Phillips, Adam, *Winnicott* (Cambridge, Mass.: Harvard University Press, 1988).

—— *Terrors and Experts* (London: Faber, 1995).

—— 'Bombs Away', *History Workshop Journal*, 45 (1998), 183–98.

Phillips, John, and Lyndsey Stonebridge (eds.), *Reading Melanie Klein* (London and New York: Routledge, 1998).

Pick, Daniel, and Lyndal Roper (eds.), *Dreams and History: The Interpretation of Dreams from Ancient Greece to Modern Pyschoanalysis* (London and New York: Routledge, 2004).

Poincaré, Henri, *Science and Method*, trans. Francis Maitland (London: Thomas Nelson and Sons, [1914]).

Poole, Adrian, 'Harrison and Marsyas' (1999), Open University, http://www.open.ac. uk/ Arts/Colq99/Poole.htm

Popper, Karl, *Of Clouds and Clocks* (St Louis, Mich.: Washington University, 1965).

Poston, Tim, and Ian Stewart, *Catastrophe Theory and its Applications* (London: Pitman, 1978).

Putnam, Michael C., *Virgil's Aeneid: Interpretation and Influence* (Chapel Hill, NC: University of North Carolina Press, 1995).

Raitt, Suzanne, *May Sinclair: A Modern Victorian* (Oxford: Clarendon Press, 2000).

Rank, Otto, *Art and Artist* (New York: Knopf, 1932).

Rapaport, Herman, *Between the Sign & the Gaze* (Ithaca, NY: Cornell University Press, 1994).

Read, Herbert, 'Psycho-analysis and the Problem of Aesthetic Value', *International Journal of Psycho-Analysis*, 32 (1951), 73–82.

Richards, David, *Masks of Difference: Cultural Representations in Literature, Anthropology and Art* (Cambridge: Cambridge University Press, 1995).

Rickman, John, *Selected Contributions to Psycho-Analysis* (1957; rpr. Karnac Books: London, 2003).

Riviere, Joan, *The Inner World and Joan Riviere: Collected Papers 1920–1958*, ed. Athol Hughes (London: Karnac Books, 1991).

—— and Melanie Klein, *Love, Hate and Reparation* (1937; rpr. New York: Norton, 1964).

Rodman, F. Robert (ed.), *The Spontaneous Gesture: Selected Letters of D. W. Winnicott* (1987; rpr. London: Karnac Books, 1999).

—— *Winnicott: Life and Work* (Cambridge, Mass.: Perseus Publishing, 2003).

Rogers, Samuel, *Human Life, a Poem* (London: John Murray, 1819).

Róheim, Gésa, *Magic and Schizophrenia* (Bloomington, Ind.: Indiana University Press, 1955).

Rosenfeld, Herbert, 'A Clinical Approach to the Psycho-Analytical Theory of the Life and Death Instincts', *International Journal of Psycho-Analysis*, 52 (1971), 169–78.

—— *Psychotic States: A Psychoanalytic Approach* (1965; rpr. London: Karnac Books, 1982).

Rudnytsky, Peter (ed.), *Transitional Objects and Potential Space: Literary Uses of D. W. Winnicott* (New York: Columbia University Press, 1993).

—— *The Psychoanalytic Vocation: Rank, Winnicott, and the Legacy of Freud* (New Haven, Conn.: Yale University Press, 1991).

Rustin, Margaret, and Michael Rustin, 'Learning to Say Goodbye: An Essay on Philip Pullman's *The Amber Spyglass*', *Journal of Child Psychotherapy*, 29 (2003), 415–28.

—— 'A New Kind of Friendship—An Essay on Philip Pullman's *The Subtle Knife*', *Journal of Child Psychotherapy*, 29 (2003), 227–41.

—— 'Where is Home? An Essay on Philip Pullman's *Northern Lights*', *Journal of Child Psychotherapy*, 29 (2003), 93–105.

Saint Jean, Robert de, *Julien Green par lui-même* (Paris: Editions de Seuil, 1967).

—— and Luc Estang, *Julien Green* (Paris: Editions de Seuil, 1990).

Sandler, Joseph, Anne-Marie Sandler, and Rosemary Davies (eds.), *André Green and Daniel Stern: Clinical and Observational Psychoanalytic Research* (London: Karnac Books, 2000).

Sayers, Janet, *Kleinians: Psychoanalysis Inside Out* (Cambridge: Polity, 2000).

—— *Divine Therapy: Love, Mysticism and Psychoanalysis* (Oxford: Oxford University Press, 2003).

Scarry, Elaine, *The Body in Pain: The Making and Unmaking of the World* (New York: Oxford University Press, 1985).

Scott, W. C. M., 'The Body Scheme in Psychotherapy', *British Journal of Medical Psychology*, 22 (1949), 137–43.

Sechehaye, M. A., *Symbolic Realization: A New Method of Psychotherapy Applied to a Case of Schizophrenia*, trans. Brabrö Würsten and Helmut Würston (New York: International Universities Press, 1951).

Segal, Hanna, *The Work of Hanna Segal* (London: Free Association Books, 1986).

—— *Dream, Phantasy and Art* (London and New York: Tavistock/Routledge, 1991).

—— 'The Function of Dreams', in Sara Flanders (ed.), *The Dream Discourse Today* (London and New York: Routledge, 1993), 100–7.

Semple, J. G., and G. T. Kneebone, *Algebraic Projective Geometry* (Oxford: Clarendon Press, 1952).

Sharpe, Ella Freeman, *Dream Analysis: A Practical Handbook for Psycho-Analysts* (1937; rpr. London: Karnac Books, 1988).

—— *Collected Papers on Psycho-Analysis*, ed. Marjorie Brierley (London: Hogarth Press, 1950).

Shelley, Percy Bysshe, *The Poems of Shelley*, Volume 2: *1817–1819*, ed. Kelvin Everest and Geoffrey Matthews (London: Longman, 2000).

Silverman, Kaja, *The Acoustic Mirror: The Female Voice in Psychoanalysis and Cinema* (Bloomington, Ind.: Indiana University Press, 1988).

Small, Helen, and Trudi Tate (eds.), *Literature, Science, Psychoanalysis, 1830–1970: Essays in Honour of Gillian Beer* (Oxford: Oxford University Press, 2003).

Smith, Lydia A. H., *To Understand and to Help: The Life and Works of Susan Isaacs* (Rutherford, NJ: Fairleigh Dickinson University Press, 1995).

Spiegelman, Art, *In The Shadow of No Towers* (New York: Pantheon Books, 2004).

Spillius, Elizabeth Bott (ed.), *Melanie Klein Today: Developments in Theory and Practice*, 2 vols. (London and New York: Routledge, 1988).

Spurgeon, Caroline, *Shakespearean Imagery* (Cambridge: Cambridge University Press, 1935).

Stehle, Phillip, *Order, Chaos, Order: The Transition from Classical to Quantum Physics* (New York: Oxford University Press, 1994).

Steiner, Riccardo, *Tradition, Change, Creativity: Repercussions of the New Diaspora on Aspects of British Psychoanalysis* (London: Karnac Books, 2000).

—— (ed.), *Unconscious Phantasy* (London: Karnac Books, 2003).

Stella, Frank, *Working Space* (Cambridge, Mass.: Harvard University Press, 1986).

Sterba, Edith, 'An Important Factor in Eating Disturbances in Childhood', *Psychoanalytical Quarterly*, 10 (1941), 365–72.

Stokes, Adrian, *With All the Views: The Collected Poems of Adrian Stokes*, ed. Peter Robinson (Manchester: Carcanet, 1981).

Stonebridge, Lyndsey, *The Destructive Element: British Psychoanalysis and Modernism* (London: Macmillan, 1998).

—— 'Bombs and Roses: The Writing of Anxiety in Henry Green's *Caught*', *Diacritics: Psychoanalysis and Trauma*, 28/4 (1998), 25–43.

Strachey, James, 'Obituary: Joan Riviere', *International Journal of Psycho-Analysis*, 44 (1962), 230.

Sutherland, John D. (ed.), *Psycho-Analysis and Contemporary Thought* (London: Hogarth Press, 1958).

Swinton, Major-General Sir Ernest, *Eyewitness: Being Personal Reminiscences of Certain Phases of the Great War, Including the Genesis of the Tank* (London: Hodder & Stoughton, 1932).

Talamo, Parthenope Bion, Franco Borgogno, and Silvio A. Merciai (eds.), *W. R. Bion: Between Past and Future* (London: Karnac Books, 2000).

Tate, Trudi, 'From Little Willie to Mother: The Tank and the First World War', *Women: A Cultural Review*, 8 (1997), 48–64.

—— *Modernism, History, and the First World War* (Manchester: Manchester University Press, 1998).

Teskey, Gordon, *Allegory and Violence* (Ithaca, NY: Cornell University Press, 1996).

Thom, René, *Mathematical Models of Morphogenesis*, trans. W. M. Brookes and D. Rand (1974; Chichester: Ellis Horwood, 1983).

—— *Structural Stability and Morphogenesis: An Outline of a General Theory of Models*, trans. D. H. Fowler (1972; London: W. A. Benjamin,1975).

Trist, Eric, 'Working with Bion in the 1940s: The Group Decade', in Malcolm Pines (ed.), *Bion and Group Psychotherapy* (London and New York: Routledge, 1985), 1–46.

Turner, John, 'Wordsworth and Winnicott in the Area of Play', in Peter Rudnytsky (ed.), *Transitional Objects and Potential Space: Literary Uses of D. W. Winnicott* (New York: Columbia University Press, 1993), 161–88.

—— 'A Brief History of Illusion: Milner, Winnicott and Rycroft', *International Journal of Psycho-Analysis*, 83 (October 2002), 1063–82.

Tustin, Frances, *Autism and Childhood Psychosis* (London: Karnac Books, 1995).

Virgil, *The Aeneid*, trans. Robert Fitzgerald (New York: Vintage, 1990).

Walton, Jean, 'Re-placing Race in (White) Psychoanalytic Discourse: Founding Narratives of Feminism', *Critical Inquiry*, 21 (1995), 775–804; rpr. in Elizabeth Abel, Barbara Christian, and Helene Moglen (eds.), *Female Subjects in Black and White* (Berkeley, Calif.: University of California Press, 1997), 223–50.

Warner, Marina, 'Anish Kapoor: The Perforate Self, or Nought is Not Nought', *Parkett*, 69 (spring 2004), 126–39.

Weiskel, Thomas, *The Romantic Sublime: Studies in the Structure and Psychology of Transcendence* (Baltimore, Md.: Johns Hopkins University Press, 1976).

Whelan, Maurice (ed.), *Mistress of her own Thoughts: Ella Freeman Sharpe and the Practice of Psychoanalysis* (London: Rebus Press, 2000).

Whyte, Lancelot Law (ed.), *Aspects of Form* (London: Humphries, 1951).

Willis, George, *The Philosophy of Speech* (New York: Macmillan, 1920).

Wilson, J. Dover, *The Essential Shakespeare* (Cambridge: Cambridge University Press, 1932).

Winnicott, D. W., *Through Pediatrics to Psycho-Analysis: Collected Papers* (1958; rpr. New York: Bruner/Mazel, 1992).

—— *The Maturational Processes and the Facilitating Environment* (1965; rpr. London: Karnac Books, 1990).

—— *Playing and Reality* (1971; rpr. London and New York: Routledge, 1991).

—— *The Piggle: An Account of the Psychoanalytic Treatment of a Little Girl* (London: Hogarth Press, 1977).

—— *Psycho-Analytic Explorations*, ed. Claire Winnicott, Ray Shepherd, and Madeleine Davis (Cambridge, Mass.: Harvard University Press, 1989).

—— *Talking to Parents*, ed. Clare Winnicott *et al.* (Reading, Mass.: Addison-Wesley, 1993).

Wolfson, Susan J., *Formal Changes: The Shaping of Poetry in British Romanticism* (Stanford, Calif.: Stanford University Press, 1997).

Wollen, Peter, *Paris Manhattan: Writings on Art* (New York: Verso, 2004).

Woodger, J. H., *Technique of Theory Construction* (Chicago, Ill: University of Chicago Press, 1939).

Woolf, Virginia, *The Crowded Dance of Modern Life*, ed. Rachel Bowlby (Harmondsworth: Penguin, 1993).

Wordsworth, Dorothy, and William Wordsworth, *The Letters of William and Dorothy Wordsworth: The Middle Years*, Part 1: *1806–11*, ed. Ernest de Selincourt and Mary Moorman, 2nd edn. (Oxford: Clarendon Press, 1969).

Wordsworth, William, *Poems, in Two Volumes, and Other Poems, 1800–1807*, ed. Jared Curtis (Ithaca, NY: Cornell University Press, 1987).

Wordsworth, William, *The Prelude 1799, 1805, 1850*, ed. Jonathan Wordsworth (New York: W. W. Norton, 1979).

—— *The Thirteen-Book Prelude*, ed. Mark L. Reed, 2 vols. (Ithaca, NY: Cornell University Press, 1991).

Wright, Elizabeth (ed.), *Feminism and Psychoanalysis: A Critical Dictionary* (Oxford: Blackwell, 1992).

Wright, Patrick, *Tank: The Progress of a Monstrous War Machine* (London: Faber & Faber, 2000).

Wulff, M., 'Fetishism and Object Choice in Early Childhood', *Psychoanalytical Quarterly*, 15 (1946), 450–71.

Wyss, Edith, *The Myth of Apollo and Marsyas in the Art of the Italian Renaissance* (Newark, NJ: University of Delaware Press, 1996).

Zeitlin, Froma, 'The Dynamics of Misogyny: Myth and Myth-Making in the *Oresteia*,' *Arethusa*, 11 (1978), 149–84.

Index